D0806237

The Dawn of Apocalyptic

The Dawn of Apocalyptic

The Historical and Sociological Roots of Jewish Apocalyptic Eschatology

by
PAUL D. HANSON

Revised Edition

Fortress Press Philadelphia

Biblical quotations, except from Isaiah 56-66 and Zechariah 9-14, are from the Revised Standard Version of the Bible, Old Testament Section, Copyright 1952, New Testament Section, First Edition, Copyright 1946, New Testament Section, Second Edition (©) 1972 by the Division of Christian Education of the National Council of the Churches of Christ in the U.S.A.

Copyright © 1975, 1979 by Fortress Press

All rights reserved. No part of this publication may be reproduced, stored in a retrieval system, or transmitted in any form or by any means, electronic, mechanical, photocopying, recording, or otherwise, without the prior permission of the copyright owner.

Revised Edition 1979

Library of Congress Cataloging in Publication Data

Hanson, Paul D
The dawn of apocalyptic.
Bibliography: p.
Includes indexes.
1. Apocalyptic literature. 2. Bible. O.T. Isaiah LVI-LXVI—Commentaries. 3. Zadokites. 4. Bible. O.T. Zechariah IX-XIV—Commentaries. I. Title.
BS646.H35 1979 296.3'3 79-17099
ISBN 0-8006-0285-4

7990F79 Printed in the United States of America 1-285

Dedicated to my beloved
mother and father
Lydia Thompson Hanson
Hans Victor Hanson

Table of Contents

Preface

Numerous have been the attempts in recent literature to define the terms *apocalypse, apocalypticism,* and *apocalyptic literature.* All too often the arguments have been conducted on such an abstract and theoretical level that they have produced definitions which must be forced unnaturally upon the literature. The present study began nearly a decade ago with form critical investigations of the ancient texts themselves. Tentative definitions only gradually began to grow out of these investigations, resulting in a number of papers, journal articles, and a doctoral thesis presented to Harvard University in 1969. Critical responses to these works have proven both stimulating and immensely helpful in an ensuing process of refining insights into the origins of the apocalyptic phenomenon in post-exilic Judaism. Seminars offered at Harvard have functioned, moreover, as a laboratory in which ideas could be tested among students who combine a lavish endowment of creative ability and a level of literary training which have led the writer to bury the notion of a dichotomy between the teaching and research roles of the university professor.

Through this process ideas grew to the point where it seemed advisable to publish them in the form of a sustained argument. It is the author's hope that this endeavor may help to refocus the discussion of apocalypticism upon the ancient texts themselves and upon the sociological matrices within which those texts took form. Too much print has been wasted on broad definitions which promise to unlock the riddle of apocalyptic without immersing either reader or writer into a single ancient text.

The reader will thus find her- or himself contemplating ancient texts throughout this book. Fresh translations, placed alongside the Hebrew text, enable the reader untutored in ancient languages to be engaged in the discussion without disadvantage. At the same time, the ancient text together with the accompanying prosodic analysis and textual notes will invite the student of ancient languages to check the conclusions of the author against the ancient sources. Except in the text critical notes, foreign scripts are eschewed in favor of English translations and transliterations of important Hebrew words, again with the general reader in mind. The translations of the texts from Isaiah 56–66 and Zechariah 9–14 are the author's, those of other parts of Scripture follow the Revised Standard Version. In the footnotes, in the case of oft-cited works, after the full reference has been given once, a short title is used thereafter; in such cases the full reference can be found in the Select Bibliography.

As I page through letters of colleagues who have taken time to contribute to the growth of an idea, I am reminded of the degree to which biblical scholarship is an international community activity. Acknowledgments could not begin to repay debts; thus I limit mention to four teachers who not only trained me in useful methods of research, but who through personal example engendered in me a deep and abiding love for the literature of the Bible, the late Gerhard von Rad and G. Ernest Wright, Brevard S. Childs, and Frank M. Cross.

Cambridge, Massachusetts *P. D. H.*
September 6, 1974

On the occasion of the reprinting of this book, I wish to thank all who, in reviews and personal correspondence, have offered helpful critique. Because this study has been adopted widely as a textbook, I have added in the appendix a general overview of Jewish and Christian apocalypticism. In classroom use instructors may find it useful to assign this appendix prior to the rest of the book.

Cambridge, Massachusetts *P.D.H.*
June 7, 1979

CHAPTER I

The Phenomenon of Apocalyptic in Israel: Its Background and Setting

To increasing numbers of observers it is becoming apparent that the dawn of a new apocalyptic era is upon us. Especially among those designated "the counter-culture," but not excluding many who continue overtly to live out their roles within the institutions of society, there is arising a profound disenchantment with the values and structures of our way of life. No longer does the optimism go unquestioned that ample education and hard work will be rewarded with all the benefits of the good life. At the heart of the matter is the collapse of confidence in the god to which twentieth-century Western man faithfully dedicated life and soul, Progress—a being infused with life by technology's discoveries and worshiped in anticipation of unlimited material return.

We now stand at a crossroads: a generation has lived out its life amidst the material affluence granted by Progress, and that generation has produced a group of children who look at the fruits of their parents' lifelong efforts and exclaim: "Vanity!" Within houses sprawling across carpets of grass and cars speeding across belts of concrete they recognize not the fruits of the good life, but the symbols of a demon who has duped a generation into believing it was imbibing soma when in fact it was drinking hemlock. In the frantic goal-oriented activity of adult society they discern not lives dedicated to the fulfillment of man's deepest needs, but lives lusting after mother earth's goods, and betraying their misdirection by transforming the mother into a whore, an earth exploited with no respect for her own health, and thereby transformed into a stinking sphere of poisonous waters and lethal air.

The continued dedication of the majority to Progress contradicts not at all the assertion that the dawn of a new apocalyptic era is upon us, for the crisis which sociologists find at the root of every apocalyptic movement is a minority phenomenon. This crisis is the collapse of a well-ordered worldview which defines values and orders the universe for a group of people, thrusting them into the unchartered waters of chaos and anomie. While the majority continues on the course defined by past norms, the apocalyptic minority calls attention to signs indicating that the course leads to perdition and offers in its place a new vision of life's values.

Accompanying the dawn of a new apocalyptic era is a renewal of interest in apocalyptic movements of the past. Within the area of biblical literature, a shift in interest is thus discernible. For decades the well-defined legal structures found in the Torah and the pre-exilic prophets supplied a reasonable moral system for a well-ordered society, making the classical prophets popular to the exclusion of the later apocalyptic writings, and causing scholars to trace the origins of normative Judaism and Christianity directly back to the prophets, dismissing apocalyptic as a fall from pure religion into the dark realm of fantasy. Any worldview which portrayed the natural order as filled with will and direction and looked upon the elemental spirits of earth, air, water, and fire as anything but vestiges of a crudely animistic mythology was untenable. But our generation, long confident in its exploitation of the natural order through technology's chains controlling the elements, was rudely awakened to a horrible spectacle. Earth, air, water, and fire, silenced for two millennia by scientific man, began to cry out to heaven for vengeance upon mortals who had polluted their home.[1] A new apocalyptic mood began to descend upon the brooding minority. Viewing the ecologi-

1. A colleague and friend, Professor J. Gerald Janzen, living in our home while we were on vacation, found the manuscript of this book on my desk, and left this marginal gloss which I quote with his permission:

cal crisis as more than a call to superficial housecleaning, they recognized that our values were perverted from the roots. Pondering over the signs, they began to look upon the universe with a new respect, even as a place charged with ominous powers and infused with a will which could not be violated by man's disrespectful exploitation of his environment. From among the ranks of such ponderers a number, experiencing complete alienation from the crumbling structures, withdrew into apocalyptic sects given to visions of the imminent collapse of this order and the dawn of a new era. These sects—the Hare Krishna, the Process—are rediscovering the vitality of the apocalyptic visions of the past; indeed, they are producing apocalyptic literature before our own eyes. The rest of us, disturbed by the signs, yet remaining within the system, account for the growing popularity of apocalypticism in the weekly magazines.

It is well that the apocalyptic literatures of the past are being rediscovered. It bespeaks a growing awareness on the part of some of a dimension to life which cuts beneath and radically calls into question the materialism which we have accepted from our god Progress. But popularity brings risks, one being the risk of inaccurate analogy, whereby we allow current interpretations of contemporary apocalyptic movements to become uncritically normative for our interpretation of ancient apocalyptic. Although certain features undeniably are shared by contemporary and ancient apocalypticists, it must never be forgotten that our world is vastly different from theirs, and symbols which are strikingly similar may have widely divergent origins and

---

The world is fouling at a rate
that ought to end an old debate
as to which element is prior—
air or water, earth or fire.
Should the criterion consist in
power to renew the rest,
the three who cannot even halt
their *own* demise lost by default.
Only fire still is pure,
and by its burning may ensure
beyond apocalypse the birth
of a new heaven and new earth—
(unless it fails to ignite the mess
and hands the verdict to chaos.)

significance in their ancient and modern contexts. For example, the current literature emphasizes the bizarre and the fantastic in contemporary apocalyptic, connecting it often with psychedelic experience, and not infrequently with the use of hallucinogenic drugs. The source of apocalyptic imagery is thereby traced to the subjective consciousness of the individual, an evaluation commonly applied as well to ancient apocalyptic. But an important difference must be remembered: while the contemporary apocalypticist must go to his subjective fantasy to derive the appropriate images, ancient man, with a worldview which we would designate mythopoeic, found his imagery in respectable religious systems. Many references to the bizarre, fantastic, disjointed, and eclectic nature of Jewish apocalyptic would be obviated were such contemporary analogies tested against historical investigation.

While thus welcoming the heightened interest in apocalyptic precipated by the contemporary *Zeitgeist,* we must temper our enthusiasm with an appeal for a rigorous application of the historical-critical method as a corrective to the type of errors which modern analogies can deliver. Both sides in the dialogue between ancient and contemporary apocalyptic will best be served when both phenomena are understood within their particular historical contexts before comparisons are drawn.

This is not to imply that the historical-critical method in itself bears the guarantee of truth. It too is vulnerable to misapplication and erroneous conclusion. Indeed, the reconstruction of the origin of apocalyptic which has been dominant for the past half-century in biblical scholarship is based on a comparative method quite as faulty as the method of contemporary analogy. Focusing on the book of Daniel as the earliest apocalyptic work, as a first step it contrasts pre-exilic prophecy with late apocalyptic by listing the characteristics of each. This yields two lists which seemingly have nothing in common. Martin Buber's contrast serves to illustrate:[2]

2. Martin Buber, *Kampf um Israel; Reden und Schriften* (Berlin: Schocken Verlag, 1933), pp. 59 ff.

	Prophecy	*Apocalyptic*
Eschatology:	Native, monistic	Foreign (Iranian) and dualistic
Object of hope:	Fulfillment of Creation	Dissolution of Creation by a different type of world
Judgment:	Coming event announced to the unrepentant; not irrevocable	Unalterable final event with firmly fixed date

The conclusion normally drawn from this method is that there is no essential connection between prophecy and apocalyptic. The discontinuity manifested by the lists is interpreted by judging apocalyptic either as a decadent late development with no real religious worth (Buber) or as a new phenomenon without primary connections to prophetic Yahwism (von Rad).[3]

The second main step in this method involves the explanation of the origins of this "new" phenomenon in Jewish religious literature. Since the contrast between prophecy and apocalyptic yields primarily dissimilarities, recourse immediately is taken to influence outside of the prophetic tradition. The most common outside source to which the origins of apocalyptic are traced is Persian dualism, especially as it was mediated by later Hellenistic influences.[4] The reason for this deduction is clear: Since apocalyptic is regarded as a new phenomenon rising in the third to

3. G. von Rad, *Old Testament Theology II,* tr. D. M. G. Stalker (New York: Harper & Row, 1965), pp. 201 ff., and *idem, Wisdom in Israel.* tr. J. Martin (Nashville: Abingdon, 1972), pp. 277-283.

4. See, for example, W. R. Murdock, "History and Revelation in Jewish Apocalypticism," *Int* 21 (1967):

> That the religion of Israel which had so recently attained the status of a truly monotheistic faith should suddenly shift to dualism is *an anomaly in the history of ideas* and cannot be understood apart from the simultaneous shift to eschatology. *Dualism and eschatology* belong together, for they constitute the two foci of a single theological system. Together they formed the core of Zoroastrianism, and they were taken up together by apocalypticism *under Iranian influence.*

P. 174 (italics added). For a similar position, see H. Ringgren, "Jüdische Apokalyptik." *RGG*[3] (Tübingen: J. C. B. Mohr [Paul Siebeck], 1949), pp. 464-466; H. Ringgren, *Israelite Religion,* tr. D. E. Green (Philadelphia: Fortress, 1966), p. 336; cf. also O. Plöger. *Theocracy and Eschatology,* tr. S. Rudman (Richmond: John Knox, 1968), pp. 26-52. and D. S. Russell, *The Method and Message of Jewish Apocalyptic* (Philadelphia: Westminster, 1964), p. 19 *inter alia.* Russell's treatment stands out from the others by drawing significant attention to the prophetic influence upon apocalyptic (pp. 88 ff.).

second century B.C., one turns to look for a third-to-second century influence to account for its dualism, determinism, etc. The logical conclusion dictated by this phenomenological approach, lacking as it is in any true historical dimension, is that Persian dualism is the primary source of apocalyptic.

The flaw in the traditional position is largely methodological, a point illustrated by a simple analogy: If one were to set a common MB II A Canaanite lamp alongside a typical lamp of the Iron II variety, the untutored bystander may fail to discern any historical connection between them. If one then filled in the typology with representatives from MB II B-C, LB I and II, and Iron I, that same bystander would recognize immediately that the Iron Age lamp develops in an unbroken continuum from the MB specimen. Our point is this: The origins of apocalyptic cannot be explained by a method which juxtaposes seventh- and second-century compositions and then proceeds to account for the features of the latter by reference to its immediate environment. The apocalyptic literature of the second century and after is the result of a long development reaching back to pre-exilic times and beyond, and not the new baby of second-century foreign parents. Not only the sources of origin, but the intrinsic nature of late apocalyptic compositions can be understood only by tracing the centuries-long development through which the apocalyptic eschatology developed from prophetic and other even more archaic native roots.

That the method we have been describing fails to understand also the intrinsic nature of apocalyptic is seen in the descriptions of apocalyptic given in the handbooks, descriptions consisting of long lists of random features gleaned from various apocalyptic works. The picture with which one is left is not only confusing, it is also misleading, for no given apocalyptic work comes close to incorporating all of the listed features. To illustrate, we offer the list found in in D. S. Russell[5] which draws heavily upon J. Lind-

5. Russell, *Apocalyptic,* p. 105.

blom:[6] transcendentalism, mythology, cosmological orientation, pessimistic historical view, dualism, division of time into eras, teaching of two eras, numerology, pseudo-ecstasy, artificial claims of inspiration, pseudonymity, esotericism, unity of history, conception of cosmic history which treats of earth and heaven, notion of primordiality, speculation on source of evil in the world, conflict between light and darkness, good and evil, God and Satan, Son of Man, life after death, individualism. How, by means of such a list, can one hope to come to an understanding of apocalyptic, or even to be able to identify a composition as apocalyptic?

Among the adverse results of the above-mentioned method are the following: (1) the sources of apocalyptic are misunderstood, (2) the period of origin is centuries off the mark, meaning that the resulting typology of apocalyptic literature is grossly inaccurate, (3) the historical and sociological matrix of apocalyptic is left unexplained, (4) the essential nature of apocalyptic is inadequately clarified.

Beside the inevitable errors attendant upon such disregard for the historical dimension in the development of apocalyptic, the flaw is exacerbated by the attempt to account for too much with a single theory. Everything in Charles's *Pseudepigrapha*[7] is to be explained by one definition. At the present state of scholarship, this claim is too sweeping.

Only an historical investigation with more modest aspirations promises to cast useful light on a confused subject. The present study focuses upon *one* strand which can be seen running at the heart of many of the so-called apocalyptic works, the strand of apocalyptic eschatology. It seeks to demonstrate that the rise of apocalyptic eschatology is neither sudden nor anomalous, but follows the pattern of an unbroken development from pre-exilic and ex-

6. J. Lindblom, *Die Jesaja-Apokalypse* (Lund: C. W. K. Gleerup, 1938), p. 102. Compare the list of characteristics, more recently, in J. Schreiner, *Alttestamentlich-jüdische Apokalyptik* ((München: Koesel, 1969), pp. 73–110 and pp. 111–164.

7. *The Apocrypha and Pseudepigrapha of the Old Testament in English*, vol. II, ed. R. H. Charles (Oxford: Clarendon Press, 1913).

ilic prophecy. Outside influences (e.g., Persian dualism and Hellenism) upon this apocalyptic eschatology appear to be late, coming only after its essential character was fully developed. They are thereby limited in their influence to peripheral embellishments.

Tracing the development from prophetic to apocalyptic eschatology will not in itself fully answer the question of the origin of every work designated "apocalyptic." It is well known that the pseudepigraphic literature is very eclectic in nature. Only studies focusing on each particular work, and indeed on each individual unit of tradition, will finally get to the base of the problem of origins by dealing not only with apocalyptic eschatology but with the origin of wisdom motifs and various foreign elements as well. Hopefully, this study will be a source of major input in such investigations, tracing as it does a strand which assumes an important position in, and indeed in our opinion, constitutes the heart of the major apocalyptic compositions. It should thus serve the iconoclastic function of exposing the untenability of many theories of origin (e.g., von Rad's theory of derivation from wisdom, and the traditional theory of Persian origin), and at the same time call attention to one significant root—and in our mind the taproot—of the major apocalyptic works.

EXCURSUS: APOCALYPTIC ESCHATOLOGY IN THE LATER APOCALYPTIC WRITINGS

Although we limit ourselves to the study of one strand within fully developed apocalyptic, namely, apocalyptic eschatology, and expect subsequent studies on the individual works to address the larger question of the origin of the apocalyptic compositions in their multifaceted totality, we anticipate such later studies by outlining, on the basis of research already completed, what seems to be the most plausible theory of origin. This theory is based on the view that apocalyptic eschatology constitutes the heart of the major apocalyptic works, a view supported by two observations: (1) The basic intent of those works seems to be that of describing to the faithful the vision of Yahweh's future saving act on their behalf. (2) The apocalyptic eschatology found at the heart of the late apocalyptic compositions can be found fully developed in all of its essentials in works of the mid-fifth century, compositions which at the same time do not yet betray any significant influence from the wisdom tradition or foreign sources (see pp. 395–401).

It would thus seem that, in tracing apocalyptic eschatology back to early prophetic roots, one is laying bare the origin of the most important current flowing into the complex phenomenon which we gather under the designation *apocalyptic*.

That such works as Daniel, 1 Enoch, and 4 Ezra contain other currents as well is undeniable, including one which, for lack of a more precise term, we call the wisdom tradition. We still await a comprehensive study tracing the wisdom material in late apocalyptic to its earlier roots. Wisdom is by nature such an amorphous tradition that it is very difficult to carry out such a study. A significant contribution in this regard is represented by Michael Stone's article, "Lists of Revealed Things in the Apocalyptic Literature" (forthcoming in the G. Ernest Wright Festschrift).

It is my tentative judgment that wisdom was wedded to the tradition of apocalyptic eschatology as a part of efforts being made by visionary circles to establish their credentials in the third and second centuries B.C. at a time when prophetic figures were being regarded with a great deal of skepticism and even animosity by many religious leaders. This search for credentials led to pseudonyms borrowed from figures of hoary antiquity like Enoch and Moses and to construction of historical resumés from earliest times down to the eschaton, all cast in the form of prediction by an ancient seer who had proven himself accurate in his predictions up to the present, and hence could be trusted for the future. The use of pseudonyms betrays the same need for legitimization in the face of challenge as that which led the Zadokites of the sixth century to establish a new genealogy by going behind their patron Zadok to the earlier figures Eleazar and Aaron. Similarly this search led to the adoption of various observations and speculations regarding the natural realm which we lump under the designation *wisdom*. By associating this learned, "scientific" material with their announcements regarding God's future dealings with his community and the peoples of the world, the visionaries were able to cloak their eschatological message in an aura of eruditeness which helped establish its authoritativeness.

When the problem is approached historically, three primary factors can be identified which account for the development of apocalyptic eschatology from earlier prophetic roots: (1) the self-identification of its protagonists with the classical prophetic tradition, (2) their following the lead of Second Isaiah in appropriating archaic league and royal mythopoeic material, but beginning to interpret it with a literalness which was carefully avoided by Second Isaiah, (3) a setting in a crisis-ridden post-exilic community struggling to adjust to the loss of nationhood and tremulous under a new threat to the unity of the community in the form of a growing schism between two factions, one visionary, the other hierocratic. These three ingredients already suggest our basic contention, that apocalyptic eschatology is the mode assumed by the prophetic tradition once it had been transferred to a new and radically altered setting in the post-exilic community. This leads to the problem of definitions, for if we argue for the unbroken continuity between pre-exilic prophetic eschatology and apocalyptic eschatology, why even retain the distinction implied by these two terms?

The reason is this: a development does occur; that is, differences do mark the opposite extremes of the continuum. It is useful, therefore, to attach names to the opposite poles, and for this purpose we retain the traditional terminology with this modification: rather than speaking simply of *prophecy* and *apocalyptic* as the two major phases in the development of the prophetic tradition, we shall use the terms *prophetic eschatology* and *apocalyptic eschatology*.[8] The advantage of this terminology lies in its underscoring both elements of continuity and change in the development. Moreover, it eschews any assumption that all of the prophetic material in the Old Testament is eschatological, even as it avoids the uncritical presupposition that every unit of tradition in the works which have come to be designated "apocalyptic" belongs to the eschatological tradition originating in the classical prophets and culminating in works such as Daniel 7–12, Revelation, and 4 Ezra. The task of clarifying the genres included in the literature which Charles gathers under the heading "Pseudepigrapha" is in its initial stages; this task is not well served by constructing theories which are too inflexible to accommodate the rich diversity of material constituting the apocalyptic literature. Moreover, much new material from discoveries in the Ju-

8. For a similar reason, we use two different terms to designate the carriers of the eschatological-apocalyptic tradition, using the standard term *prophet* for the pre-exilic carriers of eschatology and calling their post-exilic successors *visionaries*. The latter stem in an unbroken succession from the prophets, but are active in a new complex community situation which gradually alters the form of the prophetic hope which they inherited from the prophets.

dean Desert must be treated in detail before new syntheses can emerge.

Since modern scholarship does not furnish widely accepted definitions of these terms, and is characterized instead by a chaotic array of widely divergent definitions, it is necessary at the outset to clarify our terms.

Our definition of apocalyptic eschatology seeks to avoid three ill-fated means of definition which are popular in the literature, that which ignores the historical particularity of ancient Jewish apocalyptic by the hasty application of contemporary analogy; that which purports to characterize apocalyptic,[9] but fails to supply either an understanding of the essential nature of apocalyptic or a means of identifying that literature; and that which attempts to define it as a literary genre, since apocalyptic utilizes all the old traditional genres, transforming them into new, and often hybrid, forms. Our definition will instead attempt to state what we regard to be the basic essential of apocalyptic eschatology, and to state it in a way mindful of the historical dimension behind its development.

Prophetic eschatology we define as a religious perspective which focuses on the prophetic announcement to the nation of the divine plans for Israel and the world which the prophet has witnessed unfolding in the divine council and which he translates into the terms of plain history, real politics, and human instrumentality; that is, the prophet interprets for the king and the people how the plans of the divine council will be effected within the context of their nation's history and the history of the world.

Apocalyptic eschatology we define as a religious perspective which focuses on the disclosure (usually esoteric in nature) to the elect of the cosmic vision of Yahweh's sovereignty—especially as it relates to his acting to deliver his faithful—which disclosure the visionaries have largely ceased to translate into the terms of plain history, real politics, and human instrumentality due to a pessimistic view of reality growing out of the bleak post-exilic conditions within which those associated with the visionaries

9. See pp. 4–7.

found themselves. Those conditions seemed unsuitable to them as a context for the envisioned restoration of Yahweh's people.

These definitions attempt to specify the essential difference between prophetic and apocalyptic eschatology: the prophets, affirming the historical realm as a suitable context for divine activity, understood it as their task to translate the vision of divine activity from the cosmic level to the level of the politico-historical realm of everyday life. The visionaries, disillusioned with the historical realm, disclosed their vision in a manner of growing indifference to and independence from the contingencies of the politico-historical realm, thereby leaving the language increasingly in the idiom of the cosmic realm of the divine warrior and his council. Despite this difference in the form of prophetic and apocalyptic eschatology, it must be emphasized that the essential vision of restoration persists in both, the vision of Yahweh's people restored as a holy community in a glorified Zion. It is this basic continuity which compels us to speak of one unbroken strand extending throughout the history of prophetic and apocalyptic eschatology.

EXCURSUS: THE HISTORY OF PROPHECY IN ISRAEL

The basic continuity underlying the long history of prophetic and apocalyptic eschatology is best elucidated by means of a brief sketch of the history of prophecy in Israel. Comparative studies drawing attention to the connections between prophetic figures in Israel and in neighboring lands[10] have proven that Israel's prophets participated in forms and techniques of their broader cultural environment. But the essence of the prophetic movement is not comprehended by such comparative studies alone, for to the prophets fell the responsibility of serving as spokesmen for a view of reality which had been developing over a period of centuries before the first Hebrew prophet. Thus the prophets were not the inventors of Yahwism, but were themselves born of a crisis in the tenth century when Yahwism was thrust into an environment within which it could survive only by adopting new forms.

The view of reality of which the prophets were Yahweh's spokesmen therefore was characterized by emergence, change,

10. E.g., the Egyptian ecstatic Wen-Amon, the Mari *maḫḫûm*,. *bārûm*, and *āpilum*.

and development from the beginning. It is no longer possible to account for the rise of Israelite religion by hypothesizing a once-and-for-all importation of pure Yahwism into the Canaanite realm by chaste, semi-nomadic invaders at the beginning of the Iron Age. Canaanite religion was no disjointed congeries of local numina encountered by Israel for the first time at Baal-Peor. It was a highly developed and sophisticated cult whose deities were celebrated throughout the Levant. In no way could Israel's earliest ancestors have avoided contact with them.

Are we then to assume that Israel's ancestors in the period leading up to the settlement under Moses and Joshua were indistinguishable in belief from those celebrating the adventures of Baal so vividly dramatized for us in the mythic literature of ancient Ugarit? There are significant pieces of evidence which resist this assumption. Ancient Hebrew tradition distinguishes the patriarchs of Israel from the indigenous population of Canaan, pointing to a migration from the northeast as the reason for their presence in the Canaanite area. Recent studies have raised the connection of this migration to the movements of Amorite elements of the Middle Bronze Age to a high degree of probability. The available evidence for reconstructing the nature of the religion of these Amorites, however, is regrettably thin. What evidence there is suggests a religion which contrasted sharply with that of the major city-states of Mesopotamia and Canaan.[11] The cults of the latter centered around a pantheon of cosmic deities charged with regulating the cycles of the natural order. Moreover, the ritual of these cults was closely tied to the royal house, providing the current dynasty with cosmic legitimation.

Although the earliest hymnic literature of Israel bears the marks of influence from this ancient ritual, it betrays even more remarkably the emergence of a new view of reality which has cut the heart from the nature myth of the Canaanites. The God of Israel, Yahweh, is not in the first instance identified with the rainstorm in its yearly struggle to overcome the threat of drought so as to send the fructifying rains upon the land. Rather he is

11. In contrast to the cults of the major city-states, which centered around the major pantheon and its chief god who served as guarantor of the royal dynasty, the religion of the Amorites seemed to have as its essential feature a covenant relationship with a patron deity who was believed to guide a tribal group in its wanderings from one place to another in pursuit of pasturage, trade, etc. Rather than leading to notions about the immutability of royal structures and the inseparability of cult from sacred places (features of the cults of the city-states), emphasis on the patron deity led to reflection on the significance of temporal and spacial movement and of tribal genealogy (cf. the very suggestive text published by J. J. Finkelstein, "The Genealogy of the Hammurapi Dynasty." *JCS* 20 [1966]: 95-118). The existing tantalizing bits of evidence regarding the Amorites suggest a conception of deity and the relation between divine and human events which promises to shed valuable light on the backgrounds of Yahwism. but further evidence is badly needed to fill out what remains a broken picture.

recognized in events leading up to Israel's emergence as a people: a remarkable escape from the Pharaoh at the Reed Sea, sojourning among the Kenites in the Wilderness of Paran, narrow brushes with calamity finally leading to occupation of the land. The land thus occupied was identified with a promise traced from the time of the earliest Patriarch of the nation, Abraham, who migrated from the northeast in the movement of peoples which we would connect with the Amorites.

The various events of Israel's past are thus not seen as disconnected episodes, but rather as a chain leading from an early promise to a later fulfillment. And this chain comes to replace the primordial adventures of the gods of Canaan as the drama celebrated in Israel's cultic ritual, for the patron god Yahweh was confessed in Israel's pre-monarchical cult centers to be the god who had given Israel's patriarchs the promise of a land to live in as a part of his covenant with them. The cultic confession went on to trace that promise through its various stages down to its fulfillment.

While eschewing the traditional "nomadic ideal" hypothesis which traced Israel's religion to a pure desert religion transported into the crass polytheism of Canaan, we would therefore recognize probable influence from an Amorite conception of the patron deity who led his tribe through its seasonal wanderings as an ingredient in the emergence of early Yahwism. At any rate, at the earliest discernible stage of the history of Israel's religion, we recognize a confession in a God who acts in the events of history. This confession was able to reuse the motifs of the Canaanite myths with such independence as to rend them asunder, utilizing the chips and fragments to construct a new religion.

The *raison d'être* of this new religion contrasted sharply with that of the indigenous religion of the Canaanites. Far from providing cosmic legitimation of the current dynasty and guaranteeing the existing structures against change, Yahwism celebrated the god who broke the bow of the mighty and placed the poor on thrones.[12] It is not surprising that the political structure emerging from this religious climate was not a monarchy, but a confederacy which reserved the title of king for Yahweh alone, and which provided for Yahweh's rule of his people through charismatic leaders raised on a temporary basis as special needs arose.

Unlike the cults of the ancient Near Eastern city-states and empires, which linked the cosmic realm to the mundane through a king who was divine, or at least of divine parenthood, in Israel the link increasingly was provided by the integration of divine activity into the realm of history through the mediation of human

12. See the Song of Hannah (1 Sam 2:1–10) and the Song of Miriam (Ex 15:1–18).

agents, called *šōpᵊṭîm* ("judges"). The political structures of the league thus grew organically from the emergent Yahwism, with its confession that Yahweh alone was king and that he manifested his will to save primarily in the events of Israel's past. Yahweh's agent, the judge, combined in his office both religious and political responsibilities. Upon him the spirit of Yahweh descended, announcing the divine will, and it was he who led the people forth to effect the will of Yahweh thus revealed. In Israel's reevaluation of the historical realm as an arena of religious significance, Yahweh was not removed from his cosmic habitation, for he remained *yahweh ṣᵊbā'ôt,* Yahweh of the Heavenly Hosts; but his cosmic rule was integrated into the mundane realm through the agency of the charismatic judge.

This political structure, though growing out of and suited to Israel's view of divine activity, collapsed under the stress of the Philistine threat in the time of Samuel. The professional armies of the Philistine tyrants were too formidable for the men of Israel rallying behind their charismatic leader. The men of Israel demanded a king. It was as the result of Samuel's determination to save Israel's view of divine rule from being swallowed up by a foreign kingship ideal that the office of prophet was born.

The "Samuel compromise" was effected through the division of the office of judge into two separate offices; the spiritual responsibility of discerning Yahweh's will and translating the implications of his cosmic rule into the categories of history fell to the new office of the *nābî'* ("the one called"), whereas the political responsibility of carrying out the action required by this translation was invested in the office of *nāgîd,* or military leader.[13] Thus began the tension-filled coexistence of the kings and prophets of Israel. The attempts by the kings to end the division of power introduced by the Samuel compromise began with David and were carried much further by Solomon.[14] They reached a critical point in the North during the reign of Ahab, a period when the Omride dynasty was attempting to establish monarchy on the basis of a foreign ideology of kingship which left no room for the office of prophet. But, as the Elijah and Elisha stories indicate, the prophets fought back, insisting that they were spokesmen of Yahweh's will, and hence were the ones empowered with anointing and deposing kings and calling Israel to holy war. Yahweh's suzerainty could be encroached upon by the claims of an earthly king only with dire consequences according to the prophets. Though driven for a time into eclipse in the South by the high

13. See W. F. Albright, "Samuel and the Beginnings of the Prophetic Movement," *Archaeology, Historical Analogy and Early Biblical Tradition* (Baton Rouge: Louisiana State University, 1966), pp. 42–65.

14. See, for example, 2 Samuel 11 and 12, I Kings 11. and 2 Samuel 7.

form of monarchy introduced by Solomon and continued by Rehoboam and his successors, the prophetic tradition, with its mission of declaring Yahweh's suzerainty, remained active throughout the history of the Northern Kingdom. From the eighth century on it was recharged with new vitality in the South as well. In translating Yahweh's cosmic rule into the terms of contemporary history and politics, they often functioned as statesmen, as seen in their pronouncements on treaty relationships,[15] threats of war,[16] and decisions regarding internal affairs;[17] and throughout the pre-exilic period they held in tension the twin dimensions of their office, the vision of Yahweh's cosmic dominion and the translation of that vision into the idiom of their historical situation.[18]

After 587 the picture changes. Israel's political identity as a nation comes to an end. The office of kingship ends. The prophets no longer have the events of a nation's history into which they can translate the terms of Yahweh's cosmic will. Hence the successors of the prophets, the visionaries, continue to have visions, but they increasingly abdicate the other dimension of the prophetic office, the translation into historical events. At that point we enter the period of the transition from prophetic into apocalyptic eschatology.

Our approach to defining and describing apocalyptic eschatology within an historical frame of reference attempts to preserve the historical dimension essential to an understanding of the apocalyptic literature. It indicates that the visionary element which lies at the heart of apocalyptic extends throughout Israel's religious history; that is, the element of the prophet's vision of the saving cosmic activities of the Divine Warrior and his council. For instance, the early prophet Micaiah ben Imlah participated in this visionary element (1 Kings 22), relating it to the battle at Ramoth-gilead. Isaiah also participated in the visionary

15. Amos 1-2, Isaiah 30-31, Jeremiah 27.

16. Isaiah 7, Jeremiah 22, Micah 1.

17. Hosea 3, Micah 3, Jeremiah 29.

18. 2 Kings 22, Isaiah 6, Amos 7. The twin dimensions of the prophetic office are manifested also by the form of the judgment oracle. The sentence typically was cast in the cosmic language of the Holy Warrior, the indictment directed at concrete social and political events, and seeming to reflect the translating aspect of the prophetic office.

experience, and proceeded throughout his career to translate his visions into the events of the Northern and Southern Kingdoms, the Assyrian and Egyptian Empires, the state of Syria, together with their specific kings, armies, and peoples. Thus Isaiah was a true prophet, and his message was that of prophetic eschatology. The same dialectic between vision of the cosmic realm and translation into historical terms can be demonstrated in all of the pre-exilic prophets and down through the prophecy of Second Isaiah.

A study of Israel's early literature indicates, however, that the relation between the cosmic vision and the act of integrating that vision into historical realities underwent considerable change. Indeed, the earlier one goes in Israel's religious history, the more powerful the untranslated visionary element becomes, as illustrated by many of the archaic traditions of the league (e.g., Exodus 15, Judges 5, Joshua 10). This pattern suggests that Israel did not enter nationhood with a fully developed historiography; for that nation emerged from a mixture of peoples, many embracing worldviews which would not have contrasted sharply with the mythopoeic view which can be seen, for example, in the literature of ancient Ugarit. The move toward a more mythopoeic view of reality which is discernible in early apocalyptic is thus not an unexpected adventure into uncharted territory; it is a return to some of Israel's most ancient roots.

The unique significance of the prophets thus comes into focus: they were the ones responsible for historicizing Israel's religion, for integrating the cosmic vision into history, for causing myth to retreat before a more "secularized," "humanistic" worldview. In terms to be introduced below, the prophets were the ones who forged the visionary and realistic aspects of the religious experience into one tension-filled whole, allowing Yahwism to develop into an ethical religion in many ways unique in the ancient world. In this process they forced the translation of the pure cosmic vision into the terms of plain history; the result was prophetic eschatology. This accomplishment of the prophets is consonant with an aspect of the prophetic office seen most clearly in Isaiah, that in which the prophet acted as a political adviser to the king and as a statesman. Their achievement in integrating the religious vision and political realities becomes comprehensible: the structures within which they served were political ones; hence their responsibility to translate the cosmic vision into the terms of the politico-historical.[19]

It is difficult to overemphasize the revolutionary nature of the innovation effected by the prophetic movement. In a world which viewed divine activity primarily on the cosmic level, and which looked upon the flux and change of the historical realm as something to be overcome through the ritual of the cult, prophetic faith began to speak of a God who effected the salvation of his people precisely in the flux and change of history. Thus historical events were not to be denigrated as a threat to the eternal order wherein rested man's hope for salvation, but to be studied and recorded as the context within which and through which the cosmic deity Yahweh was active on behalf of his nation.

It should be noted, however, that prophetic Yahwism never eliminated all rival worldviews, as indicated especially by the psalms emanating from the royal cult of Jerusalem, a cult which preserved to a great degree the cosmic worldview of myth. Drawing heavily upon the royal ideology of Near Eastern kingship, it retained a much more static (mythic) view of reality than prophecy, and thus left the cosmic vision largely untranslated into the terms of secular history. Thus it was that the royal theology could defy political realities in claiming, for example, that Zion was unassailable and that the Davidic dynasty was eternal. This unprophetic stance, dedicated to legitimizing and preserving the existing institutions and thus opposed to the theology of radical change, accounts for the conflict often breaking out between prophet and royal court. It also clarifies why post-exilic apocalyptic writers, who were persons much

19. For a more detailed study of the development of the prophetic dialectic between vision and reality from its ancient Near Eastern roots, see the author's "Jewish Apocalyptic against Its Near Eastern Environment," *RB* 78 (1971): 31–58.

more inclined to grasp for an eternal, static order than were their prophetic forebearers, found the royal traditions so very useful in developing their message. By their time these traditions had been freed from their original setting by the fall of the monarchy.

In the eighth century Isaiah illustrates perhaps better than any other prophet the delicate balance achieved by prophetic Yahwism between the visionary element and the pragmatic integration of the cosmic vision into the events of that time.[20] Isaiah, the visionary who received his call by being drawn into Yahweh's divine council (Isaiah 6), was at the same time the statesman standing at the side of the king and relating every major event of his nation to divine will. Isaiah was permitted to look in upon the proceedings of the divine realm, but not to linger there, for unlike the seer of ancient myth, he was oriented ultimately not toward the cosmic realm, but toward the mundane: "Go, and say to the people." It is this delicate balance between vision and reality which would threaten to dissolve in the harsh times of the post-exilic era. Indeed, by the time one comes to Daniel, one witnesses another holy man permitted to view the cosmic events, but the tension is absent; cosmic realm and mundane realm represent two separate spheres which Daniel is not required to integrate: "But you, Daniel, shut up the words, and seal the book, until the time of the end."[21] (Dan 12:4).

Why was prophetic Yahwism unable to maintain the balance between vision and reality so delicately held by the classical prophets? The question is not only of historical interest, but of theological and ethical as well. The dynamism of pre-exilic prophecy is inextricably tied to the tension it maintained between allegiance to the cosmic order and responsibility to the mundane. In asking how this tension was lost in the prophetic tradition we touch upon questions which only another holy man with his head in the

20. For a more extended discussion of Isaiah, and an analysis of the prophetic tension in Jeremiah and Ezekiel, see the author's "Old Testament Apocalyptic Reexamined," *Int* 25 (1971): 459–460, 462–465.

21. Similarly, Dan 8:26; Test Levi 8:19; and 4 Ezra 12:36–38.

divine council could venture to answer; we must be content to describe certain historical and sociological factors which militated against the prophetic dialectic.

Our choice of studying the origins of apocalyptic eschatology within the conceptual framework of the tension in Yahwism between vision and reality issues from the belief that most reconstructions have erred on the side of oversimplification by treating apocalyptic as the property of one sect or party within Judaism.[22] Rabbinic texts and texts from the pseudepigrapha alike can be cited to prove that no party within Judaism was bereft of the vision we associate with apocalyptic, nor did any sect or party fail to feel the tug of responsibility to the mundane realm.[23]

Thus to structure the study of apocalyptic upon the study of the history of one particular post-exilic religious party is to describe accurately the situation in one century, only to fall into gross inaccuracy when moving to another period. For example, the Zadokites were the pragmatists of the early post-exilic period, responsible for the day-to-day maintenance of the temple cult, and given little to visions of the end-time. In studying the early apocalyptic of the sixth and fifth centuries, therefore, one studies not the Zadokite party, but a mixed group comprising followers of Second Isaiah and, it seems, including various Levitical elements which had been excluded from the temple priesthood. The untenability of the "party" theory for the origins of apocalyptic becomes clear when one then moves on to consider developments in the second century, and finds Zadokites, themselves supplanted as temple priests, belonging to the apocalyptically oriented community of Qumran.

If the party model of reconstruction fails, what model can be utilized in accounting for the dawn and rise of apocalyptic eschatology? We have adopted as a conceptual framework for the study of the post-exilic literature the field of tension between vision and reality. It relates most reasonably to sociological categories expounded by Max

22. E.g., O. Plöger, *Theocracy and Eschatology,* tr. S. Rudman (Richmond: John Knox, 1968).

23. Cf. J. Block, *On the Apocalyptic in Judaism, JQR* Monograph Series II (Philadelphia: Dropsie College, 1952).

Weber and other sociologists, categories we have adapted to the study of early apocalyptic literature below in Chapter III. The apocalyptic mentality cannot be adequately explained on the basis of the doctrines of a single religious party; we come closer to an understanding of that mentality by analyzing the relation of the various elements within Judaism to positions of control in the nation and cult at each point in post-exilic history. The visionary impulse giving rise to apocalyptic eschatology tends to be strongest among those embracing the prophetic promise of Yahweh's restoration of the faithful but at the same time witnessing the political and cultic structures of their nation falling into the hands of adversaries, thereby vitiating the possibility of fulfillment within the existing order of things. The pragmatic or realistic impulse tends to be strongest among those exercising control over political and religious structures; they often actively oppose the visionaries, viewing them as a threat to their positions of leadership.

For the purposes of our study of the rise of apocalyptic eschatology, the ideal body of literature would be one which would both enable us to isolate the visionary and realistic impulses, and at the same time to recognize the position of the protagonists of each impulse in relation to control of nation and cult. The literature of Third Isaiah (Isaiah 56–66) comes close to this ideal. This circumstance is all the more propitious inasmuch as Third Isaiah stems from the period of the dawn of apocalyptic, thus allowing us to observe the development of apocalyptic eschatology from its very beginnings.

When in Chapter II we turn to an analysis of Third Isaiah, and there witness the dissolution of the prophetic dialectic maintained by the classical prophets, it will be important to recognize that the resulting polarization of visionary and realistic elements was not without precedent. Indeed, in the broad sweep of the religious history of the ancient Near East, the dialectic of the prophets is unique, inasmuch as careful *separation* of the cosmic from the mundane characterizes the religious systems in that history. As already mentioned, ancient myth was primarily visionary, viewing the cosmic realm as the only realm of ultimate religious significance. The royal cult of Jerusalem to a large extent continued in this visionary tradition. These observations will be important when we inquire into the sources upon which apocalyptic eschatology drew in its formative stages. Alongside this positive influence on the resurgence of the visionary element in early apocalyptic was another, negative in nature, but equally important. It came from the tradition culminating in the Deuteronomic History, a tradition with deep roots in the prophetic movement, but which differed from the prophecy of an Isaiah or Jeremiah in an important respect.

The Deuteronomic History is founded squarely upon the prophetic principle par excellence, the principle of promise and fulfillment. It traces the history of Israel as a unified movement from the renewal of the partriarchal promise to Moses down to its fulfillment in Josiah. In contrast to a prophet like Isaiah, however, a critical alteration has occurred in the application of the prophetic principle. What in Isaiah was a dynamic principle, filled with the ambivalence and suspense enveloping a holy, cosmic deity and often hiding his ways from mortal eyes, became a rigid, dogmatic principle supplying the framework of a royal propaganda work and interpreting divine action with a degree of predictability and certainty which left no room for error. In a one-to-one relation, historical events were interpreted as episodes in Yahweh's direction of Israel's history toward its fulfillment in Josiah's reign. Moreover, a single, late element in Israel's legal tradition became isolated to serve as norm against which kings and kingdoms could be judged in relation to this divine direction, the law of the exclusiveness of the central Jerusalem cult.

Whereas the Deuteronomic History stands as a landmark in the development of historiography in the ancient world, and no doubt was an adequate and profound interpretation of Israel's history at the time of Josiah's reform, subsequent history proved that it was too fragile to explain the catastrophic events of the late seventh and early sixth centuries. Right at the apex of his glory, Josiah fell to Necco II and in subsequent years one horror followed the other. A theology which viewed Yahweh as predictably behind one dynasty and one cult was thrown into disarray by events destroying both that dynasty and that cult. In the Deuteronomic tradition the pendulum had swung too far toward one side of the prophetic dialectic. Yahweh's acts were tied almost exclusively to historical events, events which now contradicted the promises of the covenant. To save Yahwism from a shallow historicizing tendency, and ultimately from extinction, a new move was necessary which would reintroduce the tension of the prophetic dialectic back into Israel's faith by once again integrating the cosmic dimension of divine activity into the interpretation of the past.

In the prophecies of Jeremiah and Ezekiel, this cosmic dimension again assumes a conspicuous position. But it was especially Second Isaiah who gave formulation to the faith which was able to rescue the exiled community from despair. In powerfully dramatic terms Israel was reintroduced to a God who was creator and ruler of the entire universe. While acting in history, he was yet the God "who sits above the circle of the earth, and its inhabitants are like grasshoppers; who stretches out the heavens like a curtain, and spreads them like a tent to dwell in" (Is 40:22). Yahweh's plans had not been frustrated by Babylon; rather his plans were so lofty as often to be beyond mortal ken. Indeed, it was Yahweh himself who had given Israel to her spoilers (42:24ff), but with the express purpose of preparing for a more glorious future act (43:18–21).

Such a formulation of Israel's faith was possible by means of Second Isaiah's reintroduction of the cosmic vision into prophecy. His source was the liturgical material of the royal cult of Jerusalem, a cult by then defunct, and thus supplying material for reuse in new settings. The primary roots of this material were in ancient myth. Among the motifs in the royal liturgy, a central position was assumed by the description of Yahweh's primordial defeat of the inimical natural powers which threatened the created order, a victory repeated yearly and closely connected to the reign of Yahweh's anointed, the Davidic king. Drawing upon such material, and thereby enlarging the stage upon which the divine drama was viewed from the limited sphere of Jerusalem and those events impinging upon her to the vast universe with all of its nations and hosts, Second Isaiah answered the charge that the destruction of Jerusalem and the exile of the people were proof that Yahweh was impotent to save his people. When divine plans seemed to men to be frustrated, it was not because of limitation in Yahweh's power, but either because men's sins had brought upon them the curses of the covenant or men's limitations prevented their discerning Yahweh's saving activity in events which on the surface seemed like reversals. This cosmic nature of Israel's God Second Isaiah portrayed by means of powerful images drawn from myth. Yahweh he portrayed as the Lord of the divine council announcing the renewal of nature accompanying Israel's return to Zion (40:1ff), as the Mighty Creator stretching out the heavens like a tent for his habitation (40:22), as the Divine Warrior slaying the chaos dragon in the primeval battle (51:9–11).

This heavy borrowing from mythic material, however, did not lead Second Isaiah to break from the message of prophetic Yahwism which brought the religion of Israel away from a mythopoeic worldview, namely, that Yahweh acts through historical events and persons to save his people. Rather, what Second Isaiah did in contrast to the Deuteronomic Historian is raise the dialectic between vision and reality to a high tension. Yahweh, who dwells in the midst of the cosmic host and brings nature back to fertility, does this as an act accompanying the historical deliverance of Israel from Babylon. While stretching the heavens out as his habitation, he is also actively bringing the rulers of the earth to naught. While he slays the dragon in the primeval battle, his victory makes possible the deliverance of his nation Israel.

Perhaps the hymn to the arm of Yahweh in 51:9-11 illustrates with greatest clarity the dramatic power inherent in Second Isaiah's dialectic between vision and reality.[24] In

24. Cf., F. M. Cross, *Canaanite Myth and Hebrew Epic* (Cambridge: Harvard University, 1973), pp. 107-108.

the primordial battle Yahweh's arm slew the dragon chaos. This cosmic battle of myth, however, immediately is tied to the historical events of Israel's past: that same arm dried up the sea allowing Israel's redeemed to pass over in the exodus from Egypt. Past saving event then blends into future: there will be a second exodus, in which Yahweh again will save his people from exile. Primordial event, historical past, future salvation are all brought together into one dynamic tension-filled unity which permits Yahwism neither to be reduced to the one-dimensional historicizing of the Deuteronomic History nor to escape into the timelessness of myth. Myth is reintroduced into Israel's religion to add a cosmic dimension to a Yahwism languishing under an interpretation of divine activity which limited divine action too severely to historical events, but in such a way as to stop short of an escape into the purely visionary realm of myth.

This escape was prevented primarily because of one significant fact: though the political entity Israel was dead, the sense of nationhood was still very much alive among the exiles. Thus the prophetic office remained alive as a brief afterglow in Second Isaiah; he was conscious of being spokesman of Yahweh to his nation in its historical setting. The need to translate the cosmic vision into the categories of the politico-historical realm thus continued on into the career of Second Isaiah. Vision and reality were still integrated. While a more lofty, cosmic quality is discernible in the prophecy of Second Isaiah, yet his message is replete with historical references which bind his message to the mundane sphere. Cyrus, who serves as the surrogate of the anointed of Israel, will be Yahweh's instrument in the deliverance, Babylon will be object of Yahweh's wrath, the city of Jerusalem will be the home to which the delivered will return. This pragmatic dimension in the prophecy of Isaiah indicates that this world was still viewed optimistically as the context within which the fulfillment of the divine promises could occur. This quality of reasonable optimism was requisite for maintaining the dialectic between vision and reality.

The dawn of apocalyptic to which we now turn follows

upon the loss of this reasonable optimism. Failure of the glorious promises of Second Isaiah to find fulfillment in the post-exilic community, disintegration of the sense of nationhood in the face of a schism rending the fabric of the people, oppression at the hands of fellow Jews suffered by followers of Second Isaiah who believed themselves to be called by Yahweh to be priests of the glorious nation of the restoration, yet finding themselves crushed by the harsh realities of this world—such disappointments as these broke the optimism of prophetic eschatology with its belief that fulfillment of the vision of Yahweh's restoration of his people could occur within the context of this world. This optimism yielded to the pessimism of apocalyptic eschatology, held by people clinging to the prophetic promises of restoration, but failing to see how the order of this world could accommodate those promises, prompting them to leave the vision of restoration on the cosmic level of myth. The visionary disciples of the prophets, no longer serving as officers within a political structure, but disenfranchised from what political structures survived, came to conceive of their offices in more exclusively religious terms. Tending to "respiritualize" Yahwism by leaving their vision more on the cosmic level of the activities of the Divine Warrior and his council, they increasingly abdicated the responsibility to the politico-historical order of translating the cosmic vision into the terms of the mundane.

Once having abdicated the political side of the prophetic office, they found it increasingly difficult to maintain the dialectic of Second Isaiah between myth and history, vision and reality. The tendency to give up the prophetic task of translation into historical terms was abetted by the harsh circumstances within which the visionary group found itself in the post-exilic period. These circumstances convinced them that the politico-historical realm was overcome by evil, and was no longer a realm over which they had any control. That the element of myth should enjoy a tremendous resurgence in apocalyptic is thus understandable; once the visionary's responsibilities to a political order had become tenuous, his role returned increasingly to the spiritual role of relating the events of the cosmic realm, a role akin to that of the mythmaker. The mythic elements of Second Isaiah were torn from their mooring in history, and were interpreted with a fresh literalness. As a result, by envisioning fulfillment not on the level of historical events but within the cosmic realm of myth, a realm left unsullied by the bitter disappointments of this world, mythic motifs began to serve less the function of giving cosmic significance to Yahweh's historical acts than of offering a means of escape from the growing contradiction between glorious promise and harsh reality.

Finally, it should be emphasized that the dawn of apocalyptic is genuinely a dawning; that is, prophetic eschatology did not break into apocalyptic eschatology suddenly and without an intervening period of transition. Only gradually did the firm mooring of the prophetic message in history begin to loosen. Since Second Isaiah's use of mythic motifs points in the direction which apocalyptic eschatology would pursue while yet being fully related to the historical realm, we designate his prophecy "proto-apocalyptic." In the oracles in Third Isaiah, a harshly exacerbated community situation is reflected, and accompanying this development a move in the direction of the more rarified atmosphere of apocalyptic eschatology. Increasingly mythic motifs which in Second Isaiah were used metaphorically are applied with a literalism that offers escape from the harsh realities of this world which were contradicting the covenant promises. This collection of oracles and a number of other collections (e.g., Zechariah 9–10, Isaiah 24–27) we designate "early apocalyptic"; they stem from the late sixth and early fifth centuries. Chapters 11–14 of Zechariah will give us opportunity to trace further the transition to full-blown apocalyptic eschatology. Zechariah 14 contains an oracle which is left quite completely in the realm of the cosmic activity of the Divine Warrior and his host. It adumbrates the relation of the visionary tradition to history which characterizes late apocalyptic. The historical framework, that is, the mundane setting of events occurring in a chronological sequence, is assumed by the composition, but the attitude of the writer is one of indifference to the limitations imposed by the actual events of plain history. The saving activity is initiated and carried out by the Divine Warrior himself, and human agents appear as mere pawns in a cosmic chess game. Insofar as the elect participate in the events of the eschaton, they are absorbed into the cosmic hosts of the Divine Warrior and play no part as members of the real historical order (Zech 14:5b; cf. 9:13; 10:3–5).

The historical retrospects commonly found in late apocalyptic writings also illustrate this emancipation from the constraints of plain history: history is recounted on a grand scale, often from the beginning of the world, but the interest is far less in actual historical events than in recognition of an irresistible divine thrust pressing toward the vindication of the elect. Before this thrust empires and kings fall helplessly, and in no way are they seen as essential instruments in effecting the divine intent. The aim of these retrospects is to prove that the same sweep of divine activity discernible to the visionary in the past will continue into the future, leading finally to the eschaton. The retrospect thus is intended to verify the visionary's insight into the sovereignty of Yahweh.[25]

While the relation of the narrative to the historical order has thus become very tenuous in Zechariah 14, it is important to note that the return to myth is completed neither in this oracle nor, for that matter, in any composition within Jewish apocalyptic. As the historical resumés themselves indicate, something of the experiment of the prophets adhered stubbornly to the visionary tradition; even their cosmic vision, in its most ethereal form, continued to assume an historical framework, and even the events of the eschaton followed an historical sequence. One must wait for Gnosticism for the completion of the return to the mythic worldview, for only in that late phenomenon was the historical experiment overcome.[26]

25. See, for example, Daniel 8 and 12; I Enoch 6ff, 83–90, 93:1–10 and 91:12–17 (Apocalypse of Weeks) and the Assumption of Moses. This use of history to verify the visionary's insight into the sovereignty of Yahweh is also discernible in the Qumran commentaries.

The results of studying the origin of apocalyptic eschatology as an unbroken development out of classical prophecy are very different from the results reached by the various modifications of the traditional approach: (1) the sources of apocalyptic eschatology lie solidly within the prophetic tradition of Israel; (2) the period of origin is in the sixth to the fifth centuries; (3) the essential nature of apocalyptic is found in the abandonment of the prophetic task of translating the vision of the divine council into historical terms; (4) the historical and sociological matrix of apocalyptic is found in an inner-community struggle in the period of the Second Temple between visionary and hierocratic elements.

The method appropriate for the study of this material differs from the usual methodology, and calls for a word of explanation. In order to trace the history of the relation between vision and reality in prophetic Yahwism we developed what we call the contextual-typological method. It seeks to interpret the apocalyptic compositions within the context of the community struggle discernible behind the material studied, and it applies typological tools in analyzing the material. The typologies traced are those of poetic structure and meter, of prophetic oracle types (genres), and of the prophetic eschatology-apocalyptic eschatology continuum.

The implications of this reconstruction of the origins of apocalyptic go beyond the field of biblical studies, for we discern the matrix of the rise of apocalyptic in a post-exilic Jewish community torn between two contending elements which together represent the creative and tension-filled vital substance of Yahwism, the elements of realism and vision. These two elements, moreover, constitute the heart

26. Though overly simplified, the following typology traces the relation of the cult to history in Israel and her environment:

Early Myth (Egypt and Early Sumer):	Negation of history
Classical Mesopotamia:	History a mere reflection of the cosmic realm
Israelite League:	Myth and history in tension
Royal Cult of Jerusalem:	History a reflection of cosmic events
Prophetic Yahwism:	History affirmed as context of divine acts
Apocalyptic:	Indifference to restraints of history
Gnosticism:	Negation of history

of all ethical religions. The visionary element is the vision of a divine order transcending all mundane institutions and structures, a vision which constantly calls those institutions and structures under judgment, stubbornly refusing at the same time to become identified with them. The element of realism is concerned with the day-to-day maintenance of those same mundane institutions and structures, and with preserving continuity so as to assure a context for the continued life of the community. When separated from the realism the vision leads to a retreat into the world of ecstasy and dreams and to an abdication of the social responsibility of translating the vision of the divine order into the realm of everyday earthly concerns. When separated from the vision the realism becomes a sterile preserver of the status quo which absolutizes and eternalizes the existing order together with all of its inequities.

In Israel's religious history the prophets stubbornly integrated realism and vision into the highly creative force which was the dreaded foe of Canaanism, and thereby lifted Yahwism out of the grip of pagan myth. The history of Yahwism in the post-exilic period is the history of tension and struggle between those two elements which often led to their polarization. Within that history of tension and struggle apocalyptic was born, and its further development through the centuries and down to the Common Era occurred within that same tension-filled matrix as a result of the polarization of realism and vision. The periods when that polarization became most extreme in the history of the Second Temple represent the most rapid development of apocalyptic eschatology.

Two of the most significant of these formative periods were the sixth-fifth centuries, which will be studied here, and the second century, to be treated in a later study. But such periods of polarization are found as well throughout the recorded history of man, and thus the present work treats but one brief phase in a very long development. The eras of the primitive Church, of the Reformation, and of the last one hundred years have all witnessed the birth of apocalyptic movements as the result of the polarization of

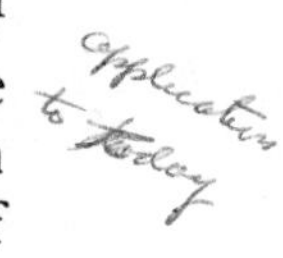

the realistic and visionary elements of religion; indeed, the present unrest in our society caused by a clash between many visionary youth and their realistic elders is a part of this same phenomenon. Each of these periods, moreover, and many periods between, have witnessed the activity of prophetic figures struggling to maintain the vital creative tension between vision and realism which is the heart of genuine ethical religion.

CHAPTER II

Isaiah 56–66 and the Visionary Disciples of Second Isaiah

A. A THIRD ISAIAH?

Of critical importance to the study of the rise of apocalyptic is that section of Isaiah designated "Tritojesaja" by Duhm in his epoch-making commentary appearing in 1892, for the oracles in these eleven chapters not only betray distinct marks of transition from prophetic to apocalyptic eschatology, but promise to elucidate the sociological situation in the post-exilic Jewish community which underlies that transition. But *caveat lector*! The material is ambiguous enough to be amenable to most any hypothesis, given an ample amount of eisegesis in support of a stubbornly held reconstruction of Israel's history in the sixth to fifth centuries. Thus C. C. Torrey can write concerning Isaiah 40–66: ". . . the twenty-seven poems are the work of a single hand; there is clearly no other possibility,"[1] whereas Artur Weiser can conclude: ". . . in Is. 55–66 we are not concerned with the work of a single prophet 'Trito-Isaiah' but with a collection of appendices to the book of Isaiah by different hands and from different times."[2] Equally as divergent as the hypotheses concerning the eleven chapters in general are the treatments of particular passages. Thus R. H. Kennett would assign 56:9–12 to the time of Antiochus Epiphanes,[3] while Paul Volz argues for a pre-exilic

1. C. C. Torrey, *The Second Isaiah* (New York: Charles Scribner's Sons, 1928), p. 203.

2 A. Weiser, *The Old Testament: Its Formation and Development*, tr. D. M. Barton (New York: Association, 1961), p. 207.

3. R. H. Kennett, *The Composition of the Book of Isaiah in the Light of History and Archaeology* (London: Oxford University, 1910), pp. 56 ff.

date.[4] The reason for such utter lack of consensus is not hard to determine: (1) in contrast to the situation in some of the other Isaianic material, here the oracles are virtually bereft of references to historical events; (2) the history of much of the period concerned is itself shrouded in darkness, large gaps remaining in our knowledge of the period from 536 to 520, and again between 516 and the middle of the fifth century.[5] The result of these two gaps is the speculative enterprise whereby scholars reconstruct the history on the basis of the oracles, and then turn to interpret the oracles within the context of that reconstructed history, an amazingly circular procedure!

Obviously. the question of methodology is a most critical one when approaching such material. It is thus best to begin with a brief summary of the history of scholarship on Isaiah 56–66, with notes on the various methodologies adopted.[6] Before Duhm's separation of Isaiah 56–66, these chapters were regarded as a part of Second Isaiah. He, however, drawing attention to the Palestinian setting of these chapters and to stylistic differences, attributed them to a prophet "Third Isaiah" who lived shortly before Nehemiah and championed the cause of the temple community against the Samaritan enemies of Ezra.[7] Although Duhm's

4. P. Volz, *Jesaia II, Kommentar zum alten Testament* (Leipzig: D. Werner Scholl, 1932), p. 207.

5. Three dates, of varying degrees of reliability, at least provide an historical framework for the period: (1) Cyrus' edict in 538 with the apparent return of exiles which ensued; (2) reconstruction of the temple from 520 until 515; (3) the reconstruction undertaken by Ezra and Nehemiah around the middle of the fifth century (this date is the least reliable of the three). With regard to biblical sources which might serve to fill out the events of this period: (1) Ezra 1–6 seems at first blush to offer the necessary data, providing a sketch of the period from the return from exile to the dedication of the temple, but the historical reliability of this source is uncertain, especially in the light of its marked theological *Tendenz;* thus it must be used with extreme caution, preferably only when corroborated by other strong evidence. (2) Haggai and Zechariah are a welcome source of information for the period circa 520. (3) Malachi sheds light on the spiritual conditions in Judah toward the middle of the fifth century. The memoirs of Ezra and Nehemiah also contribute to our knowledge of this period or a somewhat later period, depending on how one solves the problem of the dates of those two figures. (4) Finally, some of the prophecies of Jeremiah and Ezekiel afford glimpses into the conditions existing in Judah after 586.

6. Fuller treatments of the history of research can be found in the standard introductions and in the article by F. Maass, "Tritojesaja?" *Das Ferne und Nahe Wort,* Festschrift L. Rost, ed. F. Maass (Berlin: Alfred Töpelmann, 1967), pp. 151–163.

7. B. Duhm, *Das Buch Jesaia,* HAT (Göttingen: Vanderhoeck und Ruprecht,

mid-fifth-century date soon fell from favor, the history of subsequent scholarship can be seen essentially as a controversy over the questions raised by his separation of Isaiah 56–66 from the rest of the Isaianic corpus. For the sake of simplicity, the various critics can be placed in three categories: (1) those who maintain the unity of chapters 40–66; (2) those who accept Duhm's separation as well as his argument for unity of authorship in chapters 56–66 (though not necessarily accepting his fifth-century dating); (3) those who accept his separation, but reject the view of unity of authorship, recognizing instead a number of different authors ranging all the way from the seventh century to the third.

The most notable champion of the hypothesis that Isaiah 40–66 forms a unity coming from the career of one author was C. C. Torrey. In support of his argument he was able to marshal the numerous similarities in theological ideas and linguistic usage which bind these chapters together. The author in question was active in Palestine near the end of the fifth century, his work comprising twenty-seven poems which were originally written down in their present order.[8] One of the gravest flaws in Torrey's hypothesis is that his argument for a Palestinian setting for all of 40–66 necessitated deep surgery into the text, surgery unsupported by any textual evidence, since all mention of Cyrus, Babylon, and Chaldea had to be explained away as later interpolations.[9] The claims he made for metrical support are inconclusive and unconvincing.

In a recent commentary James D. Smart takes up Torrey's view anew.[10] His treatment introduces certain

1922[4]), 418–419. Duhm's whole hypothesis was accepted essentially unchanged by Marti, Cornill, Holscher, Littmann, and Pfeiffer. Typical of this group is J. Skinner, who pointed to the following conditions of the Ezra period reflected in Isaiah 56–66: (1) oppression of the poor, (2) worthless leaders of the community, (3) worldly minded priests, (4) traces of cleavage into two parties, (5) a section of the population addicted to idolatrous practices.

8. Torrey, p. 53.

9. Ibid., pp. 38–52.

10. J. Smart, *History and Theology in Second Isaiah* (Philadelphia: Westminster, 1965). Also defending the unity of Isaiah 40–66 are B. O. Banwell, "A Suggested Analysis of Isaiah XL–LXVI," *Expository Times* 76 (1964–65): 166, and M. Haran, "The Literary Structure and Chronological Framework of the Prophecies in Is.

modifications of Torrey's argument (e.g., he dates the material nearly a century earlier), but the main lines remain the same. Apparently aware that the deletion of the Cyrus passages represents for many scholars the greatest weakness in Torrey's hypothesis, Smart, in a polemical style characteristic of the work, never tires of reinforcing Torrey's argument by insisting that the attribution of messianic characteristics to a pagan monarch is an act unworthy of a prophet of God: "Frankly, who can take seriously a prophet who in God's name proclaims the impending *salvation* of humanity through the agency of a pagan conqueror?"[11] Resorting to such a level of argumentation is evidence of the fragile nature of the author's hypothesis. After one recognizes that Yahweh's use of a pagan nation or monarch as an instrument of his activity is a notion entirely at home in Yahwism,[12] and also appreciates how great an impact, loaded with eschatological significance, the defeat of Babylon and the envisioned return to Jerusalem must have had on the *gôlāh,* one comes to realize that the idea of Cyrus as an instrument of Yahweh, far from calling the seriousness of Second Isaiah's message into question, is a notion fully worthy of a prophet of God.

One senses the excessive influence of an hypothesis upon the interpretation again when Smart comes to treat the dynamic "second exodus-conquest" passages. Since it is meaningless for a prophet living with his people in Palestine to speak literally on a way prepared for them by Yahweh for their return to the land, Smart must interpret such passages as a vision of Yahweh's theophany, having nothing to do with Yahweh guiding the people back to the land.[13] Similarly, references to the wilderness which Yahweh will transform are not interpreted as descriptions of the barren region through which the people, under Yahweh's protection, would pass on their return to Palestine,

40-48," *VT* Suppl IX (1963): 127-155. Older works, alongside that of Torrey, which upheld the unity of the second half of Isaiah, include E. König, *Das Buch Jesaja* (Gütersloh: C. Bertelsmann, 1926), and L. Glahn, vol. 1 in L. Glahn and L. Koehler, *Der Prophet der Heimkehr* (Giessen: Alfred Töpelmann, 1934).

11. Smart, *History,* p. 24; cf. pp. 115-118.

12. Cf. Is 10:5ff; Jer 25:9; cf. also the Balaam stories in Nu 22-24.

13. Smart, *History,* p. 46.

for if Second Isaiah meant that, "he was a muddleheaded prophet who gave men bad advice."[14] From this one would have to infer that "muddleheads" also invented the stories of God's protection of his people in the wilderness in Exodus and Numbers, and that Ezra was a "muddlehead" to expect Yahweh to protect him and his cortege in their return to Palestine.[15] The fundamental error underlying all of Smart's untenable suggestions is his failure to recognize the centrality of second exodus typology in Second Isaiah's message, whereby this prophet of hope equates the imminent return of the *gôlah* from Babylon with the passage from Egypt and the entry into the land of promise. The rebirth of Israel would recapitulate the earlier birth of the nation.

The commentaries of Torrey and Smart illustrate the price which must be paid for advancing the hypothesis that Isaiah 40–66 forms a unity, the price of massive surgery on the text and highly contrived argumentation to alter the most obvious sense of the material. One is led to conclude that a less violent explanation must be found for the elements held in common between Isaiah 40-55 and 56–66. For the differences between these two sections are as deep as they are significant:[16] (1) The setting of 40–55 is Babylon, that of 56–66 is Palestine. (2) The mood of 40–55 is one of excited expectation of an imminent return, that of 56-66 is one of bitter controversy and disappointment after that return has already occurred. (3) In 40–55 the entire nation is object of the promise of salvation, whereas in 56–66 salvation is reserved for one segment of the nation. This is reflected, e.g., in the reinterpretation of the "servant" Israel of Second Isaiah as the "servants" comprising only the faithful remnant. (4) In 40–55 the polemic against idolatry is carried on in a humorously ironical manner, while in 56-66 that polemic becomes sardonic and bitter. (5) As closer examination will illustrate, 56–66 represents a point more advanced on the typology of prophet-

14. Ibid., p. 75.

15. Ezr 8:21ff.

16. The exceptional position occupied by 57:14–21 and 60–62 will be considered below.

ic genres, as well as on the continuum from prophetic eschatology to apocalyptic eschatology. (6) Stylistic and metric differences are in evidence, as will also be demonstrated below.

Finally, a very satisfactory explanation of the numerous thematic and stylistic elements common to both sections is found when one adopts the view that the authors of the oracles in 56–66 stand in the tradition of Second Isaiah, even as the latter can be viewed as belonging to a tradition stemming from the eighth-century Isaiah. To be certain, one can argue that all of the above differences could be attributed to the development through which one prophet passed during a long career, and no absolute evidence can be advanced to disprove such a notion.[17] Ultimately, one must be guided by the explanation which seems to account most naturally for most of the data. The present writer feels that viewing chapters 56–66 as later material stemming from a Second Isaiah tradition accounts least forcedly both for the elements in common and for the differences between the two sections.

The scholars who accept this division in turn fall into two groups, those accepting Duhm's view of unity of authorship in Third Isaiah, and those feeling that Isaiah 56–66 represents material from a number of authors.

Karl Elliger[18] has advanced the most vigorous argument in favor of seeing Isaiah 56-66 as the work of a single author—a disciple of Second Isaiah of the first generation after the return who also edited the work of his master, leaving his imprint on the material in 42:18-43:7; 43–46; 48:1-11; 51:1-16; and 52:1-6, and adding from his own oracles chapters 47; 48:17-19; 49:22-26; 50:1-3; and chapters 54-55.[19] Elliger's argument is a very intricate one,

17. Using a similar methodology, one can attribute the entire book of Isaiah to one prophet, as is done, e.g., by O. Allis, *The Unity of Isaiah* (Philadelphia: The Presbyterian and Reformed Publishing Co., 1950), and E. Young, *Who Wrote Isaiah?* (Grand Rapids; Eerdmans, 1958).

18. Elliger, *Die Einheit des Tritojesaia* (Stuttgart: W. Kohlhammer, 1928); *Deuterojesaja in seinem Verhältnis zu Tritojesaja* (Stuttgart: W. Kohlhammer, 1933); "Der Prophet Tritojesaja," *ZAW* 49 (1931): 112-141.

19. A more popularized version of Elliger's position is given by W. Kessler, *Gott geht es um das Ganze* (Stuttgart: Calwer, 1960). Positions similar to Elliger are also held by E. Sellin, *Einleitung in das altes Testament* (Leipzig: Quelle und Meyer,

based on linguistic and stylistic evidence, and one's first impression is that he has presented a formidable case. When one examines his evidence systematically, however, it becomes obvious that the matter is not so conclusive as his assertions would lead one to believe.[20] For example, when he finds literary similarities connecting a passage in 56–66 with the Second Isaiah corpus, he either argues that the particular passage in question was written by Second Isaiah, or that it represents Third Isaiah's imitation of his master, Second Isaiah, i.e., he can opt for whichever alternative fits his hypothesis. Moreover, his argument is very circular inasmuch as he uses characteristics collected not only in chapters 56–66 to claim a passage for Third Isaiah, but also ones collected from sections in Second Isaiah which he earlier had claimed for the Third Isaiah corpus, e.g., 47 and 52:13–53:12. Finally, when a passage fails to fit into his reconstruction, he does not hesitate to dismiss it as an interpolation, on occasion even resorting to an idealistic dogmatism to argue that a chapter like 47 is too legalistic and vindictive to be worthy of a great prophet like Second Isaiah. One is led to conclude that the argument from linguistic, lexicographical, and stylistic data is incapable of settling the question of authorship in one direction or the other. That Elliger's study demonstrates that certain similarities on these levels do tie the bulk of Isaiah 56–66 together can be granted, but, as we shall argue later, this is best considered as evidence that the material all belongs to a common tradition rather than as proof that it all derives from a single hand. This view has the added advantage of accounting for both the similarities *and* the differences existing between Second and Third Isaiah.

Finally, the largest group of critics accepts Duhm's division, but denies unity of authorship to Isaiah 56–66.[21] In a

1925), and J. Meinhold, *Einführung in das alte Testament* (Leipzig: Alfred Töpelmann, 1919).

20. Paul Volz has exposed the weakness inherent in Elliger's methodology in *Jesaia II*, pp. 197 ff. Elliger's rebuttal is in his *Deuterojesaja*, pp. 278–303.

21. E.g., K. Budde, *Die Heilige Schrift des AT* (Bonn: Verlag von Peter Hanstein, 1922⁴); A. van der Flier, *Jesaja II*, Tekst en uitleg (Groningen: 1926); R. P. P. Auvray-J. Steinmann, *Isaie*, La Sainte Bible (Paris: Les Editions du Cerf, 1951); G. Fohrer, *Das Buch Jesaja III*, Zürcher Bibelkommentare (Zürich/Stuttgart: Zwingli, 1964).

sense, one finds within this group some of the most balanced treatments of the material, largely because their approach can be more objective, not being guided by a rigid hypothesis regarding authorship. Only two of the most significant of these commentaries can here be mentioned for the purpose of methodological considerations. The first is a highly respected commentary of several decades ago written by Paul Volz.[22] As the commentaries discussed in the above two groups illustrate the danger common to them, namely, of beginning with an hypothesis regarding authorship, followed by the attempt to fit each oracle into that hypothesis, so Volz's commentary illustrates a prevalent methodological weakness in this group, that of utilizing obscure or even fictitious historical references to date each oracle in complete isolation from the other material in 56–66. Thus the reference to Gad and Meni in 65:11–12 leads Volz to a Hellenistic date for that passage, whereas 63:7–64:11 seems to reflect for him the conditions soon after the fall of Jerusalem, prompting a date circa 586. This method is sound wherever relatively reliable historical allusions are found, but such are almost totally absent from Isaiah 56–66. Gad and Meni had admirers long before the Hellenistic period, and the lament in 63:7–64:11 could fit perfectly into the conditions of the dark period described by Ezra at the mid-fifth century, or into the bleak conditions of the mid-sixth century.

The most recent commentary of the group which accepts Duhm's division but denies unity of authorship is that of C. Westermann.[23] This form critic does not escape the old question of authorship and, after searching for the *ipsissima verba* of Third Isaiah, he attributes to him those sections which many critics have felt were written by Second Isaiah, so closely do they stand to the latter in style and content, namely, chapters 60–62 and 57:14–20; he also believes Third Isaiah to have written 65:16b–25, 66:6–16, and perhaps 58:1–12. Alongside these words of Third Isaiah he

22. Volz, Jesaia II.

23. C. Westermann, *Isaiah 40–66*, tr. D. M. G. Stalker (Philadelphia: Westminster, 1969 [first German edition, 1966]).

finds three other later levels of tradition in chapters 56-66.[24]

Without considering further works, the above survey should illustrate the wide range of interpretations possible in the critical treatment of Third Isaiah, thereby bringing into focus the problem of methodology. One can observe that virtually all criticism of Isaiah 56-66 has gravitated around the question of authorship raised by Duhm. This preoccupation with the problem of authorship is an unhappy one, since it polarizes the critics into the positions described, whereas it seems likely to the present writer that the truth lies somewhere in between. That is, it is hard to deny completely the force of Elliger's argument for the unity underlying Isaiah 56-66, for there are distinct themes, lexicographical features, and stylistic characteristics which persist throughout the material. Nor are Smart and Torrey entirely misdirected in recognizing common features running throughout the larger collection Isaiah 40-66. Finally, Volz and all of those holding related positions must also be given their due, for undeniable

24. Ibid, pp. 296-308. The method generally used by critics who set out to establish the original corpus of Third Isaiah recurs in Westermann's commentary. First, the nucleus of that corpus is identified (in Westermann's case comprising chapters 60-62). Then only those other passages which agree in theme (promise of salvation to the whole nation, with foreign nations sharing in the salvation event) and tone (conciliatory) with this nucleus are credited to Third Isaiah. The method is to be faulted especially because of its rigidity. The entity Third Isaiah becomes absolutely static. Since he is conciliatory to the whole nation in chapters 60-62, he may not be held responsible for the charges leveled in chapter 59 against transgressors. Since he is generous in his attitude toward foreigners in chapter 60, he could not have recited the oracle in 63:1-6. Such imposition of rigid categories bespeaks in no way the complexities of the community situation in the early post-exilic period, during which the people were thrust from disappointment to despair, were constantly forced to alter the form of their hopes, were cast under the power of foreign powers which changed whimsically from hostile to benign to aggressive without warning or apparent reason. Something of the rigidity of a literary critic like Duhm, with his distinction between oracles of judgment (pre-exilic) and oracles of salvation (post-exilic) lingers on in a form-critic like Westermann. Viewing the prophecies of Third Isaiah as the products of a community living amidst very complex conditions alone seems able to free one from this rigidity. For when the inquiry is directed toward the sociological matrix producing the literature, both the ceaseless reduction of the material into ever smaller units and the equally futile search for the historical kernel of the anonymous prophet Third Isaiah become unnecessary. For the attention shifts toward the broader creative power of the religious group developing this literature against the background of a particular prophetic tradition and within the context of distinct social pressures. An organic quality in the corpus becomes expected and intelligible, and exact divisions between what one author wrote and the writings of another become less significant (even if such divisions could be established with any degree of certainty) than origin within one religious group.

differences do separate many of the units of prophecy in 56-66 from each other. The very fact that each of these three lines of interpretation continues tenaciously to reappear in the literature already suggests that legitimate insights are found in each. But how is one to get beyond the impasse evidenced by current scholarship? We move to consider several methodological questions in the hopes of laying the basis for a fruitful new line of inquiry.

We begin with a very elementary fact, the significance of which has been neglected in the literature: both Second and Third Isaiah, in contrast to the earlier prophetic corpora, are anonymous collections. They point toward a period when imposing literary figures go into eclipse: the process of literary creation, collection, and transmission becomes a collective rather than an individual enterprise. If the critic is to get at the original intention of the material, he must be aware of the significance of this development. Secondly we note that Isaiah 56-66 does betray a peculiar sort of unity, the adhesive ingredients of which go beyond mere editorial links bridging otherwise independent units. For a distinct unity of basic themes is evident, as is a definite similarity in the community situation underlying most of the material. Yet these similarities are not of the type which would suggest unity of authorship; for example, one author may stand behind chapters like 59 and 66, while it is very unlikely that 63:7-64 could be attributed to that same author. The question of authorship simply is inadequate in dealing with the type of unity binding this material together.

There is, however, a level of inquiry which does seem to be adequate, one which takes seriously the anonymous character of the material and recognizes the underlying unity as that which stems from a common tradition and a common community situation. This level of inquiry, utilizing the contextual-typological method described in the previous chapter, alone seems capable of accounting both for the common elements which the defenders of the Third Isaiah hypothesis marshal as evidence, and for the differences upon which the "atomists" base their case. It also takes cognizance of the force behind Torrey's and Smart's argument, for it recognizes that the tradition reflected in Isaiah 56–66 develops out of the message of Second Isaiah.[25] At the same time it avoids the forceful handling of the text often necessitated by the various hypotheses of authorship, and is sensitive instead to the important sociological factors effecting both the form and content of the literature.

In applying the contextual-typological method, we shall proceed as follows: Each unit of tradition will be investigated to determine form, dominant themes, and function, and to establish connections with other prophetic material, either in Isaiah 56–66 or elsewhere. Two dominant characteristics will become evident in this investigation: (1) An eschatological ideal of the community and its destiny, and of Yahweh's relation to that community, runs throughout this material, an ideal which stands in full harmony with the theology of Second Isaiah. (2) Based upon this ideal is a pervasive polemical element, varying in degree from mild reprimand (64:7) to acrimonious attack (57:3ff). Throughout, this polemic is in defense of the eschatological ideal, and is directed against an apparently uneschatological rival position which stands in sharp contrast. These characteristics will emerge in the course of a literary analysis, the first discernible in the recurrent themes of the material, the second communicated by the specific forms in which those themes have been cast.

The next step will involve the move from the literary analysis to extrapolation of the community situation reflected by the material, a move which involves a methodological crux: when, and on what basis, can one draw historical conclusions from a literary corpus? It would be safer to leave this move unattempted; this, however, would necessitate forfeiting the most significant aspect of the in-

25. For the view that an "Isaiah school" developed from the prophetic activity of Proto-Isaiah (cf. Is 8:16–18), later to be perpetuated by both Second Isaiah and the Third Isaiah group, see H. Birkeland, *Zum hebräischen Traditionswesen* (Oslo: Jacob Dybwod, 1938), pp. 39–40. Two recent commentaries develop this view: J. Muilenburg, "Introduction, Exegesis," *Isaiah,* IB 5 (New York: Abington, 1956), and G. E. Wright, *The Book of Isaiah,* The Layman's Bible Commentary (Richmond: John Knox, 1964).

quiry. For Isaiah 56–66 represents a stage in Israel's prophetic literature when classical prophetic forms are undergoing transformation into apocalyptic forms; if one can penetrate through this literary phenomenon to the underlying community situation, it is likely that valuable insight will be gained into the rise of Jewish apocalyptic, and especially of the transformation of prophetic eschatology into apocalyptic eschatology.

Since any move from literary analysis to historical situation involves an element of speculation, the critic must be fully aware that he has entered an area where dogmatism has no place. Yet, no area breeds as much dogmatism as an uncertain area like sixth- and fifth-century prophecy, since diminishing evidence is often accompanied by increasing claims. The inevitable conclusion is not that one must opt for complete neutrality, for such caution leads to a leveling of all evidence producing a picture as false as the wildest hypothesis. Somehow the tightrope must be walked between the speculative nature of, let us say, Morgenstern's treatment of Zerubbabel[26] and the extremely cautious reconstruction of the fifth and sixth centuries offered by Peter Ackroyd.[27] The former goes far beyond the evidence; the latter is insensitive to some of the most significant evidence, that is, he treats all of the literature of the period as pretty much representing the same mainstream of orthodoxy. The latter alternative is best countered not by new speculations, but by appeal to hard evidence, such as the fact that one of the essential *literary* characteristics of Isaiah 56–66 is its polemical thrust. The significance of this fact is enhanced in light of the polemical nature of other literatures of the period in question, e.g., Haggai, Ezra, and additions to Ezekiel and Zechariah. When one considers the post-exilic literature as a whole, it becomes apparent that two very divergent streams of tradition are emerging. An historical reconstruction that leaves

26. J. Morgenstern, "A Chapter in the History of the High Priesthood," *AJSL* 55 (1938): 1–24, 183–197, 360–377.

27. P. R. Ackroyd, *Exile and Restoration* (Philadelphia: Westminster, 1968). A similar leveling of divergent tradition is found in Th. Chary, *Les Prophètes et le Culte* (Paris: Desclée, 1955).

such evidence unaccounted for is not a cautious reconstruction, but an incomplete, or even falsifying one.

With these hazards clearly in mind we shall attempt to move from the literary analysis to a reconstruction of the situation giving rise to this literature. We shall argue that the first result gained by the literary analysis, namely, that of a unified eschatological ideal running throughout the material, betrays an origin in a community of those remaining faithful to the tradition stemming from Second Isaiah. The second result of that analysis, that of the polemical form assumed by much of the material, will be used to identify the nature of the struggle in which this community is embroiled. The identity of the group being attacked will be sought on the basis of the accusations made in the polemic, leading to the conclusion (tentative and to be tested further in Chapter III) that the opponents belong to an uneschatological group which controls the official cult, and threatens to compromise the eschatological ideal which the prophetic group espouses. Dramatic traces of oppression at the hands of the official community will be discerned. It will be argued that both the transformation occurring in the form of the prophetic oracle and the development of prophetic eschatology toward apocalyptic eschatology are intimately related to the oppression suffered by this minority. Also related to this opposition is a more vindictive spirit, and a narrowing of the modest universalism found in Second Isaiah.

This approach to the last eleven chapters of Isaiah has the added advantage of answering questions raised in connection with the transmission history of the book of Isaiah. In seeking the factors which brought together this diverse material, we come to recognize the unbroken thread of a religious group vitally interested in the prophetic literature, especially that of Second Isaiah. It is from the promises made in that literature that the members of this group derive their identity and hope. The "Servant" Israel of Second Isaiah becomes further democratized, as they recognize themselves as the "Servants" of Yahweh, the true Israel. As they live from that literature, and await the fulfillment of its promises in their midst, they revitalize it by reapplication and amplification. At an early period they summarize Second Isaiah's message in a program of restoration (60–62); in other cases they quote from or allude to words of the master, applying his thoughts to their new situation (58:8b//52:12b; 59:1//50:2; 62:10//40:3f). We thus discern signs that we are dealing with a living, ongoing tradition, restlessly seeking new applications as the situation changes.

But the ongoing situation in most cases has clearly left its mark, in terms of a development in the form of the oracle, in terms of a development in the direction of apocalyptic eschatology, even in terms of modifications in prosodic structure. It is on the basis of such changes, and with the use of typological considerations, that the attempt can be made to place the oracles of Third Isaiah in a relative chronology. This attempt must be considered tentative in light of the uncertainty of much of the evidence, especially when it comes to detail. In its broad lines, however, it is likely that the relative chronology thus established will be reasonably accurate; for example, Isaiah 60–62 stems from a period close to the time of Second Isaiah, while 63:4–64:12 is later, but still considerably prior to chapter 65. Whether we can place chapters 65, 66, and 56:9–57:13 in proper sequence is much less certain, but the question is not critical for the argument as a whole, since the community situation reflected in the last mentioned three passages is very similar.

In any case, the present ordering of Isaiah 56–66 is clearly the result of later redaction. The stages of the *Traditionsgeschichte* leading to this final ordering can only be suggested here. Since the material in 56–66 was so intimately related to Second Isaiah, often assuming the form of a commentary on that corpus, it is natural that it finally came to be identified with the Isaianic tradition. We can conjecture that the fusion was effected already by the community from which the new oracles originated, for they likely transmitted their interpretation and reapplication of Second Isaiah with that work itself. Occasionally the considerations guiding their redactional activity can be detected, e.g., 65:1ff may have been placed as a reply to the question with which the unit 63:7–64:19 ends. Because these oracles—sharply critical of the official party though they were—came to be bound so inseparably to the Isaianic corpus, they came to be preserved by the very hierocracy which they originally attacked, one of the evidences for the great flexibility which characterized Judaism, all claims to the contrary notwithstanding.[28]

B. THE IDEAL COMMUNITY ENVISIONED BY THE DISCIPLES OF SECOND ISAIAH

1. *Isaiah 60–62*

Metrically, stylistically, and thematically the units found in chapters 60, 61, and 62 are inextricably related, a fact recognized by all critics in spite of their wide disagreement on questions of authorship, date, and interpretation. No argument is necessary, therefore, in defense of our treating these three chapters together.

EXCURSUS: TEXTUAL RECONSTRUCTION AND PROSODIC ANALYSIS

The poetic compositions studied in this chapter and in Chapter IV have been reconstructed with three aims in mind: (1) restoration of as original a form of the text as present evidence permits; (2) analysis of the internal structure of the poetry by diagraming the prosodic units which comprise each composition; (3) analysis of the metric structure. More must be said concerning the latter two aims.

In analyzing the internal structure, we have diagramed the prosodic units by assigning a letter to each significant grammatical element of a colon. Parallel grammatical elements in succeeding cola receive the same letter, but with sublinear numbers to indicate their order of occurrence. In the case of a grammatical element which is identical to its parallel antecedent, the identical letter and number are used. When two elements are derivatives of the same Hebrew root, the distinction is indicated by placing an

28. The great flexibility characteristic of Judaism is evidenced by its exposition of a passage like Is 52:9–53:12, a passage which assumed a central position in visionary circles of the sixth and fifth centuries. As the Targum Jonathan indicates, passages like this were reinterpreted in a way which made them perfectly compatible with the dominant theological thinking of the rabbis.

acute accent over the letter (e.g., Is 60:1, אורי $=a_1$, אורך $=\acute{a}_1$). The length of the prosodic units varies from the short bicolon and tricolon to units embracing a dozen cola and more. Whatever its length, however a prosodic unit develops a tightly knit unit of thought held together by parallelism. repetition of grammatical elements, assonance, paronomasia, and similar poetic devices. (In the outlines of the internal structure and meter, short double lines will be used to divide between prosodic units, short single lines between bi- and tricola within prosodic units, and a long line between strophes).

Such systematic analysis of internal structure promises to become an important tool for the dating of Hebrew poetry, for the development of the canons of poetic composition is analogous to the development of paleographic style in writing and shape in pottery. Thus even as typologies of pottery and writing have been established, it should be possible to establish a typology of poetic structure as well. Until now only the broad outlines of that typology are apparent, and much additional work must be done until the details are filled in. It is clear, however, that the classical canons of Hebrew prosody, borrowed from Canaan, were based on the dominance of the parallel bi- and tricolon. The last flourishing of those canons came in the poetry of Second Isaiah.

The sixth- and fifth-century material being studied in this thesis is very important in the study of the typology of poetic structure, for not only are new genres and new modes of prophetic eschatology being developed, but new canons of poetic structure as well. Some may consider this development a disintegration of the earlier pure forms. However conceived, the development is in the direction away from the dominance of the simple bi- and tricolon toward longer, more baroque prosodic units. A parallel development away from the simple bi- and tricolon as the basic prosodic unit toward longer more baroque units seems to characterize the long history of Akkadian poetry as well. The structural analysis in this thesis must be considered tentative, and the conclusions drawn from the analysis concerning typology and dating even more tentative. But it may suggest the direction in which further study can be pursued.

A greater degree of precision has already been achieved in the third area mentioned, the analysis of metric structure. The system of scanning adopted here is based on syllable count rather than on the Ley-Sievers system of accentual scanning, and offers a more reliable means of revealing the symmetry or asymmetry between cola. For example, according to the accentual system two cola may appear imbalanced with a 3:2 pattern, whereas syllable count reveals that they are equal. The longer cola can be designated l (*longum*), the shorter b (*breve*), with about seven syllables being the dividing line between them. (Cf. F. M. Cross, "The Song of the Sea and Canaanite Myth," *Journal for Theology and the Church* 5 [New York: Harper Torchbooks, 1968], especially n. 12, pp. 4–5; for a brief but excellent discussion of the various methods which have been used to analyze Hebrew prosody, the reader is referred to D. N. Freedman's "Prolegomenon" to the new edition of G. B. Gray's *The Forms of Hebrew Poetry* [KTAV, 1972]: vii–liii).

Each of these three aims is a part of one process, inasmuch as structural and metric considerations cannot be divorced from textual criticism. And, in turn, all three are part of the one unified

---

60

1 Arise, shine, for your light has come,
the glory of Yahweh has risen upon you;
2 though darkness covers the earth
and a deep darkness the peoples,
yet over you Yahweh now rises
and his glory is seen upon you;
3 nations will come to your light
and kings to your rising brightness.
4 Look around and see,
they all gather and come to you;
your sons will come from afar,
your daughters will be carried in arm.
5 Then you will see and be radiant,
your heart will be excited and full.
The abundance of the sea will be turned to you
and the wealth of the nations will come to you;
6 a host of camels will cover you,
the young camels of Midian and Ephah,
all of them will come from Sheba;
they will bear gold and incense,
the praise of Yahweh they will announce;
7 all the flocks of Kadar will gather to you,
the rams of Nebaioth will be at your service.
They will be accepted graciously upon my altar
and I will glorify my beautiful house.
8 Who are these that fly like a cloud,
like doves to their cotes?
9 For the ships are gathering themselves to me
with the vessels of Tarshish at their head,
to bring your sons from afar,
their silver and their gold with them,
for the name of Yahweh your God,

task of exegesis, since lower criticism cannot be carried on apart from considerations of higher criticism, and vice versa.

In our reconstruction of the poetic texts in the present chapter and Chapter IV, we will not note in the text textual emendations merely involving the dropping of the conjunction, the definite article, the direct object marker, and the like (all common late additions to poetic texts), and also those involving the changing of converted perfects to imperfects (late editing of the texts betrays a preference for the converted form). Omissions and additions are indicated by brackets ([ ]), change of word order by an acute and a grave accent around the word or words affected (´ `).

60:1

	קומי אורי כי בא אורך	a	a_1	b	$á_1$	8	1:1::1:1::1:1::1:1
	כבוד יהוה עליך זרח		Á	c	b_1	8	
2	הנה [ ][a]חשך יכסה ארץ		a_2	b_2	d	7	
	וערפל לאמים		a_3		D	7	
	ועליך יזרח יהוה		c	b_1	a_4	7	
	כבודו עליך יראה		a_5	c	b_3	8	
3	הלכו גוים לאורך		b_4	d_1	a_1	8	
	ומלכים לנגה זרחך			d_2	A_1	8	
4	שאי סביב עיניך וראי	a	b	a_1		9	1:1::1:1
	כלם נקבצו באו לך		d	e	e_1	8	
	בניך מרחוק יבאו		d_1	f	e_1	8	
	בנתיך על צד תאמנה[b]		d_2	f_1	e_2	9	
5	אז תראי ונהרת	a	b	b_1		7	1:1
	פחד ורחב לבבך		b_2	b_3	c	8	
	יהפך עליך חמון ים	a	b	c		8	1:1::1:1:1:1:1::1:1
	חיל גוים יבאו לך[c]	c_1	a_1	b_1		7	
6	שפעת גמלים תכסך		C		a_2	8	
	בכרי מדין ועיפה		c_2	d	d_1	8	
	כלם משבא יבאו		c_3	d_2	a_1	8	
	זהב ולבונה ישאו		c_4	c_5	a_3	9	
	תהלת יהוח יבשרו		C_1		a_4	9	
7	כל צאן קדר יקבצו לך		c_6	d_3	a_5	9	
	אילי נביות ישרתונך		c_7	d_4	a_6	10	
	יעלו [ל]רצון [על][d]מזבחי	a	b	c		9	1:1
	ובית תפארתי אפאר		C	d		8	
8	מי אלה כעב תעופינה	a	b	c		9	1:1
	כיונים אל ארבתיהם		b_1	D		9	
9	כי לי [צ][e]יים יקוו	a	b			7	1:1
	אניות תרשיש בראשנה	A		c		9	
	להביא בניך מרחוק	a	b	c		9	1:1
	כספם וזהבם אתם		b_1	b_2	c_1	8	
	לשם יהוה אלהיך	a	B			8	1:1

for the Holy One of Israel who glorifies you.
10 Foreigners will rebuild your walls
and their kings will serve you.
For in my anger I struck you,
but in my goodwill I have pitied you.
11 And your gates will be open continually,
neither day nor night will they be closed;
that the wealth of the nations may be brought to you,
and their kings conducted as captives.
12 The nation which will not serve you will perish,
and that kingdom will be utterly destroyed.
13 The glory of Lebanon will come to you,
the cypress, the plane and the pine together,
to adorn the site of my sanctuary,
that I may glorify the resting place of my feet.
14 Your oppressors will come unto you,
your despisers will fall at your feet.
They will call you "City of Yahweh,"
"Zion of the Holy One of Israel."
15 Though you have been abandoned,
hated, with none passing through,
I will make you majestic forever,
a joy from one generation to the next.
16 You will suck the milk of the nations,
the breasts of kingdoms you will suck.
You will know that I am your Savior
and your Redeemer the Mighty One of Jacob.
17 Instead of bronze I will bring gold,
instead of iron I will bring silver,
instead of wood, bronze,
instead of stone, iron.
I will make your officers Peace,
your rulers Righteousness.
18 No longer will violence be heard in your land,
nor destruction and ruin in your territory.
But you will call your walls "Salvation,"
your gates "Praise. . . . "
21 Your people shall all be righteous,
they shall possess the land forever,
guardians of the plantation of Yahweh,
of the work of his hand, for his ornament.
22 The smallest will become a clan,
the least significant a mighty nation.
I will hasten it in its time.

	לקדוש ישראל כי פארך		B_1	c		9	
10	בנו בני נכר חמתיך	a	b	c		9	1:1
	ומלכיהם ישרתונך		b_1	a_1		9	
	כי בקצפי הכיתיך	a	b			7	b:b
	וברצוני רחמתיך	a_1	b_1			7	
11	ופתחו שעריך תמיד	a	b	c		10	1:1
	יומם ולילה לא יסגרו	c_1	c_2	a_1		10	
	להביא אליך חיל גוים	a	b	c		8	1:1
	ומלכיהם נהוגים		c_1	a_1		7	
12	הגוי[ ]לא יעבד[ ]ך יאבד[ ]	a	b	b_1		9	1:1
	[והממלכה] חרב [ת]חרב[ ] [f]	a_1	B			9	
13	כבוד לבנון אליך יבוא	A	b	c		9	1:1
	ברוש תדהר ותאשור יחדו	a	a_1	a_2	d	10	
	לפאר מקום מקדשי	a	b	c		8	1:1
	ומקום רגלי אכבד	b_1	c_1	a_1		8	
14	הלכו אליך [ ]מעניך	a	b	c		10	1:1
	השתחוו על [ ]רגליך [ ]מנאציך [g]	a_1	b_1	c_1		11	
	קראו לך עיר יהוה	a	b	c		7	b:b
	ציון קדוש ישראל		b_1	C		7	
15	תחת היותך עזובה	a	b	c		7	b:b
	שנואה ואין עובר		c_1	d	e	7	
	שמתיך לגאון עולם	a	b	c		7	b:b
	משוש דור ודור		b_1	C		5	
16	ינקת חלב גוים	a	b	c		6	b:b
	שד מלכים תינקי	b_1	c_1	a		7	
	ידעת כי אני מושיעך	a	b	c		9	1:1
	וגאלך אביר יעקב		c_1	B		9	
17	תחת נחשת אביא זהב	a	b	a_1		7	b:b:b:b
	ותחת ברזל אביא כסף	a_2	b	a_3		7	
	ותחת עצים נחשת	a_4		a		6	
	ותחת אבנים ברזל	a_5		a_2		7	
	שמתי פקדתך שלום	a	b	c		8	1:b
	נגשיך צדקה		b_1	c_1		6	
18	לא ישמע עוד חמס בארצך	a	b	c		9	1:b
	שד ושבר בגבוליך		b_1	b_2	c_1	7	
	וקראת ישועה חומתיך	a	b	c		9	1:b
	שעריך תהלה[ ] [h]		c_1	b_1		6	
21	עַמֵּךְ כלם צדיקים	a	b	c		7	1:1
	לעולם יירשו ארץ		d	e	f	7	
	נצר[י] מטע [יהוה]	a	b	c		7	1:1
	מעשה ידו[ו] להתפאר [i]		b_1	c_1	d	8	
22	הקטן יהיה לאלף	a	b	c		7	1:1
	הצעיר לגוי עצום	a_1		C		7	
	אני [ ]בעתה אחישנה	rubric				9	1

61: 1 The Spirit of the Lord Yahweh is upon me,
for Yahweh has anointed me,
to bring good news to the poor he has sent me,
to bind up the brokenhearted,
to proclaim freedom to captives,
release to those in prison,
2 to proclaim a year of favor from Yahweh,
a day of deliverance for our God,
to comfort all who mourn,
3 to give them a crown instead of dust,
oil of gladness instead of mourning robe,
praise instead of a despondent spirit,
to call them righteous nobles,
the plantation of Yahweh, for his ornament.
4 They will rebuild the ancient ruins,
they will raise up devastated places of old,
they will restore desolate cities,
devastations of the past generations.
5 Strangers will stand and graze your sheep,
foreigners will be your plowmen.
6 You will be named the priests of Yahweh,
ministers of our God.
You will feed on the wealth of the nations,
and grow fat in their abundance.
7 Because their shame was twofold,
and they inherited insult as their portion,
they will inherit twofold in their land,
eternal joy will be theirs.
8 For I Yahweh love justice,
I hate robbery with burnt offering.
I will faithfully grant their reward,
and make an eternal covenant with them.
9 Their progeny will be renowned in the nations,
and their offspring among the peoples.
All who see them will acknowledge them,
for they are a people blessed by Yahweh.
10 I will rejoice greatly in Yahweh,
my soul will exult in my God.
For he has clothed me in garments of salvation,
he has wrapped me in a cloak of righteousness,
as the bridegroom prepares a garland
and the bride adorns herself with her jewels;
11 for as the earth brings forth its shoots
and a garden makes its seeds flourish,
so Yahweh will cause righteousness to flourish
as well as praise before all nations.

61:1	רוח אדני יהוה עלי	a	B	c		8	1:1::1:1::1:1::1:1
	יען משח יהוה אתי		d	b	c_1	7	::1:1:1:1::1:1
	לבשר ענוים שלחני		e	f	d_1	10	
	לחבש לנשברי לב		e_1	F		8	
	לקרא לשבוים דרור		e_2	f_1	g	9	
	ולאסורים פקחקוח			f_2	G	8	
2	לקרא שנת רצון ליהוה		e_3	g_1	b	10	
	ויום נקם לאלהינו			g_2	B_1	9	
	לנחם כל אבלים[ ] [j]		e_4	F_1		7	
3	לתת להם פאר תחת אפר		e_5	f_3	g_3 h	8	
	שמן ששון תחת מעטה אבל [k]			G_1	H	7	
	תהלה תחת רוח כהה			G_2	H_1	7	
	וקרא [l] להם אילי צדק		e_6	f_3	g_4	8	
	מטע יהוה להתפאר			g_5	I	8	
4	ובנו חרבות עולם	a	b	c		8	1:1:b:b
	שממות ראשנים יקוממו	b_1	c_1	a_1		10	
	חדשו ערי חרב	a_2	B			6	
	שממות דור ודור		b_2	C		6	
5	עמדו זרים ורעו צאנכם	a	b	a_1	c	5:5	b:b:1
	ובני נכר אכריכם[ ] [m]		B	A		9	
6	[ ] כהני יהוה תקראו	a	b	c		9	1:1
	משרתי אלהינו[ ] [n]	a_1	B			8	
	[o] [מ]חיל גוים תאכלו	a	b	c		7	1:1
	ובכבודם תתמר[א]ו [p]	A		c_1		9	
7	[כי היתה] [q] בשת[ ]ם משנה	a	b	c		8	1:1::1:1
	וכלמה יר[ש]ו [r] חלקם	b_1	a_1	c_1		9	
	[ ]בארצם משנה יירשו	d	c	a_1		8	
	שמחת עולם תהיה להם	c_2	a	d_1		8	
8	כי אני יהוה אהב משפט	a	b	c		9	1:1
	שנא גזל בעולה [s]		b_1	c_1	d	7	
	נתתי פעלתם באמת	a	b	c		10	1:1
	וברית עולם אכרות להם	b_1	a_1	d		9	
9	ונודע בגוים זרעם	a	b	c		8	1:1
	צאצאיהם בתוך עמים		c_1	B		8	
	כל ראיהם יכירום	a	b	b_1		7	1:1
	כי הם זרע ברך יהוה		c	d	e	7	
10	שוש אשיש ביהוה	A	b			6	b:1
	תגל נפשי באלהי	a	c	b_1		8	
	כי הלבישני בגדי ישע	a	b	c		8	1:1::1:1:1:1::1:1
	מעיל צדקה יעטני	b_1	c_1	a_1		8	16
	כחתן יכ[י]ן [t] פאר		d	e	f	7	
	וככלה תעדה כליה		d_1	e_1	f_1	9	16
11	כי כארץ תוציא צמחה		d_2	e_2	f_2	7	
	כגנה זרועיה תצמיח		d_3	e_3	f_3	9	16
	כן [ ] [u] יהוה יצמיח צדקה	g	a_2	c_2		8	
	ותהלה נגד כל גוים		C_3	H		8	16

62: 1 Concerning Zion I will not keep silent,
concerning Jerusalem I will not desist,
until her victory goes forth as a bright light,
and her salvation flames as a torch.
2 Nations will see your deliverance,
and all the kings your glory;
And you will be called by a new name
which the mouth of Yahweh will designate.
3 You will be a beautiful crown in Yahweh's hand,
a royal diadem in the hand of your God.
4 You will no more be called "Abandoned,"
nor your land "Desolate";
you will be called "My Delight is in her,"
and your land "Married,"
for Yahweh takes delight in you
and your land will be married.
5 As a young man marries a virgin
your Lord will marry you,
and as the bridegroom rejoices over his bride
your God will rejoice over you.
6 Upon your walls, Jerusalem,
I have appointed watchmen.
All day and all night
they will never be silent.
You who remember Yahweh
do not rest,
7 nor give him any rest

until he has made Jerusalem

a praise in the earth.
8 He has sworn by his right hand,
and by his mighty arm:
I will not give your grain
as food for your enemies,
nor will foreign men drink
your wine for which you toiled;
9 those who harvest it will eat it
and they will give praise to Yahweh;
those who gather it will drink it
in my holy courts.
10 Pass through, pass through the gates,
prepare a way for the people,
build up, build up the highway,
clear it of stones,
lift up, lift up a signal
over the peoples.

62:1	למען ציון לא אחשה	a	b	c		7		1:1
	למען ירושלם לא אשקוט	a_1	b_1	c_1		9		
	עד יצא כנגה צדקה	a	b	c		8		1:1
	וישועתה כלפיד יבער	c_1	b_1	a_1		10		
2	וראו גוים צדקך	a	b	c		7		1:1
	וכל מלכים כבודך		B	c_1		8		
	וקרא לך שם חדש	a	b	c		7		1:1
	פי יהוה יקבנו		d	e	f	8		
3	היית עטרת תפארת ביד יהוה	a	b	c		10		1:1
	צניף מלוכה בכף אלהיך		b_1	C		10		
4	לא יאמר לך עוד עזובה	a	b	c		9		1:1::1:1::bb
	ולארצך לא[ ] [v] עוד שממה		B	c_1		9		
	לך יקרא חפצי בה	b	a_1	c_2		7		
	ולארצך בעולה		B	c_3		7		
	כי חפץ יהוה בך		$\acute{c}_2$ d	b_1		6		
	וארצך תבעל		B	$\acute{c}_3$		6		
5	כ[ ]בעל [w] בחור בתולה	a	b	c		8		1:1::1:1
	יבעלך [אד]ניך [x]	a	B			7		
	ומשוש חתן על כלה	$\acute{a}_1$	b	c_1		8		
	ישיש עליך אלהיך	a_1	B	c_2		7		
6	על חומתיך ירושלם	a	b	c		8		1:b
	הפקדתי שמרים		d	e		6		
	כל יום וכל לילה	a	a_1			6		b:b
	תמיד לא יחשו	a_2	b			5		
	מזכרי יהוה	a	b			5		b:b:b:b:b
	אל דמי לכם		c	d	e	5		
7	אל תתנו דמי לו		C	d	e_1	7		
	עד יכונן / עד ישים } ירושלם		f	g	h	7		
	תהלה בארץ [y]			h	i	5		
8	נשבע [ ]בימינו	a	b			6		b:b
	ובזרוע עזו		B			6	12	
	אם אתן דגנך[ ]	a	b	c		6		b:b::b:b::b:b::b:b
	מאכל לאיביך		c_1	d		6	12	
	אם ישתו בני נכר	a	b_1	d_1		7		
	תירושך יגעת בו		c_2	e	f	6	13	
9	מאספיו יאכלהו		d_2	c_1		7		
	והללו יהוה			g	h	6	13	
	ומקבציו ישתהו		d_3	b_1		7		
	בחצרות קדשי			i	j	6	13	
10	עברו עברו בשערים	a	a	b		8		1:b::1:b::1:b
	פנו דרך עם		a_1	c	d	4	12	
	סלו סלו מסלה	a_2	a_2	c_1		7		
	סקלו מאבן		a_3	e		5	12	
	הרימו [הרימו] נס	a_4	a_5	c_2		7		
	על[י] עמים			f	g	4	11	

11 This Yahweh announces
to the end of the earth:
say to the daughter of Zion:
here comes your salvation!
12 They will be called "The Holy People,"
"Yahweh's Redeemed,"
and you will be called "Sought-out,"
"City-not-abandoned."

TEXTUAL NOTES

a) Dropping the article with LXX. Hebrew poetry, as it has been handed down to us, is replete with various particles which are common to Hebrew prose, but are not original in classical Hebrew poetry, especially the את direct object marker, the relative particle אשר, the definite article (when having demonstrative force, it is often original), and, in many cases, the *waw* conjunction. It is not possible to delete these particles with as much confidence in late sixth- and especially fifth-century poetry as in pre-exilic poetry, since the classical canons are yielding during this period to various pressures, including the pressure of prose style. In our material, however, we shall generally assume that the presence of these particles is due to the later prosaizing of the text and, especially when supported by metric considerations, we shall delete them without further discussion in the notes.

b) As it stands in the MT, *tē'āmanāh* is an incomprehensible form. If it is to be taken as a nip'al of *'mn,* a dagesh must be added to the *nûn.* Arabic attests a root *'mm,* "to go," which would be a good parallel with *b'.* Finally, LXX seems to be translating the nip'al of *nś',* an apparent ancient variant supported by 1QIsa[b]. With evidence like this it is impossible to be certain of the best solution, though the basic meaning of the bicolon is not at stake.

c) As in most of the prophetic books, the versions in Third Isaiah are rarely helpful in offering strong, independent variants to uncertain readings in the MT. In this respect the LXX is especially disappointing, often being a very free (almost paraphrastic) rendering of its Hebrew *Vorlage,* as in the case of this verse.

d) Emending on the basis of LXX, 1QIsa[a], Pesh, Tg, and some Hebrew mss.

e) Only the change of *'āleph* to *ṣādê* is required to restore this line to a sense parallel to the second colon of the bicolon.

f) V. 12 is usually considered a gloss, with two reasons submitted as evidence, the extraordinarily long meter and the harsh view toward the foreign nations. The latter reason is not conclusive, since the nations are the object of Israel's exploitation

11	הנה יהוה השמיע	a	b	c		6		1:b::1:b
	אל קצה ארץ		d	e		4	10	
	אמרו לבת ציון		c_1	d_1	e_1	6		
	[z] הנה ישעך בא[ ]	a	f	g		5	11	
12	קראו להם עם קדש	a	b	c		7		1:b::1:b
	גאולי יהוה			C		5	12	
	לך יקרא דרושה	b_1	a_1	c_1		7		
	עיר לא נעזבה			C_1		5	12	

elsewhere in chapter 60 (by implication throughout the chapter, explicitly in v. 11b and v. 14). The former reason carries more weight, although the long meter may have resulted from a scribal error which placed the subjects of both cola in the first colon, and then necessitated the change of the verbs from singular to plural. When the subject of the second colon is returned to its original position, a regular meter is restored.

g) V. 14a seems to contain several glosses. Through their deletion it is possible to restore a satisfactory parallel bicolon. LXX has a shorter text, but it likely stems from the free handling of the Hebrew rather than from a variant Hebrew *Vorlage*.

h) As indicated by the prosaic style, which completely disrupts the meter and prosodic structure, and the apocalyptic theme, vv. 19–20 constitute a later interpolation (cf. footnote 33).

i) As the wide divergence among the versions indicates, the corruption of the text of 60:21b is ancient (cf. I. F. M. Brayley, "Yahweh Is the Guardian of His Plantation," *Bibl* 41 [1960]: 275–290). It is impossible to restore the original text with confidence, and the text we reconstruct is offered as a reasonable conjecture, utilizing what clues can be gained from the versions, and from metric and prosodic considerations. The first stichos of the bicolon as preserved by the MT is short (four syllables); IQIsa^a contains יהוה after מטעו, and is the basis for that part of our emendation (see 61:3c). The LXX reads נצר as referring to the people of the preceding bicolon. We are reading it as a plural participle construct, referring to the people. Since *waw* and *yod* are commonly confused, the restoration of ידו is plausible.

j) לשום לאבלי ציון seems to be a variant to לתת להם which has found its way into the text. Metrically the latter is the superior reading.

k) Reversing the last two words. If the MT division is retained, a very unbalanced 5:9 meter results.

l) Reading as a qal infinitive, according to the pattern throughout the preceding verses.

m) אכריכם and כרמיכם are apparently ancient variants which have been combined in our text.

n) The original bicolon seems to have been filled out on the basis of a fuller prose syntax, a judgment supported by the shorter reading preserved by LXX.

o) The colon is short in the MT, and the loss of this *mem* could have resulted from a haplography after לכם, once the latter came into the text.

p) The Hebrew is unintelligible. Deriving the verb from מרא seems reasonable.

q) A conjectural emendation instead of תחת, on the basis of sense, meter, and parallel structure.

r) An emendation proposed by J. L. McKenzie, *Second Isaiah,* Anchor Bible (Garden City: Doubleday, 1965), p. 180. In favor of this conjecture and the one in q) is the parallel structure which results, with the repetition of both verbs in the corresponding imperfect in the next two lines.

s) The translations and commentaries emend the pointing to read בְּעַוְלָה and can claim the support of the versions. We are not convinced that the Masoretic interpretation can be rejected so easily. The contrast between cultic observance and violence is too central a feature in the polemic of the Third Isaiah material (e.g., 58:3–4 and 66:3) to permit one to dismiss the MT ("I hate robbery with burnt-offering") without strong internal support. But as the parallels indicate, such support is missing. The contrast is found elsewhere in prophecy as well, for example, Is 1:13: "I cannot endure iniquity and solemn assembly." Moreover, the preposition ב does not read smoothly in the emended text, leading some scholars to further emend the ב to ו.

t) MT יכהן is unintelligible here.

u) As commonly, an expansion of the divine name.

v) As suggested by the meter, the repetition of the verb is probably an expansion. The structure here is parallel to v. 4b.

w) With LXX and 1QIsa[a].

x) The absurd picture of Zion's sons marrying their mother is usually corrected by the emendation to בנך. But metrically, this reading is unsatisfactory (five syllables). We propose אדניך, the expected parallel to the following אלהיך (cf. Is 51:22, et al.); this reading suits well the context of marriage. It is not difficult to understand, in a sentence with as many roots with initial *beth* as this, how the אד was replaced by ב.

y) Good metric structure is restored by recognizing עד יכונן and עד ישים as ancient variants.

z) The meter (1:1) suggests that 11c is intrusive (cf. Is 40:10).

The question of authorship of Isaiah 60–62 has been a matter of much debate, with scholars attributing the section to one of three figures: Second Isaiah, Third Isaiah, or some third prophetic figure. Since the discussion here, as with the rest of Isaiah 56–66, seems to be stalemated, and since the old line of inquiry offers little hope of advancing our understanding, it seems wise to shift attention away from the question of authorship and to ask the questions raised by the contextual-typological method. From the start this much seems evident: there are striking features which Isaiah 60–62 holds in common with Second Isaiah in contrast to Third Isaiah; other characteristics of 60–62 reveal close affinities with Third Isaiah; still other features seem to be unique, standing between the two. A satisfactory interpretation of Isaiah 60–62 should account for all of these facts.

We turn first to the evidence gained from analysis of the internal structure, meter, and style of these three chapters. It is recognized widely that they betray remarkable affinities on this level with Second Isaiah, and our analysis bears this out. The basic building block of the internal poetic structure is the bicolon, and even where rather long prosodic units are constructed (e.g., 60:1–2; 61:10b–11), they are readily divisible into parallel bicola. The meter is quite regular throughout, with a mixture of metric schemes—a common characteristic of archaic poetry—being used effectively in some strophes (e.g., the fourth strophe of chapter 60 and the first of chapter 62). The third and fourth strophes of chapter 62 exemplify a very regular metric and prosodic structure producing a fine archaizing effect.

Alongside such examples of an archaizing style close to that of Second Isaiah are features which foreshadow the development seen in later parts of Third Isaiah toward a more irregular, baroque style. One of these features is a type of prosodic unit producing a very prosaic, list-like effect, e.g., 60:17. Another is the grotesque mixing of metric patterns found in the last half of the fifth strophe of chapter 60 and in the first half of the second strophe of chapter 61. It is significant that precisely in these more irregular sections the tendency found in the other parts of chapters 60–62 to echo words of Second Isaiah is absent. Instead we find a new range of vocabulary with a uniqueness of its own. Later we shall notice that these sections are unique in another way: they develop themes constituting a program which moves beyond Second Isaiah through application of older material to a new setting. Prosody thus proves to be key to an important observation: those sections which tend to be most archaizing prosodically are the sections which also stand thematically closest to Second Isaiah; in them we discern the tendency to reiterate the message of the great prophet of the exile. The sections (60:17–21 minus the interpolated vv. 19–20 and 61:4–6) where this archaic style breaks down, however, are sections which begin to develop themes unique to Third Isaiah.[29] They form the heart of what we shall recognize as the visionary group's program of restoration. It would thus seem that in the latter sections the disciples of Second Isaiah are moving out on their own, thereby foreshadowing the prosodic features and themes developed further by visionary followers of Second Isaiah in Isaiah 56–59 and 63–66.[30]

With regard to meter and internal structure, Isaiah 60–62 can thus be placed in a typology somewhere between Second Isaiah and the later Third Isaiah material which we shall consider below.

When the content is considered, a similar comparison presents itself, for thematically most of Isaiah 60–62 bears close affinities with Second Isaiah. The message is still the pure promise of restoration to the whole nation (62:10–12 = 40:8–11; 52:7–10), promise based upon the theme of pardon (60:10b, 15 = 40:1–2; 44:22; 54:7–8). As

29. We shall use "Third Isaiah" as a designation for Isaiah 56–66 without thereby implying that the entire section, or even a large part of it, is to be attributed to one author. The unity implied by our use of this designation is a unity of tradition, not of authorship.

30. A third stage in the typology of prosody is represented by the interpolated verses in 60:19–20, where the classical canons are abandoned altogether; here too our judgment regarding the typology of Hebrew prosody is corroborated by the content of the verses, for they express a dualism which is a feature of Jewish apocalyptic eschatology of the fifth century and after.

in Second Isaiah Yahweh promises that Zion's children will be gathered from the nations (60:4, 9 = 43:5-7; 49:12, 18, 22), and that the wealth of the nations will flow to her (60:5-7, 16 = 45:14). Indeed, even foreign kings will join in the service of Zion (61:10f = 49:7b, 23). Jerusalem will be rebuilt in unprecedented glory, a promise expressed in very material terms (60:13, 17 = 54:11-12). The restored city will be secure from the threat of hostile nations, for all of her foes will be destroyed (60:12, 14; 62:8 = 41:11-13; 51:21-23; 54:14-17). In these ideal conditions, she will find fulfillment of the ancient promise of being fruitful and multiplying (60:22 = 49:19-21; 54:1b-3), and will enjoy Yahweh's eternal covenant (61:8 = 54:10; 55:3). Thus blessed, she will carry out Yahweh's commission of being a light to the nations (60:3 = 49:6). Her former shame will cease (62:4-5 = 45:17; 54:4-8). As in Second Isaiah (48:11; 49:26b; etc.) all this is done for the sake of Yahweh's glory (60:16, 21).

Such parallels make it obvious that Isaiah 60-62 still participates profoundly in the world of Second Isaiah, a fact made even clearer when some of the points are considered at which this picture of restoration differs from the rest of Third Isaiah: (1) Whereas Second Isaiah and 60-62 are exuberant announcements of Yahweh's salvation, other oracles in Third Isaiah struggle to explain why that salvation has been delayed. (2) Whereas in Second Isaiah and 60-62 Israel's judgment is past history,[31] and the message is one of salvation based upon Yahweh's pardon, the oracles of Third Isaiah announce a future judgment which must precede the restoration. (3) Also in the latter, the restoration is announced not to the whole nation, but solely to one segment of Israel, while the other segment is threatened with destruction. That new message in the later Third Isaiah material led to notable changes in the prophetic genres, whereas in chapters 60-62 the genres are continuous with those found in Second Isaiah.

31. The harsher words directed to Israel by Second Isaiah never constitute a judgment of Israel, but rather a rebuke for lack of faith which is always intended to return Israel to true trust in Yahweh.

All of these points demonstrate that Isaiah 60–62 manifests pronounced affinities with Second Isaiah in contrast to the rest of Third Isaiah. If this were the full picture, one might place 60–62 at the center of the prophecy of Second Isaiah. However, the total picture also includes subtle points which indicate that chapters 60–62 represent an advance beyond the central prophecy of Second Isaiah in the direction of the rest of Third Isaiah.

One point of difference between Second Isaiah and Isaiah 60–62 concerns the terms in which the promise of restoration is stated. Although Second Isaiah frequently draws upon mythic material to underscore the universal, and even cosmic, significance of the return to Zion, in the prophecy stemming from Babylon he never fails to preserve the dialectic between plain history and the cosmic meaning behind that history. For while he is always explicit that Israel's salvation stems ultimately from Yahweh, he nevertheless recognizes this activity unfolding in concrete historical events involving historical personages, like the conquests of Cyrus and the fall of Babylon. In 60–62 the picture of restoration has begun to dissolve that dialectic by moving beyond the historical in its plainest terms, as seen already in 60:1 f where Yahweh's theophany is described in the image of light invading darkness, an image left without ties to historical agents or events. The picture is developed further: Zion will be glorified, her foes will be removed, the wealth of the nations will flow to her, kings will serve her, all her inhabitants will be priests; in a word, the disorder of chaos (*ḥāmās* in 60:18) which marked the collapse of the created order in primeval times (Gen 6:11, 13) will be removed from the land.[32] This entire glorious picture of shalom is painted without relation to the events and leaders of plain history. Within the typology of prophetic eschatology, this section would lie somewhere between the proto-apocalyptic eschatology of Second Isaiah and the early apocalyptic eschatology of Isaiah 65 and 66. That the

32. Cf. G. von Rad, "The City on the Hill," in *The Problem of the Hexateuch and other Essays*, tr. E. W. Trueman Dicken (New York: McGraw-Hill, 1966), p. 238.

eschatology of 60–62 has not developed as far toward apocalyptic as, for example, Isaiah 65:17–25 is clear in the absence of any alterations or disruptions in the realm of nature, or of any trace of dualism.[33]

That 60–62 must be regarded as distinct from Second Isaiah is also suggested by a concern expressed in these chapters which is absent in Second Isaiah, but vitally important in Third Isaiah, namely, the concern with the possession of the land (60:21; 61:7), a matter which will receive more attention below.

Finally, a distinct difference of perspective separates 60–62 from the prophecy of Second Isaiah. Already the absence in 60–62 of the polemic against the gods of the nations which played such an important part in Second Isaiah suggests a new setting. One senses that the author of 60–62 no longer stands with his feet on foreign soil nor does he gaze over a vast wilderness through which he believes Yahweh would lead his people to that beloved city beyond the horizon. The section sounds instead like the fervent hope of a community, intimately acquainted with

33. 60:19–20, which would be a clear exception, is recognized above on prosodic grounds to be an interpolation. It belongs to a later period when the restoration of the true Israel, which was then suffering "days of mourning," was construed in dualistic terms, involving a radical transformation of the realm of nature, and even a supplanting of the polarities established in the primeval times (Gen 8:22; cf. 65:17 ff and Zech 14:6–7). The highly irregular meter and prose-like style of these two verses verify our judgment that they are secondary:

The sun will no longer be your light by day,
nor for brightness will the moon shine on you by night;
but Yahweh will be your everlasting light,
your God will be your glory.
Never again will your sun set,
nor your moon withdraw itself;
but Yahweh will be your everlasting light,
and your days of mourning will be ended.

לא יהיה לך עוד השמש לאור יומם	a	b	c	d	11
ולנגה [הלילה] ᵃ הירח לא יאיר לך	d_1	c_1	a_1	b	11
והיה לך יהוה לאור עולם	a'^{1}	b	c_2	d_2	10
ואלהיך לתפארתך	c_3	d_3			9
לא יבוא עוד שמשך	a_2	c			6
וירחך לא יאסף	c'_1	a_3			8
כי יהוה יהיה לך לאור עולם	c_2	a	b	d_2	10
ושלמו ימי אבלך	e	f	g		8

[a]supplied with 1 QIsa[a], LXX, Old Latin and Tg.

the words of Second Isaiah, which now finding itself in Palestine seeks to reaffirm the promise of restoration made by Yahweh through his spokesman of the exile. Indeed, one can perhaps best describe the difference between Second Isaiah and Isaiah 60–62 by characterizing the former as the prophet's announcement of the imminent second exodus-conquest whereby Yahweh would lead the exiles back to Zion in a manner reminiscent of the first exodus, and by characterizing the latter as a *program of restoration* written by a group which has returned to Zion, a program based to be sure on the earlier message of Second Isaiah. That Isaiah 60–62 is based on Second Isaiah's proclamation has already been indicated; it remains to be demonstrated that it actually is programmatic in nature.

As widely recognized, chapter 60 is basically a homogeneous unit throughout, with only two or three verses disputed. Verses 1–9 renew the promise of restoration for Zion found in Second Isaiah, with one notable difference: return from exile is no longer mentioned. The people are *in* Zion, and they await the theophany of the Divine Warrior Yahweh and the resulting glorification of the city and the ingathering of those still scattered among the nations. The direction of the promise makes this clear: they are asked to lift up their eyes to see their children coming *to* them (v. 4), even as the wealth of the nations will come *to* them (vv. 5-7). There follows in 60:10–22 a description of the manner in which the salvation promised in verses 1–9 would occur, forming the first part of a post-exilic program for restoration. Verses 10, 11, and 13 provide for the rebuilding of the walls and the sanctuary, a rebuilding to be carried out by Yahweh himself with the aid of foreigners and their kings. The city is secured from foreign aggression as all enemies are destroyed or brought to submission (vv. 12, 14). After these provisions have established the external conditions of restoration, the internal reorganization is delineated: Zion's officers will be Peace, her rulers Righteousness (v. 17b). Violence will no longer be heard in the land, so that the walls will be called Salvation, the gates Praise (v. 18). As for the people, they shall all be righteous, they shall possess the land forever, they shall become a mighty nation (vv. 21-22).

Whereas chapter 60 betrays the attempt to remain close to the language, style, and themes of Second Isaiah by adapting his message to the new post-exilic setting, it gives no clue to the identity of an actual prophetic figure behind this reiteration, and in 60:4 even word-for-word repetition, of the message of the earlier prophet. Rather than shedding light on the mission of a prophet in the traditional sense, the chapter seems to bring into focus the hopes and plans of a community deriving its identity from the message of an earlier prophetic figure.

In contrast to the anonymous style of chapter 60, the next unit in 61:1-3 is a first person narrative which seems to afford a glimpse into the career of the "prophet," Third Isaiah. Understandably it is used as a key passage in many characterizations of the prophet.[34] Closer scrutiny of these three verses, however, leads one to question whether one can discern the personality of an identifiable prophet on the basis of these words. For these verses betray the form of a catena of themes taken from Second Isaiah.[35] What sort of prophet is he who merely echoes the thought of an earlier prophetic figure? It should be apparent that we are not witnessing a new outpouring of the classical prophetic spirit here, but rather the studied reiteration of an earlier prophet's message. This being the case, it seems impossible—and of little consequence—to determine whether the one thus reiterating the earlier message is an individual, or a group speaking collectively. What does seem possible—and significant—to determine is how this reiteration of words from the Servant Songs of Second Isaiah func-

34. Westermann, p. 366, even uses 61:1-3 to describe the prophet's self-consciousness : "These words show that Trito-Isaiah was very much aware that he had received a call. Right away they make clear that, after the exile, prophecy, vigorous prophecy, made a fresh start in his hands."

35. 61:1 develops the theme found in 42:1 of Yahweh's investing his servant with his spirit. The bringing of good news (pi'el of *bśr*) is at the heart of Second Isaiah's message (40:9, 41:27, 52:7). The mission of mercy in 61:1-2 expands on that attributed to the servant in 42:5-9. Further, compare *šᵊnat rāṣôn* with 49:8 and *rûᵃh kēhāh* with 42:3-4. Cf. W. Zimmerli, "Zur Sprache Tritojesajas" in *Gottes Offenbarang* (München: Chr. Kaiser, 1969), p. 227.

tions in its new setting in Isaiah 60–62, a section which we have designated as a program of restoration.

In seeking to identify the function of this first person account, we should be mindful of its context, for it follows immediately after the first part of the program of restoration (60:1–22), and leads without a break into a section developing some of the aspects of that restoration program (61:4–11). When considered against the background of the repeated echoing of the words of the Servant Songs in these verses, this position suggests that the function of this unit is the critical one of lending authority to the program of restoration by relating it unmistakably to the commission of the Servant of Second Isaiah. The fact that the *'ebed yahweh* became a central figure in the thought of the visionaries of the post-exilic period—a fact which will be established later in this chapter—lends credence to this view. In a time when a rival program of restoration was being propounded,[36] and when many were even questioning Yahweh's willingness or power to save, it would have been imperative for the visionaries of Isaiah 60–62 to produce credentials. Whether originally written[37] by a spokesman for the visionaries or by a group of leaders, Is 61:1–3 is thus a reiteration of the commissioning of the servant of Second Isaiah intended to legitimate the program of restoration developed in Isaiah 60–62; it boldly proclaims the belief that the mission of the servant was living on in this post-exilic community. If the designation of the servant as Israel in 49:3 is original (and there are no conclusive grounds, metric or other, to the contrary), the collective interpretation of the servant which we find here was an original element already in the Servant Songs themselves, thus offering post-exilic disciples of Second Isaiah a most natural and useful image to develop further in defining and legitimizing their identity and mission. If, on the other hand, Israel is a later addition, it most likely stems from the

36. See p. 71.

37. That we are dealing with written composition is indicated both by the complexity of the prosody and by the studied use of allusions to and quotations from Second Isaiah.

same hands which produced 61:1-3, for the manuscript evidence proves that the reading, if not indeed original, represents a very early interpolation. In either case, 49:3 lends support to a collective interpretation of 61:1-3.[38] In answer to all those who despaired of Yahweh's power to save, the visionary community bore witness to a message of salvation which revivified the proclamation of the servant of Yahweh in the post-exilic period. In them, the new servants of Yahweh, the prophet's office—now collectively construed—of mediator between Yahweh and his covenant community lived on. To the impoverished, brokenhearted, imprisoned, to those mourning and despondent, in a word, to all who saw little evidence of the dawning of Second Isaiah's glorious promises, the word was one of imminent healing and salvation.

To be sure, in using words of a proclamation originally spoken in a context remote from the present one, some of the earlier terms applied only in an altered sense. In Second Isaiah the good tidings (*biśśēr* in 40:9 and 52:7) concerned an announcement of a deliverance which had already been effected, whereas in the new context they bore the promise of a future transformation; in Second Isaiah the captives promised release (42:7; 49:9) were exiles in Babylonia, a meaning no longer applicable to those in Zion.[39] These and similar incongruences add support to a collective interpretation of the function of Is 61:1-3.

Another way in which the collective adaption of Israel's prophetic heritage manifests itself in the early post-exilic period is in the democratization of all of the traditional offices. In the section introduced by the prophetic commission (61:4-11), we first hear of the physical rebuilding of Zion and then are told about the priests who will officiate in the restored community: the people would be named

38. The alternation between first person singular and plural in the communal lament in 63:7-64:11, which derives from the same visionary group at a slightly later period, demonstrates further how the community in question can adopt either form of narrative, since it thinks of itself both collectively as Yahweh's servant and individually as "your servants" (63:17).

39. Cf. Westermann, pp. 366-367.

"priests of Yahweh," which represents an astonishing democratization of the formerly exclusive sacerdotal office and its amalgamation with the prophetic office producing a symbiosis reminiscent of the career of Moses. The needs of these prophet-priests would be supplied by foreigners (vv. 5-6); their relationship with Yahweh would be secured by an everlasting covenant and sealed by the fulfillment of the ancient patriarchal promises (vv. 7-9). In a remarkable adaption of ancient promises which resists being limited to any exclusive tradition—even the royal symbols are democratized and applied to the people (62:3)—we recognize the efforts of a new reform group consisting of diverse elements to establish their program as normative for the entire nation.

Chapter 62 develops further the program of restoration; as in 61:1-3 we find a reiteration of themes from Second Isaiah[40] which bespeak the efforts of the visionaries to establish their program of restoration as the legitimate continuation of the servant's mission. As is common in Third Isaiah, the old themes do not fit the new context in their original sense.[41] The note of urgency is unmistakable in this chapter, possibly suggesting a later period when opposition to the program was being voiced. Thus elaboration of the themes of the reform program—the restored community will be called by a new name (v. 2), the covenant will effect a marriage between Yahweh and the land (vv. 4-5)—is interspersed with the emphatic claim that Yahweh had not abandoned his people, but was about to turn to deliver them. Verses 6 and 7 vividly describe the situation out of which Isaiah 60-62 arises, even as they develop further the collective understanding of the prophetic office recognized in 61:1-3. The deliverance promised by Second Isaiah has not yet come, and because men speak of Yahweh's abandoning his people, the matter of mediating between the savior and the people grows critical. In verses 6 and 7 Yahweh appoints the officers who are to act as

40. Eg., 62:10a-40:3; 62:10b-49:22; 62:11-40:10; 62:6f-49:16.

41. For example, see Zimmerli's discussion of 62:10-11 in "Sprache," p. 221.

mediators in this critical period. They are designated as "watchmen," and their intercession is to go up without ceasing until the day of deliverance arrives. What we surmised in connection with 61:1-3 here receives corroboration. In the mind of the visionary community, the solitary office of prophet in the new setting of the post-exilic period has been widened to encompass a broader group, the watchmen. Here we find the leaders of the visionary group accounting for their commission to a prophetic task, that of witnessing on behalf of the people before Yahweh until the restoration plan developed in chapters 60-62 is fulfilled. The age of the solitary prophet has given way to the age of the visionary community.

We have witnessed a significant development in this section, for two of the basic features of apocalyptic are seen emerging: (1) The period of the fresh outpouring of the prophetic spirit yields to the studied reapplication of the words of former prophecy. (2) The individual office of prophet develops toward a collective office according to which the community of visionary leaders claims as a body to continue the office of the servant of Yahweh. In a typological sequence, we recognize this occurring first through the collective interpretation of the image of the servant (a phenomenon already present in Isaiah 40-55 and developed in 61:1-3 and 62:1), and then moving into a phase of democratization where the office of prophecy—together with the other traditional pre-exilic offices—is broadened and applied to the entire community. Later in our study we shall witness another phase whereby the democratized office of prophecy is subsequently narrowed to apply only to the faithful within Israel (the *ʿăbādîm* and the *bəḥûrîm*, "servants" and "chosen") in a conscious exclusion of other elements of the community which opposed the reform program of the visionaries.

62:10-11 brings together several of the points raised above. In catena fashion it presents quotations from Second Isaiah which summarize the message developed in chapters 60-62. The reverence felt for the words of the exilic prophet is manifested most clearly here, for words are repeated in spite of the fact that they ill suit the new situation. The original divine council setting of the prologue of Isaiah 40 is lost, and instead of comprising a commission to be carried out by heralds of the heavenly court (40:3), verse 10 takes on the form of an admonition to the faithful. Moreover, no longer is the preparation to be made for the dramatic passage of Yahweh through the wilderness as he leads forth the exiles in a second exodus; not a way for Yahweh, but for the people is called for. The concrete picture of the return from exile in Second Isaiah is transformed into an obtuse metaphor (is the highway a way toward restoration? a path for further returnees?). Verse 11, which draws its language from 40:9–10, similarly transforms into a pale abstraction a specific commissioning of heralds who are to announce the arrival of the victorious Warrior Yahweh. While lacking the sublime poetic beauty of the original master and ill fitting the new context, this section nevertheless bears witness to the struggling efforts of the post-exilic prophetic community to reaffirm Second Isaiah's proclamation of salvation to an age little disposed to hearing about the God Yahweh. The unsympathetic critic could fault such writing as poor imitation, the product of a committee approach paraphrasing an older classic; the critic who recognizes God's word coming to expression even in the groping efforts of the epigon can speak of the prophetic faith which seeks "in new periods to speak in such manner that the validity of earlier proclamation becomes comprehensible."[42]

If our interpretation is correct, we have discovered the beginning of the path which the prophetic tradition would follow in the post-exilic period, a path which would lead it from embodiment in a distinct office of individuals called by Yahweh as his messengers to incorporation into the vocation of a group of visionaries. Thus the prophetic tradition entered the period of early apocalyptic, characterized by anonymity and the studied reapplication of older prophecies, thereby giving rise to an attitude toward past

42. Zimmerli, "Sprache," p. 233.

writings which began to lay the foundation for the formation of a canon.[43] The need felt by the apocalyptic groups to legitimate their message, after passing through a period of anonymous reapplication of older themes, would later give rise to another legitimization device, pseudonymity, whereby the message of the seers is placed in the mouths of saints who lived in the period when the prophetic spirit yet moved men to prophecy.

When the visionary restoration plan which we have just examined is compared to Ezekiel 40–48, it becomes apparent that we have in the Bible two rival programs of restoration, and that the visionary program, based on the message of Second Isaiah, was written in conscious opposition to that originating with Ezekiel and adopted by the hierocratic group led by the Zadokites. If our judgment is accurate that two distinct lines of tradition can be traced running parallel to each other through the sixth and fifth centuries, it is not surprising to find that each of these traditions includes its own plan for the restoration of the Yahweh cult and the community. That Ezekiel 40–48 represents such a program from a group strongly imbued with priestly concerns is generally accepted. Comparison of that program with Isaiah 60–62 presents strong evidence in favor of our thesis that this section represents a rival program.

One could contrast the restoration programs in Isaiah 60–62 and Ezekiel 40–48 by referring to the former as the dream of visionaries, to the latter as the blueprint of hierocratic realists or pragmatists.[44] This impression is consonant with the origins which we would recognize behind these two plans, Isaiah 60–62 coming from a prophetic group highly charged with the dramatic eschatological mes-

43. Other steps along this path toward canon are found in Zech 1:4 and 7:12, Ezek 38:17, and Dan 9:2.

44. No single set of terms expresses adequately the contrast we wish to draw between the two parties which we recognize taking form behind the restoration programs in Isaiah 60–62 and Ezekiel 40–48, and only reluctantly do we adopt the terms visionary/realist (see pp. 211 ff. for other terminology). These terms do, however, capture the essential character of the two tendencies traceable in Judaism down to the Common Era and beyond. On the one hand, the visionaries fervently long for divine intervention to usher in a radically new order, and on the basis of their vision of an ideal new age to come, they proclaim judgment upon existing structures. On the other hand, the realists, as the contemporary leaders of the

sage of Second Isaiah, Ezekiel 40–48 reflecting the views of the priestly circles which had officiated over the First Temple. Two sharply contrasting mentalities are reflected, one the mentality of officials responsible for the rebuilding and maintenance of the day-to-day life of the temple community, the other of an idealistic or even fanatical band eagerly longing for the glorification of Zion, and confident that Yahweh would soon act to accomplish what man alone could not.[45] Thus the former plan is firmly grounded in mundane realities, seeking to establish the conditions necessary for Yahweh's dwelling among his people through concrete ordinances (*ḥuqqôt*) and judgments (*mišpāṭîm*), whereas the latter is a highly idealized picture threatening to become detached from the practical problem of fulfillment within the limitations of historical realities.

These contrasting mentalities are brought into sharp focus when one compares the corresponding details within the two programs:[46] (1) The leaders of the prophetic community are Peace and Righteousness (Is 60:17b), those of the hierocracy are the various officials of the priestly and civil hierarchies, headed by the high priest and the prince. (2) The promise of the visionary is that *the whole nation* "will be named the priests of Yahweh, the ministers of our God" (61:6); the realist carefully regulates: ". . .mark well

present institutions, are dedicated to the preservation of those structures, and to the details involved in operating a cult and nation which is very much a part of the real world. We also refer to the tradition of the realists as the hierocratic tradition, since it is a tradition dominated by the temple priests, whereas the tradition of the visionaries will sometimes be referred to as the prophetic tradition, inasmuch as its inspiration is derived from the prophets, and even down to late apocalyptic its kinship to prophecy is evident. These terms, however, must be regarded as conceptual tools, and no more, for if held too rigidly they could lead to error. For example, late apocalyptic includes detailed descriptions of history and historical institutions which are very realistic in appearance, even as Ezekiel 40–48 indicates that a hierocratic program can be cast in the form of a vision. The latter example serves further as warning against viewing Weberian ideal types in a rigid manner; even as Ezekiel, the father of the hierocratic tradition, includes many of the traits of the visionary, so too the later representatives of the two traditions will not be pure examples of the visionary or realistic type, but merely approximations of one or the other. For "visionary" and "realist" do not designate rigid parties, but rather ideological tendencies which can be traced through the literature of the post-exilic period.

45. Karl Mannheim's categories of "Ideology" and "Utopia" apply very well to the contrasting mentalities embodied by these two groups (cf. Chapter III, B).

46. Ezekiel 40-48 includes additions to the basic Ezekielian work (see Chapter III). At this point comparison will be made to the program in its final form.

those who may be admitted to the temple and all those who are to be excluded from the sanctuary. . .; [the Levites] shall not come near to me, to serve me as priest. . ." (44:5, 13); ". . .the sons of Zadok. . .alone among the sons of Levi may come near to the Lord to minister to him" (40:46; cf. 44:15). (3) The visionary exults, "Your people shall all be righteous. . ." (60:21); "They will be called 'The Holy People'. . ." (62:12); the realist meticulously explains that holiness is reserved for the few and that it must be safeguarded by ordinances: when the Zadokites leave the inner court, "they shall put off the garments in which they have been ministering, and lay them in the holy chambers; and they shall put on other garments, lest they communicate holiness to the people with their garments. . . .They shall teach my people the difference between the holy and the common. . ." (44:19, 23). A special holy place is designated where the priests are to boil the offerings, "in order not to bring them out into the outer court and so communicate holiness to the people" (46:20). (4) The visionary announces: "The glory of Lebanon will come to you, the cypress, the plane, and the pine together, to adorn the site of my sanctuary, that I may glorify the resting place of my feet" (60:13); the realist draws up architectural plans, exact in every detail, for the new temple, and lays it before the people to build it (43:10–12). (5) The visionary proclaims, "Foreigners will rebuild your walls, and their kings will serve you," whereas the attitude of the realist could be summarized in the old maxim: "God helps those who help themselves."

To summarize, the hierocratic program is designed to regulate carefully the cultic life of the community, to safeguard the holiness which is reserved for the few, and thereby to restore the circumstances in which Yahweh could be expected to tabernacle with his people. In Isaiah 60–62 the sealed gates (Ezek 44:1ff) are cast open, for *all* the people will be righteous and holy. The obsession with the minute details of the rebuilt temple is replaced by a glorious vision of a restored Zion, the tedious measurements of the dimensions of walls and gates yield to walls called "Salvation," and gates "Praise." And this whole glorious restoration is to take place not because of any priestly efforts to regulate the holy, but because ". . .your light has come, the glory of Yahweh has risen upon you" (60:1). Yahweh's initiative alone accounts for the blessed transformation.[47]

Intimately tied to this basic contrast in the substance of these two programs is the stylistic contrast. The most obvious difference is that the program of Ezekiel 40–48 is written in prose, whereas Isaiah 60–62 is written in archaizing poetry. The contrast can be drawn further between the realistic style of Ezekiel 40–48, in which every detail is filled out with the painstaking care of Courbet, and the impressionistic style of the Isaianic program where a few bold brush strokes pass over the finer detail leaving much to the imagination, adding a dimension of depth akin to a work of Monet.

Such a comparison of Isaiah 60–62 with Ezekiel 40–48 strongly suggests that the prophetic community living in the promises of Second Isaiah here set out their ideal program for the restoration of Zion. Point for point, it covers the same problems as Ezekiel 40–48: rebuilding of walls and sanctuary, the officials of the community, membership in the priesthood, the problem of holiness. Even the conclusions of the two versions are parallel, providing the new name which will be given to Zion: "And the name of the city henceforth shall be, The Lord is there" (Ezek 48:35); "And you [Zion] will be called 'Sought out,' 'City-not-abandoned'" (Is 62:12). By thus covering the very issues raised by Ezekiel 40–48, the prophetic version seems to be contesting the validity of Ezekiel's program, offering instead its own visionary program for a glorious Zion which Yahweh would create. This program, based on the message of Second Isaiah, underlies the prophetic activity recorded in Third Isaiah. The situation within the community

47. The contrast between the visionary and realistic program is not captured by reference to the spirituality of the visionary and the materialism of the realist; the vision of Isaiah 60–62 is one of vast material riches flowing into Zion (e.g., 60:5–7); the program of Ezekiel also spoke of great future prosperity (e.g. 47:1–12).

reflected in those oracles will be a changing situation, and the eschatological vision of Israel's future found in them will be a vision developing steadily in the direction of apocalyptic. But the basic program, the central vision of what Yahweh's community is to be like, remains the same: it is to be a *righteous and holy* community restored to a glorious Zion; it is to be a *nation of priests, in possession of the land* and *in control of Yahweh's holy mountain;* it is to be *secure* from the threat of enemy harassment. And all this will be fulfilled, not because of human effort, but because *Yahweh will act* directly on behalf of his people.[48]

When these two programs of restoration are contrasted, confrontation and finally conflict between their protagonists seem almost inevitable, for when the hierocratic group gained ascendancy, their restoration attempts must have compromised and belittled all which the visionaries considered sacred. Hardest of all to accept was that they themselves were excluded from the restoration for which they so fervently longed, for, according to the final redaction of the theocratic program of Ezekiel 40–48, holiness was limited to the Zadokites; only the sons of Zadok could enter the holy place. Consequently, the visionaries soon came to realize that they were losing what they considered their rightful inheritance in Yahweh's holy mountain. The only comfort which their leaders could give them was that though others now controlled Zion, men who derided them for their visions (Is 66:5), Yahweh would not leave them comfortless, but would yet restore them to their proper possession and fulfill their dream (Is 65:17-25; 66:6-16; 57:13).

When the bitter discouragement experienced by the prophetic group is considered, it is totally comprehensible how their dream increasingly tended to dissolve the radical tension Second Isaiah had maintained between the mythical and the concretely historical, and how the optimism

48. This unity of the basic themes does not receive adequate attention in Westermann's reconstruction, where the divisions between the different parts of Isaiah 56–66 are accentuated to the neglect of the unity. We propose that one accounts best for the multifariousness of the material by recognizing throughout Third Isaiah the same basic restoration plan, which is obliged to adapt itself as conditions change.

dominating the message of Second Isaiah, and still permeating the program in Isaiah 60–62, faded away and yielded to a harsh vindictiveness. Thus in these two programs we have the seeds of the two currents which run parallel throughout subsequent Jewish history, currents which, to be sure, were not exclusive of one another. For both are essential elements of one faith, but were often tragically polarized into two imbalanced extremes, resulting in tension and even conflict as visionary parted company

---

57:14 Build up, build up, clear the way,
remove every obstacle from the way of my people.
15 For thus says the Most High, the Exalted,
whose home is eternity and whose name is holy;
I dwell in a lofty and holy place,
but also with the oppressed and the lowly,
to give new life to the lowly,
to revive the heart of the oppressed.
16 For I will not contend forever,
nor will I be angry without end.
For the spirit would grow faint before me,
even the souls which I have made.
17 I was vexed with his violent injustice,
I struck him, hiding myself in anger.
And he went wandering in his own way,
18 I have seen his ways.
Yet I will heal him and lead him,
I will fill him with consolation,
....
19 Peace, peace to the far and the near,
says Yahweh, and I will heal him.
20 But the wicked are like the restless sea
which cannot be still;
its waters stir up mud and slime.
21 There is no peace, says my God, for the wicked.

TEXTUAL NOTES

a) The meaning of this word in the present context is uncertain. Many translators (among them Torrey and RSV) render it "proceed," a translation supported by LXX, V, and Pesh, but not attested in Hebrew.

b) Comparison of the MT with IQIsa[a] and the versions suggests that two ancient variants stand behind the various readings:

with realist, and realist disassociated himself from visionary.

2. *Isaiah 57:14–21*

A second, shorter section of Isaiah 56-66 is closely related stylistically and thematically to chapters 60-62, and typological considerations place it within the same general period. We shall therefore turn to an examination of Isaiah 57:14-21.

	Text	Structure				Meter	Prosodic Units
14	סלו סלו פנו דרך	a	a	a_1	b	7	1:1
	הרימו מכשול מדרך עמי		a_2	b_1	c	9	
15	כי כה אמר רם ונשא	a	b	b_1		8	1:1
	שכן עד וקדש שמו		B	B_1		8	
	מרום וקדוש אשכון	a	a_1	b		7	1:1::1:1
	ואת דכא ושפל רוח		c	c_1		8	
	להחיות רוח שפלים		d	e	c_2	7	
	להחיות לב נדכאים		d	e_1	c_3	7	
16	כי לא לעולם אריב	a	b	c		7	1:1
	ולא לנצח אקצוף	a	b_1	c_1		7	
	כי רוח מלפני יעטוף[a]	a	b	c		8	1:1
	נשמות אני עשיתי	a_1	b_1	d		8	
17	בעון בצעו קצפתי	a	a_1	b		8	1:1
	אכהו הסתר וקצף		b_1	c	c_1	8	
	וילך שובב בדרך לבו	a	b	c		9	1:1
18	דרכיו ראיתי		c_1	d		6	
	וארפאהו ואנחהו	A	A_1			9	1:1
	ואשלם נחמים לו	a	b	c		8	
19	c..............................	..	....			=	
	שלום שלום לרחוק ולקרוב	a	a	b	b_1	11	1:1
	אמר יהוה ורפאתיו		c	d	e	8	
20	והרשעים כים נגרש	Addition Prose					
	כי השקט לא יוכל						
	ויגרשו מימיו רפש וטיט						
21	אין שלום [ ] לרשעים						

וְקָצֹף הַסְתֵּר and וָאֶקְצֹף וְאַסְתִּר (cf. A. Rubinstein, "Isaiah LVII–17 ואקצף הסתר and the DSIa Variant," *VT* 4 [1954]: 200, and S. Talmon, "Aspects of the Textual Transmission of the Bible in the Light of Qumran Manuscripts," *Textus* 4 [1964]: 117). The variant with infinitive absolutes recommends itself for metric and stylistic reasons.

c) No satisfactory solution has been found for this colon.

In a manner similar to Isaiah 60–62, the composition in 57:14–19 (20–21 will be discussed below) betrays close affinities, metrically, stylistically, and thematically, with Second Isaiah. The meter consists of a regular "1" pattern throughout, with the archaic bicolon structure predominating. Stylistic features reminiscent of Second Isaiah are the repetition of initial elements of a verse (v. 14: סֹלּוּ סֹלּוּ; v. 19: שָׁלוֹם שָׁלוֹם),[49] and the expansion of the introductory formula through various modifiers, especially relative clauses (v. 15a).[50] Finally, the thematic development is closely akin to that of Second Isaiah, with a joyous message of comfort and healing to the whole nation based on the motif of Yahweh's pardon of Israel's waywardness. These features, also noted in 60–62, closely tie this passage to the thought of Second Isaiah.

But again there is another dimension of the passage which points toward Third Isaiah, namely, the note that Yahweh, who inhabits eternity, nevertheless dwells "with the oppressed and the lowly" (cf. 66:1–2). This dimension adumbrates a special concern in Third Isaiah for an element within the community which, in contrast to the proud men of position, are variously designated "the humble," "the oppressed," "those who tremble at my word," and "my servants."

All of these features indicate that 57:14–19, like 60–62, stands midway between the message of Second Isaiah and the other oracles of Third Isaiah. But this bridging function is seen with even greater clarity when verses 20–21 are considered, two verses which both meter and theme prove to be secondary. For the meter switches from the regular 1:1 to 1:b, and the consistently parallel structure of the rest of the passage collapses. When our interpretation of the rest of Third Isaiah is anticipated, it becomes apparent why this addition was affixed to the passage. In its original form the passage promised pardon and salvation for Israel as a whole. But as we shall soon recognize, the remainder of the material in Isaiah 56–66 indicates that conditions in Israel

49. E.g., Is 40:1; 51:9; 51:12, 17; 52:1, 11.
50. E.g., Is 42:5; 43:1; 44:2, 24; 45:18.

soon worsened for the visionary group, for they encountered strenuous opposition and even oppression from the normative cult. In such changed circumstances, they could no longer announce Yahweh's promise of salvation to the whole nation; the promise had to be qualified, with peace and healing reserved for the righteous; "but the wicked are like the restless sea . . . there is no peace, says my God, for the wicked."

Examination of this secondary addition appropriately brings this section of Chapter II to a conclusion. It bridges the gap between the ministry of Second Isaiah and the later struggles of the post-exilic community reflected in the bulk of Third Isaiah. For the next section takes us a step further away from Second Isaiah in our typology, further away, however, only in regard to the changing situation, for the program for restoration in Isaiah 60–62, based on the teachings of Second Isaiah, remains throughout Third Isaiah the ideal toward which the visionary group aspires. Indeed, even when the harsh realities of frustration and oppression seem to vitiate that dream of their possession of a glorified Zion, they stubbornly refuse to submit to those historical realities. Instead they call upon the Warrior God Yahweh to bring them victory even when the unambiguous message of plain history is that they have already been defeated. This clinging to a restoration hope, in spite of opposition and defeat, provides the context for the development of apocalyptic eschatology which we shall trace in the following pages. For disintegrating historical circumstances prompted new modes of conceptualizing that restoration hope. As the visionaries discovered that preservation of their hope made it increasingly tempting to detach their vision from the events of plain history, those new conceptual modes developed in the direction of apocalyptic eschatology.

C. THE IDEAL UNDERMINED BY OPPOSITION (63:7–64:11)

Is 63:7–64:11 is cast in the form of a liturgy. More specifically, it stands in closest relation to the communal lament, as comparison with a composition like Psalm 44 indicates. As is characteristic of the material of Third Isaiah, however, the traditional genre of the lament is treated loosely, with less attention being given to the "pure" form of the old genre than to the new demands which the altered post-exilic situation are placing upon traditional modes of expression.

As it now stands the liturgy is tightly bound to chapter 65, for in 63:7–64:11 the congregation addresses Yahweh in the form of a complaint, ending with the troubled query, ". . .can you remain unmoved, Yahweh, keeping silent and oppressing us inordinately?" The word of Yahweh in

---

63: 7 I will recount the covenant promises of Yahweh,
the marvelous deeds of Yahweh,
according to all he has done for us,
the great goodness to the house of Israel
which he granted them according to his mercy
and the magnitude of his covenant promises.
8 For he said, Surely they are my people,
children who will not deal falsely,
and he became their savior
9 in all their distress.
Not a messenger, nor an angel,
but his own Presence saved them;
in his love and in his pity
he himself redeemed them;
he lifted them up and bore them
throughout the days of old.
10 But they rebelled and grieved
his holy spirit.
Therefore he turned to be their enemy,
he himself fought against them.
11 Yet I will recall the days of old,
of Moses and his people.
Where is he who brought up from the sea
the shepherds of his flock?
Where is he who placed in their midst
his holy spirit;
12 causing to go at Moses' right hand
his glorious arm,
dividing the waters before them
to establish for himself a name,

65:1-25 in the present redaction of the material seems to furnish the answer for that query. Yet, the main theme of the complaint, the withdrawal of Yahweh from his people because of their sin, is not taken up in chapter 65. Rather, an attack on cultic abuses is found. Thus Is 63:7-64:11 must be treated independently of chapter 65.

As for the internal unity of the liturgy thus delimited, it can confidently be maintained, on the basis of literary parallels (e.g., Psalms 36, 74, 77, 79; Lamentations 1-5), that the recitation of the *magnalia dei* in 63:7-14 is an original introduction to the lament which follows in 63:15ff.

	Text	Structure			Meter	Prosodic Units
63:7	חסדי יהוה אזכיר	a	b	c	6	b:b
	תהלת יהוה	A	b		5	
	כעל כל גמלנו [ ]	a	b	c	7	b:b::b:b
	[a] רב טוב לבית ישראל		b_1	D	7	
	גמלם כרחמיו		c	b_2	7	
	וכרב חסדיו		B		6	
8	ויאמר אך עמי המה	a	b	c	8	1:b::1:b
	בנים לא ישקרו		b	D	7	
	ויהי להם למושיע	a_1	c_1	e	8	
9	בכל צרתם		f	g	5	
	לא צר [b] ומלאך	a	b	b_1	5	b:b::1:b::1:b
	פניו הושיעם		b_2	C	5	
	באהבתו ובחמלתו		D	D_1	9	
	הוא גאלם		b_3	C_1	4	
	ינטלם וינשאם		C_2	C_3	9	
	כל ימי עולם		e	f	5	
10	והמה מרו ועצבו	a	b	b_1	9	1:b
	רוח קדשו		c	d	4	
	ויהפך להם לאויב	a	b	c	9	1:b
	הוא נלחם בם	A	b_1		4	
11	ו[א]זכר [c] ימי עולם	a	b		8	1:b
	משה [ו]עמו [d]		b_1	b_2	5	
	איה המעל[ה] [e] מים	a	b	c	7	1:b
	רעי צאנו		d	e	4	
	איה השם בקרבו	a	b_1	c_1	7	1:b
	רוח קדשו		d_1	e_1	3	
12	מוליך לימין משה	a	b	c	7	1:b::1:b::1:b::1:b::1:1
	זרוע תפארתו		D		5	
	בוקע מים מפניהם	a_1	e	b_1	7	
	לעשות לו שם[ ] [f]		f	d	5	

13 making them walk through the deeps
like a horse in the desert?
14 like cattle going down into the valley
the Spirit of Yahweh gave them rest;
thus you led your people
to establish for yourself a glorious name.
15 Look down from heaven, and see,
from your holy and glorious habitation.
Where is your ardor and your might,
the yearning of your pity and mercy?
Do not hold back, for you are our father!
16 though Abraham does not acknowledge us,
and Israel does not regard us,
you, Yahweh, are our Father,
our Redeemer from of old is your name.
17 Why do you permit us to stray from your ways
and harden our hearts against fearing you?
Return, for the sake of your servants,
the tribes of your inheritance.
18 For a brief time your holy people held possession,
but our adversaries have desecrated your sanctuary.
19 We have become like those never ruled by you,
those not called by your name.
Oh, that you would rend the heavens and come down—
before you the mountains would melt!
64: 1b to make known your name to your adversaries—
before you the nations would tremble!
2 as you perform unexpected wonders—
before you the mountains would melt!
3 From of old no ear has heard,
no eye has seen a god besides you,
who acts for those who await him,
4 meets with rejoicing those doing righteousness,
those keeping in mind your ways.
You were angry, for we were sinners,
. . . ., for we were rebels.
5 We were all like unclean men,
all of our righteous deeds like filthy clothing.
We have all withered like leaves,
and our sin bore us away like the wind.
6 There is none calling upon your name,
rousing himself to cling to you.
For you have hidden yourself from us,
you have delivered us up to our sin.
7 And yet, Yahweh, you are our Father,
we the clay, you the potter,
the work of your hand, all of us.

13	מוליכם בתהומות	a	b_2			7	
	כסום במדבר [ ] [g]		h	b_3		5	
14	כבהמה בבקעה תרד		h_1	b_4	i	9	
	רוח יהוה תניח[ם] [h]		D_1	$á_2$		6	
	כן נהגת עמך	$á_3$	e_1			7	
	לעשות לך שם תפארת		f	D_1		8	

15	הבט משמים וראה	a	b	a_1		8	1:1
	מזבל קדשך ותפארתך		b_1	c	c	11	
	איה קנאתך וגבורתך	a	b	b_1		12	1:1
	המון מעיך ורחמיך		B	b_2		10	
	אל [ת]תאפק [i] כי אתה אבינו	a	b	c		10	1:1:1::1:1
16	כי אברהם לא ידענו		d	e	f	9	
	וישראל לא יכירנו		d_1	e	f_1	9	
	אתה יהוה אבינו		B	c		7	
	גאלני מעולם שמך		C	b_1		10	
17	למה תתענו מדרכיך	a	b	c		10	1:1
	תקשיח לבנו מיראתך		B	c_1		10	
	שוב למען עבדיך [j]	a	b	c		7	b:b
	שבטי נחלתך			C		6	
18	למצער ירשו עם קדשך	a	b	c		10	1:1
	צרינו בוססו מקדשך		c_1	b_1	d	10	
19	היינו מעולם לא משלת בם	A	b	c		11	1:1
	לא נקרא שמך עליהם		B	c_1		8	

	לוא קרעת שמים [ו]ירדת	a	b	a_1		9	1:1::1:1::1:1
	מפניך הרים נזלו [ ] [k]		c	b_1	a_2	9	
	להודיע שמך לצריך	a_3	b_3	d		9	
	מפניך גוים ירגזו		c	b_2	a_4	9	
2	בעשותך נוראות לא נקוה	a_5	B			11	
	[ ] [l] מפניך הרים נזלו		c	b_1	a_2	9	
3	ומעולם לא שמעו[ ][m]ה אזן	a	b	c		9	1:1
	עין לא ראתה אל[ ] [n] זולתך		c_1	b_1	d	10	
	[ה]עשה למחכה לו	a	b	c		8	1:1:1
4	פגע[ ] ששו[ן] עש[י] צדק [o]	a_1	b_1	c_1		7	
	[ו]דרכיך יזכרו[ן] [p]		c_2	B		8	
	הן אתה קצפת ונחטא	a	b	c		9	1:1
	ונ[פ]שע [q]	?	?	c_1		?	
5	ונהי כטמא כלנו	a	b	c		9	1:1
	וכבגד עדים כל צדקתינו		B	c_1		10	
	ונבל כעלה כלנו	a_1	b_1	c_2		9	1:1
	ועוננו כרוח ישאנו		c_3	b_2	d	11	
6	ואין קורא בשמך	a	b	c		7	b:b
	מתעורר להחזיק בך		b_1	d	c_1	7	
	כי הסתרת פניך ממנו	a	b	c		10	1:1
	ותמ[ג]ננו [r] ביד עוננו	a_1	d	e		11	

7	ועתה יהוה אבינו אתה	a	b	c	b_1	5:5	bb:bb:1
	אנחנו החמר אתה יצרנו	b_2	c_1	b_1	c_2	5:6	
	ומעשה ירך כלנו		C	b_3		9	

8 Let not your anger go to extremes, Yahweh,
do not remember our sin forever,
for look, we are your people, all of us.
9 Your holy cities have become a desert,
Zion has become a desert,
Jerusalem a desolation;
10 Our holy and glorious house
in which our fathers prayed to you
has been consumed by fire;
everything in which we delight is in ruins.
11 Given all this can you remain unmoved, Yahweh,
keeping silent and oppressing us inordinately?

TEXTUAL NOTES

a) The LXX does not have the conjunction here.

b) Reading צִיר with LXX.

c) It is hardly possible to read Yahweh here as subject. C. C. Torrey (*ad loc.*) translates it as an impersonal third person, "Then one recalled. . ." In light of the apparent parallel to v. 7, we adopt the emendation of Karl Elliger and Paul Volz (*ad loc.*) to the first person singular.

d) משה עבדי is an attractive variant found in a few Hebrew manuscripts, and in Syriac. Since, however, what follows is concerned with the people, it seems best to supply the conjunction (LXX, V) and retain the עמו.

e) Read with 1QIsa.[a] MT is conflate.

f) An expansionary gloss.

g) A gloss.

h) There is disagreement among the versions between a singular or plural suffix. The plural is probably original (LXX, Pesh, Tg), though a collective singular is certainly not excluded by Hebrew usage.

i) Torrey, among others, proposes this very plausible emendation with the attendant restoration of the prosodic structure.

j) This colon has given rise to numerous attempts at emendation (cf. Muilenburg, *ad loc.*), since the plain sense of the Hebrew contradicts what most interpreters consider to be the historical background of the passage, namely, the destruction of the Babylonians in 587. Against such an understanding, the למצער would hardly apply, since the period during which Israel had possession of the Solomonic temple was longer than "a little while." Of the emendations offered, that proposed by Marti and Torrey (*ad loc.*) is the most clever: למה צערו רשעים קדשך, "Why do evil men desecrate thy sanctuary?" But the objections to this reading are

8	אל תקצף יהוה עד מאד	a	b	c		8	1:1:1
	ואל לעד תזכר עון	c_1	a_1	d		8	
9	הן הבט נא עמך כלנו	a_2	e	f		10	
	ערי קדשך היו מדבר	A	b	c		9	1:1:1::1:1:1::1
	ציון מדברהיתה	a	c	b_1		7	
	ירושלם שממה	A_1	C_1			8	
10	בית קדשנו ותפארתנו	A_2	A_3			9	
	אשד הללוך אבתינו		d	e	f	10	
	היה לשרפת אש		b_2	C		7	
	כל מחמדינו היה לחרבה	A_3	b_2	C_2		10	
11	העל אלה תתאפק יהוה	a	b	c		9	1:1
	תחשה ותעננו עד מאד		b_1	b_2	d	10	

very formidable: (1) It has absolutely no support in the versions. (2) Throughout the history of the transmission of this text, the final long vowels would have been marked by *matres lectionis*. Hence, one must assume gross scribal error if one is to accept this emendation. (3) **צער** in the sense proposed is unattested in biblical Hebrew, and recourse must be taken to the Aramaic dialects, and late Hebrew influenced by Aramaic. (4) The resulting parallel is too redundant to be natural: **מקדש//קדש**. (5) The text as it stands makes perfectly good sense, requiring no emendation.

More must be said about the last objection, since the type of emendation offered by Torrey, involving gross emendation and recourse to obscure uses of a root, is defensible only when the text does not yield to a reasonable translation, or when the metric structure is disrupted. But the colon as found in the MT presents no difficulties: (1) The temporal ל reflects a perfectly acceptable, though often misunderstood, usage. (2) The type of dual service rendered by the object in the second colon is in keeping with good Hebrew prosody, where the parallelism is maintained by balancing one syntactic member in the first stichos with a different syntactic member in the second: adverb-verb-subject::subject-verb-object. Here the adverb למצער is balanced by the object, **מקדשך**, the latter serving as object of both verbs. Furthermore, **ירש** is such a well-established technical term that it can be used absolutely (e.g., Gen 20:10; Dtn 1:21; 2:24). (3) The passage as it stands is saturated with the major concerns of the tradition in which it is embedded, and thus fits so flawlessly into its context that emendation cannot be achieved without disrupting badly the thrust of the entire unit. This will become evident in the interpretation which follows. Here it need only be observed how smoothly the notion of inheritance in v. 17b flows into that of possession in v. 18. Moreover, of central concern throughout Third Isaiah is the issue of inheritance and possession of the sanctuary (e.g., 57:13; 61:7; 65:9, 11) and the concept of a holy people (e.g., 62:12).

The LXX offers a very interesting variant which would represent: למצער ירשנו הר קדשך. But MT is to be preferred, being the *lectio difficilior,* since the alteration of עם to הר is easily traceable to the influence of the technical term הר הקדש. Moreover, it is well known that the Greek translators usually failed to understand the canons of Hebrew prosody, which suggests that they felt the need to supply ירש with an object, something most easily achieved through a change of עם to הר and a slight alteration of the verb.

k) The bicolon in 64:1a gives the appearance of an expansionary gloss, being metrically short and disrupting the internal structure in 63:19b–64:2 (i.e., act of Yahweh/theophanic refrain, thrice repeated). We read עמסים in the first colon following 1QIsa[a] (see A. Guillaume, "Some Readings in the Dead Sea Scroll of Isaiah," *JBL* 76 [1957]: 42):

כקדח אש (ע)מסים	a b c	7 as fire kindles brushwood
מים תבעה אש	c_1 a_1 b	4 as fire boils water.

l) An addition easily explained by influence from ירדת מפניך, etc., in 63:19b. The fact that all the commentators delete 64:2b (3 b) stems from the failure to recognize the poetic structure of 63:19b–64:2.

m) The confusion in this colon would have occurred when a noun - verb sequence came to be interpreted as two verbs.

n) Using the shorter form for "god."

o) This colon has obviously suffered corruption in the MT. We restore it on the assumption that it ran parallel to the preceding colon.

p) Following LXX.

q) This colon is hopelessly corrupt. The versions offer scant help. None of the suggested emendations is convincing (cf. S. H. Blank, "'And All Our Virtues' – An Interpretation of Isaiah 64:4b–5a," *JBL* 71 [1952]: 149–165).

r) With LXX.

There are a number of facts regarding the genre and approximate date of Is 63:7–64:11 which can be established at the outset. Belonging to the genre of the communal lament, it is closely related to the laments found in the book of Lamentations, and betrays affinities with several Psalms, especially 44, 74, and 79. Zech 7:1–17 and 8:18–19 permit us to extrapolate with a reasonable degree of certainty the general situation behind these laments: they were recited by the community remaining in Palestine in the period following the catastrophe of 587. Exactly when is impossible to determine, although one can observe that in general the memory of the catastrophe seems vivid in this literature; a date somewhere around the middle of the sixth century suggests itself. The same vividness of memory supports the view that these laments arose in Palestine, and not among the Babylonian exiles. It is not possible, however, to move beyond these generalities without closer investigation, for once again the commentators are broadly divided over the question of authorship when they deal with Is 63:7–64:11.

In seeking to avoid the impasse resulting from preoccupation with questions of authorship, we again apply the tools of the contextual-typological method of inquiry. First, what can be said about the internal structure, meter, and style of the composition? On the surface, the semblance of the archaic parallel structure is preserved, with the bicolon dominant and with an occasional tricolon adding to the archaic effect. The use of the 1:b *qînah* in 63:7–14 adds a limping, lament-like quality to the first two strophes which is effective. When we carry the analysis below the surface, however, it becomes very apparent that the quality of the poetry is far inferior to that of Second Isaiah, Is 57:14–19, and the archaizing sections of Isaiah 60–62. Enjambment abounds, the words are in general lacking in imaginative quality, and the total effect is quite prosaic. Yet isolated sections manifesting a better quality of poetry are not lacking, for example, the short Divine Warrior Hymn in 63:19b–64:2, where the archaizing prosody can be explained on the basis of the hymn's heavy dependence on older theophanies.[51] The meter as a whole remains quite regular, although the choice of 1 and b cola seems rather whimsical in places (e.g., 60:9 and 63:17).

The composition, judged on the basis of structure, meter, and style, is thus typologically later than Second Isaiah, Isaiah 60–62, and 57:14–19; however, it falls earlier in the

51. Cf. Ju 5:4–5 and Ps 18:8–16.

typology than the other oracles of Third Isaiah which we have yet to consider. This conclusion agrees with a picture which will grow clearer as we study other dimensions of this lament: we recognize here the emergence of a poetic tradition which, while betraying roots in earlier prophecy (especially Second Isaiah), nevertheless, is moving toward a unique prosody and thematic development which are increasingly distinguishable from earlier models.

We turn to an overview of the themes incorporated in the various sections of this particular lament, before addressing the problem of the particular community setting which it reflects. Drawing on the same pattern as Psalm 44, the lament begins with a summary of the *magnalia dei* which dramatizes Yahweh's early acts to save his people in fidelity to his covenant promises (vv. 7-9). The period referred to is the time of the exodus, a time – as remembered in early traditions like Exodus 15—when Yahweh's covenant relationship with his people was intimate and direct, unmediated by the elaborate structures of kingship and temple cult:

> Not a messenger, nor an angel,
> but his own Presence saved them;
> in his love and in his pity
> he himself redeemed them;
> he lifted them up and bore them
> throughout the days of old. (v. 9)

The underlying tone of this verse is archaizing, reflecting the desire to hark back to a period antedating the institutions which led the people from one rebellion against Yahweh to the next. We already discern the source which the creators of this material drew upon. That source was Israel's earliest traditions (e.g., Exodus 15) which celebrated "the days of old" when Yahweh acted directly on behalf of his people, when "his own Presence" saved and redeemed them (cf. Ex 33:14).

In contrast to this idyllic celebration of "the days of old" stands the memory of the more recent past characterized by the people's rebellion and the shocking result: Yahweh became their enemy and fought against them! It is neither possible nor helpful to attempt to pin down this reference to a particular period or event, for it tersely covers the entire span from the end of the idyllic pre-nationhood period celebrated in verses 7 through 9 to the tragic present within which the community finds itself. Israel's entire history as a nation was one of grieving "his holy spirit"!

But the lament, as if repulsed by the thought of that long history of rebellion and divine enmity, hastens back in verses 11-14 to "the days of old" by celebrating the idyllic era with words which are unprecedented in earlier prophetic material, a sure indication that the group creating the lament here loosens its relation to earlier conventions to give expression to its unique self-understanding: "Yet I will recall the days of old, of Moses and his people." The community of the idyllic period of the past is identified as "Moses and his people." This exalting of Moses as the ideal leader is remarkable, and its significance will be discussed below. The disturbing contrast between the golden era of Israel's primitive period and the subsequent period down to the present is accentuated by a series of questions:

> Where is he who brought up from the sea
> the shepherds of his flock?
> Where is he who placed in their midst
> his holy spirit;
> causing to go at Moses' right hand
> his glorious arm,
> dividing the waters before them
> to establish for himself a name,
> making them walk through the deeps
> like a horse in the desert? (vv. 11-13)

These questions draw attention to the nerve-center of the community reciting this lament: their sense of identity and their criticism of the existing situation are based upon their idyllic picture of the events of Israel's most distant past, especially the events centering around the great deliverance at the sea. But even as they live from the memory of those ancient traditions, they move in directions of their own: Yahweh's presence they uniquely interpreted as "his holy spirit" (vv. 10, 11, 14), and Yahweh's motivation they identified as the establishing of his "glorious name" (vv. 12, 14).

The disjuncture between the vivid memory of Yahweh's direct acts of salvation in the past and the deplorable conditions of the present issues forth in an ardent appeal for a *return* to the conditions of the idyllic, primitive period:

> Look down from heaven, and see,
> from your holy and glorious habitation. . . .
> Return, for the sake of your servants,
> the tribes of your inheritance. (vv. 15a, 17b)

With this entreaty begins the lament section itself, which extends from 63:15 to 64:11, and is constructed loosely with impassioned pleas for help interspersed with lines of complaint. Already in the progression from the historical resumé to this plea for Yahweh's return we recognize a familiar pattern by which oppressed sectarian groups in widely divergent historical periods have sought to resolve the tension between brilliant hopes for the future and harsh present realities which threaten to crush those hopes, that pattern being an ardent longing for a return to a past golden era. A yet more advanced stage of this pattern is a harking back even beyond the historical events of the dim past to the timeless, primordial events of myth which offer total escape from the harsh realities of this world. At points in the lament section proper we appear to be on the threshold leading from the longing for the golden age of the past to the stage in the pattern which harks back to the primordial events of myth:

> Oh that you would rend the heavens and come down—
> before you the mountains would melt!
> to make known your name to your adversaries—
> before you the nations would tremble!
> as you perform unexpected wonders—
> before you the mountains would melt!

Against the background of this overview of the main sections of the composition, we turn to the question of the community situation reflected by this lament. Within the early post-exilic community, what group is raising this impassioned voice to Yahweh? Who are the adversaries against whom they so bitterly complain and call down Yahweh's wrath?

In approaching these questions we should bear in mind the observation made above that the lament in 63:7–64:11 bears closest affinities with compositions arising during the exile, compositions stemming, however, not from the Babylonian exiles, but from those who remained in Palestine.[52] This observation relates to the current scholarly consensus that the Chronicler draws an overly simplified picture when he depicts the entire community of religiously elite being removed by the Babylonians with only an inferior rabble of syncretizers being left in the land (2 Chr 36:20f). Passages like Jer 41:5f and I Kgs 8:33 suggest that definite activity continued to be carried on at the site of the temple ruins after the fall of Jerusalem. Supporting these hints is a significant body of literature coming from the Palestinian community during the years of the exile.[53] We can no longer accept uncritically the picture found in Ezra that the concern for restoration after the national catastrophe was limited to the group of exiles returning with Sheshbazzar under the Persian mandate in 538. Historians of the period must remain open to hints of a situation which was a good deal more complex than that portrayed by Chronicles, Ezra, and Nehemiah.

The lament in 63:7–64:11 seems to be a part of this more complex situation. The passage as a whole betrays

52. See above, pp. 86–87.

53. E. Janssen, *Judia in der Exilszeit* FRLANT 69 (Göttingen: Vandenhoeck und Ruprecht, 1956) has gathered the evidence supporting the thesis that a very active community of those faithful to Yahweh existed in Palestine throughout the years of the exile. Literature arising from the Palestinian community includes the book of Lamentations, Isaiah 21, the Deuteronomic History, Obadiah, and a number of Psalms. He estimates that the total number of those exiled in 587 did not exceed five thousand, leaving a goodly number of Yahwists in the land (pp. 34–35). Though his thesis probably goes too far in minimizing the catastrophic effect which the events of the early sixth century had on Palestine (cf. W. F. Albright, *The Biblical Period from Abraham to Ezra* [New York: Harper Torchbooks, 1949], pp. 85–86, it is a useful corrective to the view that all Yahwistic activity ceased in Palestine during the years of the exile.

unmistakable signs which tie it to the tradition of Second Isaiah already recognized behind the program of restoration in Isaiah 60–62. For as in Second Isaiah (e.g., 40:4f) and Isaiah 60–62 (60:1; 62:11), the community in 63:7–64:11 awaits deliverance as a day in which Yahweh himself will appear in glory to save his people (63:9; 64:3f; cf. 40:25f; 41:21ff, 28f). In this lament, as in Isaiah 65, Second Isaiah's enigmatic figure of the servant is further democratized to apply to the faithful within Israel (63:17). Finally, two central concerns in Isaiah 60–62 and other parts of Third Isaiah are present here, the concern with possession of Zion (63:18; cf. 60:21; 61:7; 57:13; 65:9), and with the holiness of the people (63:18; cf. 62:12).

Although these basic themes persist as constants from Second Isaiah, through Isaiah 60–62, and now into Is 63:7–64:11, further analysis indicates that they are undergoing readaptation to a changing situation. As was already noticeable in Isaiah 60–62 (e.g., 62:1ff), what in Second Isaiah was a confident announcement of the imminent salvation has here become a desperate cry for Yahweh to act (63:11ff, 15, 19b–64:3, 8–12). It seems apparent that the salvation has been delayed, driving the people to the brink of despair.

In another startling way, the situation seems to be deteriorating: what in Isaiah 60–62 were but faint hints of a narrowing of the salvation hope to a segment within Israel (61:3) in this lament grow into ominous signs that a fatal rift is threatening to divide the community. Thrice in the midst of the plea for help the cry goes up to Yahweh, "You are our Father." This repetition alone strongly implies that someone is contesting this claim, and this implication is verified by words coming between two of those cries:

> Do not hold back, for you are our Father!
> though Abraham does not acknowledge us,
> and Israel does not regard us,
> you, Yahweh, are our Father,
> our Redeemer from of old is your name. (63:15b–16)

The referent of the designations *Abraham* and *Israel* can be taken most naturally as the central Israelite community of this period, that is, the group returning from exile under the leadership of the Zadokite priests. The remarkable reference to God as Father, which appears only in this lament, arises from a desperate clinging to Yahweh by a group whose ancestral fathers (Abraham and Israel as eponyms of the nation) have rejected them.[54] A conflict is thus reflected between the central community and the group protesting in the oracle that it is not being acknowledged by that normative, Zadokite community. The correctness of this interpretation will become increasingly apparent as the rest of Third Isaiah comes under scrutiny, an interpretation which has already been suggested by indications that the community behind this material has for some time been concerned to disassociate itself from the old names for the nation like Israel and Abraham. For example, Is 62:2: "And you will be called by a new name which the mouth of Yahweh will designate," and Is 62:12: "They will be called 'The Holy People,' 'Yahweh's Redeemed.'" This same concern will be recognized later as well, e.g., Is 65:15, "You will leave your name as a curse, but my servants will be called by a new name." In other words, Israel was becoming a designation with very negative connotations for this group—a very startling development, indeed—and hence the search through tradition for new designations free from the stigma attaching itself to the old, new designations like "My servants" (63:17; 65:8 f, 13 ff; 66:14), "My chosen" (65:9, 15, 22), "the Priests of Yahweh" (61:6), "My Delight is in Her" (62:4), "Married" (62:4), and in 63:15 and 64:7, even the designation which had hitherto been eschewed because of its mythic connections, "our Father."

Further evidence of this growing rift is found in 63:17b, where the plea for Yahweh's intervention is supported with the phrase, "for the sake of your servants, the tribes of your inheritance." The reference to "your servants" is very significant here, for, as chapter 65 will show, it is the term

54. Cf. the polemic in the Gospel of John 8:12–59, where Jesus speaks of God as his Father, and the Pharisees are quoted as saying: "Abraham is our Father" (v. 39).

which comes to designate the faithful remnant within Israel in contrast to the defiled majority. In 65:8 the same phrase is used, and it acts as a commentary on 63:17b: ". . .so I will act for the sake of my servants, in order not to destroy the whole." A distinction within Israel has already established itself in the minds of the community behind these passages. They regard themselves as standing in a special relationship to Yahweh, and thus can appeal for help "for the sake of your servants." The rift apparent in 63:17 does not seem to be as deep, however, as it does in Isaiah 65; for while in the latter it has come to divide the servants, who shall be saved, from the others, who are promised damnation in the strongest terms, in this lament confession is still made on behalf of, and hope still seems to be held out for the entire nation (64:5–9). This fact is one of the reasons why we place this lament at an early point in our relative chronology.

In connection with the numerous new names which the protesting group can be seen applying to itself, a feature within the recitation of the *magnalia dei* introducing the lament becomes noteworthy. The purpose of that introductory recitation seems to be that of underscoring the now contested fact that their history stands in unbroken connection with the earliest history of the nation, making them the rightful heirs of the ancient promises.[55] The remarkable feature in that recitation is the prominent position assumed by Moses, who normally is not found in the summaries of Israel's *Heilsgeschichte*.[56] Here, after the tragic first chapter of Israel's history which concluded with Yahweh's turning against Israel because of the nation's disobedience, Moses is portrayed as the one through whom Yahweh saved his people (vv. 11, 12). When the lament

55. Their claim to membership in the nation is also advanced in the archaic designation, "the tribes of your inheritance," in v. 17b; cf. Ps 74:2, Jer 10:16//51:19. Similarly archaizing are the terms used by the visionary authors of the compositions in Zechariah 9–14, e.g., "clans of Judah" (12:5, 6) and "tents of Judah" (12:7).

56. G. von Rad, *The Problem of the Hexateuch and Other Essays*, tr. E. W. T. Dicken (New York: McGraw-Hill, 1966), pp. 1–13; M. Noth, *A History of Pentateuchal Traditions*, tr. B. W. Anderson (Englewood Cliffs: Prentice-Hall, 1972), pp. 156–157.

asks where the one is who thus led Moses and his people, it compares the situation of the community rejected by Abraham and Israel to the dire straits within which Moses and his people found themselves. As verses 15, 19, and 64:1f indicate, the disenfranchised group pleads for a mighty act of Yahweh to save them even as Moses and his people were saved. This leads to the attempt to identify further the group drawing upon the prophetic tradition of Second Isaiah in protesting the central community's failure to acknowledge their membership in Israel, and citing their kinship to Moses as evidence of the legitimacy of their claim. When it is recalled that the *gôlāh* group which seized the leadership of the restoration efforts in the last half of the sixth century was dominated by the Zadokites, and when it is further noted that the chief target of the Zadokites in their struggle for leadership was the Levites,[57] a plausible explanation of this remarkable reference to Moses suggests itself.

The Mushite background of many of the Levites is well known, for once the Mushites were removed from a central position in the Solomonic temple, they were amalgamated with the ranks of the Levites. Upon the return to Palestine of the Zadokite-dominated *gôlāh* group, conflict was almost inevitable with the Levitical priests who had remained in the land and who were likely the ones who carried on the activity around the altar site during the dark years of the exile. What we are suggesting is this: the party registering the protest in 63:7–64:11 against their exclusion from the cult included, perhaps among various other dissident elements, Levitical priests who found that the Zadokite program left no room for them in the restoration cult. The fact that the central concern of the Third Isaiah material is the *priestly* concern of possession of Zion[58] supports the hypothesis, as does the observation that the conceptual world of Third Isaiah, though still participating profoundly in the prophecy of Second Isaiah, is permeated much more

57. See Chapter III.
58. See pp. 152–153.

deeply by priestly concepts than the latter,[59] indicating that many priests had entered the ranks of the disciples of Second Isaiah. Also fitting well into this hypothesis of a Mushite-Levite element within the group protesting against the temple party returning from exile is the Mushite family background of Jeremiah of Anathoth, a prophet who took an unpopular stand against the temple theology of the Zadokite party of his time.

Against the background of our hypothesis of a conflict between the Zadokite group returning from exile with the hierocratic program for restoration and the dissident Levitical-prophetic group resisting the official program the cryptic verse 63:18 becomes intelligible: "For a brief time your holy people held possession, but our adversaries have desecrated your sanctuary." As noted above, designations like "your servants," "tribes of your inheritance," and "your holy people" were adopted by the dissident group to distinguish themselves from the remainder of the Israelite people. In the context of this inner-Israelite conflict, the antithetical parallel "our adversaries" applies most naturally to the Zadokite priestly party.[60] Does not the verse then refer to a time during the exile when the Levitical group had charge of the temple site, and is not this short time now contrasted to the new situation after the returning Zadokite group has seized control of the sanctuary? We shall leave this suggested interpretation in the form of an hypothesis, to be tested against further evidence, an hypothesis, however, which relates remarkably well to the major concern of the remaining oracles of Third Isaiah, namely, the struggle to regain control of Zion (e.g., 65:9: "My chosen will inherit it and my servants will dwell there"; 57:13b: "But he who seeks refuge in me will inherit the

59. Cf. Chary, *Prophètes, passim.*

60. Note that צר is used also in Ezra to designate the opponents in the inner community struggle. The evidence gathered by F. M. Cross has made it impossible to consider any longer an interpretation of the Third Isaiah material against the background of the Samaritan conflict ("Aspects of Samaritan and Jewish History in Late Persian and Hellenistic Times," *Harvard Theological Review* 59 [1966]: 201–211).

land, he will take possession of my holy mountain").[61] Moreover, there is evidence elsewhere that the control of the *gôlāh* group over the temple site was not achieved without a struggle.[62] However, the actual overt struggle over the temple site would have been brief, for the claim to sole authority raised by the returning *gôlāh* group was given teeth by an official Persian mandate, and once the Persians threw their full support behind the hierocratic program, as they did upon the accession of Darius Hystaspes, there was little on the political level that the Levitic-prophetic group could do to resist. But their hope was not crushed, for even as they affirmed in their restoration program that Yahweh himself would direct the rebuilding, so now in the face of crushing opposition from within the community they believed that Yahweh ultimately would intervene to give them victory over their adversaries. Whereas they were obliged to acknowledge defeat within the political arena, and were soon to be convinced that the present cult had been wrested irrevocably from their control, they began to raise their vision to a more dramatic

61. One can almost speak of the Third Isaiah group's concern with possession of Zion as an obsession from the early formulation of their program based on Second Isaiah (60:7, 21–22; 61:7), to the somewhat later lament (63:17b–19), to the late polemical material (57:13; 65:1–10). That a bitter struggle for control over Zion is being fought is an undeniable conclusion to be drawn from this strongly polemical Third Isaiah material, and a strong argument in favor of the above reconstruction of the situation within the community in the exilic and post-exilic period is that this reconstruction satisfactorily explains the background of that struggle. Further traces of the struggle may be discerned in Ezr 4:1–4.

62. Ezr 3:2 ff recounts the earliest attempts to restore the temple area by the hierocratic group which returned under Sheshbazzar. The key figures emerging in this activity are Jeshua and Zerubbabel, who led their kinsmen in building "the altar of the God of Israel, to offer burnt offerings upon it." The author makes clear that this was the authorized altar, for it was built "as it is written in the law of Moses the man of God," which probably refers to some form of the Pentateuch. The account continues, "They set the altar in its place, for fear was upon them because of the peoples of the lands. . . ." The latter is the designation used by the Chronicler to cover all elements which were in the land upon the return of the official *gôlāh.* Thus the Levitical-prophetic group protesting in Isaiah 63–64 their exclusion from the restoration cult would also be so designated, suggesting that Ezr 3:2ff may preserve a memory of the struggle for the temple site between those who occupied the site during the exile and the Zadokite *gôlāh* group which seized the restoration initiative after their return. This struggle would then be the background of the protest in 63:15–16: "Do not hold back, for you are our Father! though Abraham does not acknowledge us, and Israel does not regard us, you, Yahweh, are our Father. . . ." and of the cryptic lament, "For a brief time your holy people held possession, but our adversaries have desecrated your sanctuary" (63:18). (Cf. Janssen, *Juda,* pp. 102–103, and Ackroyd, *Exile,* pp. 28–29.)

restoration which Yahweh would achieve once he had punished the usurpers.

This visionary character of their faith is expressed in the section following the lament, where they fervently plead for Yahweh to return to his ancient mode of action by intervening directly on their behalf. They turn to that tradition which suited so perfectly the visionary nature of their hope as they express their plea in the theophanic imagery of the Divine Warrior Hymns. Stemming ultimately from the mythic cycles of the Canaanites, and having had a marked influence on Israel's earliest literature—an influence which increased greatly within the royal cult in the period of the monarchy—the imagery of the Divine Warrior was adapted to prophecy in a fresh way by the Second Isaiah, and from that point became the chief carrier of the eschatological faith of the post-exilic visionary tradition.[63] In verses 63:19b–64:2 the plea takes the form of three lines, each followed by a refrain dramatizing the natural phenomena accompanying the theophany.[64] The plea itself runs: "Oh, that you would rend the heavens and come down, . . . to make known your name to your adversaries, . . . as you perform unexpected works." The central object of the plea is for Yahweh to reveal himself to his adversaries, that is, the ones who have deprived them of a position in the cult, the "Abraham-Israel" which refuses to acknowledge "your servants," "your holy people." Though thus defeated, this group does not lose hope that Yahweh will act to restore them to their rightful inheritance, for Yahweh alone is the God "who acts for those who await him, meets with rejoicing those doing righteousness, those keeping in mind your ways" (64:3–4). Expressed in these lines is a note of comfort and assurance—seemingly unjustified by the actual situation—that ultimately Yahweh would act on behalf of the faithful, a note running

63. See F. M. Cross, "The Divine Warrior in Israel's Early Cult," *Biblical Motifs*, ed. A. Altmann (Cambridge: Harvard University, 1966), pp. 11–30; *idem, Myth*, pp. 105–110; P. D. Miller, Jr., *The Divine Warrior in Early Israel*, Harvard Semitic Monographs 5 (Cambridge: Harvard University, 1973); and the author's "Jewish Apocalyptic," pp. 36–57.

64. See textual notes "k" and "l" above.

throughout the Third Isaiah material (e.g., 57:13; 59:20; 65:9f; 66:7-14) and then on into the vast literature we designate as apocalyptic.

Analysis of the lament in 63:7–64:11 thus yields the following conclusions: it was written from within the visionary tradition which stemmed from Second Isaiah and was summarized programmatically in Isaiah 60-62. At the same time it reveals that the former confidence that Yahweh would soon restore his people upon Zion as a nation of priests living in righteousness has been replaced by a situation in which this prophetic group finds itself being denied its rightful possession and position of leadership in the restoration by what has come to be a powerful opposition party. In this situation they raise their complaint to Yahweh.

The remaining material which we shall examine from Third Isaiah will represent further chapters in this struggle between visionary and hierocratic factions within the post-exilic community, for while the former never gave up faith that Yahweh would come to dispose of their enemies and return them to their rightful heritage, they did not wait in silence. As long as they felt that Zion was being defiled, their representatives would preach Yahweh's word of judgment, a word which would become more and more acrimonious. Accompanying that word of judgment against the wicked in Israel, however, would be a word of comfort to the righteous, reaffirming the original promises of Second Isaiah and Isaiah 60-62. But in a situation which grew increasingly oppressive, where the chances for an actual historical return to Zion became increasingly bleak as the hierocratic party gained an ever firmer control of the cult, that promise, though unchanged in substance, underwent change in form. Thus in the context of this historical struggle we shall be witnessing the transformation of the eschatology of Second Isaiah—within which the dialectic between history and myth was held intact—into an emerging apocalyptic eschatology which threatened to dissolve the prophetic dialectic by returning Yahwism to the pure vision of myth. The study of this development promises to cast new light upon the perplexing riddle of the historical background of the apocalyptic literature which flourished from the second century B.C.E. to the second century of the Common Era.

D. TENSION WITHIN THE COMMUNITY GROWS (58 AND 59)

1. Isaiah 58:1–12

Is 58:1–12 forms a self-contained unit both metrically

58: 1 Cry out aloud, hold not back,
lift up your voice like a trumpet,
proclaim to my people their guilt,
to the house of Jacob their sins.
2 They inquire of me daily,
they delight in the knowledge of my ways,
as if they were a nation doing righteousness,
not abandoning the justice of its God;
they ask me for just ordinances,
they delight in drawing near to God.
3 Why do we fast, but you do not see,
afflict ourselves, but you do not know it?
Look, on your fast day you pursue pleasure
and oppress all your workmen.
4 Look, you quarrel and strive when you fast,
and strike the poor with the fist.
But your fasting thus regularly
will not make your voice heard on high.
5 Is this the sort of fast I choose,
a day for a man to afflict himself,
to bow down his head like a rush,
lying down on sackcloth and ashes?
Is this what you call a fast,
a day acceptable to Yahweh?
6 Is not this the sort of fast I choose,
to loose the fetters of injustice,
to remove the thongs of the yoke,
to set free the oppressed,
and break every yoke?
7 Is it not to share your bread with the hungry,
to bring home the homeless poor;
when you see one naked, to clothe him,
and not to turn from your own flesh?

(1:1 throughout) and thematically (dealing with the theme of fasting). Only verses 13–14 give rise to the question of originality, since they deal with the issue of the sabbath in a way suggesting a later period. These two verses bear striking similarities to 56:1–8, and may well have been added along with the redactional framework 56:1–8 and 66:18–24.

	Text	Structure			Meter		Prosodic Units	
58:1	קרא בגרון אל תחשך	a	b	a_1			8	1:1::1:1
	כשופר הרם קולך	c	a_2	b_1			8	
	הגד לעמי פשעם	a_3	d	e			7	
	לבית יעקב חטאתם		D	e_1			7	
2	אותי יום יום ידרשון	a	b	c			7	1:1::1:1::1:1
	דעת דרכי יחפצון	A		c			7	
	כגוי [ ]צדקה עשה		d	e	f		7	
	משפט אלהיו לא עזב			E	f_1		8	
	ישאלוני משפטי צדק		c_2	E_1			8	
	קרבת אלהים יחפצון		E_2	c_1			8	
3	למה צמנו ולא ראית	a	b	c			9	1:1
	ענינו נפשנו ולא תדע		B	c_1			10	
	הן ביום צמכם תמצאו חפץ	a	b	c^1			9	1:1
	וכל עצביכם [a] תנגשו		C	b_1			9	
4	הן לריב ומצה תצומו	a	a_1	b			9	1:1
	ולהכות באגרף רש [b]		a_2	C			8	
	[ו]לא תצומו כיום	a	b	c			7	1:1
	להשמיע במרום קולכם		d	e	f		8	
5	הכזה [ ]צום אבחרהו	a	b	c			8	
	יום ענות אדם נפשו		b_1	d	e		7	
	הלכף כאגמן ראשו			d_1	f	e_1	8	mixed
	ושק ואפר יציע			e_2	e_3	d_2	6	
	הלזה תקרא צום	a_1	c_1	b			6	
	ויום רצון ליהוה		b_1	g	h		7	
6	הלא זה צום אבחרהו	a_2	b	c			8	
	פתח חרצבות רשע			d_3	E		6	
	התר אגדות מוטה			d_4	E_1		7	
	ושלח רצוצים חפשים			d_5	E_2		8	
	וכל מוטה תנתק[ ] [c]			E_3	d_6		7	
7	הלא פרס לרעב לחמך		a_3	d_7	E_4		10	
	ועניים מורדים [d] תביא בית			E_5	D		10	
	כי תראה ערם וכסיתו			E_6	d_8		9	
	ומבשרך לא תתעלם			e_4	D_1		9	

8 Then your light will burst forth like dawn,
and your healing will come quickly;
your righteousness will proceed before you,
the glory of Yahweh will guard you from behind.
9 Then you will call, and Yahweh will answer,
you will shout, and he will say, Here I am.
If you abolish the yoke from among you,
the accusing finger, the malicious word,
10 and you give your bread to the hungry
and satisfy the need of the oppressed;
Then your light will rise in the darkness,
and your dark shadows will be like noon.
11 Yahweh will always guide you,
he will satisfy you in desert places,
he will invigorate your bones;
and you will be like a watered garden,
like a spring of water,
whose waters never fail.
12 Your ancient ruins will be rebuilt,
you will raise up the old foundations.
You will be called "Repairer of the breach,"
"Restorer of ruins for habitation."

TEXTUAL NOTES

a) עצבים is obscure. Two עצב roots are attested in biblical Hebrew, the most frequent with the basic meaning of "hurt, grieve," the other appearing most frequently in nominal form meaning "idol." The latter meaning does not apply here; hence attention focuses on the former. The verbal element in the colon can be translated, "you exact (something)," or "you drive (someone)." MT seems to be opting for the latter, pointing the noun object as a *nomen agentis.* BDB therefore suggests the meaning "toiler," as one who grieves under his task. On the basis of LXX (ὑποχείριοι— - "those under one's power," "debtors") and V (*debitores*) Duhm conjectured עבטיכם. The present state of the evidence makes a conclusive judgment impossible, though the alternative offered by BDB has the advantage of requiring no emendation.

b) With LXX. For ταπεινός = רָשׁ, cf. 1 Sam 18:23. The conjunction is found in about fifty mss.

c) Singular with LXX, Old Latin, Vg.

8	אז יבקע כשחר אורך	a	b	c		9	1:1::1:1
	וארכתך מהרה תצמח	c_1	b_1	a_1		10	
	והלך לפניך צדקך	a_2	b_2	c_2		10	
	כבוד יהוה יאספך		C	a_3		8	
9	אז תקרא ויהוה יענה	a	b	c		8	1:1
	תשוע ויאמר הנני	a_1	c_1	b_1		9	
	אם תסיר מתוכך מוטה	a	b	c		8	1:1::b:b
	שלח אצבע ודבר און		C	C_1		8	
10	ותפק לרעב [לחמך] [e]	a_1	b_1	c_1		7	
	ונפש נענה תשביע		B	a_2		6	
	וזרח בחשך אורך	a	b	c		8	1:1
	ואפלתך כצהרים		C	b_1		9	
11	ונחך יהוה תמיד	a	b	c		8	1:1:1::1:b:b
	והשביע בצחצחות נפשך	a_1	d	e		10	
	ועצמתיך יחליץ		E	a_2		7	
	והיית כגן רוה		f	d_1	g	8	
	וכמוצא מים			d_2	g_1	5	
	לא יכזבו מימיו			h	g_1	7	
12	[נ]בנו[f] ממך חרבות עולם	a	b	C		10	1:1
	מוסדי דור ודור תקומם		C_1	a		8	
	וקרא לך גדר פרץ	a	b	c		8	1:1
	משבב נתי[צ]ות [g] לשכת [h]		C	d		8	

d) Though apparently intended by the Masoretes as a passive participle of מרד, the sense would suggest that the original was a form of רוד, perhaps the hop'al part., מוּרָדִים (cf. LXX: ἀστέγους, "houseless," and Vg: *vagos,* "wandering").

e) The difficulties in this colon are most easily solved by regarding נפשך as the result of a dittography of the following word and restoring לַחְמְךָ with Pesh. LXX has both words: *καὶ δῷς πεινῶντι τὸν ἄρτον* (+*σου* A) *ἐκ ψυχῆς σου* (except *α'σ'θ'* have only *ψυχην σου*).

f) Nip'al following LXX. ממך חרבות means simply "your ruins" (cf. Torrey, *ad loc.*).

g) A simple emendation involving one letter, and resulting in an excellent parallel (cf. G. R. Driver, "Notes on Isaiah," *Von Ugarit nach Qumran,* Eissfeldt Festschrift, eds. J. Hempel and L. Rost [Berlin: Alfred Töpelman, 1958], p. 48; *idem,* "Linguistic and Textual Problems, Isaiah XL-LXVI," *JTS* 36 [1935]: 405).

h) Concerning vv. 13–14, see p. 101.

As is typical of the material in Third Isaiah, there is nothing approaching a consensus among the scholars regarding the date and authorship of Isaiah 58. The two factors usually drawn into discussions concerning the setting of this oracle are the phenomena of fasting dealt with and the mention that "your ancient ruins shall be rebuilt" (v. 12). Regarding fasting, it is argued by some that the oracle must stem from the period between 536 and the time of Zechariah, since it was during this time that the four fasts mentioned in Zech 7:5 and 8:19 were practiced; 536 is set as the *terminus a quo* since Palestine forms the background of the oracle, 520 the *terminus ante quem* because Zechariah reports the abolishment of these fasts. The argument for the *ante quem* dating has some force. The 536 date is more questionable, since it rests uncritically upon the Chronicler's schema of the return.

The second factor, reference to the "ancient ruins" in verse 12, is less useful. It is cited in defense of a date *circa* 530, being interpreted as an indication that the temple still lay in ruins. Duhm and those adopting his views, however, interpret it as referring only to the walls of the city which were not rebuilt until the middle of the fifth century. The verse offers no help whatsoever, inasmuch as it accommodates either interpretation.[65] We again dispense with such attempts to determine an absolute date, turning instead to the question of the typology of prosody and the relative date it may suggest, then to the question of the traditions to which the unit belongs, finally asking whether any reflection of the situation within the community can be ascertained.

The internal structure, meter, and style of chapter 58 represent a further departure from the prosody of Second Isaiah. There are places where the parallel structure of the bicolon is maintained, and where the poetic quality is quite good, especially in the third strophe (vv. 8–12). The reason

65. Duhm's further argument for the 460 date is that the background of the oracle is that delineated in Neh 5:1ff, namely, a time of famine where sons and daughters had to be given as slaves in trade for food, and likewise lands and homes. If this line of argumentation has any validity, it would be more plausible to compare the background of our oracle to the economic conditions suggested by Hag 1:5.

for this is not hard to recognize: in verses 8–12 the author is drawing heavily upon Second Isaiah in renewing the eschatological promise found in the message of that great prophet. But in the other two strophes, and especially in the second (vv. 5–7), the author is formulating his own message within the context of harshly altered community circumstances, and the structure, meter, and style are given a new stamp. We now shall examine the second strophe in greater detail.

All that can be said about the meter of this section is that it is utterly mixed, with no pattern being apparent. The parallel structure of the bicolon has also broken down, but in contrast to the patternlessness of the meter, a new type of prosodic structure can be seen emerging to replace the old. It is a very complicated prosodic structure based on an interweaving of recurring grammatical elements which may stem from an attempt to achieve an archaizing effect, but which fails to achieve that end. For whereas repetition was used in archaic oral composition for refrains, or to construct catalogues of fine poetic quality, the repetition found here is much more prosaic, much more contrived, serving to bind together long prosodic units with an end effect which is indelicate and baroque. The prosodic unit extending throughout the second strophe is bound together by two devices: (1) by repetition of the interrogative element (a, a_1, a_2, a_3) and (2) by expansion in a list-like fashion of the infinitive (and occasionally finite verb) element and the object element (d and e, respectively). Another baroque prosodic unit is found in verse 2, being comprised of two bicola followed by a third which binds together chiastically the verbal elements of the first colon with the object elements of the second.

We thus find in this chapter structural features which point to developments away from the austere beauty of early Hebrew poetry, including the intricate interweaving of grammatical elements which becomes more and more contrived, repetition serving less the purpose of refrain than of binding together long prosodic units, and the prose-like succession of elements in long lists. It is hard to avoid the conclusion that these characteristics betray a move away from the influence of oral composition toward canons more purely literary in character. This development can be traced back to Second Isaiah, whose poetry betrays distinct marks of literary composition, even though the simple beauty of early poetry is in part maintained as an archaism. This archaic quality is lost to an increasing extent in the typology we are tracing. Isaiah 58 represents a further stage on that typology.

The form of this oracle betrays a transformation of one of the oldest classical oracle types, the judgment oracle dealing with the theme "obedience is better than sacrifice." In the pre-exilic prophets (e.g., Am 5:21–24; Is 1:10–17) this oracle type comprises two main sections: (1) indictment for false cultic practices and (2) threat of judgment, or admonition. The form-critical analysis of the present oracle reveals that it is transitional between this classical type and the salvation-judgment oracle which develops in the last part of the sixth century and which we shall discuss below.

The oracle begins in the manner of the classical oracle, verse 1 being the commission of the prophet (cf. Is 6:9; Jer 2:2; 4:5), followed in verses 2–5 by the judgment itself (vv. 2–4a: indictment, v. 4b: sentence). But the elements of the oracle are very loosely conceived; elements of the disputation (reminiscent of Second Isaiah) expand the indictment section, and the sentence is followed in verse 5 with further disputation. The next section in verses 6–7 can be compared to the admonition section which sometimes concluded the classical oracle, but it leads to a conclusion of the oracle in verses 8–12 which is best designated as a very developed promise of eschatological salvation. This salvation section is dominated by the images of light and darkness, which derive from Second Isaiah and are an indication of the relative lateness of this oracle. The long list of promises, covering both traditional promises and innovative ones applying only to the post-exilic situation, is unlike anything found in the pre-exilic oracles.

Taken as a whole the oracle adumbrates the salvation-judgment oracle which comes to characterize the post-exilic period: (1) The judgment section in verses 2–5 is directed toward those who fast falsely, those who consider themselves righteous in cultic observances yet combine these cultic observances with oppression and violence, leading to the judgment that their fast will not "make your voice heard on high" (v. 4). (2) The section in verses 6ff is directed toward those who would fast in a way pleasing to Yahweh by acts of mercy, leading to words of salvation and promise: "Then you will call, and Yahweh will answer" (v. 9).

This transformation in form is very significant, for it represents a transitional point at which the function of the prophetic oracle is being radically altered. Verses 1-5, if taken by themselves, strongly recall the past history of the prophetic oracle, where the entire nation was addressed either with a word of salvation or with a word of judgment. Where salvation and judgment oracles were found juxtaposed in the classical period Israel was still treated as a unit, for the judgment aspect was directed against the nations, the salvation aspect at Israel.[66] But that classical form, with one word directed toward the nation as a whole, is strongly qualified when the salvation section (vv. 6-12) is taken into consideration, for implied is a dichotomy within the nation whereby one element is threatened with judgment while the other is promised salvation. We must regard this oracle as transitional, since that dichotomy is not yet complete. Indeed, at several points tension between the classical form

66. This juxtaposition of judgment words against Israel's historical enemies and salvation words to Israel is common in classical prophecy, and indicates that judgment versus those enemies usually implied salvation for Israel. See, for example, Isaiah 18, where vv. 1-6 announce judgment on Ethiopia, v. 7 salvation for Zion; Is 28:1-4, judgment against the Northern Kingdom, vv. 5-6 salvation for Judah (vv. 5-6); Jer 46, containing judgments against various nations, and concluding with a word of salvation to Israel (vv. 27-28). Similarly, Jer 50:17f, 51:5; and Ezek 36:8ff contain salvation words for Israel which follow words of judgment on the nations. Moreover, the overall structure of several of the prophetic books verifies this connection between oracles of judgment against the nations and salvation to Israel. This is true especially of Ezekiel: 1-24= judgment against Judah and Jerusalem; 25-32 = judgment against the nations; 33-39= promise of salvation to Judah and Jerusalem. Similarly the LXX of Jeremiah where the oracles against the nations found in chapters 46-51 of the MT come after 25:13 and are then followed by words of salvation to Israel. In Isaiah 12-23 oracles of judgment against the nations are interspersed with words of promise to Israel, illustrating this same connection. In contrast to this pattern which sets Israel off against the nations, we shall trace the development in Third Isaiah whereby the scope of the prophetic oracle shifts from a *rîb* encompassing the nations to one involving, in the first instance, Israel alone. In this new development the line of division effected by the oracle will divide Israel itself into two segments.

and the later mutation is evident; for example, contrast the commission referring to "my people" as a unit with the division of the people into the wicked and the righteous implied by the juxtaposition of verses 2-5 and 6-12. Moreover, the use of the Torah style to introduce the word of salvation blunts the dichotomy by intimating that reception of the promise of salvation is contingent upon obedience to the Torah, thus leaving the *possibility* of salvation open to the *whole* nation while categorically promising it to no *one* group. In oracles to be considered below, the transformation will be carried to its conclusion, for the dichotomy will become absolute with judgment to one element and salvation to the other being stated categorically and unconditionally, e.g., 65:13: "See, my servants will eat, but you will go hungry. . ."

Underlying this mutation in the form of the oracle is an alteration in the situation within the community, an extremely important fact virtually ignored in the commentaries. The next task is thus to determine the tradition to which the oracle belongs, and then to inquire into the community situation underlying the oracle.

The fact that this oracle is imbued with the language and themes of Isaiah 40-55, 60-62, and 63:7-64 demonstrates that we are again within the Second Isaiah tradition. This is seen, for example, in the terms used to describe the coming salvation: (1) in verses 8a and 10b light is used as a symbol of that salvation (cf. 42:16; 51:4; 60:1-3); (2) verse 8b is a paraphrase of 52:12b; (3) verse 12a is a paraphrase of 61:4a. Again, the Second Isaiah tradition is recognized in the concern for the restoration of Zion (58:12; 52:7-10; 60:10, 13; 62:7; 64:10f). The acts of mercy describing the true fast are reminiscent of the servant of Second Isaiah (42:6-7; 49:9f) and of his counterpart in 61:1ff. The playing down of the cultic in favor of the concrete acts of mercy is also a characteristic of the Second Isaiah tradition.

The polemical nature of this chapter is unmistakable, and the accusations made against the offenders promise to afford a glimpse also of the second party in the dispute, at least as they are seen through the eyes of the prophetic group. Above all, one is struck by the emphasis upon the self-righteousness of those being attacked; they obviously regard themselves as religiously elite and impeccable in matters concerning the cult. Verses 2-5 leave no doubt that their righteousness is based on meticulous conformity to the prescribed observances of the official cult: (1) "They inquire of me daily"; *dāraš* is a *terminus technicus* for inquiring of Yahweh's will through the proper cultic channels (Am 5:4-6; Zeph 1:6; Is 8:19; 31:1; Jer 21:2; 37:7; Ezek 29:1, 3; 2 Chr 25:15, 20; I Sam 28:7; etc.). (2) "They delight in the knowledge of my ways." Mal 2:7 suggests that such knowledge was also the property of cultic personnel. (3) "As if they were a nation doing righteousness" provides the key to an understanding of the attack; their righteousness is a sham righteousness (cf. 57:12), a contrived act of self-deception, for in fact they are a nation "abandoning the law of its God" (cf. 65:11). (4) The exquisite irony of the polemic comes out beautifully as the accusation that they have abandoned the justice of Yahweh is followed immediately by reference to their cultic activity, "they ask me for just ordinances." They have forsaken the *mišpat* of Yahweh ("justice," in the sense of, e.g., Is 61:8) in their very act of seeking the *mišpātîm* of the cult ("ordinances," in the sense of, e.g., Lev 26:46), that is, they have turned their backs on true religion in their self-righteous obsession with the particulars of cultic observance. (5) "They delight in drawing near to God." Again, *qārab* is a *terminus technicus* of the cult for the priests' drawing near to Yahweh in the sanctuary, and it is hardly a mere accident that this technical usage is a central concept in the language of P and Ezekiel.[67] Indeed, the entire enterprise described in verse 2 is the priestly activity around the cult, betraying the same obsessions with statutes and ordinances which characterize the hierocratic tradition.

Verse 3a is a quotation from the priestly party which

67. Nu 17:5 (EVV 16:40): ". . .so that no one who is not a priest, who is not of the descendants of Aaron, *should draw near* to burn incense before the Lord. . ." Ezek 44:15-16: "But the Levitical priests, the sons of Zadok, who kept the charge of my sanctuary when the people of Israel went astray from me, *shall come near* to me to minister to me, and they shall attend on me to offer me the fat and the blood, says the Lord God; they shall enter my sanctuary, and they shall *approach* my table, to minister to me, and they shall keep my charge." (See also Lev 9:7, 8; 16:1; 21:17f; 22:3; Nu 17:28 [EVV 17:13]; 18:3; et al.)

betrays the motive behind their meticulous observances; their entire enterprise is aimed at attracting Yahweh's attention and bending his will in their favor. After they have staged their performance, and nothing happens, their reaction is reminiscent of the priests of Baal in the contest on Mount Carmel: they complain bitterly when the deity fails to react. The comparison of their use of the cult to pagan practices is not remote, for the same superstitious understanding of the efficacy of cultic manipulation underlies both.

Verses 3b and 4a uncover the reason why, in the eyes of their critics, their cult is illegitimate: (1) it represents a pursuit of their own pleasure; (2) it combines cult with oppression and violence. The irony is again exquisite when in verse 3b the same root (*ḥpṣ*) which in verse 2 is used to describe their cultic activity ("*delight* in the knowledge of my ways," "*delight* in drawing near to God") is used to describe why that cultic activity is abortive: "on your fast day you pursue *ḥpṣ*"; though giving the appearance of conscientiously taking delight in Yahweh, they are merely intoxicated with self-delight. Then in good prophetic fashion, the real condition of their relationship to God is revealed by their actions toward those under their power: they oppress their workmen[68] and combine cult with strife and violence. Hence the judgment in verse 4b: "But your fasting thus regularly will not make your voice heard on high." Verse 5 summarizes the indictment of the preceding verses that outward observances do not constitute a cult acceptable to Yahweh. It also serves as a bridge to the next section, as is indicated by the structural analysis according to which verses 5–7 comprise one continuous structural unit.[69]

After examining the affinities of the attacking and attacked groups with biblical traditions known from other parts of the canon, we have been able to demonstrate lines of connection between this composition and the Second Isaiah tradition. Beyond that, there are very striking

68. Or "creditors"; see textual note "a" above.
69. See p. 101.

affinities between the description given of the party attacked and the cultic interests of the hierocratic party. The oracle makes it very clear that the ones attacked are those in the position of control over their fellows, from which position they are able to oppress them and deal violently with them. They are also described as the self-righteous, religiously elite, obviously in control of the cult, representing, it would seem, the normative cult. Their cultic activities are described as attempts to coerce Yahweh to act on their behalf, and they complain when he does not respond. In contrast, the description of true cultic behavior derives from the tradition of Second Isaiah, and manifests the ethos of the humble and broken of spirit.

After thus suggesting the general identity of the two opposing traditions represented in the chapter, we next seek to probe the community situation in which they were active. Already, the element of polemic inherent throughout the oracle identifies that situation in a very general sense. But what other clues can be discerned?

The key to understanding the setting of this oracle is to be found in the judicial sentence (v. 4b) appearing in the judgment section and in the promises (vv. 8–9; 10b–12) belonging to the salvation section. For a comparison of the judgment word with the salvation words discloses both the issue at stake and the background against which that issue has arisen.

First, in regard to the issue at stake, a comparison of verse 4b with verse 9 indicates—as does the theme of fasting permeating the entire oracle—that the question of the true versus the illegitimate cult is the burning problem. As for the cult of the group in control, a description of that cult and of the behavior of its adherents is followed by the verdict, "But your fasting thus regularly will not make your voice heard on high." Conversely, after the true cult (= the fast of merciful deeds) of the humble is described, the promise is given, "Then you will call, and Yahweh will answer, you will shout, and he will say, 'Here I am.'" Thus the oracle answers in no uncertain terms which cult, in the eyes of the visionaries, is acceptable to Yahweh.

Secondly, the background against which the question of the true versus the illegitimate cult has arisen is elucidated by comparison of the remainder of the salvation promises (vv. 8, 10b–12) with the complaint of the cultic party (v. 3a). The latter would imply that the self-righteous ones have been conducting their cultic rites so as to coerce Yahweh to act, though the type of action they desire is not mentioned. Comparison with the promises, however, makes it amply clear that the action desired is related to restoration of the post-exilic community. They complain that Yahweh has failed to secure that restoration in spite of their meticulous observances in the cult. The prophet replies that their maintenance (= defilement) of the cult will not cause their voice to be heard on high, i.e., will not result in the restoration. Indeed, the implicit accusation against the leaders of the normative cult is unmistakable, namely, that by their defilement of the cult they are the ones guilty of impeding the restoration and thus of prolonging the present miserable conditions.

The oracle then goes on to describe the true cult which can expect Yahweh's intervention on its behalf, and to those who adhere to this cult of meekness and mercy it renews the promise for restoration as it was described in the program of restoration of the Second Isaiah tradition (Isaiah 60–62). It will be a restoration initiated not by human cultic observances, but by a theophany of Yahweh (vv. 8, 10b) resulting in the renewal of the faithful (v. 11) and the restoration of Zion (v. 12).

Further consideration of the community situation being reflected in Isaiah 58 must be deferred until comparative material from other oracles has been brought into the discussion, material which will demonstrate that we are

---

59: 1 His hand is not too short to save,
nor his ear too dull to hear.
2 But your iniquities have made a gulf
between you and your God,
and your sins have hidden the Presence
so that you are not heard by your Lord.

here dealing with the same struggle for control of the cult which was seen to underlie the lament in Isaiah 63:7–64:12, a struggle between Levitic-prophetic elements on the one hand and the normative hierocratic group on the other. Here, as throughout this material, we are unable to determine the degree of distortion in the description which one group gives of the other. We must remind ourselves repeatedly that we are tracing the struggles of the post-exilic period not through the eyes of objective reporters, but through the interpretations of first one party in the struggle and then the other. The value of such an exercise, however, is evident: by following those interpretations, we can witness the unfolding of apocalyptic eschatology and even discern some of the circumstances and attendant frustrations which led to that transformation of the prophetic tradition.

2. Isaiah 59:1–20

Apart from verse 21, which is regarded as a secondary prose addition by nearly all exegetes, chapter 59 is a homogeneous composition.[70] Volz's view that the unity of the chapter represents only a secondary liturgical unity will be refuted below. The oracle, to be sure, does not preserve the austere form of the classical judgment oracle, but combines various elements in a baroque fashion. But this is to be accounted for in terms of the development of the prophetic genres in late prophecy rather than in terms of secondary liturgical fusion.

70. This is the view of many scholars, including Muilenburg, Fohrer, Elliger, McKenzie, and Westermann.

	Text	Structure	Meter	Prosodic Units
59:1	הן לא קצרה יד[ו] [a] מהושיע	a b c	10	1:1
	ולא כבדה אזנו משמוע	a_1 b_1 c_1	<u>10</u>	
2	כי אם עונתיכם [ ][b]מבדלים	a b c	10	1:1::1:1
	בינכם לבין אלהיכם	d D	<u>9</u>	
	וחטאותיכם הסתירו פנים [c]	b_1 c_1 e	10	
	מכם משמוע [אדניכם][d]	d_1 D_1	<u>9</u>	

3 For your hands are defiled with blood,
and your fingers with iniquity,
your lips utter falsehood,
your tongue mutters wickedness.
4 No one makes accusation justly,
no one judges honestly;
trusting in vanity and uttering falsehood,
they conceive trouble and give birth to wickedness.
5 They hatch adders' eggs
and weave the spider's web;
anyone eating of their eggs dies,
the stinking (egg) hatches out (as) a viper.
6 Their webs are worthless as clothing,
one cannot cover oneself with their products,
their products are wicked works,
violent deeds are in their hands,
7 their feet chase after evil,
they hasten to pour out innocent blood,
their thoughts are wicked plots,
havoc and ruin they leave in their wake,
8 the way of peace is unknown to them,
there is no justice in their paths,
they make their trails crooked,
none passing over them knows peace.
9 Therefore justice is far removed from us,
and righteousness cannot overtake us.
We look for light, but all is darkness,
for brightness, but we walk in gloom;
10 we grope like blind men for the wall,
like men without sight we feel our way;
we stumble at noon as if it were dusk,
we smell, though healthy men, like dead men;
11 we growl like bears, all of us,
and moan continually like doves;
we look for justice, but it does not come,
for salvation, but it is far removed from us.
12 For our faults are many in your sight
and our sins testify against us,
for our faults are with us
and we know our iniquities:
13 rebellion and denial of Yahweh,
backsliding from following our God,
conceiving thought of oppression and revolt,
murmuring from the heart lying words.
14 Thus justice has turned back

3	כי כפיכם נגאלו[e] בדם	a	b	c		9	1:1::1:1
	ואצבעותיכם בעון	A		c_1		9	
	שפתותיכם דברו שקר	a_1	b_1	c_2		8	
	לשונכם עולה תהגה	a_2	c_3	b_2		8	
4	אין קרא בצדק	a	b	c		5	b:b
	אין נשפט באמונה	a	b_1	c_1		7	
	בטוח על תהו ודבר שוא	a	b	a_1	b_1	5:4	bb:bb
	הרו עמל והוליד און	a_2	b_2	a_3	b_3	4:4	
5	ביצי צפעוני בקעו	a	b	c		8	1:1::1:1
	וקורי עכביש יארגו	a_1	b_1	c_1		9	
	האכל מביציהם ימות	d	a	e		9	
	והזורה תבקע אפעה[f]	a_2	c	b_2		9	
6	קוריהם לא יהיו לבגד	a	b	c		8	1:1:b:1:1:1:1:
	ולא יתכסו במעשיהם		B	a_1		9	1:1:1:1:1
	מעשיהם מעשי און	a_1	a_1	d		6	
	פעל חמס בכפיהם	a_2	d_1	e		7	
7	רגליהם לרע ירצו	a_3	c_1	b_1		8	
	וימהרו לשפך דם נקי		b_2	C		10	
	מחשבותיהם מחשבות און	a_4	a_5	d		9	
	שד ושבר במסלותם		d_2	d_3	e_1	8	
8	דרך שלום לא ידעו		e_2	d_4	b_3	7	
	אין משפט במעגלותם		d_5	e_3		8	
	נתיבותיהם עקשו להם		e_4	b_4	f	10	
	כל דרך ב[ם][g]לא ידע שלם		F	b_3	d_4	9	
9	על כן רחק משפט ממנו	a	b	c		9	1:1
	ולא תשיגנו צדקה	A	b_1			9	
	נקוה לאור והנה חשך	a	b	c		9	1:1::1:1::1:1::1:1
	לנגהות באפלות נהלך	b_1	c_1	a_1		10	
10	נגששה כעורים קיר	a_2	d	b_2		7	
	כאין עינים נגששה		D	a_2		9	
	כשלנו בצהרים כנשף	a_3	e	d_1		9	
	בא[שנו] שמנים כמתים[h]	a_4	e_1	d_2		8	
11	נהמה כדבים כלנו	a_5	d_3	g		8	
	וכיונים הגה נהגה		d_4	A		8	
	נקוה למשפט ואין	a	b_3	h		9	
	לישועה רחקה ממנו		b_4	H		9	
12	כי רבו פשעינו נגדך	a	b	c		10	1:1:1:1::1:1:1:1
	וחמאתנו ענתה בנו	b_1	a_1	c_1		10	
	כי פשעינו אתנו		b	c_2		8	
	ועונתינו ידענום		b_2	a_2		9	
13	פשע וכחש ביהוה	b_3	b_4	c_3		8	
	נסוג מאחר אלהינו	b_5	C			8	
	דבר[י] עשק וסרה הרו	D	b_6			8	
	והגו מלב דברי שקר[i]	b_7	c	d		8	
14	והסג אחור משפט	a	b	c		7	1:1:1:1:b:b

and righteousness stands far removed,
for truth has stumbled in the squares
and uprightness is unable to enter;
15 truth is lacking
and the repentant is robbed.
Then Yahweh saw it with his own eyes
and he realized that there was no justice,
16 he saw that there was no man. . .
was appalled that there was no one to intervene.
So his own arm brought him victory
and his righteousness upheld him.
17 He put on righteousness as a breastplate,
the helmet of salvation on his head,
garments of vengeance as his dress,
and he wrapped himself in jealousy as a cloak.
18 According to deeds he will repay,
wrath to adversaries, due payment to his enemies.
19 Thus they will fear Yahweh's name from the west,
and his glory from the rising of the sun.
For he will come like a rushing stream
which is driven by the breath of Yahweh;
20 he will enter into Zion as Redeemer
for those of Jacob who turn from sin.

TEXTUAL NOTES

a) Expansion through addition of the divine name is common; the fullness of this colon would lead us to conjecture that such is the case here.

b) A prosaizing expansion.

c) Retaining the absolute with MT, since פניו in the versions appears to be a later interpretation.

d) This colon is short in the MT. Our conjecture is based on the structure of verse 2, where the parallel is between bicola. Hence we propose the addition of אדניכם parallel to אלהיכם.

e) The MT pointing is a conflation of the pu'al and nip'al. The consonantal text recommends the latter.

f) For the etymology of זור = "stink," see P. Wernberg- Møller, "A Note on זור 'to stink,'" *VT* 4 (1954): 322–325.

g) Reading plural with Pesh, Tg and Vg.

h) This emendation of F. M. Cross restores שנו which would have been lost by haplography before שמנ (cf. W. F. Albright, who proposes that 'Esmûmîm is here an abstract plural meaning "health" derived from the Sidonian god of healing, Eshmun; *Yahweh and the Gods of Canaan* [New York: Doubleday and Co., 1968] p. 187).

	צדקה מרחק תעמד	c_1	b_1	a_1		8	
	כי כשלה ברחוב אמת	a_2	b_2	c_2		8	
	נכחה לא תוכל לבוא	c_3	a_3	d		8	
15	תהי אמת נעדרת		c_2	a_4		6	
	סר מרע משתולל		C	a_5		6	
15b	וירא יהוה בעיניו	a	b	c		7	b:b:b:b
	וי[ד]ע כי אין משפט[j]	a_1	d	e		7	
16	וירא כי אין איש	a	d	e_1		5	
	ישתומם כי אין מפגיע	a_2	d	e_2		7	
	ותושע לו זרעו	a	b	c		7	1:1
	צדקתו היא סמכתהו		c_1	A		8	
17	ילבש צדקה כשרין	a	b	c		8	1:1:1:1
	כובע ישועה בראשו		c_1	b_1	d	8	
	בגדי נקם תלבשת[k]		c_2	b_2	d_1	7	
	ויעט כמעיל קנאה	a_1	c_3	b_3		8	
18	כעל גמלות כעל ישלם	a	b	a	c	5:5	bb:bb
	חמה לצריו גמול לאיביו[ ][l]	d	e	d_1	e_1	5:5	
19	וייראו ממערב שם יהוה	a	b	c		8	1:1
	וממזרח שמש כבודו		B	c_1		8	
	כי יבוא כנהר צר	a	b	c		7	b:b:b:b
	רוח יהוה נססה בו		d	e	f	7	
20	בא לציון גואל	a	g	h		6	
	לשבי פשע ביעקב[ ]		I	g_1		7	

---

i) Verse 13 is a four-line prosodic unit dominated by infinitives. As it stands in the MT, however, this verse betrays metric difficulties. The first bicolon balances eight syllables against ten; the second, six against ten. The conjunction beginning the second colon can be considered secondary. But the real imbalance comes in the third and fourth cola. The difficulty is solved by dividing the bicolon between הרו and והגו, and reading דברי rather than דבר. The result is a very balanced unit with good parallelism and fine chiasm.

j) In v. 15b both meter and parallel structure have been disrupted (meter 10:4; structure: two verbs/no verb). Balance and good sense are restored by merely supposing that an original וידע from the second stichos has been misplaced, and under the force of its new context, the ד has been changed to ר.

k) Rather than regarding the rare word תלבשת as a gloss, D. N. Freedman has offered a much more plausible emendation by regarding וילבש as a dittography (as adopted by McKenzie, *Second Isaiah,* p. 170).

l) Deleting 18c as a gloss, with most critics. It probably reflects secondary influence of Second Isaiah on the text. The colon is not in LXX.

The attempt to date Isaiah 59 on the basis of historical allusions or the types of abuses attacked is futile, since this oracle offers no reliable historical "handle," and the moral abuses mentioned are of a piece with those attacked by the prophets since Amos. The application of typological tools, however, gives some basis to suggest a date shortly after that of Isaiah 58, which would accord well with the community situation reflected by the oracle. It would be uncautious to be dogmatic about the relative chronology at this point, however, since the results of both the typological investigation and the inquiry into the community situation are more meager than in the case of most of the other oracles in Third Isaiah. In the final analysis, our reconstruction would not be altered in the least if Isaiah 59 were placed, let us say, before chapter 58 in the relative chronology, for the contribution which this oracle makes to our understanding of the development of prophetic genres and eschatology in the general period of the last half of the sixth century bears little relation to the question of exact dates.

Regarding meter and internal structure, what was said about chapter 58 applies with equal force to the present composition. Increasingly, the parallel structure of the bicolon is yielding to the longer, more baroque prosodic unit, and the meter is becoming more erratic. Verses 9b–11 serve as an example of the longer prosodic unit which is challenging the preeminent position long held by the bicolon in Hebrew poetry (cf. also vv. 6–8). It is bound together by the development of the verbal element (a) throughout. Verse 13 illustrates the list-like sequence found with increasing frequency in the late-sixth-century poetry.

The composition is not bereft, however, of poetic quality reminiscent of an earlier age, as is indicated by the Divine Warrior Hymn in verses 15b-20. But this section again illustrates that the archaic canons are retained most conspicuously in sections which draw most heavily on the themes and motifs of earlier traditions. In those sections which sever close ties with earlier models a new type of prosody becomes evident.

Since the switch from reproach to lament in verse 9 and from lament to theophany in verse 15b leads some critics to argue that originally independent units have been secondarily fused into a liturgical composition,[71] our treatment of the chapter as a unity must be defended. It is first important to recognize that the structure of literary genres is as subject to transformation over the centuries as is the structure of prosodic units. This does not mean that a priori every complex unit from the sixth century must be regarded as original; for example, though 63:7-65 now seems to form a unity, it is apparent that chapter 65 was added to the original lament in 63:7-64 only secondarily. It does mean, however, that great risks are involved in the attempt to establish the limits of post-exilic prophetic units on the basis of pre-exilic models. Those limits legitimately can be determined only on the basis of internal evidence and comparison with other oracles from the same period. When this is done one recognizes a development analogous to that characterizing the history of the prosodic unit: the tendency, as seen already in Second Isaiah, is toward greater length and a higher degree of complexity. For example, we have seen that in Isaiah 58 elements of judgment oracle, Torah, and salvation oracle were all fused by the author into an indivisible whole, thus adumbrating the emergence of a new genre, the salvation-judgment oracle.

This development in the sphere of prophetic genres is discernible again in Isaiah 59. Verses 1–8 constitute an element which closely resembles the indictment section of the classical judgment oracle, but rather than the expected sentence of judgment in verse 9, a communal lament is introduced. This literary phenomenon can be explained as the product of secondary redaction only if the critic forces the oracle to conform to pre-exilic patterns; as soon as the oracle is allowed to remain within the context of its post-exilic community situation, an indivisible connection between verses 1–8 and verse 9 becomes apparent. In verses 1–8 the group living from the message of Second Isaiah

71. E.g., Volz, *Jesaia* II, pp. 230-231.

attacks the evils of the defiled cult community; then in verses 9-15a they lament the delay in the salvation and restoration caused by the sins of the defiled (note the *'al-kēn* ["therefore"] of v. 9). Finally in verses 15b-20 the sentence of judgment which was deferred in verse 9 to make room for the lament is finally introduced, but again in an unclassical manner and with a changed substance, for it takes the form of a Divine Warrior Hymn and not only pronounces judgment on the enemy but promises salvation to the faithful. Nevertheless, this section also is bound inextricably to the preceding, for here the *mišpat* and *ṣedāqāh* withheld in verses 1-8 and longed for in verses 9-15a are promised, since Yahweh will intervene where no man was able to help. When taken as a whole, this chapter represents our first fully developed example of a salvation-judgment oracle, a late genre which becomes one of the chief characteristics of the Third Isaiah material.

The identification implied above between the two groups behind this oracle and those behind chapters 63:7-64 and 58 must now be substantiated. We turn first to examine the evidence for the identification of the group being attacked. At first blush, the issue at stake in chapter 59 may appear to differ from that in 58, for whereas the latter chapter revolved around the problem of the true versus the defiled cult, chapter 59 seems to concern itself with social evils. But closer examination reveals the parallelism between the polemics in the two chapters: the catalog of social evils in 59:3-8 is not offered in isolation, but supplies the reason for the defilement of the normative cult and the resulting delay in the restoration; that list has its exact parallel in 58:3b-4.

59:1 therefore introduces (as did 58:2) a prophetic attack on the defiled, and therefore ineffectual cult. The members of that cult are complaining that Yahweh's hand is too short to save and his ear too dull to hear, that is, they are complaining about his failure to give answer to their cultic intercession by ending the dismal conditions within the post-exilic community and hastening the restoration. The complaint answered by this oracle is thus of a piece with

58:3: "Why do we fast, but you do not see, afflict ourselves, but you do not know it?" Even as the prophet in chapter 58 countered that it was no fault of Yahweh that their cult was ineffectual, but that the fault was to be found in their own iniquity, so too here: "but your iniquities have made a gulf between you and your God, and your sins have hidden the Presence, so that you are not heard by your Lord." The parallel to 58:4b is again striking: "But your fasting thus regularly will not make your voice heard on high." As in chapter 58, the choice of terminology in 59:2 verifies that the issue at stake is the defilement of the normative cult, for the term "your sins have hidden the Presence (*pānîm*)" is an obvious *terminus technicus* of the cult.[72] It was in the cultic realm that the worshiper addressed Yahweh through priest or prophet, and because of the abiding presence of the *pānîm*, Yahweh's reply was received. But our prophet declares that this *pānîm* has become hidden from them by their sins, for their hands are defiled with blood. Allying himself with the classical prophets, he draws upon words Isaiah used in condemning the defiled cult of his day: "I will hide my eyes from you . . . your hands are full of blood." The object of attack is the same mixing of self-righteous ritual acts with the acts of violence and injustice which were described in chapter 58. Such a mixing defiles the hands of the worshipers, and renders their cult invalid and an abomination to Yahweh.[73]

Verse 5 illustrates with two images the defilement of these self-righteous worshipers: they are not snakes according to outward appearance, and yet they hatch adders' eggs. Similarly, the evil they spread throughout the community is like a rotten egg with a viper inside, very white and pure looking on the outside, but fatal to the one who is deceived by outward appearances into eating it (cf. the imagery in the polemical woe passages in Mt 23, especially vv. 27-28). These shocking images, matched repeatedly in

72. Cf. Ex 28:29-30; 39:8; 33:12-17; Lev 24:3-8. See also H. Odeberg, *Trito-Isaiah* (Uppsala: A. B. Lundequistska Bokhandeln, 1931), p. 177, and R. E. Clements, *God and Temple* (Philadelphia: Fortress, 1965), p. 27.

73. Cf. Is 66:3-4.

this material by equally shocking ones, indicate the degree of bitterness harbored by those making the attack against the priestly leaders controlling the cult.

With regard to the controlling group, it is clear that we are dealing with the same adherents of the normative cult which were encountered in chapter 58. This group complains that Yahweh does not regard their cultic observances, self-righteously denies any share of the fault that the restoration is delayed, and mixes ritual practices with personal violence and flagrant breach of justice. The oracle declares that the cult of that group is cut off from Yahweh, and warns in no uncertain terms that the faithful are to beware lest they be deceived by the ostensible righteousness of its leaders, for behind their facade of purity is a venom which threatens to destroy the entire community.

In verses 9–15a, the minority group raises its lament to Yahweh, and again the themes and concepts comprising their lament are telltales of the tradition to which they belong. Already in verse 1 their dependence on the message of Second Isaiah is manifested (cf. Is 50:2). And now, when they lament that the promised salvation has been delayed because of the apostasy of the defiled group controlling the cult, they express that promised salvation in the familiar terms of Second Isaiah, terms which had subsequently been compiled programmatically in Isaiah 60–62. Second Isaiah had earlier announced the comforting words of Yahweh: "Listen to me, my people, and give ear to me, my nation, for a law will go forth from me, and my *justice* for a light to the peoples; my *deliverance* draws near speedily . . .,"[74] but now the faithful view a nation rent asunder by a defiled cult and they lament, "Therefore *justice* is far removed from us, and *deliverance* cannot overtake us." Second Isaiah had promised that Yahweh would turn "the darkness before them into light,"[75] but the defilement of the apostates has turned that promise into the corresponding curse: "We look for light, but all is darkness, for brightness, but we walk in gloom." Second Isaiah had promised

74. 51:4f; see 42:1, 34; 45:8; cf. 62:1, 2.

75. 42:16; see 51:4; cf. 60:1–3, and note the very close parallel in 58:10b.

that Yahweh's Servant would "open the eyes that are blind" (42:7, 16), but the faithful, in a troubled time resembling anything but restoration, complain, "We grope like blind men for the wall, like men without sight we feel our way." There seems little room for doubt that we are dealing again with the literature of the prophetic tradition stemming from Second Isaiah.

In verses 12-13 the prophetic community moves from lament to confession, in keeping with the usual order of that genre. This section of the oracle is concluded in verses 14-15a with a summary of the lament describing the complete collapse of righteousness in the land.

The indictment (vv. 1-8) and the lament (vv. 9-15a) together paint a very bleak picture, indicating how hopelessly remote the prophetic community found itself from the brilliant promises of Second Isaiah. Only a gross misunderstanding of the prophetic group from which this material stems, however, could lead one to regard the following section in verses 15b-20 as secondary.[76] For not only does the repetitious reference (five times) in these verses to the justice, righteousness, and salvation for which the community longed in verses 9-15a tie the two sections together, but the very belief of that group that the restoration would be the result of divine initiative demands such a conclusion as this. The relation of verses 1-15a to 15b-20 can be compared to the transition occurring in an earlier composition which we examined: in the verses prior to 63:19 the plight of Yahweh's "Holy People" had been lamented; they had been left no share in the inheritance of Israel, they had lost control of Zion to their adversaries; their lament reaches its climax with the cry: "We have become like those never ruled by you, those not called by your name." But suddenly the bitter complaint bursts forth in a fervent plea for the Divine Warrior's intervention in an earth-shaking theophany to save the faithful remnant: "Oh, that you would rend the heavens and come down—before you the mountains would melt!—to make known your

76. Contra B. Stade, *Geschichte des Volkes Israel*, vol. 2 (Berlin: G. Grote, 1888), p. 81.

name to the adversaries—before you the nations would tremble! . . ." Now in chapter 59 we again encounter this transition from lament to appeal to the Divine Warrior: in a situation where historical realities have vitiated the restoration plans of the prophetic group, they hark back to an archaic genre dating from the days of the league and stemming originally from the world of mythopoeic thought, the Divine Warrior Hymn, which celebrates Yahweh's conflict against his enemies and his glorious victory. The form in which this hymn reaches the prophetic circles of the sixth century results from the melding of ancient league hymns like Exodus 15 and royal hymns like Psalm 48.[77] It follows a ritual pattern reflecting earlier use in the cult:

15b-16a	Threat
16b-18	Conflict—victory
19	Manifestation of Yahweh's universal reign
20	Procession to Zion and the Salvation of the repentant

The choice of that archaic hymnic form is fully understandable in light of the theology of the prophetic circle and in considering the sociological circumstances within which they found themselves. As has been noted above, from the early program of restoration in Isaiah 60-62 on down, this circle had expressed the belief that the restoration would come solely as a result of Yahweh's mighty saving activity, and what form better portrayed Yahweh acting alone against humanly impossible odds to save his people than the archaic Divine Warrior Hymn? Moreover, use of that archaic form served well the purpose of demonstrating their solidarity with early Israel. Earlier they had protested, in the face of being rejected by "Israel" and "Abraham" (that is, by the normative community threatening to displace them from their inheritance in Israel), that they were true sons of Yahweh (63:16), and in their fervent plea to Yahweh to help them they recalled that

77. Cf. the author's *Jewish Apocalyptic*, pp. 43-44. The antecedent history of the Divine Warrior Hymn adopted by early apocalyptic will be discussed at length on pp. 299-316.

glorious period when Yahweh the Divine Warrior most dramatically intervened to save his people, the period of "Moses and his people" when he "divided the waters before them . . ." (63:11-12). Now in the face of oppression from a powerful group controlling the cult and depriving them of an inheritance in Zion, and in the circumstances of having no earthly powers to call upon, it is patently clear why this group claiming to be the true people of Yahweh would identify themselves again with Israel's forefathers—men who also had found themselves fighting against impossible odds for possession of the land—and hark back to that most archaic of Israelite forms, the Divine Warrior Hymn celebrating the ritual conquest, to express their faith in Yahweh's ultimate intervention on their behalf.

The form was particularly suited to their purposes in that it announced both Yahweh's judgment upon the enemy and his salvation to his chosen people. To be sure, its new function introduced changes: the old line between people and enemy was the line dividing Israel from the nations; in its new context, the line came to divide between two segments *within Israel,* the prophetic circle, and the adherents of the defiled cult, a change which had far-reaching effects, even upon the form of the prophetic oracle.[78] A second alteration came in the temporal framework, the original Divine Warrior Hymn celebrating Yahweh's acts of the past, the new adaption being eschatologized to refer to a mighty act of the future. But in essence the threat facing the prophetic group was the same as that which faced the ancestors of Israel as they looked upon the strong fortified walls of the Canaanite cities and called upon the Divine Warrior to aid them (cf. Ex 15; Josh 10-11; Ju 5). Their beloved land was also controlled by the enemy, and though that enemy in fact comprised fellow Israelites, yet they regarded those brethren as essentially no different from the Canaanites, as the shocking accusations throughout the oracles of Third Isaiah indicate. Helpless to

78. See below, p. 150.

save themselves, they therefore appealed to the Divine Warrior to come in might to reconquer the land for them.

When seen in the context of the rapidly changing situation within the Israelite community which we have been tracing, this adoption of the archaic genre of the Divine Warrior Hymn by the exilic and post-exilic prophetic group can be recognized as a powerful factor behind the transformation of prophetic eschatology into apocalyptic eschatology.[79] This thesis requires explanation.

As mentioned earlier, the original home of the Divine Warrior was the cosmic realm of myth, a realm torn between the contending forces of fertility and sterility. Though Israel's earliest literature betrays the influence of mythopoeic thought,[80] it was the achievement of the pre-exilic prophets to keep at bay the notions and practices of Canaanite religion. They interpreted Israel's relation to the divine in the categories of Yahweh's guiding his people in history. Similarly, the eschatology which grew out of this prophetic religion was remarkably free of mythical elements: salvation was construed as the reestablishment of the historical people Israel in their land. It was otherwise with the royal theology of the Jerusalem court, where the ancient myth and ritual pattern was combined with the archaic league tradition of the ritual conquest. This new formulation of an ancient hymnic pattern apparently was used in royal festivals commemorating the enthronement of the Davidide (and the reign of Yahweh), and celebrating the victory of Israel's Heavenly King in overcoming the dark powers of sterility, a victory which guaranteed the fertility of the land and the prosperity of the people[81] After the collapse of the Southern Kingdom Second Isaiah borrowed from the then defunct royal cult the Israelite version of the conflict myth, and applied it to his prophetic message of the restoration which would soon return the

79. See the author's "Zechariah 9 and the Recapitulation of an Ancient Ritual Pattern," *JBL* 92 (1973): 37–59.

80. See Cross, *Myth*, p. 99–105.

81. Ibid., pp. 91-99.

people to Zion.[82] This application of mythic material to the prophetic message marks the important first step in the direction of apocalyptic, and hence our designation of Second Isaiah's message as proto-apocalyptic.

The effect of this application of mythic material to prophecy was profound, for, without allowing Yahwism to slip back to the timeless, unhistorical framework of myth, it added a cosmic dimension to the divine act which hitherto had been absent in prophecy. In Isaiah 40 the divine council is portrayed transforming all of nature as the curse is removed from the land, and the way is prepared for the Second Exodus and the procession to Zion. In Is 51:9-11 the battle of Yahweh (Baal) against Yamm is recalled to add a cosmic dimension to the Second Exodus announced by the prophet. The remarkable cosmic change throughout nature which Yahweh's new act would inaugurate leads the prophet to divide history into two periods, the past which was to be forgotten and the future "new thing" which Yahweh was about to perform (Is 43:18-19).

In spite of this profound application of myth in his prophecy stemming from the exile, Second Isaiah never relaxed the dialectic he had effected between myth and history. The reason why he was able to maintain that dialectic is clear: the goal which the divine act was to achieve was for Second Isaiah the concretely historical one of restoring the historical entity Israel in its historical land of Palestine. This historical goal meant that Second Isaiah was deeply interested in the events of history and the historical leaders of his time. An event of the realm of plain history would provide the context of the divine act, namely, the fall of the Babylonian Empire; a conqueror of the historical realm would be Yahweh's instrument of saving his people,

82. See R. Rendtorff, "Die theologische Stellung des Schöpfungsglaubens bei Deuterojesaja," *ZThK* 51 (1954): 3-13; and C. Stuhlmueller, "The Theology of Creation in Second Isaias," *CBQ* 21 (1969): 429-467. These writers are basing their studies on the earlier works of J. Begrich and S. Mowinckel, who thoroughly documented the influence of the royal liturgy on Second Isaiah; see especially J. Begrich, *Studien zu Deuterojesaja*, ThB 20 (München: Chr. Kaiser, 1963 [Neudruck]., pp. 80-95; S. Mowinckel, *He that Cometh*, tr. G. W. Anderson (New York: Abingdon, 1955); *idem, The Psalms in Israel's Worship*, tr. D. R. Ap-Thomas (New York: Abingdon, 1962), 2 vols.; *idem, Psalmenstudien II. Das Thronbesteigungsfest Jahwäs und der Ursprung der Eschatologie* (Khristiania: Dybwad, 1922).

namely, Cyrus.[83] The people thereby saved would have the concrete vocation of being Yahweh's witness to the neighboring nations. Thus the cosmic activity which Second Isaiah portrays is always anchored tightly to the realm of plain history, and this realm is taken in utter seriousness as the context of the salvation event.

If Isaiah 34–35 and 60–62 come from Second Isaiah himself after his return to the land of Palestine, the transformation which ultimately would threaten to dissolve the tension between myth and history begins with the great teacher himself. If the other possibility proves to be true, namely, that these passages come from disciples in the period immediately after Second Isaiah, then the transformation begins after his ministry. Even as the prosody of these two passages proves that they are very close to Second Isaiah, so too the transformation away from the dialectic in Second Isaiah is minimal. For example, in 60–62 the goal of the divine activity is still the restoration of the people in their historical city (60:13; 62:6–9). Nevertheless, important changes are adumbrated. In both 34–35 and 60–62 there is a growing indifference to the concrete events of plain history; mention of foreign lands and kings has lost all particularity (34:5ff; 60:10, 12, 16), and the treatment of mythic motifs has become much more excessive, with little effort apparent to relate them to the events of plain history (34:3f, 11–17). The dialectic of Second Isaiah, whereby he constantly anchored the mythic embellishment in the historical (e.g., 51:9–11), is no longer held so rigidly. The impression one gets of 34–35 and 60–62 is that of a much more visionary view of the restoration than that held (at least originally) by Second Isaiah. These passages seem more visionary in the sense of being more aloof to the realities of the common historical process.

83. Second Isaiah's skillful infusion of cosmic significance into historical events is seen clearly in the passages dealing with Cyrus, whom Yahweh "stirred up from the north . . . , from the rising of the sun" (41:25; cf. 41:2; 46:11); for an interpretation of the mythical dimension of these passages in the light of Psalm 19A, see K. Koch, "Die Stellung des Kyros im Geschichtsbild Deuterojesajas und ihre überlieferungsgeschichtliche Verankerung," *ZAW* 84 (1972): 352–356.

To be sure, the visionary element was present in Second Isaiah, but it never threatened to become detached from the particulars of plain history. In these two passages, however, we hear of Yahweh's sacrificial slaughter of Edom, but Edom has been reduced to a symbol (34:5ff). We learn of the return to Zion of the redeemed, but the image is no longer tied to the concrete historical entity Israel with a definite responsibility for the political order (35:8ff); of officials called "Peace" and "Righteousness," but without real political vocations (60:17), and of people possessing the land forever (60:21) and being priests of Yahweh (61:6), but without any responsible relation to the nations. In a word, the view of the restoration of the nation is beginning to sever itself from the historical order in the plainest sense, and is moving to a level where responsibility to the political order is becoming a matter of growing indifference, where Israel's vocation is no longer seen in terms of her responsibility to the other nations, but more in terms of the offices in the new age to come. Prophetic eschatology is beginning to be transformed into apocalyptic eschatology.

In Isaiah 34-35 and 60-62 the circumstances influencing this transformation are not yet clearly visible. They do, however, come into much sharper focus in later oracles from the visionary tradition. In chapters 63:7-64:11, 58, and 59, we have seen signs of a further weakening of the dialectic between myth and plain history. In 63:19b-64:2 the cry is heard for the direct intervention of the Divine Warrior against the adversaries, with no effort to relate that intervention to events in the political order. In 58:8-12 restoration is promised in glowing terms—light replacing darkness, unfailing springs of water, the rebuilding of the ruins—again without relation to actual historical events and figures. Finally, in 59:15b—20, after the dismal situation of the total collapse of justice in the community has been decried, salvation is announced as the direct result of a theophany of the Divine Warrior which will be visible from the rising of the sun to the far west, with no effort being made to relate this divine activity to human instruments like Cyrus or the servant of Second Isaiah.

Isaiah 63:7–64:11, 58, and 59 also have revealed the sociological circumstances within the community abetting this development. The prophetic group building upon the thought of Second Isaiah no longer has before its eyes the national entity Israel, held captive in a foreign land but looking to the imminent return, as the goal of their restoration hope. The return has occurred, but the restored nation has not proven to be the holy nation promised by Second Isaiah and described by the visionary program of restoration of the prophetic group. Second Isaiah had still addressed himself to, and identified himself as leader of, the entire people Israel, and he spoke of a redemption affecting the entire nation. The prophetic circle now found itself an oppressed minority within Israel, persecuted by a majority dominated by a priesthood claiming exclusive control over the national cult, yet straying ever farther from the vision seen by the prophetic group of what it meant to be Yahweh's "Holy People." It thus became increasingly difficult to view the restoration as the renewal of the historical Israel in the historical Jerusalem, for the historical Israel had become a defiled assembly, and the historical Jerusalem was hopelessly polluted by a cult condemned by Yahweh.

Under such circumstances, where the object of the restoration hope was no longer the entire nation, but an oppressed minority within it, the pressure became great to upset the delicate balance between myth and history maintained by Second Isaiah. For the latter that balance was still possible, for his partition between the old epoch and the new divided one nation's history into two periods, a period of judgment and exile and a period of restoration. On both sides of the partition the historical entity *Israel* was the object of Yahweh's activity. For the post-exilic visionary group the division was radically changed: the old era came to *include the historical Israel* which had returned from exile, for it remained defiled, whereas the new era was pushed into the future, the salvation of that new era being narrowed to a small segment separated out from the nation as a whole. The division, in short, was between the present evil world and the blessed world to come. The historical anchorage of the new era became increasingly vitiated by the disintegrating conditions within which the historical Zion had fallen into the firm grasp of the defiled majority. As it became increasingly difficult to view the restoration of the oppressed remnant within the strict limits of plain history—inasmuch as the historical realm seemed irrevocably removed from their control—the vision of restoration began to eschew the harsh realities of the present political order by describing the awaited salvation in categories unconditioned by historical realities. Thus the dialectic maintained by Second Isaiah between history and myth began to dissolve. In the mythic material which earlier had served only to enhance an historical understanding of Yahweh's saving activity, the visionary group began to recognize a new way to conceive of the restoration hope which historical circumstances had crushed so harshly.

Thus within the context of this disintegrating situation, where the hope of an actual restoration of the historical entity Israel was increasingly being vitiated by political realities, the influx of mythic materials into the prophetic tradition now began to threaten the historical orientation of classical prophecy by offering an escape into a vision unencumbered by the limitations imposed by political realities. The prophetic group found itself tempted to use myth as a means of moving beyond history in its plainest terms to a vision of its own bliss freed from the weighty vocation of serving within the political order, freed from the necessity of interpreting divine activity in relation to the real events of human history as in Second Isaiah. This escape is the flight from the historically oriented eschatology of prophecy into apocalyptic eschatology. It does not yet involve the dissolution of the terrestrial order as such, as would occur in certain Gnostic works, for the new era is still described in terrestrial terms.[84]

84. While recognizing the profound influence that mythic elements had upon Jewish eschatology, whether these elements were borrowed directly or through the

What is lost, however, is the sense of vocation which in Second Isaiah always bound the redeemed to responsibility for the present political order. The redeemed in the visionary group of the post-exilic period feel responsible only to their own eschatological circle, which makes it possible for them to remain aloof from the political sphere. Prophetism has here begun to move out of the national cult toward exclusive sectarianism, ceasing to address the world of political realities and narrowing its vision to the sanctified community of the new era, giving up interpreting divine activity within the context of plain history and choosing instead to announce deliverance to the faithful in terms highly influenced by mythology and disinterested in considerations of human instrumentality and historical contingency. The end result of this development was the death of prophecy, and the birth of apocalyptic eschatology. Isaiah 59 is an important point along the path of that development.

After this rather extended discussion of the impact of myth upon post-exilic prophecy, we return to the Divine Warrior theophany in 59:15b–20. The picture of the social order sketched by the indictment and lament in verses 1–15a is that of the complete breakdown of justice and righteousness. The degree of the disillusionment felt by the followers of Second Isaiah is seen in utmost clarity in verses 9–10 where the promise of restoration in Second Isaiah's prophecy and in Isaiah 60–62 is turned inside out into the

mediation of earlier Israelite institutions, we must never overlook the thorough transformation to which these elements were subjected in being drawn into Yahwism, even in late post-exilic times. This can be illustrated especially in connection with the phrase commonly used to describe the relation of Jewish apocalyptic to ancient Near Eastern myth: *Endzeit wird Urzeit,* for to translate *wird* in terms of total identification is very misleading. In borrowing mythic forms such as the Divine Warrior Hymn, the prophets and apocalyptic seers never departed completely from the temporal framework of the classical period of prophetic thought. For while the *Urzeit* of myth was recurrent and bound up with the cycles of nature, the *Endzeit* of late prophecy and apocalyptic was construed as occurring once-and-for-all and as a culmination of the long history of Yahweh's relationship to his people. The mark left on such borrowings from mythopoeic sources is seen in another regard: in myth the divine acts celebrated in the cult ritual are allowed to run parallel to the events of the historical realm; the two orders are not obliged to integrate. In apocalyptic eschatology, even in its late phase, a degree of integration occurs in the sense that the events of the end-time are construed as the fulfillment of the historical process, and not occurrences which leave the mundane realm to pursue its parallel course uninterruptedly.

corresponding curse to describe the existing conditions. It is difficult to conceive of a bleaker picture of total depravity, of the complete victory of evil. Clearly the visionary group could no longer hope for the fulfillment of their program within such historical conditions. It is not surprising that their vision began to move beyond the realm of plain history.

In contrast to the bleak picture of a fallen social order, the conquest of the Divine Warrior is portrayed in cosmic terms breaking all limitations imposed by political realities and unrelated in any way to the particulars of history.[85] Recognizing "no justice," "no man," "no one to intervene," he arms himself and proceeds to achieve a victory which breaks all national boundaries. In the classical oracle, judgment would have been limited to the wicked leaders of the cult who had been indicted for their sins; here all limitations dissolve as a judgment is portrayed which is universal in scope, extending from the west to the rising of the sun. The questions of how judgment could be effected through the instrumentality of human agents and historical events is no longer a vital concern. Thus when Second Isaiah's promise of Yahweh's royal procession to Zion as redeemer is renewed in verse 20, Zion in this new cosmic context suddenly seems to be elevated to a plane far above the Zion defiled by the illegitimate priesthood attacked by the oracle. Thus the flight of the visionary group into a realm freed from the restraints of historical realities and removed from responsibility to the political sphere is clearly evident.

The mythic structure underlying the hymn, fusing the league tradition of ritual conquest with the royal motif of the procession to Zion, no longer is limited to the function of enhancing the historical interpretation of divine activity, but has begun to serve as a vehicle for a new interpretation of divine activity in terms elevated above the historical realm in the plainest sense, an interpretation which would

85. By its very nature, the context of the Divine Warrior Hymn is the cosmic sphere. See, for example, the Baal cycle and the *Enūma eliš,* Dtn 33:2-5, 26-29; Josh 10:12-13; Ju 5; Psalm 68; 2 Sam 22:7-18/Ps 18:7-18; and Hab 3:3-15. Cf. F. M. Cross, "Yahweh and the God of the Patriarchs," *HTR* 55 (1962): 256; and Miller, *Divine Warrior,* pp. 196 ff.

ultimately undermine the political dimensions of the prophetic office by summoning the faithful to a realm of salvation unencumbered by responsibility to the socio-political order. In its disparagement of the political and social order as beyond redemption and fallen to evil, and in its vision of a redemption removed from that political and social order, this new interpretation has come close to adopting also the dualistic worldview of myth, the worldview picturing an old order of sterility which must be destroyed to make way for a new order of fertility. This dualistic worldview would never be able to supplant completely Israel's historical understanding of divine activity, but as the contrast between verses 1-15a and 15b-20 illustrates, and as 65:17-25 will corroborate, the availability of the ancient gospel of myth within a context of oppression and *Weltschmerz* presented the visionaries with a tempting means of resolving the tension between brilliant visions of salvation and bitter disappointment—the flight into the timeless repose of myth.

E. THE SCHISM WIDENS, VINDICTIVENESS INCREASES, HOPE IS DEFERRED, AND THE SEEDS OF APOCALYPTIC ESCHATOLOGY ARE SOWN (65:1-25)

As explained in section C above, Isaiah 65 was originally an independent unit, only secondarily fused with 63:7-64 into a liturgical composition. As for the unity of the chapter itself, there are certain formal marks which some exegetes[86] use to divide the chapter into three separate units: in verse 7 the concluding formula "Yahweh says" (*'āmar yhwh*) and in verse 8 the introductory formula "Thus Yahweh says" (*kōh 'āmar yhwh*) would represent the first division; in verse 13, what Elliger[87] calls an introductory formula "Therefore, thus says the Lord Yahweh" (*lākēn kōh 'āmar 'adōnāy yhwh*) would mark the beginning of the third section, which then concludes with the closing formula in verse 25 "Yahweh says" (*'āmar yhwh*). These formulae, helpful as a guide to division in other prophetic corpora, are quite useless in Third Isaiah where they are often found at

86. E.g., Elliger, *Einheit*, pp. 33 ff.
87. Ibid, p. 35.

the center of units which by no means can be divided, and are usually lacking where divisions are obvious. Often, as in the case of verse 7, metric and other considerations indicate that the formula is a secondary intrusion into the text. As for the formula in verse 13 it is rather an imitation of the formula used in the classical form of the judgment oracle to introduce the threat.[88] Therefore, the question of the integrity of the chapter as a single unit must be decided on the basis of other factors.

When we examine the structure of Isaiah 65, we find many features which demonstrate that it is a tightly knit unit: (1) Verses 1f and 10 constitute an *inclusio* with the contrast between "my people who seek me" and "a stubborn and rebellious people" to whom "I was ready to be sought" but "who did not seek me." (2) Verses 10 and 11 bind together the first and second section of the oracle with the contrast between "my people who seek me," and "but you, who have abandoned Yahweh . . . ," the type of contrast used repeatedly in Third Isaiah (e.g., 57:2-3). A similar unifying contrast is between the "inheritors of my mountain" in verse 9 and those "who have forgotten my holy mountain" in verse 11. (3) Verses 12 and 24 again manifest conscious contrasts which serve to unify that section: "For I called, but you would not answer, I spoke, but you would not hear," "Before they call, I shall answer, while they are yet speaking, I shall have heard." (4) Taken as a whole, the structure of the chapter resembles many of the oracles of "Third Isaiah," alternating words of judgment against the wicked (1-7, 11-12, half of 13-15) with words of promise to the faithful (8-10, half of 13-15, 16-25). As we suggested in the last section, this structure of the oracle grows out of a new situation within the community of post-exilic Israel, and those who disarticulate oracles such as chapter 65 on the basis of the contrast between judgment and salvation words fail to recognize a major characteristic of this material. (5) The divine first person is used throughout. On the basis of these features, we conclude that 65:1-25 is an original prophetic unit (with two minor additions, as indicated by the textual notes).

88. E.g., Is 5:24; 7:14; 8:7; 29:14; 30:13.

65: 1 I was ready to be sought by those not asking for me,
I was ready to be found by those not seeking me,
I said, "Here I am, here I am"
to a nation which did not call on my name,
2 I spread forth my hands all day long
to a stubborn and rebellious people,
who walk in a path that is not good
following their own devices,
3 a people who provoke me to anger
before my very Presence continually,
who offer sacrifices in the gardens,
burning incense upon altars,
4 who sit in tombs
and spend the night in secret places,
who eat the flesh of swine,
a polluted soup in their dishes,
5 who say, "Keep your distance,
approach me not, or I will communicate holiness to you."
Such men are a smoke in my nostrils,
a fire which burns continually.
6 See, it is written before me:
I will not remain silent, but I will repay
7 those who burned incense upon the mountains
and insulted me upon the hills;
I will measure out their due upon their head
and will repay their full reward into their lap.
8 Thus Yahweh says:
Just as, when new wine is found in the cluster,
they say, "Destroy it not, for it contains blessing";
so I will act for the sake of my servants
in order not to destroy the whole.
9 I shall bring forth descendants from Jacob,
and from Judah inheritors of my mountain.
My chosen will inherit it
and my servants will dwell there.
10 Sharon will become a pasture for flocks,
and the valley of Achor a place for herds to lie
for my people who seek me.
11 But you, who have abandoned Yahweh,
who have forgotten my holy mountain,
who set a table for Gad,
who fill cups of mixed drink for Meni:
12 I will commit you to the sword,
and all of you shall succumb to the slaughter.
For I called, but you would not answer,

	Text	Structure				Meter	Prosodic Units
65:1[a]	נדרשתי ללוא שאלו[ני]	a	b	c		9	1:1::1:1::b:b:b:b:
	נמצאתי ללא בקשני	a_1	b	c_1		9	b:b:1:1:1:1:1:1:1
	אמרתי הנני הנני	a_2	d	d		9	
	אל גוי לא קרא [b] בשמי		b_1	c_2	e	8	
2	פרשתי ידי כל יום	a_3	d_1	f		7	
	אל עם סורר [ומורה][c]		b_2	c_3	c_4	7	
	ההלכים דרך לא טוב			c_4	E	7	
	אחר מחשבתיהם				E_1	7	
3	עם המכעיסים אותי		b_3	c_5	e_1	7	
	על פני תמיד			e_2	f_1	5	
	[d] [ה]זבחים בגנות		b_4	c_6	g	7	
	מקטרים על [מ]לבנים[e]			c_7	g_1	8	
4	הישביש בקברים			c_8	g_2	8	
	ובנצורים ילינו			g_3	c_9	8	
	האכלים בשר חזיר			c_{10}	E_2	8	
	[f] [מ]רק פגלים [g] [ב]כליהם			c_{11}	E_3	9	
5	האמרים קרב אליך			c_{12}	E_4	9	
	אל תגש בי כי קדשתיך			E_5	h	9	
	אלה עשן באפי	a	b	c		7	1:b
	אש יקדת כל יום		B	d		5	
6	הנה כתוב לפני	rubric					
	לא אחשה כי אם שלמתי[ ][h]	ab	ab			8	1:1:1::1:1
7	אשר קטרו על ההרים	b_1	cd			9	
	ועל הגבעות חרפוני	D	c_1			10	
	מדתי פעלתם [ב]ראש[ם]	a_2	e	d_2		10	
	[ושלמתי גמולם] על חיקם	a_1	e_1	d_3		10	
8	כה אמר יהוה	rubric					
	כאשר ימצא התירוש באשכול			proverb		12	
	ואמר אל תשחיתהו כי ברכה בו					12	
	כן אעשה למען עבדי					8	
	לבלתי השחית הכל					7	
9	והוצאתי מיעקב זרע	a	b	c		8	1:1
	ומיהודה יורש הרי [i]		b_1	C		8	
	וירשוה בחירי	A	b			8	1:1
	ועבדי ישכנו שמה	b_1	a_1	c		9	
10	והיה שרון לנוה צאן	a	b	c		9	1:1:1
	ועמק עכור לרבץ בקר		B	c_1		8	
	לעמי דרשוני		d	e		7	
11	ואתם עזבי יהוה	a	b	c		8	1:1::1:1
	השכחים הר קדשי		b_1	C		7	
	הערכים לגד שלחן		b_2	d	c_1	8	
	הממלאים למני ממסך		b_3	d_1	c_2	9	
12	ומניתיכם לחרב	a	b	c		7	1:1
	וכלכם לטבח תכרעו	b_1	c_1	a_1		8	
	יען קראתי ולא עניתם	a	b	c		9	1:1::1:1

I spoke, but you would not hear;
you did what I consider evil,
what displeases me, that you chose.
13 Therefore, thus says the Lord Yahweh:
See, my servants will eat
but you will go hungry,
see, my servants will drink
but you will go thirsty.
14 See, my servants will rejoice
but you will be put to shame,
see, my servants will sing out for joy of heart
but you will cry out for sadness of heart,
and you will howl with a broken spirit.
15 You will leave your name as a curse,
but my servants will be called by a new name.
16 One blessing himself in the land will bless himself
by the God Amen.
One taking an oath in the land will swear
by the God Amen.
For the former troubles will be forgotten,
they will be hidden from my eyes;
17 for now I create new heavens
and a new earth,
and the former things will not be remembered,
nor will they come to mind;
18 rather be glad and rejoice forever
over that which I create,
for now I create Jerusalem "Rejoicing"
and her people "Gladness,"
19 and I shall rejoice over Jerusalem
and be glad over my people.
No more will be heard in her the sound of weeping
or the sound of a cry;
20 no more will there be an infant that dies,
or an old man not living out his days.
One dying at a hundred will be considered young,
the sinner dying at a hundred is accursed.
21 They will build houses and settle down,
plant vineyards and eat;
22 they will not build for someone else to settle in,
not plant for someone else to eat.
As the days of a tree will be the days of my people,
and they will enjoy the works of their hands.

	רברתי ולא שמעתם	a_1	b_1	c_1		8	
	ותעשו הרע בעיני	c_2	d	e		8	
	בלא חפצתי בחרתם		D	c_3		8	
13	לכן כה אמר אדני יהוה	rubric					
	הנה עבדי יאכלו	a	b	c		8	1:b::1:b::1
	ואתם תרעבו		b_1	c_1		6	:b::1:1:1
	הנה עבדי ישתו	a	b	c_2		7	
	ואתם תצמאו		b_1	c_3		6	
	הנה עבדי ישמחו	a	b	c_4		8	
	ואתם תבשו		b_1	c_5		6	
14	הנה עבדי ירנו ממוב לב	a	b	c_6		11	
	ואתם תצעקו מכאב לב		b_1	c_7	d	10	
	ומשבר רוח תילילו			d_1	c_8	8	
15	הנחתם שמכם לשבועה[ ][j]	a	b	c		9	1:1
	ולעבדי[ ] יקרא שם אחר	b_1	a_1	c_1		10	
16	מתברך בארץ יתברך	a	b	a		8	1:b::1:b
	באלהי אמן		c	d		6	
	ונשבע בארץ ישבע	a_1	b	a_1		8	
	באלהי אמן		c	d		6	
	כי נשכחו צרות ראשנות	a	B			9	1:b::1:b:1:b:
	נסתרו מעיני	a_1	c			6	1:b:1:b:1:b
17	הנני בורא שמים חדשים		d	E		9	
	וארץ חדשה			E_1		5	
	ולא תזכרנה ראשנות	A	b			9	
	לא תעלינה על לב	a_2	c_1			6	
18	כי אם שישו וגילו עדי עד		f	f_1	g	10	
	[על][k] אשר אני בורא		e	d		7	
	הנני בורא ירושלם גילה		d	e_1	f_1	10	
	ועמה משוש			e_2	f	5	
19	וגלתי בירושלים			f_1	e_1	8	
	וששתי בעמי			f	e_2	6	
	לא ישמע בה עוד קול בכי	a	b	c		9	1:b::1:1
	וקול זעקה			C		5	
20	לא יהיה משם עוד עול ימים	a_1	b_1	c_2		9	
	וזקן לא ימלא ימיו			c_3	d e	9	
	כי נער בן מאה שנה ימות	a	b	c		9	1:1
	חוטא בן מאה שנה יקלל[l]	a_1	b_1	c_1		10	
21	ובנו בתים וישבו	a	b	a_1		9	1:1::1:1
	נטעו כרמים ואכלו[ ] [m]	a_2	b_1	a_3		10	
22	לא יבנו ואחר ישב	a	c	a_1		8	
	לא יטעו ואחר יאכל	a_2	c	a_3		9	
	כי כימי [ ]עץ ימי עמי	a	b	a	b_1	4:4	bb:1
	ומעשה ידיהם יבלו[n]	a_1	b_2	c		9	

23 My chosen will not labor in vain,
they will not bear children for calamity.
For they shall be a race blessed by Yahweh,
and their children with them.
24 Before they call I shall answer,
while they are yet speaking I shall have heard.
25 The wolf and the lamb will pasture together,
the lion will eat straw like the ox,
and dust will be the serpent's food.
They will do no harm and no destruction
in all my holy mountain, says Yahweh.

TEXTUAL NOTES

a) The suffix, found in 1QIsa[a], LXX, Old Latin, Pesh, and Tg was possibly lost in most of the Hebrew mss by haplography (note the *nûn* beginning the following word).

b) Context makes קָרָא preferable, that is, the active with the versions, rather than the passive of the Masoretic pointing, which may reflect influence from 63:19.

c) A word has been lost in the MT. LXX adds *καὶ ἀντιλέγοντα*. The Hebrew word was likely ומֹורָה (C. C. Torrey, *ad loc.*).

d) 1QIsa[a] and LXX have the pronoun, which could be interpreted as grounds for restoring המה in the MT, especially since the colon is metrically short. However, the pattern in this prosodic unit is for the participle beginning each bicolon to have the definite article. Q and LXX would then be interpreted as an expansion on the article.

e) The versions differ widely in their readings of 3b. The MT reading is translated variously as "burning incense upon bricks," or "on the roofs," or emended to read "upon the mountains." Behind the MT we would see מלבנים, since incense altars would be the natural place for burning incense (confusion of ה for מ is a common scribal error; see also M. Dahood, "Textual Problems in Isaiah," *CBQ* 22 [1960]: 408). The LXX reads, "and burn incense on bricks," thus far agreeing with MT, but then goes on, "to demons which do not exist" (*τοις δαιμονιοις α ουκ εστι*), which is apparently a rendering of הישבים of verse 4, based on a variant preserved in the Lucianic tradition (*τοις ουκ ουσιν*) which itself owes its existence to an error. It should be *οικουσιν*, a literal rendering of the Hebrew (I. L. Seeligmann, *The Septuagint Version of Isaiah* [Leiden: E. J. Brill, 1948], pp. 30 ff.). But the problem posed by MT and LXX is nothing compared to the "shocking variant" offered by 1QIsa[a], וינקו ידים על האבנים, which Arie Rubenstein translates, "and suck the hands upon the stones," taking

23	בחירי לא ייגעו לריק	a	b	c		9	1:1
	ולא ילדו לבהלה		b_1	C		9	
	כי זרע ברוכי יהוה המה	a	b	c		9	1:1
	וצאצאיהם אתם			c	d	7	
24	היה טרם יקראו ואני אענה	a	b	c	d	11	1:1
	עוד הם מדברים ואני אשמע	a_1	b_1	c	d_1	11	
25	זאב וטלה ירעו כאחד	a	a_1	b	c	9	1:1:1
	ואריה כבקר יאכל תבן	a_2	a_3	b_1	d	9	
	ונחש עפר לחמו		a_4	d	e	7	
	לא ירעו ולא ישחיתו	A	A_1			9	1:1
	בכל הר קדשי אמר יהוה		b	c	rubric	9	

"hands" to be a euphemism for the phallus, similar to 57:8 ("Notes on the Use of the Tenses in the Variant Readings of the Isaiah Scroll," *VT* 3 [1953]: 94–95). W. H. Brownlee (*The Meaning of the Qumran Scrolls for the Bible with Special Attention to the Book of Isaiah* [New York: Oxford University, 1964] pp. 234–235), who favors this reading over MT ("because the variant is shocking, we may regard it as preserving an original reading"), carries out the image further by translating stones as "testicles."

Professor Cross (private communication) points out that the 1Q orthography for the root ינק would be ויינקו, and that the root in the Q reading is thus נקה, "empty, pour out." Pointing out the use of יד = כף "incense spoons," he translates, "they empty their incense spoons on stones," which suits the context well. It is possible that Q here preserves a very ancient, possibly even original reading. Since LXX here supports MT, however, and the MT reading offers a good parallel to "sacrificing in gardens" and prepares for the mention of "smoke in my nostrils" in verse 5b, we retain the MT reading.

f) Reading the Qere, supported by 1QIsa^a, LXX, Tg, Vg. Even with this correction, the exact meaning of the term is not certain, though it must be some sort of forbidden food.

g) Required by the context, and deriving support from 1QIsa^a, Vg, and Tg.

h) The last three words of verse 6 and 7a appear to be a clumsy gloss using phrases from the rest of verses 6 and 7 and the traditional formula, "their iniquities and the iniquities of their fathers." Telltales of the disruption at this point are the collapse of what has been to this point a regular meter, the breakdown of the prosodic structure, and the sudden switch to second person suffixes.

ושלמתי על חיקם	a	b	7
עונתיכם ועונת אבותיכם יחדו	c	C	15
אמר יהוה	x	x	

i) Reading הָרִי, i.e., singular. It seems strange that the usual emendation, following the note in BH, is to change the following pronominal suffix to the plural, while a much stronger case can be made for our proposal: (1) "Inherit my mountain" is a technical phrase in the salvation oracles of Third Isaiah (57:13c; 65:9, 11a, 26; 66:20), and it is always singular. (2) The phrase is a conscious adaptation of the technical term, "my mountain of heritage." (3) The singular agrees with the singular suffix on וירשוה, of which it is the antecedent (in sixth-century orthography ה would have been the normal *mater lectionis* for the masculine suffix ô [< uh]). (4) A final argument is based on the form of the salvation-judgment oracle used in this material, where salvation words are followed by the corresponding judgment word (e.g., v. 13 ff). Thus the promise, "I will bring forth descendants from Jacob, and from Judah inheritors of my mountain," is followed in verse 11 with: "But you, who have abandoned Yahweh, who have forgotten my holy mountain . . . ."

j) Meter (14:9:10), structure (a b c d: e f: d_1 g h) and sense all indicate that verse 15b is corrupt. The bicolon is restored once לבחירי and לעבדיו are recognized to be ancient variants, and the phrase והמיתך אדני יהוה is removed as a gloss. The suffix on לעבדיו would have been changed from the first to the third person after the gloss had entered the text.

k) Lost by haplography after עדי עד.

l) The text as it stands seems to yield tolerable sense, both cola of verse 20b illustrating that death at one hundred will be unnatural. (For a different interpretation requiring a slight emendation, cf. G. R. Driver, *JTS* 36 [1935]: 406; Torrey, p. 470, regards verse 20 as a later addition.)

m) Both the meter and the parallel with the preceding colon indicate פרים is a gloss. Note also that the same parallel occurs in the next bicolon, again without the object.

n) The meter is restored if בחירי is read with the next colon.

Once again we have before us an oracle bereft of any reference which might allow one to attach to it a precise date. This is not to say that attempts have not been made to date the oracle on that basis. For instance, Paul Volz uses the mention of Gad and Meni in verse 11 as evidence for a second-century date.[89] This and many similar late dates have been disproven by manuscript evidence from Qumran. In what follows we shall marshal further arguments

89. Volz, pp. 284–285. Cf. Glahn, *Prophet*, vol 2; pp. 94–95.

against the late dates which one finds assigned to this chapter in the older literature.

The poem in chapter 65 represents a significant step further away from Second Isaiah in the typology of poetic structure and meter. The meter is so bad through most of the poem that it must be accounted for either as a breakdown of the archaizing style of Second Isaiah or as the result of later prosaizing and glossing on an immense scale. The evidence suggests that what is being witnessed is in fact the breakdown of earlier canons of prosody, for a consistent pattern has become discernible in the poems we have studied thus far in the breakdown not only of the meter but of the internal structure and literary genres as well.

The prosodic unit extending throughout verses 1-5a illustrates this breakdown on the level of internal structure, for it manifests a synthetic development of thought based on sequential repetition of grammatical elements resulting in a cumbersome and monotonous style which bears no resemblance to the formal beauty of Second Isaiah's poetry; adding to the grotesqueness of the total effect is a chaotic meter. A similar list based on repetition of participles appears in verse 11. The prosodic unit in verses 13-14 is based on another type of monotonous repetition, and again the meter is erratic. This evidence leaves little doubt that the poem lies at a greater distance from Second Isaiah on the typology of poetic structure and meter than any of the poems studied earlier.

The form of this oracle incorporates a feature found in chapters 58 and 59, the juxtaposition of salvation and judgment words. At the same time it appears that chapter 65 represents a somewhat later point on the typology of prophetic genres than those two chapters, since the fusion of judgment and salvation elements seems to be more complete. Whereas a certain tension between the classical form (directing the word of judgment toward the whole people) and the new form (distinguishing between recipients of judgment and salvation within Israel) was still recognized in Isaiah 58, in chapter 65 the distinction between the two parties and the corresponding juxtaposition of judgment and salvation words are basic to the entire unit.[90] Verses 13–14 indicate how complete that fusion of judgment and salvation oracles has become. Moreover, the conditional element in chapter 58 which blunted the dichotomy between the recipients of salvation and of judgment is now absent; the sentence of judgment to one group and the promise of salvation to the other are offered unconditionally and categorically, an observation on the form critical level which betrays a deepening of the schism within the community.

The structure of this salvation-judgment oracle is the following: verses 1–7 are an indictment (vv. 1–5) and sentence (vv. 6–7) on "a stubborn and rebellious people" guilty of defiling the cult; verses 8–10 are a promise of salvation to a group variously called "my servants," "my chosen," and "my people who seek me." Verses 11–12 turn to another indictment and sentence against those "who have abandoned Yahweh, who have forgotten my holy mountain." This juxtaposing of judgment and salvation words is then intimately drawn together in a rapid series of salvation-judgment words in verses 13–15. The judgment segment in each case is introduced with "But you" (*wᵊʼattem*), exactly as was the judgment section in verse 11 (see also the same feature in 57:3). The intimate tie between salvation and judgment words achieved by this series, "See, my servants . . . but you . . . " (*hinnēh ʿăbāday . . . wᵊʼattem . . .*) is of central importance in the form critical analysis of the Third Isaiah material, for like no other passage it proves how inseparably bound the salvation and judgment elements have become in the prophetic oracle of this period. The juxtaposition of salvation and judgment words in verses 13–15 is of a piece with the juxtaposition of salvation and judgment words in the oracles in chapters 58, 59, 66, and 57:3–13.

90. The designation *ʿam* ("people") might lead one to assume that verses 1–7 are addressed to Israel as a whole, in the manner of the classical prophets. But *ʿam* is not used here in the technical sense meaning Israel, but as a designation for the group rebelling against Yahweh in contrast to the group faithful to Yahweh. This is seen by comparison of verse 2 with verse 10: "a stubborn and rebellious people (*ʿam*)" / "my people (*ʿam*) who seek me."

Against the critics who would attribute the combination of judgment and salvation in these chapters to later redaction and would therefore remove sections like 57:13c and 65:8-10 as secondary additions, we would maintain that it is just as arbitrary to separate those salvation words from the corresponding words of judgment as it would be to separate the series of blessings introduced with "See, my servants . . . " in verses 13-14 from the curses introduced with "but you . . . ." The rapid succession of judgment and salvation words found running throughout these oracles represents a key development in the prophetic genres of the post-exilic period. It is not surprising that the resulting oracle is considerably longer than the average oracle of the classical period, for as the structural analysis has indicated, we here most probably are dealing with literary composition, a phenomenon already present in Second Isaiah. Much of the dividing of the Third Isaiah material into short, classical-length units is thus based on a misunderstanding of the development of prophetic genres in the post-exilic period. Methodologically, this does not mean that every lengthy unit that has been handed down to us by tradition must be considered a priori to be original; secondary fusing of originally independent units does account in cases for existing units (e.g., 63:7-65). It does mean, however, that if internal features (such as those identified earlier in chapter 65) hold together a lengthy composition in an indivisible unity, pre-exilic standards must not be applied to justify disarticulation of that composition into smaller units. Recognition of these characteristics of the post-exilic salvation-judgment oracle leads us to affirm the originality also of verses 16b-25; indeed, the sequence of judgment and salvation sections in verses 1-16a serves as introduction to the final salvation section in 16b-25.

After recognizing the close connection between this oracle and those discussed earlier with regard to prosodic structure and form, we are not surprised to find that the two opposing parties also seem identical to those locked in the polemic in Isaiah 63:7-64; 58; and 59. Already, observations on the strictly form critical level suggest a situation where the rift between the two groups has deepened even more, for the salvation and judgment elements are delivered unconditionally to two different groups, with no apparent qualification or compromise. It now remains to examine the judgment and salvation words for light they can throw on the two traditions represented in this polemic and on the situation within the community.

With regard to the prophetic tradition to which this oracle belongs, all of the concerns expressed reflect the concerns we have come to identify with the tradition stemming from Second Isaiah; possession of the land, control of Zion, abundant progeny, being called by a new name, and bitter polemic against the self-righteous majority which controls and is defiling the central cult. How a changing situation has altered the guise which these basic concerns assume will be discussed below. But first the party condemned by the oracle will be examined.

The first seven verses of the chapter give a shocking description of the self-righteous majority, a description which is consonant with and complementary to the picture of them given by the earlier oracles. It is again a picture of a group very actively engaged in sacred activities, but they are activities which infuriate rather than please Yahweh. The beginning of the oracle seems to address the same charge answered by chapters 58 and 59 that Yahweh has withdrawn from the people, leaving them in the bleak circumstances of the early post-exilic period. Four times, in different ways, Yahweh insists that the fault does not lie on his side, for he has been accessible to them. Then a series of participial clauses uncovers the reason for the delay in the restoration, namely, the defiled cult, and the "stubborn and rebellious people" directing that cult who provoke Yahweh to anger before his very Presence (*pānîm*). The passage is again saturated with the technical language of the cult, as well as with phrases reminiscent of earlier attacks of the prophetic group against those they regard as apostates; e.g., although Yahweh makes himself present, they do not call on his name (cf. 64:6). As chapter 58 also makes clear, this does not imply that they neglected cultic activities, for it is precisely before Yahweh's *pānîm* (cf. 59:2b), i.e., in the cult, that they provoke him to anger.

Verses 3–4a enumerate their defiled cultic practices, using what is probably the strongest traditional language available to the author to suggest defilement. The language is not meant to be taken any more literally than the charge in 59:5–6 that they hatch adders' eggs and spin spider's webs, or the indictment in 57:5–8 that they sacrifice their children and build a harlot's bed on a hilltop. In treating such symbolical language, the exegete's task is to discern the actual abuses being attacked with this symbolical, hyperbolical language, a task which can be met with greater success in some cases than in others. In the case of 59:5–6 the general meaning of the images is clear: the party being attacked, though ostensibly righteous, is treacherously dangerous to the community. In this chapter the references to "offering sacrifices in gardens" and "burning incense upon altars" equate the cult of those attacked with Canaanizing sacrificial practices (cf. 66:3 and 57:5). Verse 4a suggests necromantic features of the Canaanite funerary cult, while the dietary practices of verse 4b constitute violations of Mosaic law.

Our treatment of these abominations as symbols of illegitimate practices in the central cult is firmly supported by the context. Verse 3a introduces this list of abominations with the charge that this people provoked Yahweh "before my very Presence (*'al pānay*) continually," which is the technical term for the central sanctuary, where Yahweh's Presence tabernacled.[91] According to the prophetic group, the adherents of the cult conduct themselves in a manner comparable to pagans not in the *bāmôt* of pagan deities, but precisely where Yahweh's Presence is revealed in order to be reverenced and feared. Verse 5, which follows immediately on the list of abominations, again indicates that those attacked are not rabid paganizers, but the religiously elite leaders of the normative cult who regard themselves as having an exclusive claim on holiness, "who say, 'Keep your distance (*qərab 'ēleykā*), do not approach me (*'al tiggaš bî*) or I will communicate holiness to you (*kî qədaštîkā*).'" It is hardly an accident that this short sentence contains three of the

91. See note 72.

cardinal technical terms in the priestly language of the hierocratic tradition to express the special sanctity of the Zadokite priesthood. A more biting attack on the central tenet of that tradition can hardly be imagined than equating their special sanctity with paganizing practices.

It has already been observed how the program of restoration in Isaiah 60–62 looked for the day when the people "shall *all* be righteous" and "shall be called the priests of the Lord" (60:21; 61:6), and how this view was fated to come into conflict with the program which would finally emerge as victor, represented by Ezekiel 40–48. It is well to recall a few of the passages from the Ezekiel program that embody the exclusive claim of the Zadokite priests which is here bitterly opposed by the prophetic circle. These passages use precisely those technical terms which are found in verse 5a. First, stated negatively, are instructions that none, save the Zadokites, may enter the holy area: "and mark well those who may be admitted to the temple and all those who are to be excluded from the sanctuary . . . " (then comes the list, foreigners, uncircumcised, and even the Levites): "They [i.e., the Levites] shall not come near (*yiggəšû*) to me, to serve me as priest, nor come near (*gešet*) any of my sacred things. . . ." Then positively, "but the Levitical priests, the sons of Zadok . . . shall come near (*yiqrəbû*) to me . . ." (Ezek 44:5, 13, 15). How exclusive was this Zadokite right of access to the Holy, and what precaution had to be taken not to include others in this holiness, is then made clear: "And when they go out into the outer court to the people, they shall put off the garments in which they have been ministering, and lay them in the holy chambers, *lest they communicate holiness to the people* (*yəqaddəšûʾet hāʿām*) . . ." (Ezek 44:19).[92] When one compares this last phrase with :

92. Numerous similar passages could be cited to illustrate this exclusive claim of the Zadokites, e.g., Ezek 42:13 ff; 44:23; Lev 10:1–17; and the P stratum of the narrative of the Korahide rebellion (Numbers 16–17). Numbers 18 also explicates the exclusive right of the Zadokites to holiness; the Levites "shall not come near to the vessels of the sanctuary or to the altar, lest they, and you, die." They may attend to the duties of the tent, but "no one else shall come near you" (*wezār lōʾ yiqrab ʾalêkem;* cf. Is 65:5; *qerab ʾēleykā ʾal tiggaš bî*). Finally the exclusiveness of the normative priestly party is manifested in a somewhat different way in Ezr 4:1–3, where the "adversaries" approached Zerubbabel and were told: "You have nothing to do with us in building a house to our God; but we alone will build to the Lord the God of Israel. . . ." Since the Chronicler lumps all who do not belong to the

"Keep your distance (*qᵊrab 'ēleykā*), do not approach me (*'al tiggaš bî*), or *I will communicate holiness to you* (*kî qᵊdaštîkā*)," and further realizes that *nāgaš* (Ex 24:2; 28:43; 30:20; 34:30; Lev 21:21, 23; Nu 4:19; 8:19; 44:13; Ezek 44:13; see also 2 Chr 29:31), *qārab* (Ex 40:32; Lev 9:7f; 21:17; 22:3; Ezek 40:46; 42:14; 45:4) and *qādaš* in the pi'el (Ex 28:3, 41; 30:29f; 40:13; Lev 8:12; 16:19; Ezek 44:19; 46:20) are all key technical terms in P and Ezekiel, it becomes difficult to escape the startling conclusion that precisely the priestly group which based its restoration efforts on the hierocratic program is here object of a most bitter attack. There is evidence elsewhere that the polemic was fought just as bitterly from the other side.[93] The irony of the attack culminates in verse 5b, for after all of the cultic activities of the defiled group have been enumerated, and their arrogant self-righteousness has been so vividly expressed in verse 5a, Yahweh declares that far from producing a pleasing smell with all their sacrifices, "such men are a smoke in my nostrils, a fire which burns continually." The judgment on the cult of the priestly group could not be more unequivocal: "a people provoking me to anger before

official party into such categories as *'am hā"āreṣ* and *ṣārîm*, it is difficult to identify the ones being opposed, but the Third Isaiah material indicates that at least one prophetic group strenuously resisted the exclusive claim of the Zadokites, insisting that they were the true priesthood entitled to the land, and that the normative party was in fact the defiled group.

93. See Chapter IV. Intriguing in this connection are certain late additions to Numbers 16–17. Korah and his associates protest: "You have gone too far! For all the congregation are holy, every one of them; why then do you exalt yourselves above the assembly of the Lord?" Moses replies: "In the morning the Lord will show who is his, and who is holy, and will cause him to come near (*qārab*, hiph.) to him . . . , and the man whom the Lord chooses shall be the holy one. You have gone too far, sons of Levi!" Then after asking them why they should be dissatisfied with the task Yahweh has given them, Moses concludes: "And would you seek the priesthood also?. . ." After the rebels have been punished with death, their censers "were hammered out as a covering for the altar, to be a reminder to the people of Israel, so that no one who is not a priest, who is not of the descendants of Aaron, should draw near to burn incense before the Lord, lest they become like Korah and his company. . . ." This account is obviously of polemical intent, and not only is an example of the type of exclusiveness and self-righteousness attacked by Isaiah 65, but parts of it may stem from the other side of the same polemic.

A comparison of several passages in the program of restoration (Isaiah (60–62) with Numbers 16–17 is very suggestive: the program states, "Your people shall all be righteous" (60:21) and "They will be called 'The Holy People'" (62:12); similarly, in Numbers 16 the Korahides insist, "All the congregation are holy, everyone of them," against which democratizing tendency the official priestly position is set: "The man whom Yahweh chooses shall be the holy one. You have gone too far, sons of Levi!" Again, the program announces to the entire people: "You will be named the priests of Yahweh," whereas in Numbers 16 the priestly protest is placed in the mouth of Moses: "Would you seek the priesthood also?"

my very *pānîm* continually," "a smoke in my nostrils." It is the same judgment on the cult found in 58:4b and 59:2, and which we will also find in chapter 57. The formal sentence then follows in verses 6–7.

In keeping with the salvation-judgment oracle form which we have seen emerging in the Third Isaiah material, the judgment word against the defiled cult in verses 1–7 is followed by a word of salvation to the prophetic group in verses 8–10. It is introduced in verse 8 by an image which is of highest significance as a key to the development taking place both in the literary genres of prophecy and in the development of prophetic eschatology in the direction of apocalyptic. First, regarding the genres of prophecy: the image of the grape cluster, the good parts of which are saved and the bad destroyed (an eschatological image comparable to the parable of the Wheat and the Tares) illustrates with utmost clarity why the new prophetic genre, the salvation-judgment oracle, came to replace the classical forms (where the judgment oracle and the salvation oracle were two separate genres). For no longer are two separate entities the easily distinguishable objects of Yahweh's wrath and mercy; no longer can a pure judgment word be delivered to the nations, and a separate salvation word to all Israel, or a pure judgment word to all Israel. The oracles no longer distinguish between groups defined by national boundaries, which means that the individual salvation or judgment word no longer encompasses an entire nation. Rather the line cuts through one nation, and thus in an oracle delivered to that nation, salvation and judgment words must be spoken simultaneously. We recognize a clear instance of the influence which a new sociological setting has upon the literary forms of a literature: a new situation demanded a new form of prophetic oracle, thereby leading to the conception and development of the salvation-judgment oracle.

This change in form is accompanied by a shift away from prophetic eschatology in the direction of apocalyptic eschatology. For what happens to a nation's eschatology which hitherto was construed in the historical terms of Yahweh's restoration of the nation to its original political autonomy and integrity when that nation is no longer a recognizable historical entity, when the historical boundary demarcating Israel from the nations is replaced by the spiritual boundary setting Israel off from Israel? In the last section we recognized the beginning of the alteration which the changed situation necessitated: with the aid of concepts borrowed from myth, restoration was seen more and more as an event of the new era, an event losing connections with the concrete realities of history, an event removing the elect from any relation of responsibility to the present political order, an event no longer interpreting divine action in the historical terms of Yahweh directing the destiny of nations and kings, but tending to be viewed in terms of a more direct forensic intervention whereby Yahweh separates the righteous from the wicked. Thus in the present image Yahweh promises that he will not destroy the good with the bad in the cluster which is Israel but, in eliminating the bad through judgments like those found in verses 1–7, he will save and restore his servants. So long as those servants felt that their program, as expressed in Isaiah 60–62, could be the basis for the restoration, their eschatology could maintain the dialectic between myth and history, and could preserve a vital connection with the political order. But we have come to realize that the visionary group faithful to the tradition of Second Isaiah has become an oppressed minority opposed by a powerful hierocratic group.

As already indicated by 59:9–15, and now clarified by this oracle, the present order was evil, necessitating radical changes before the hoped for restoration could occur. Thus, the image of the grape cluster taken together with the delineation of the restoration which follows betrays the increased influence of myth as the picture of restoration moves away from the brilliant promises of Second Isaiah in the direction of the cataclysmic descriptions of full-blown apocalyptic: (1) The restoration would be preceded by a mighty act of judgment by Yahweh which would fall not along the national lines of classical prophecy, but along spiritual lines separating the righteous from the wicked, thus adumbrating the universal judgment of later apocalyptic. (2) The restoration would occur not in the present order, which is tainted by evil, but only after a series of cosmic upheavals through which Yahweh would create a new order purged of evil; these cosmic events would go beyond the human realm to effect even the world of nature so as to establish a suitable natural setting for the restoration people. Where that effect upon the natural sphere became the central concern in the description of the events of the restoration—as it occasionally did in early and middle apocalyptic—the influence of mythic dualism became so profound as to endanger Israel's historical interpretation of Yahweh's saving activity.

The image of the grape cluster introduces the salvation promise to the faithful (vv. 9–10) which was prepared for by the preceding judgment on the apostates. That promise, betraying the tendencies toward apocalyptic mentioned above, and disclosing more evidence concerning the community situation underlying the oracle, must now be considered in detail.

The first elements of the promise deal with two of the central concerns of the program of restoration in Isaiah 60–62 (evidence that we are still within the Second Isaiah tradition), namely, promise of descendants (cf. 60:22) and of inheritance of Yahweh's holy mountain Zion (cf. 60:21; 61:7). In the section on Isaiah 60–62, we noted how very concerned the followers of Second Isaiah are with inheriting Zion, where they would live as priests in charge of the cult (60:7; 61:4–7). In 63:18, a possible reference to their apparent loss of possession of Zion to adversaries of the prophetic circle is recognized. It is very understandable that this oppressed group, distressed with their loss of control of the cult and with their exclusion from the priesthood, would in the first instance associate Yahweh's final act with the restoration of Zion to their possession. Moreover, their protest that they are the true descendants of ancient Israel (cf. 63:11–17; 64:8f) is supported by the reapplication of the patriarchal promise of progeny and land to their group (65:9), and by the parallelism that Yahweh would bring forth descendants from Jacob, and inheritors from Judah. Their contention that they are the true descendants of Yahweh's people is supported as well by the application to their group of two key designations used by Second Isaiah for the restored Israel, "my servant," and "my chosen."

In 45:4 Yahweh summons Cyrus to saving action "for the sake of my servant Jacob, and Israel my chosen." Again in 42:1 he introduces his servant: "Behold, my servant, whom I uphold, my chosen, in whom my soul delights," as also in 41:8: "But you, Israel, my servant, Jacob, whom I have chosen . . . " (cf. also 41:9; 44:21; 49:3). It is obvious that the prophetic group is identifying itself with the servant, the chosen, who according to Second Isaiah is to be recipient of and agent in Yahweh's final redemptive act, an identification which we observed earlier in 61:1-3 where it functions to legitimize the mission of the visionary group. But once again borrowing from the prophetic tradition is accompanied by adaptation to an altered situation, for no longer are "my servant" and "my chosen" applied to the entire nation, but they are narrowed to a small circle of faithful in the midst of an Israel whose leaders oppress them; hence the change from the collective singular to the plural form of these words. Thus even the borrowing of technical terms and the alteration in the form and application of those terms take their place alongside the transformation of prophetic genres and the mutation in eschatological modes of expression as indicators of the development which we have been tracing within the post-exilic community. The glorious promises of Second Isaiah which applied to the servant Israel have been narrowed to a small segment within Israel, and the classical forms of the judgment and salvation oracles have been fused to account for the new division within the people.

Verse 10 supplements the promise of descendants and possession of Zion with an idyllic picture of a transformed world which will provide the paradisiacal setting for the restored people. This transformation is made possible only by the preceding judgment on the wicked and adumbrates the changes in the natural sphere which come to characterize much of the late apocalyptic literature as the dualistic worldview of myth exerts its influence upon the earlier eschatology of the prophets. It will be the peaceful habitation of "my people who seek me."

We are reminded of the harsh narrowing of the restoration hope again by the use of terminology, for the promise can no longer be given to "my people," meaning the whole nation, but the term must be qualified, limiting the promise to "my people who seek me." And immediately the rest of the *'am* must be accounted for with a juxtaposed word of judgment (vv. 11-12). They are the ones "who have abandoned Yahweh, who have forgotten my holy mountain," in contrast to the "inheritors of my mountain," "my people who seek me" in verses 9-10. The two factions thus contrasted are identical with those met repeatedly in this material, and the burning issue is again the prostitution of the cult. The adherents of the defiled cult have abandoned Yahweh, have "forgotten my holy mountain" through their cultic aberrations, and the aberrations are again symbolized by pagan abominations (v. 11b). The sentence of judgment follows in verse 12, together with a supporting indictment which again stresses that it is no fault of Yahweh that conditions are as they are, for he has been actively calling, but the apostates would not hear, but rather choose what displeased Yahweh. As comparison with the use of *bahar* ("choose") and *ḥāpaṣ* ("delight") in 66:3-4 indicates, this passage refers to the illegitimate cultic practices which they have elected to follow.

In verses 13-15 a section interweaves the salvation and judgment elements of the first half of the oracle as tightly as the warp and woof in the loom. It demonstrates that those two elements are inseparable in this new type of prophetic genre, justifying the designation *salvation-judgment oracle.* The particular nature of the blessings and curses comprising this section is significant against the community background discernible behind the Third Isaiah material: represented in the contrasts eat/go hungry, drink/go thirsty, rejoice/be put to shame, joy of heart/sadness of heart, curse/new name, is a "turning of the tables" in the eschaton, when the faithful prophetic group oppressed by the apostates would be vindicated and blessed, while the tormentors would receive their just deserts. This series of contrasts delineates most graphically the social upheaval tearing into the fabric of the Judahide community of the late sixth century.

Verse 15 indicates that in that new age to come, while the apostates will leave their name as a curse, Yahweh's servants will be called by a new name. We have noticed above[94] how this tradition repeatedly associates the time of fulfillment with Yahweh's giving a new name to the elect. As 63:16 indicated, normative Israel and Abraham did not acknowledge the prophetic group, meaning that they could be restored to their rightful inheritance only under completely altered circumstances. This fact is brought out here in several different ways: first, by the "turning of the tables" implied by the blessings and curses in verses 13–15, next by the new name to be given to the elect in the eschaton (15c), then by the mention that "the former troubles will be forgotten" (16c); all indicating that a new era will replace the old, and in that new era, the hardships of the old, the oppression of the majority, the scorn and ridicule, the hunger and anguish, in a word, "the former troubles," utterly will be forgotten.[95] Finally, the most magnificent description of this new era follows in verses 17–25: the old situation in which the defiled control the cult and oppress the faithful is replaced by new conditions in which the faithful are restored to Zion to live in peace, a passage of paramount importance for the study of the development of prophetic eschatology into apocalyptic eschatology. In this passage one of the cardinal doctrines of the apocalyptic literature finds its earliest clear formulation, the doctrine of world epochs. In the delineation of the new heavens and new earth which would replace the old, the influence of mythical dualism, with its disparagement of the old world order in favor of the new order which would replace it, reaches a high water point within early apocalyptic. It does not represent the end of the development of that doctrine, for later the two world epochs found here splinter into a multiplicity of different stages. Nor does it mark the beginning of the development of that doctrine, for which reason

94. See p. 93

95. These three descriptions of a new epoch with completely altered conditions lead in an unbroken way to the climactic expression of that new epoch in verses 17–25, further indication that it is wrong to sever that section from the preceding as a later apocalyptic addition, as Westermann (pp. 407–411) and most other commentators do.

we shall consider briefly its background in earlier prophecy before turning to the analysis of Is 65:17–25.

The formulation in chapter 65 of the concept of a new world epoch, where evil is eliminated from the human sphere by judgment and from the natural realm by a new creation, represents another case where the community behind the Third Isaiah material draws upon the tradition of Second Isaiah. For that great prophet of the exile gave the first classic expression to the idea that the restoration would introduce an act of Yahweh which would be so gloriously new that the old era of the past would be forgotten: "Remember not the former things, nor consider the things of old. Behold, I am doing a new thing; now it springs forth, do you not perceive it? I will make a way in the wilderness and rivers in the desert" (Is 43:18–19; cf. 48:6–7).[96] Here we find expressed the division of history into the era of the former things and the era of Yahweh's glorious new act which would supercede it. The contrast underscores how qualitatively superior to any former act Yahweh's new saving act would be. When we compare this bold statement with the reverence for the saving history of the past which forms the cornerstone of the pre-exilic cult, we gain a fair impression of the incredible impact which the catastrophic events of the last years of the Kingdom of Judah had upon the prophetic faith.[97] The source of the

96. Regarding "former things," cf. 41:22; 42:9; 43:9, 18; 46:9; 48:3; "things of old," 43:18; "new thing(s)," 42:9; 43:19; 48:6. Cf. C. R. North, "The 'Former Things' and the 'New Things' in Deutero-Isaiah," in *Studies in Old Testament Prophecy*, ed. H. H. Rowley (Edinburgh: T. and T. Clark, 1950), pp. 111–126, and B. W. Anderson, "Exodus Typology in Second Isaiah," in *Israel's Prophetic Heritage*, eds. B. W. Anderson and W. Harrelson (New York: Harper & Row, 1962), pp. 177–195, for a complete study of the frequent occurrences of the concepts *former things* and *new things* in Second Isaiah. Cf. also N. C. Habel, "'Yahweh, Maker of Heaven and Earth': A Study in Tradition Criticism," *JBL* 91 (1972): 334–336.

97. Gerhard von Rad observes that Is 43:16–19 contains words "which the pious in particular must have felt to contain an element of blasphemy" (*Old Testament Theology* II, tr. D. M. G. Stalker [New York: Harper & Row, 1965], p. 249). Israel was being admonished to concentrate so intently on Yahweh's new act of salvation that the former things, the events of the saving history from the promise to Abraham to the exodus and on through the monarchy, i.e., the events which formed the heart of Israel's cultic confessions, should no longer be remembered! This can only mean that for Second Isaiah an epoch had come to an end. The destruction of the temple and the exile which resulted from Israel's history of sin had placed a caesura in the history of Yahweh's relation to his people. The events before that caesura were no longer to be remembered, for they had led to destruction. To be anticipated instead were the events of the future, which would lead to salvation. Von Rad remarks, "Never before had a prophet so sharply

incipient dualism which underlies the division of world history into epochs in Isaiah 65 stems from two aspects of Second Isaiah's message: his contrast between the old and the new born of the catastrophic events of the early sixth century, and his in-depth borrowing of motifs from the cosmogonic myth intended to glorify Yahweh over his rivals and to celebrate his unlimited power to save. For once the contrast between old and new was related to the conflict myth, resulting in an equation between the chaos monster and the faithful community's enemies of the past and present, the seed was planted which would mature later into the full-blown concept that the period of the past down to the present represented an epoch tainted with evil, which, like the dragon, would have to be destroyed and replaced by a new world.

Second Isaiah can thus be seen as providing the background for the dualism and the division of history into epochs found in rudimentary form in Is 65:16c–25. But the latter represents a very significant development beyond Second Isaiah, who utilized the dualism and division into epochs to draw attention to the profound significance of events taking place within the context of plain history.[98]

---

marked off the inauguration of the eschaton, nor so strictly dissociated it from all Jahweh's previous actions in history" (p. 248). Is 43:18–19 brings us to the threshold of the apocalyptic doctrine of world epochs, the former epoch being one of destruction, the latter being a glorious era of salvation (cf. Ph. P. Harner, "Creation Faith in Deutero-Isaiah," *VT* 17 [1967]: 303–304). The development of this doctrine and its underlying dualism would be greatly abetted in the prophetic tradition once Second Isaiah's metaphorical use of mythic motifs yielded among his disciples to a more literal application of the conflict myth to the situation of the post-exilic prophetic community.

98. A study of the uses of *bārā'* ("create") in Second Isaiah exemplifies how carefully that prophet moored his use of cosmic and "creation" imagery to the events of history. In bold paeans of praise, he could celebrate the God who created the cosmic hosts (40:26), the ends of the earth (40:28), darkness and light (45:7), who stretched out the heavens (45:12), but in each of these cases the celebration of the cosmic acts of Yahweh is related to the historical events which would inaugurate Israel's salvation (see C. Stuhlmueller, "The Theology of Creation in Second Isaias," *CBQ* 21 [1959]: 447–451). Thus *bārā'* can also refer to the historical event of the exodus which Yahweh creates (41:20). 45:8 illustrates how in Second Isaiah Yahweh's creative acts in the natural realm and the historical are inseparably fused.

In Third Isaiah *bārā'* occurs in 57:19 and in our present passage (65:17–18). In 65:17 an archaic liturgical formula (Gen 14:19; Ps 115:15; 134:3; 121:2; 124:8; 146:5, 6a; see Habel, "Yahweh," pp. 321–337) is remolded, partly on the basis of Second Isaiah's reapplication (*ōseh* > *bōrē*) and partly on the basis of the heightened eschatology of the followers of Second Isaiah. The formula no longer recalls Yahweh's creative act of the past, but announces: "for now I create *new* heavens and a *new* earth." That this heightened eschatology which moved in the direction

Tying together the old epoch and the new in one historical continuum was the one historical entity Israel. For Second Isaiah lived at a time when Israel as a nation was still viewed as an object of Yahweh's saving activity. While the summons to forget the former things served to integrate the tragic events of 587 into Israel's interpretation of saving history and to accentuate the glory of the imminent new act, it implied neither a negation of the existing world as irredeemably evil nor an absolute break in the historical process. But for the disciples of Second Isaiah, a pessimistic view of historical realities led to the belief that such a break between the present evil age and the world to come was a necessary precondition for salvation. Historical continuity was no longer assured by a political entity Israel seen as object of Yahweh's saving acts on both sides of the division between past and future. The Israel of the past was an enemy of Yahweh; the Israel of the future was rent by schism.

To an increasing extent, as the community situation grew ever bleaker for the visionary group, the old era took on the character of utter corruption, which apparently was seen to permeate even the world of nature. The mythic dualism, dividing reality into good and evil epochs, was no longer confined to the role of underscoring the brilliance of the new act which Yahweh was about to perform. Rather the ontological equation, present era = evil, future era = good (limited to the chosen), was taken with increasing seriousness, for the visionary group could understand the present situation only as unmitigated evil, and had come to be completely disillusioned with the prospects of realizing its ideal program of restoration in the present world. Al-

---

of a dualistic worldview issues forth from the fountainhead of Second Isaiah's prophetic utterances is indicated by the echoing of the words of 43:18a in 65:17b*a* and by the likelihood that the source of the idea of the "new" creation is to be found in 43:19: *hinnî ʿōśeh ḥădāšā(h)* ("Now I am doing a new thing").

That the tension preserved in Second Isaiah between Yahweh's cosmic creative acts and his creative acts within the historical community is not completely dissolved in Third Isaiah—as it never would be, even in fully developed apocalyptic compositions—is recognized in the use of *bārāʾ* in 65:18b: "for now I create Jerusalem 'Rejoicing' and her people 'Gladness.'" The creative act of Yahweh is still related to the historical community, but unlike the case in Second Isaiah where it is developed with careful attention to specific events, agents, and circumstances, this relation seems to receive only token expression, lacking in specificity of application to actual historical conditions.

ready 59:15c–20 indicated the direction toward which they were forced to look for the hope of ultimate fulfillment of their ideal, toward a new, decisive act of Yahweh in which he would first eliminate the evil through destruction of the old order and then establish a new order of justice. Since the object of that saving act was no longer Israel as a whole, but only a faithful remnant, it is obvious that that act could no longer be delineated strictly within the context of plain history, but would increasingly be seen within the context of the cosmic-mythic sphere of the Divine Warrior.

Isaiah 65 makes even clearer the pattern discernible in Isaiah 59. The present world is evil, and is no suitable context for the realization of the prophetic hope. Forgiveness of Israel's sin and restoration of the nation in her former habitat are a possibility vitiated by the harsh realities. Evil has become too deeply rooted to allow for a purely historical restoration. Rather, the judgment sections of 65:1–16 indicate that all the wicked in the land would have to be removed by a dramatic act of Yahweh: "I will commit you to the sword, and all of you shall succumb to the slaughter" (v. 12a). Nor is the evil limited to the human sphere alone, but has even penetrated the world of nature; ethical dualism has begun to lapse into ontological dualism. The creation myth used by Second Isaiah to heighten the significance of Yahweh's new historical act here is largely released from an historical context, and viewed within the mythic framework as an end in itself. In the eschaton Yahweh will not only purge the human sphere, but will also "create new heavens and a new earth." In the context of a very bleak historical situation, the danger has become very great that Israel's historical interpretation of divine intervention will dissolve under the pressure of myth. The disparagement of the present order as unmitigated evil and the promise of a new creation threaten to dissolve the dialectic that earlier prophets had maintained between the primordial events and the historical events of the present (e.g., Is 51:9–11), events which were seen to be typologically related but never equated. Here the primordial events threaten to merge with the eschatological events in the timeless "now" of the cult. The salvation of myth, construed as flight from the historical realm of change to the eternal repose of the divine sphere, exudes its powerful appeal anew as a weary circle of visionaries longs for a new creation which would supplant an old era of decay with a new era of shalom.

The essential characteristics of apocalyptic eschatology are drawn together into a coherent whole in Isaiah 65: the present era is evil; a great judgment separating the good from the evil and marking the crossroads between the present world and the world to come is imminent; a newly created world of peace and blessing ordained for the faithful lies beyond that judgment. These teachings of world epochs, universal judgment, and a modified dualism are the basic components of later apocalyptic eschatology. To be sure, they will be elaborated extensively, the world epochs developing into a highly complex system, the judgment becoming universal and finally cosmic, the dualism becoming more radical. But the important fact is that, already at the end of the sixth century, the basic schema of apocalyptic eschatology has evolved in Israel and that the whole development is perfectly comprehensible within the history of Israel's own community and cult. Hasty recourse to late Persian influence is therefore unnecessary and unjustifiable in the search for the origins of the basic eschatology of Jewish apocalyptic.

The picture of the new heavens and new earth which Yahweh will create to replace the realm tainted by the defiled cult stands in unmistakable continuity with the program of restoration in Isaiah 60–62. To be sure, a tendency which was only inchoate in that program is here nearly full blown, the tendency to elevate the restoration hope to a realm whose connections to the events of plain history become extremely tenuous. Although the picture of a restored Jerusalem, which in Second Isaiah was firmly tied to the historical realm, and in Isaiah 60–62 still was restrained by historical moorings, has here largely been cut loose from the historical sphere, nevertheless the basic underlying hopes remain those expressed by Second Isaiah and Isaiah 60-62. Central to that hope is the restoration of Jerusalem to its former glory (v. 18//52:7–10; 60:1-17). Her people will live securely in joy and peace (v. 19//35:8-10; 45:17; 51:3, 11; 60:15-18) free from the fear of enemy attack (vv. 21-22//51:22f; 54:15-17; 60:12, 14). Her children will be abundant and blessed (v. 23//54:1-3; 60:21-22) and will enjoy the fruit of their labors (vv. 21-22//62:8), and in stark contrast to the present defiled cult (vv. 1, 12) the future cult will be one in vital relationship to Yahweh (v. 24//60:7; 61:6).

The basic hopes of the prophetic circle thus remained in essence the same from the time shortly after the ministry of Second Isaiah to the period of oppression represented by the present oracle. But the context within which the fulfillment was to occur had shifted from the context of the real historical events of the nation Israel—both within her community and with foreign nations—to a context which seems detached from participation in the political order. The effort to relate the activity of the deity to the events of plain history has been abandoned. Myth has provided a means of envisioning the restoration on a plane insulated against the frustrations of an historical order which had demonstrated itself to the visionaries to be completely hostile. Though the essence of the prophetic promise is thus retained, the relinquishment of the task of interpreting the prophetic message and the corresponding vocation of the chosen people within the historical context heralds the death of prophecy and the birth of apocalyptic eschatology.

F. CONTROVERSY OVER THE BUILDING OF THE TEMPLE AND EXPULSION FROM THE CULT (66:1-16)

There is little agreement among scholars concerning the division of chapter 66 into original units. Duhm, Elliger, Volz, and Westermann find a number of separate units.[99] Kissane sees verses 1-16 as a unity,[100] while Torrey regards the entire chapter as a single composition.[101] To begin with

99. Duhm, (pp. 481-482): vv. 1-4, 5-11, 12-17, 18-22, 23-24. Elliger, *Einheit* (pp. 36 ff): vv. 1-4, 5-11, 12-16, 17-24. Volz (p. 288): vv. 1-2, 3-4 + 17, 5-6, 7-16 + 18-24. Westermann (pp. 362 ff): vv. 1-2, 3-4, 5, 6-16, 18-24.

100. E. Kissane, *The Book of Isaiah*, vol. 2 (Dublin: Browne and Nolan, 1944), *ad loc.*

101. Torrey, pp. 471-472.

the area of optimal agreement, the majority of scholars seem correct in judging that verses 17–24 are to be interpreted separately from the preceding. We are dealing here with a level of tradition found also in 56:1–8. We suggest that when the visionaries of a period later than the time of origin of the oracles in Third Isaiah collected and redacted those oracles, they added a framework consisting of 56:1–8 and 66:17–24. A clue to the period of this redactional activity may be offered by thematic similarities tying these two passages to Zechariah 14 (especially verses 20–21), a composition written from the visionary perspective probably between 475 and 425 (cf. below, Chapter IV, H).

We are unable, however, to concur with the scholars who go on to divide verses 1–16 into four or five separate units, for underlying that atomizing tendency is the application of pre-exilic norms to determine the length of oracles coming from a later period. On the basis of those pre-exilic norms, the major criterion for dividing the material is the distinction between salvation and judgment oracles. For example, a line is usually drawn between verses 4 and 5, where the discourse moves from a sentence of judgment upon the apostates to a word of comfort and salvation to "those who tremble at his word." But as we have recognized in chapters 58, 59, and 65, and as we shall note again in 56:9–57:13, the prophetic oracle during this period has been developing a unique form, the chief characteristic of which is precisely this rapid oscillation between salvation and judgment words (e.g., 65:7–8, 10–11, 13–15; 56:12–57:1; 57:13b–c). It is impossible to regard these alternations as the result of secondary redactionary activity, as proven by verses like 65:13–15 and 66:14b. In the face of such abundant evidence that the prophetic genres have been developing in new directions, it seems best to approach the question of delimiting units on the basis of post-exilic evidence rather than pre-exilic models.

In this approach to the question of delimitation, the balance of probability favors viewing verses 1-16 as a closely knit unit. Verses 1-4 constitute a prophetic indictment and sentence against an allegedly defiled group which is building a temple. At the heart of that attack is inserted a contrasting word of salvation to the one "who trembles at my word" (v. 2b). After the sentence against the apostates in verse 4 the discourse suddenly returns in 5 to those "who tremble at his word." In keeping with the pattern of the salvation-judgment oracle, this word of comfort immediately reverts to a word of judgment against the apostates. The remainder of the oracle develops further the two elements of salvation and doom; verse 6 judgment; verses 7-13 salvation and comfort; verse 14 again interweaves the salvation of the preceding verses with the judgment which follows in verses 15-16. The movement of the entire oracle is very effective as it interweaves the harsh attack against the offenders with words of comfort to those suffering persecution. A very effective climax—reminiscent of the climax in 59:15b-20—is reached in verses 15-16 with Yahweh the Warrior coming in a dreadful theophany to execute judgment. As comparison of the end of verse 6 with the last part of 14 indicates, this theophany is the event toward which the whole oracle has been striving. But before it could actually be portrayed, the rather extended section of comfort and salvation in verses 7-14 is necessary, in that the latter clarifies the ultimate purpose behind Yahweh's mighty demonstration of power, namely, the final deliverance of the oppressed community.

66: 1 Yahweh says this:
The heavens are my throne,
and the earth is my footstool.
What is this house which you would build for me,
and what is this throne dais?
2 All of these things my hand has made,
and all of these things are mine.
But upon this one I will look, the humble,
who is broken in spirit and trembles at my word.
3 Who slaughters an ox and kills a man,
who sacrifices a lamb and breaks a dog's neck,
who presents an offering and (offers) swine's blood,
who burns incense and blesses an idol;
Surely these have chosen their own ways,
they have taken delight in their abomination;
4 so I in turn will choose hardships for them,
and will bring what they dread upon them.
For I called, but no one would answer,
I spoke but they would not hear:
they did what I consider evil,
what displeases me, that they chose.
5 Hear the word of Yahweh,
you who tremble at his word.
Your brethren say, who hate you,
and thrust you out for the sake of my name:
"Let Yahweh display his glory that we may see!"
But I will make you rejoice, while they shall be confounded.
6 Listen! An uproar from the city,
a shout from the temple;
the voice of Yahweh paying in full
due reward to his enemies.
7 Before she went into labor
she bore a son,
before labor pains came upon her
she brought forth a boy.
8 Who has ever heard anything like this,
who has ever seen such a thing?
Can a land be born in one day,
is a nation brought forth in a moment?
For no sooner was Zion in labor
than she brought forth her sons.
9 Shall I open the womb and not bring forth? asks Yahweh,
or shall I who bring forth close the womb? asks your God.

	Text	Structure				Meter	Prosodic Units
66:1	כה אמר יהוה	rubric					
	שמים כסאי	a	b			5	b:b
	וארץ הדם רגלי	a_1	B			6	
	אי זה בית אשר תבנו לי	a	b	c		8	1:1
	ואי זה מקום מנוחתי	a	B			9	
2	כל אלה ידי עשתה	a	b	c		8	1:1
	והיו לי [a] כל אלה[ ]	c_1	b_1	a		7	
	ואל זה אביט אל עני	a	b	a_1		8	1:1
	נכה רוח וחרד על דברי	a_2	A			10	
3	שוחט שור מכה איש	a	b	a_1	b_1	3:3	bb:bb:bb:bb
	זובח שה ערף כלב	a_2	b_2	a_3	b_3	3:3	
	מעלה מנחה דם חזיר	a_4	b_4	A		4:3	
	מזכיר לבנה מברך און	a_5	b_5	a_6	b_6	5:4	
	גם המה בחרו בדרכיהם	a	b	c		10	1:1::1:1
	בשקוציהם נפשם חפצה	c_1	a_1	b_1		10	
4	גם אני אבחר בתעלליהם	a_2	b	c_2		10	
	ומגורתם אביא להם	c_3	b_2	d		9	
	יען קראתי ואין עונה	a	b	c		8	1:1::1:1
	דברתי ולא שמעו	a_1	b_1	c_1		8	
	ויעשו [ ]רע בעיני	c_2	d	e		7	
	ב[ ]לא חפצתי בחרו		D	c_3		8	
5	שמעו דבר יהוה	a	b			6	b:b
	החרדים אל דברו		d	b_1		7	
	אמרו אחיכם שנאיכם	a	b	c		10	1:1
	מנדיכם למען שמי			c	d	8	
	יכבד יהוה ונראה	a	b	c		8	1:1
	ושמחתכם [b] והם יבשו	c_1	b_1	a_1		10	
6	קול שאון מעיר	a	b	c		5	b:b::b:b
	קול מהיכל	a		c_1		4	
	קול יהוה משלם	a	b_1	d		6	
	גמול לאיביו			e	f	6	
7	בטרם תחיל	a	b			4	b:b::b:b
	ילדה [ילד] [c]		b_1	C		4	
	בטרם יבוא חבל לה	a	B			6	
	המליטה זכר		B_1	c_1		5	
8	מי שמע כזאת	a	b			5	b:b
	מי ראה כאלה	a_1	b_1			6	
	היוחל ארץ ביום אחד	a	b	c		8	1:1
	אם יולד גוי פעם אחת	a_1	b_1	c_1		8	
	כי חלה גם ילדה	a	a_1			7	b:b
	ציון בניה		b	c		5	
9	האני אשביר ולא אוליד	a	b	b_1		9	1:1

10 Rejoice with Jerusalem,
be glad for her, all you who love her,
rejoice with her greatly
all you who mourn her!
11 That you may suck and be satisfied
from her consoling breast,
that you may savor with delight
from her full teat.
12 For thus says Yahweh:
Now I am sending prosperity to her like a river,
and like a rushing stream the glory of nations.
Like an infant you will be carried on the hip,
and upon the lap you will be fondled;
13 like a son comforted by his mother,
so I will comfort you,
and in Jerusalem you will be comforted.
14 At the sight your heart will rejoice,
and your bones will flourish like the grass.
It will be known that Yahweh is with his servants,
but his wrath is with his enemies.
15 For Yahweh is about to come in fire,
and his chariots will be like the hurricane;
to pay back his anger in scorching heat,
and his threat with flames of fire.
16 For Yahweh will execute judgment with fire,
and with his sword against all flesh,
and those slain by Yahweh will be many.

TEXTUAL NOTES

a) Reading the possessive pronoun with LXX, which apparently was lost from the Hebrew by haplography.

b) Reading ושמחתכם instead of בשמחתכם, since the conjecture of Torrey (p. 473) restores sense and metric structure.

	יאמר יהוה	rubric					
	אם אני מוליד ועצרתי	a_1	b_2	b_3		9	
	אמר אלהיך	rubric					
10	שמחו את ירושלם	a	B			8	1:1::b:1
	וגילו בה כל אהביה	a_1	b	c		9	
	שישו אתה משוש	a_2	b_1	d		6	
	כל מתאבלים עליה		C	b_2		8	
11	למען תינקו ושבעתם	a	b	c		8	1:b::1:b
	משד תנחמיה		d	e		6	
	למען תמצו והתענגתם	a	b_1	c_1		10	
	מזיז כבודה		d_1	e_1		5	
12	כי כה אמר יהוה	rubric					
	הנני נטה אליה כנהר שלום	a	b	c	d	11	1:1
	וכנחל שוטף כבוד גוים		C	D		9	
	[כ]ינקת[d] על צד תנשאו	a	b	c		9	1:1::1:1:1
	ועל ברכים תשעשעו		B	c_1		9	
13	כאיש אמו תנחמנו	a_1	d	c_2		10	
	כן אנכי אנחמכם		d_1	$\acute{c}_2$		8	
	בירושלם תנחמו		B	$\acute{c}_2$		10	
14	וראיתם ושש לבכם	a	b	c		9	1:1
	ועצמותיכם כדשא תפרחנה	c_1	d	b_1		10	
	נודעה יד יהוה את עבדיו	a	b	c		10	1:1
	וזעמ[ו] [e]את איביו		b_1	c_1		7	
15	כי הנה יהוה באש יבוא	a	b	c		9	1:1
	וכסופה מרכבתיו		b_1	D		8	
	להשיב בחמה אפו	a	b	c		8	
	וגערתו בלהבי אש		c_1	B		8	
16	כי באש יהוה נשפט	a	b	c		7	1:1:1
	ובחרבו את כל בשר	a_1	D				
	ורבו חללי יהוה		e	d	b	7	

c) Emended on the basis of the parallel in v. 7b. The lines are very short at this point, producing a staccato effectively conveying the agitated excitement of the announcement.

d) Conjecture, on basis of the parallel in v. 13a, and the sense.

e) *Ad sensum.*

A very lively debate has been carried on in the commentaries over the question of the date of Isaiah 66, a debate focusing on the tantalizing but cryptic words in verse 1 directed against a house being built for Yahweh. Before enumerating the more plausible of the alternatives proposed, we shall ask whether considerations related to the form, meter, and prosodic structure of the oracle are able to shed any light on the date of this oracle relative to those already studied.

The meter of this poem is more chaotic than in any of the other poems thus far examined, suggesting a relatively late date. As for the internal structure, the prosodic unit in the first half of verse 4 illustrates the list-like sequence which we have discovered elsewhere in the Third Isaiah corpus.[102] The most striking feature of the poem, however, is its prosaic nature. A good proportion of the poem is written in bicola in an apparent archaizing effort, but the feel for the archaic parallel bicolon has been all but lost, as verses like 2b and 5 indicate. In those verses where tolerable parallel structure is maintained older models are visible directly below the surface (e.g., vv. 15–16). Meter and internal structure would thus place the poem at a point near chapter 65 in the typology.

Regarding the typology of prophetic genres, the poem falls at a point beyond chapter 59, but approximately coincident with chapter 65 and 57:3–13, inasmuch as it represents the salvation-judgment oracle in its fully developed form, with a rapid succession of juxtaposed salvation words and sentences of judgment. To these typological considerations will be added later another from a different level of inquiry, since the future hope of this oracle corresponds closely to that in chapter 65 on the continuum from prophetic to apocalyptic eschatology.

After noting where the typological considerations would place chapter 66 in a relative chronology, we now turn to enumerate briefly the most significant proposals made with regard to the absolute date of the oracle. Duhm (together

102. See pp. 118 and 143.

with those espousing his views, such as Karl Marti)[103] fits the chapter into his mid-fifth-century dating of Third Isaiah by interpreting verses 1-2 as an attack by the temple community on the Samaritans of Ezra's time who wish to build a rival to the Jerusalem temple. Sellin and Elliger,[104] on the other hand, draw on Ezr 4:2f and Hag 2:14 in arguing that the prophet is opposing the participation of the syncretistic people of the land in the rebuilding of the temple by the returned *gôlāh* in 520. Both of these proposals are purely hypothetical, resting upon very slim evidence from problematical sources like Ezra, and buttressed by speculative reconstruction. That the Haggai and Ezra material is germane to the problem is not to be denied. However, it must not determine the interpretation of 66:1ff, but must be interpreted independently of the latter before comparisons are drawn. Paul Volz[105] offers a corrective to this type of hypothetical reconstruction in arguing that one must remove the interpretation of this text from the bias of any Third Isaiah hypothesis. When one does this, he maintains, it becomes apparent that 66:1f repudiates temple building as such, and belongs to a tradition reaching from 2 Sam 7:5f through the Psalms 40, 50, 51, and 69, and finally culminating in John 4:24. While we would agree that the prophetic attack in 66:1f has a prehistory, we would maintain that a thorough study of the passage must include inquiry into the setting and function of *this particular* attack. Volz's suggestion that it *may* be related to the temple building of 520 does not grow out of or receive support from a careful inquiry into the community situation giving rise to this attack. The anti-temple impulse instead is seen as a floating motif which crops up at various points throughout the Old and New Testament. Westermann severs 66:1-2 even more completely from any historical setting by arguing that verses 1a, 2a, and 2b are actually an in-

103. Karl Marti, *Das Buch Jesaja,* Kurzer Hand-Commentar zum Alten Testament (Tübingen: J. C. B. Mohr [Paul Siebeck], 1900, pp. 406 ff.

104. Elliger, "Einheit," pp. 107-108; E. Sellin, *Geschichte des israelitisch-jüdischen Volkes II* (Leipzig: Von Quelle und Meyer, 1932), pp. 15 ff.

105. Volz, p. 288.

dependent psalm-word which cannot be connected to any actual setting in the community.[106] The approach of Volz and Westermann, while serving as a warning against subjective reconstruction based on tenuous evidence from other biblical sources, is itself guilty of ignoring the relation of the verse to its context, and of passing over the form-critical question of *Sitz im Leben* by leaving the passage in suspension. For while Westermann may be right in perceiving a psalm-word in 66:1–2, and while Volz is probably correct in recognizing an antecedent tradition behind these verses, it is equally important to note that when the prophets draw upon older sayings and tradition, they do so in addressing particular situations within their community. Thus it is not enough to identify the prehistory of the tradition being adopted; even more important is the inquiry into the use to which the prophet is putting the traditional material in his particular situation.

The present context of the anti-temple word is by no means bereft of clues to that historical situation. The most significant clue is found in the internal structure of the controversial verses 1 and 2 themselves: Yahweh declares his universal majesty, and then makes an inquiry which represents a harsh attack on those addressed, "What is this house which you would build for me . . .?" That this attack actually involves a rejection of the cult of those being addressed is made clear by the juxtaposed word of acceptance directed toward another group: "But upon this one I will look, the humble, who is broken in spirit and trembles at my word." The structure is based upon the contrast between two religious stances, the one centered around the formal worship of the temple, the other based on an attitude of humility and fear before Yahweh. This underlying dual structure is ubiquitous in chapters 58, 59, 65, and 56:9–57:13. For example: "Is this the fast that I choose, a day for a man to afflict himself, to bow down his head like a rush, lying down on sackcloth and ashes?//Is not this the

106. Westermann, pp. 412–414.

sort of fast that I choose, to loose the fetters of injustice. . .to share your bread with the hungry. . .?" (58:5-7). Or: "I spread forth my hands all day long to a stubborn and rebellious people . . . a people who provoke me to anger before my very Presence continually//Sharon will become a pasture for flocks . . . for my people who seek me" (65:2f, 10). Or: "For I called, but you would not answer//Before they call, I shall answer" (65:12, 24). Or: "Whom did you dread and fear when you were false to me, and did not remember me//.But he who takes refuge in me shall possess that land" (57:11, 13).

We could go on to give many more examples of this contrast between these two religious stances, one acceptable to Yahweh, one not, but the above should suffice to illustrate that the structure underlying 66:1-2 is precisely that underlying all of the salvation-judgment oracles in Third Isaiah, a structure reflecting a very definite situation in the community. In each case the prophetic spokesman announces Yahweh's rejection of the normative cult, and then balances his attack with a word of Yahweh's acceptance of the faithful minority. To draw—as Westermann does—upon psalms like 50 and 113 as evidence that the saying in 66:1-2 is independent of its immediate literary context and removed from any concrete polemic seems to be a reversal of sound methodology, for in contrast to such psalms, where the question of setting is patently a moot one, 66:1-2, in its context, offers very definite clues to the setting. Thus, if one wishes to bring psalms like 50 and 113 into the discussion, one might profitably inquire whether the Third Isaiah material may not clarify the origin of those psalms, rather than use the psalms to prove that 66:1-2 is a floating motif. That the visionary theology finding expression in 66:1f is thoroughly at home in the message of Second Isaiah and his school is illustrated by passages like 40:26; 57:15; and 63:15.

Rather than base the interpretation of the beginning of this oracle on speculative reconstructions from outside evidence on the one hand, or on the other treat it in absolute isolation as a theological impulse passing through the centuries and cropping up like a Platonic form in Samuel, the Psalms, or the Gospel of John, we believe the soundest approach is that of interpreting 66:1–2 in the context of the present oracle and of the other oracles of Third Isaiah because of the close affinity of the internal structure of these two verses with the other oracles of Third Isaiah. For the internal structure common to these several oracles betrays a common communal origin, a common struggle between the hierocratic party and the visionary group for control of the restoration cult. Naturally we are not able to advance irrefutable proof that each of these oracles belongs to the same community struggle as it unfolded over a period of some thirty years. However, when the cumulative evidence from prosodic analysis, form criticism, and the study of the development of ideas all points to a common matrix, sobriety recommends that both speculative hypothesis from tenuous outside evidence and atomistic interpretation which isolates the passage from all historical context be eschewed in favor of the contextual-typological approach which we have chosen.

After thus discerning on the basis of the Third Isaiah material itself that we are dealing in chapter 66 with the struggle between the prophetic group carrying on the tradition of Second Isaiah and the hierocratic group controlling the cult, we can legitimately proceed to inquire whether other biblical sources stem from or preserve a record of this same struggle. Fortunately, the activities of the hierocratic group are better preserved for the period of the temple rebuilding than for any other period in the sixth or fifth centuries. Thus ample material is available for the purposes of reconstructing the theology of the temple party being opposed in Isaiah 66.[107]

On the basis of comparison with other sources, especially the books of Haggai and Zechariah, Isaiah 66 can be dated with confidence circa 520 B.C., that is, in the period of the

107. See Chapter IV.

rebuilding of the temple. Although the typological considerations dealing with prosodic structure, genres, and the development of apocalyptic eschatology which we have discussed in connection with each of the above oracles did not yield absolute dates for those oracles, they did establish a rough relative chronology. Isaiah 60–62 was seen to stem from a period not far removed from the height of Second Isaiah's career, when the struggle within the community had not yet developed, and the hope of the prophetic group still focused on the restoration of the historical community on the basis of their ideal program. The tension and finally the bitter struggle which can be traced through Isaiah 63:7–64, 58, 59, 65, and 66, as manifested in the content of the oracles as in the development of the salvation-judgment oracle and the eschatology, require a fairly lengthy span of time during which the hierocratic party, after having returned from exile (ca. 538), gained complete control of the cult, forcing the prophetic group increasingly into the position of an oppressed minority. This relative chronology synchronizes well with the dating of Isaiah 66 at the time of the temple building by the normative cult in 520.

The most energetic champion of the temple party's cause known to us through the surviving literature was Haggai. The fact that he was a prophet building his message upon a fervent eschatology serves warning against a simplistic caricature of all supporters of the hierocratic program as unprophetic. Indeed, aspects of Haggai's prophecy come close to the spirit of Second Isaiah and his early disciples (as expressed in Isaiah 60-62): he looks for the imminent restoration of the community (2:6), to be accompanied by the influx of the tribute of the nations (2:7–9). Moreover, Haggai's central concern with the rebuilding of the temple is not absent from the visionary program of restoration (cf. 60:13). On the basis of these facts alone one might expect to find Haggai in close alliance with the visionary group expressing its aspirations in Isaiah 56–66. Deeper probing, however, leads us to quite the opposite conclusion. In Is

66:1–2 we have a direct repudiation of the temple building campaign of Haggai: "What is this house which you would build for me?"[108]

This harsh repudiation of one prophetic witness by another fits into the phenomenon common in Israel from the time of Micaiah ben Imlah's confrontation with the two hundred court prophets of Ahab to Jeremiah's continuous struggles with Hananiah and the other "false" prophets: inner-prophetic controversy. In Haggai the visionary followers of Second Isaiah encountered a figure placing the prophetic office in the service of a restoration program with the following characteristics: (1) as study of Haggai and Zechariah indicates, it is a program developing the features of Ezekiel 40–48; (2) Zerubbabel, scion of David and appointee of the Persians, was to be the royal head of the restored community, a plan greeted with messianic enthusiasm;[109] (3) Joshua, of the Zadokite priesthood, was to be the high priest. This specific restoration program, applying carefully the details of Ezekiel 40–48, was offered by Haggai as the key which would unlock the heavens and usher in the eschaton long awaited by the despairing post-exilic community. Ezekiel had prophesied the blessings of the restoration era in the following terms:

I will send down the showers in their season; they shall be showers of blessing. And the trees of the field shall yield their fruit, and the earth shall yield its increase, and they shall be secure in their land . . and I will provide for them prosperous plantations so that they shall no more be consumed with hunger in the land. . . . (34:26–29)

108. Cf. J. Smart, "A New Interpretation of Isaiah 66:1–6," *The Expository Times* 46 (1935): 420 ff., and *History,* pp. 281 ff., whose hypothesis of the authorship of Isaiah 56–66 by Second Isaiah necessitates his dating the chapter circa 538 on the basis of the allusion in Ezr 3:8ff to an earlier attempt to rebuild the temple. His hypothesis causes him to deal with the Haggai material in a forced manner, identifying Haggai as spokesman of a religious point of view similar to that criticized years earlier by Second Isaiah (66:1ff). If one concludes that Haggai's temple theology is of the type which Is 66:1ff is attacking, how much more natural to relate both Haggai and Isaiah 66 to the same period, i.e., 520.

109. In Hag 2:23 the technical royal terms *'abdî* ("my servant," cf. 2 Sam 3:18, Ezek 34:23–24 and 37:24) and *ḥôtām* ("signet ring," cf. Jer 22:24), together with the verb *bāhar* ("choose"), draw attention to the messianic overtones of the book. The messianic themes in Zechariah 1–8 will be considered later.

But because the people had not carried out Ezekiel's temple program, the blessings bound up with the temple[110] were countermanded by the covenant curses:

You have looked for much, and lo, it came to little . . . Why?. . . .Because of my house that lies in ruins. . . .Therefore the heavens above you have withheld the dew, and the earth has withheld its produce. And I have called for a drought upon the land and the hills, upon the grain, the new wine, the oil, upon what the ground brings forth, upon men and cattle, and upon all their labors. (Hag 1:9–11)

In the face of this curse, Haggai proclaims his key in no uncertain terms: ". . .build the house, that I may take pleasure in it and that I may appear in my glory, says the Lord" (1:8). The results will be dramatic:

For thus says the Lord of hosts: Once again, in a little while, I will shake the heavens and the earth and the sea and the dry land; and I will shake all nations, so that the treasures of all nations shall come in, and I will fill this house with splendor, says the Lord of hosts. The silver is mine, and the gold is mine, says the Lord of hosts. The latter splendor of this house shall be greater than the former, says the Lord of hosts; and in this place I will give prosperity, says the Lord of hosts. (Hag 2:6–9)

It is remarkable how the oracles we have preserved from Haggai are preoccupied with the removal of the curse and the ushering in of the blessings tied to the temple program: "Pray now, consider what will come to pass from this day onward. Before a stone was placed upon a stone in the temple of the Lord, how did you fare?" (2:15, 16aα). Then he repeats the curses: drought, blight, mildew, and hail ruining the grains and wines. But the turning point comes with the laying of the temple foundation:

Consider from this day onward, from the twenty-fourth day of the ninth month. Since the day that the foundation of the Lord's

110. "And on the banks, on both sides of the river, there will grow all kinds of trees for food. Their leaves will not wither nor their fruit fail, but they will bear fresh fruit every month, because the water for them flows from the sanctuary. . . ." (Ezek 47:12).

temple was laid, consider: Is the seed yet in the barn? Do the vine, the fig tree, the pomegranate, and the olive tree still yield nothing? From this day on I will bless you. (Hag 2:18-19)

There is no mistaking the fact that Haggai's oracles comprise a powerful propaganda piece for the official restoration program presided over by Zerubbabel and Joshua. When the restoration hopes of the visionary followers of Second Isaiah are contrasted with the program developed by Haggai, the inner-prophetic controversy which ensued is very understandable: (1) If our earlier arguments are correct, that Ezekiel 40-48 and Isaiah 60-62 document rival programs of restoration from the exilic period, and that Haggai was the energetic spokesman of the former, whereas the Third Isaiah group built their hopes upon the latter, the conflict between the oracles of Haggai and Isaiah 66 is already plausible. (2) In contrast to the detailed realism of Ezekiel's program, the visionaries delineated the restoration in very vague terms, attributing all to Yahweh's glorious acts rather than spelling out particular historical details. How would they react to Haggai's word that Zerubbabel was the "servant" and "signet" ring appointed by Yahweh, a prophecy directly contradicting Jeremiah's prophecy in 22:24-30?[111] It seems likely that they would react wrathfully to this as further evidence of the hierocratic attempt to supplant Yahweh's restoration plan with their own, a reaction exacerbated by the fact that Zerubbabel's appointment by the Persians could be construed as the attempt to replace Yahweh's sovereign guidance over the restoration with the patronage of an alien power. Whether Jeremiah's curse against Jehoiakim and his offspring would have added to their hostility toward Zerubbabel cannot be determined. (3) That the newly built temple would be presided over by a Zadokite priest would have irritated the sensitive feelings of the visionary group even more than Zerubbabel's messianic designation, for, as we have seen and shall continue to recognize, the visionaries of Third

111. See K. Baltzer, "Das Ende des Staates Juda und die Messias-Frage," *Studien zur Theologie der altestamentlichen Überlieferungen,* ed. R. Rendtorff and K. Koch (Neukirchen, Neukirchener, 1961), p. 38.

Isaiah look upon themselves as the legitimate heirs to the priesthood of the restoration temple; if our suggestion is correct that these visionaries included Levitical (Mushite) rivals of the Zadokites, the hostility seems even more inevitable.[112]

This contrast between the prophecy of Haggai and the position of the visionary followers of Second Isaiah leads us to discern a situation where the latter bristle in wrath in the face of an equation: "Build the house" and "I will give prosperity," an equation springing from a view of cultic orthopraxy which seems to threaten the doctrine of divine sovereignty at the heart of the visionary program. Was this not an attempt to force Yahweh's hand, exuding the same spirit found in the protest of the orthodox in Is 58:3: "Why do we fast, but you do not see?" The visionaries would have believed so, especially as the temple reform grew in popularity. Ezr 6:16 describes the celebration of the rebuilt temple and is perhaps accurate in depicting it as an extremely popular event among the populace. At that celebration the passover "was eaten by the people of Israel who had returned from exile, and also by everyone who had joined them and separated himself from the pollutions of the peoples of the land. . . ." To the visionary group, smarting under opposition and the frustration of their glorious restoration hopes, such a temple and restoration would have been a travesty of the true temple and community of Yahweh, built by a defiled priesthood and flooded by masses bent on inaugurating the eschaton by proving their acceptability through the Zadokite orthopraxy.

The question of whether the visionary minority's restoration cult would have assumed forms essentially different from those they now opposed is not a question which can be answered. The observation which we *are* able to make, however, is very plausible from a sociological point of view: The *actual* cult which undermines their own restoration plans they now oppose on the basis of their *ideal* vision of Yahweh worship. This response is in keeping with what we

112. See pp. 94-96.

can reconstruct of the situation. The normative party has already frustrated their plan for the restoration of Zion by removing them from any part in the leadership of the community. Now bolstered by a popular following resulting from the preaching of Haggai and Zechariah, that party is in a position to build their shrine upon the holy mountain which the visionaries considered their rightful inheritance. Already the visionaries have opposed the cultic practices and attitudes of the majority party, calling them defiled and aimed at inaugurating the eschaton on the basis of human initiative, and have posited an eschatological view of salvation inaugurated and achieved by Yahweh alone. In 520, the year of our present oracle, the battle comes to a head as the temple building gets under way. In the face of a claim that completion of the priestly temple program would be followed by the eschaton, the visionaries cry out in protest, reiterating their sentences of judgment against a defiled cult and restating their vision of Yahweh's act on their behalf.

Within the context of this struggle in the year 520 the protest in Isaiah 66:1–2 finds its elucidation: in a grandeur reminiscent of Second Isaiah, Yahweh points to the heavens and the earth which are his throne and footstool and then asks, "What is this house which you (plural) would build for me?"[113] Then in contrast to those who propose to build the temple, Yahweh singles out the one whom he accepts, "the humble, who is broken in spirit and trembles at my word," which, as 66:5 indicates, refers to the oppressed minority faithful to the prophetic tradition.

In no uncertain terms, the God of this oracle rejects the temple of the hierocratic party, bringing to a climax a century-long struggle between two concepts of salvation, that nurtured by a visionary tradition which placed sole emphasis on the great imminent acts of Yahweh and that promulgated by the temple priests which emphasized cultic

113. Placed alongside each other, Is 66:1 sounds very much like a direct answer to Hag 1:8:

bᵊnû habbāyit wəʾerṣeh bô wəʾekkabᵊdā	Build the house that I may take pleasure in it and appear in my glory.
ʾê zeh bayit ʾăšer tibnû lî	What is this house which you would build for me?

orthopraxy. For in marshaling this visionary perspective in their resistance to the temple program, the disciples of Second Isaiah are reiterating a position dating back to the Davidic monarchy when Nathan, after having been commissioned by Yahweh, goes to the king and asks: *ha'attāh tibneh lî bayit ləšibtî* ("Would you build me a house to dwell in?" [2 Sam 7:5b]). His query is echoed in the query of Yahweh in Isaiah 66:1: *ê zeh bayit 'ašer tibnû lî* ("What is this house which you would build for me?"). It seems possible that the allusion to the Nathan incident is intended as corroboration from ancient tradition for the prophetic group's attack. Between those two prophetic words against the temple from the tenth and the sixth centuries lies a long history of tension between prophet and temple cult. A few examples of this history are found in Am 5:21-24; Mi 3:12; and Is 1:10-11. This tension reaches a climax in Jer 7:1ff; 11:14f; 13:13; and 26:1ff. In Second Isaiah, the temple plays virtually no part in the restoration hope. Against the background of this prophetic tradition, it is understandable how the prophetic group following in the tradition of Second Isaiah could find justification to utter the rejection of the temple found in 66:1; the sanctuary has come under the control of a rival priestly party which they feel would perpetuate a temple just as defiled and idolatrous as that condemned by Jeremiah and rejected by Yahweh in the catastrophe of 587.

Immediately after this rejection of the temple, the prophetic oracle goes on to assail the sacrificial cult belonging to that temple. Verse 3 is intimately related to passages like 65:4-5 and 57:5-10, passages collecting images from the most shocking examples of pagan defilement and then equating these abominable practices with the cultic activities of the opposition group. The equation which is implied elsewhere is stated explicitly in the present oracle by juxtaposing the temple rite and the pagan practice with which it is compared.[114] Sacrifice of an ox in this cult is no better

114. Muilenburg, pp. 761-762, has argued that comparison between the temple and pagan practices is not intended, but rather the combining of the former with the latter is object of attack. But this interpretation is not defensible in light of the parallel structure of the poetry, or even on the basis of Hebrew syntax, according to which the meaning clearly is that of equating the two members. This is how it was interpreted by LXX, Vg, and 1QIsa^{a}.

than murder, sacrifice of a lamb than of a dog; offering of the *minhah* is equivalent to a libation of swine's blood, burning of incense to worshiping an idol. The condemnation is a very reckless one and is understandable only within the context of the bitter polemic which we have discerned mounting throughout Third Isaiah. The practices of the temple party are no less abominable than the most shocking of pagan rites! Though perhaps more extreme than any other attack in the canon, the tactic of assailing a rival cult by comparing it to pagan idolatry has a long history, indeed is the standard means by which such an attack is mounted. For example, the Mushites in Exodus 32 impugn the Aaronid priesthood by connecting it with Canaanite idolatry; or when the hierocratic party mounts its counterattack on the Levitical priests, it does so by charging that they went astray after their idols (Ezek 44:10). Of course the book of Jeremiah is replete with such allusions to archaic Canaanite practices.

Neither the new temple nor the cultic practices which will fill it will hasten the day of Yahweh, for the cult of the hierocratic group is not a cult which is derived from Yahweh. It is rather an illegitimate cult which has forcefully evicted Yahweh's true priests and seized Zion. The cult being attacked is not from Yahweh, but is a man-made abomination: "Surely these have chosen their own ways, they have taken delight in their adominations."

In chapters 57 and 58 Yahweh asks concerning the illegitimate cult: "Will these things appease me?" "Is such the fast that I choose?" In each case the query is answered with a scathing attack and threat of judgment. In the present oracle Yahweh again inquiries: "What is this house which you would build for me?" Again judgment follows the rejection of that cult: "So I in turn will choose hardships for them, and will bring what they dread upon them" (v. 4).

In the characteristic pattern of the salvation-judgment oracle the discourse suddenly switches in verse 5 to "you who tremble at his word," i.e., the faithful group, clinging in spite of oppression to the eschatological message of the prophets, which in verse 2b received the promise of Yahweh's favor. Again the conflict between them and their priestly oppressors is hinted at in the words of Yahweh which follow (see textual note "b"):

> Your brethren say, who hate you,
> and thrust you out for the sake of my name:
> "Let Yahweh display his glory, that we may see!"
> But I will make you rejoice, while they shall be confounded.

Underlying this passage seems to be the schism which in the sixth century came to cut so deeply into the post-exilic community, dividing Israelite against Israelite as visionaries and realists parted company. Not some foreign enemy is the threat to the faithful, but their very brethren, the priestly group in control of the cult; if our interpretation of this difficult verse is correct, it seems to reflect a point at which the hierocratic majority casts the visionaries out of the cult. Thus is consummated the fear expressed by the complaint in 63:16: "Though Abraham does not acknowledge us, and Israel does not regard us, you, Yahweh, are our Father. . . ."

Hinted at may be an historical event which greatly exacerbated the division in the community which is portrayed symbolically by the image of the grape cluster in 65:8, and which influences both the form of the salvation-judgment oracle and the perceptible shift from prophetic to apocalyptic eschatology during the last half of the sixth century. That event was the expulsion of a prophetic group from the official cult.[115] The underlying reason for that expulsion may be discerned in the jeering remark of the brethren: "Let Yahweh display his glory that we may see!" The target of this derision seems to be their eschatological fervor, a fervor expressed, for example, in their program of restoration in Isaiah 60–62 and in the apocalyptic message of 65:17–25. Although this text is not transparent enough to become the basis for an elaborate reconstruc-

115. Muilenburg, p. 764, notes that נדה "in later Talmudic usage acquired the technical meaning of excommunicate in reference to expulsion from the synagogue."

tion,[116] it is not unlikely that it reflects a point around 520 B.C. when the tension already seen inherent in the contrast between the programs of restoration of Ezekiel and the Second Isaiah school and increasing in later oracles, finally reached the breaking point.

The realists, regarding the restoration as assured by their orthopraxy, mock the visionaries who await Yahweh's victorious entry into Jerusalem to usher in a new and glorious age. Scoffing at such pie-in-the-sky dreaming, they cast the fanatics from the cult, so as to avert any hindrance which might delay their restoration plans. The division between the "servants" and the apostates which would be effected on the day of judgment according to the salvation-judgment oracle is apparently not purely the product of the prophetic group's imagination; for it is a division which has become a social reality as a result of their expulsion from the cultic community. To the visionaries the word of Yahweh must have seemed actively at work effecting the judgment of the divine prophecies in the very events they are experiencing. For in rejecting the eschatological message which taught that the future salvation could be initiated by Yahweh alone, the priestly group is placing itself under the condemnation of all efforts aimed at forcing Yahweh's hand.

"But I will make you rejoice, while they shall be confounded." The jeers of the skeptics are met by a terse salvation-judgment word, comparable to those in 65:13–15. The tables will be turned, and the threat will not wait long for fulfillment, for verse 6 announces the imminent judgment which will befall the wicked, while verses 7ff proclaim the salvation which awaits the faithful. Verse 6 is an announcement of battle which reverberates with a mood of excitement, as reflected by the thrice repeated *qôl* and the terse meter. Right at the heart of Israel's sickness, within the temple area which is now being defiled by the plans of the wicked, Yahweh as Warrior roars and renders recom-

116. Whether Torrey's conjecture is accepted, or whether the MT is read unchanged (as in RSV), the verse supports the hypothesis here proposed (see textual note "b").

pense to his enemies. Then immediately follows the eschatological word of promise to the faithful that their salvation will come just as swiftly as the judgment upon the wicked. For although their oppression at the hands of the apostates makes their present condition very grim, Yahweh would not cause a son to be conceived and then hinder its birth, and so after promising salvation to the faithful, he will not fail to fulfill this promise. The child will be born!

The metaphor of Zion miraculously and suddenly giving birth to a new nation emphasizes how abruptly the new era will arrive. As underscored by 65:17ff, the break between the old era of evil and the new era of blessing will be radical. Thus we notice here the same movement away from an eschatology firmly related to historical events toward an apocalyptic view emancipated from the restraints of historical contingencies. The new heavens and new earth of chapter 65 are equivalent to the "land which is to be born in a day," and the "nation brought forth in a moment." The break will be complete as the wicked are cut off by judgment, and the new nation is suddenly born, the nation of those faithful to the prophetic hope. It is a nation brought forth supernaturally and destined for a new paradisiacal realm, a realm which verses 12–14 indicate is untouched by the uncertainties of the political arena and unencumbered by Israel's former vocation of becoming involved in the destiny of other nations. The stubborn realism of the prophets by which they insisted upon relating the activity of Yahweh to an historical context is abandoned here as in chapter 65, for the future of the faithful is portrayed in the paradisiacal terms of prosperity flowing to Zion like a river, of her people being fondled like an infant, of their bones flourishing like the grass.

Verse 6 already intimated what 14b–16 now dramatically demonstrates, that the prophetic group is adopting a powerful traditional element which, in being applied to a community situation torn by upheaval, is abetting the development of prophetic eschatology in the direction of the mythic dualism of apocalyptic eschatology. That traditional element, as already seen in 59:15b–20, is the hymnic development of the Divine Warrior motif. Verse 14b sets the stage by referring to the judgment of Yahweh which will reverse the existing evil situation and thereby prepare for the new era of blessedness for the servants. It is expressed tersely in the now familiar form of the salvation-judgment word: "It will be known that the hand of Yahweh is with his servants, but his wrath is with his enemies." Then the Divine Warrior appears in verses 15–16, and his conflict is described in dramatic terms which illustrate vividly both the mythic background of the motif and the manner in which it is altering the nature of the prophetic group's eschatology. The hymn pictures Yahweh as the storm god familiar to ancient Near Eastern mythology. As Baal in the Ugaritic texts bears the epithet "rider of the clouds" (*rkb ʿrpt*), and Marduk (*Enūma eliš* IV:50) is described mounting the storm-chariot as he sets out to battle Tiamat, Yahweh too goes to battle with chariots "like the hurricane" (v. 15, cf. Am 1:34; Ps 18:9//2 Sam 22:9). The weapon of fire, produced by the lightning bolts carried in the quiver of the storm god (cf. *Enūma eliš* IV:39f; Nu 21:27–30; Ps 18:17ff//2 Sam 22:7ff; Ps 50:3; Dtn 33:2), is also borne by the Divine Warrior Yahweh as he goes forth to "execute judgment with fire" (v. 16).

When we view the oracle as a whole, we see clearly how this Divine Warrior motif, applied to the struggle of the prophetic group, became a significant factor in the development of apocalyptic eschatology. In a grim situation where the hopes for the historical fulfillment of their restoration plans had utterly collapsed, in a situation where the harsh realities of history denied them a part in the land they felt was rightfully theirs, they appealed to the Hero of the Conquest, the Divine Warrior Yahweh. But the ensuing historical victory, which in the Conquest period bound Israel's vision to the historical realm and thus firmly restricted the influence of the cosmic-mythic Divine Warrior motif to embellishment of what remained an historical worldview, could not be duplicated by the visionaries. Victories in the historical sphere were harshly denied them, and thus it is not surprising that they fell to a danger their ancestors had avoided: they borrowed the Divine Warrior motif not merely as an embellishment of an historical faith but rather as a new way of interpreting reality which ultimately would threaten to dissolve the dynamic dialectic maintained by Second Isaiah between history and myth. The effort to interpret divine events within the context of history would be abandoned in favor of awaiting an unmediated act of the Divine Warrior which would destroy the old evil order and introduce the new one.

Such a faith would emerge in a fully developed form only in a later period; yet the essential elements of apocalyptic, the world epochs, the universal judgment, and the dualism, are all nascent in the present chapter, as in chapter 65. For this oracle teaches that : (1) the present era is dominated by evil, vitiating all hope that the existing order can be redeemed; (2) a great judgment is imminent, in which Yahweh will commit his enemies to destruction, but will deliver those faithful to him; (3) beyond that judgment lies a new era of prosperity and blessing, when the evil world will be supplanted by a paradisiacal realm ordained for the faithful. At one notable point, the Divine Warrior Hymn in chapter 66 reveals an element bringing the prophetic eschatology even closer to apocalyptic than the oracles previously considered: "for Yahweh will execute judgment with fire, and with his sword *against all flesh*" (v. 16). The picture of judgment here enters the cosmic realm of the Divine Warrior even more fully than 59:15b-20, for Yahweh's judgment will encompass "all flesh." To separate this reference to universal judgment from the preceding as Westermann does[117] is arbitrary in the extreme, for it is precisely at this point in Israel's history where social upheaval has caused the classical division between Israel and the nations to retreat before a new spiritual division between the wicked and the righteous, and where the cosmic-mythic motif of the Divine Warrior has been introduced in an attempt to comprehend the new chaos, that one expects the inception of the concept of universal judgment along purely spiritual lines.

117. Westermann, p. 418.

One final element in this oracle becomes ubiquitous in later apocalyptic; to be sure, not absent even in early prophecy, it is the element of comforting an oppressed group which finds no ray of hope in the grim realities of this world.[118] The promise of an imminent intervention in which Yahweh would turn the tables, destroying utterly the oppressors and giving birth in an instant to an era of peace and prosperity for the faithful, served to comfort and encourage the prophetic community which was bitterly disillusioned because of the delay in the restoration promised by Second Isaiah. This function of comforting and consoling is seen clearly in the image of the sudden, miraculous birth of the new nation in the joyous hymn in verses 10–11 and in the promise in 12–14: "Like a son comforted by his mother, so I will comfort you. . . ."

G. THE CONFLICT GROWS ACRIMONIOUS (56:9–57:13)

The Torah in 56:1–8 must be separated from the following, for it represents a later level of tradition. We suggested earlier that it is part of a redactional framework added to the oracles of Third Isaiah when they were gathered into a collection. The division of the rest of chapters 56 and 57 is more difficult to determine. Westermann follows Ewald[119] and Volz in treating 56:9–12; 57:3–6; and 57:7–13a as pre-exilic compositions, since in each case the people as a whole, or the leaders as representatives of the people, are being addressed.[120] The argument is based on massive surgery of the text which is indefensible. First, 57:1–2 can be separated from 56:9–12 only if the contrast drawn between the wanton leaders and the righteous men who suffer because of their neglect is completely overlooked; but the contrast between leaders of the community and oppressed men of faith lies at the very heart of the Third Isaiah material. It is also central to the Second Zechariah material

118. Cf. Russell, *Apocalyptic*, pp. 17–18.

119. G. H. A. von Ewald, *The Prophets of the Old Testament*, IV, tr. J. F. Smith (Edinburgh: Williams and Norgate, 1880), pp. 321 ff.

120. Westermann, pp. 316–325.

which will be studied in Chapter IV, material which is closely related to Third Isaiah. For example, Zech 10:1-2 attacks the "teraphim" and the diviners who mislead the people. "Therefore they (the people) withdraw like sheep, they are afflicted for want of a shepherd." 56:9-57:2 thus must be treated as a whole, a conclusion strengthened by the rhyming, refrain-like sequence binding the unit together (vv. 56:10, 11 and 57:1):

lōʾ yādāʿū hābîn
lōʾ yādāʿū habîn
bəʾên ʾîš mēbîn

Further, it seems impossible to separate 57:3-6 from 7-13, for those verses together comprise a single attack on a cult which is equated with Canaanite paganism. Finally, at the end of that composition, verse 13b is often the victim of the exegete's scalpel.[121] What underlies this surgical procedure is the old prejudice tracing back to Duhm that judgment and salvation words never appear together in original prophetic units. We have sought to prove, on the basis of verses like 65:13-14, the untenability of this judgment in the case of the Third Isaiah material, material in which the juxtaposition of salvation and judgment words is the single most noteworthy formal characteristic. Moreover, internal evidence corroborates this conclusion that verse 13b cannot be removed from the oracle, since the ironic treatment of the root *nḥl* (inherit/wadi) in verse 6 is picked up and resolved in 13b.

After recognizing in 56:9-57:2 and 57:3-13 two prophetic compositions which cannot be broken down into smaller units, we ask what is the relation between the two. The evidence is not unambiguous. On the one hand 56:9-57:2 seems to constitute a complete composition: the beasts (foreign nations) are summoned to devour (v. 9), and then an indictment against the different leaders of the community furnishes the explanation of why the land is vulnerable to foreign attack; the leaders have neglected their duties and have sought only to satisfy their own lust

121. Ibid., p. 325.

and greed (vv. 10–11). Verse 12 invokes a proverb to characterize their uneschatological philosophy of *carpe diem*, sardonically introduced with the same word used in verse 9 to summon the beasts. Then the attention turns to the victim of this deplorable social disintegration, the righteous man who dies and finds peace only in the grave (57:1–2). Although this lament forms a fitting conclusion, 57:3 begins with the same formula (*wə'attem*) used in 65:11, 13, and 14 as a transition between a salvation word to the faithful and a judgment word to the wicked. In those cases the transition was definitely internal. These two pieces of evidence seem best reconciled if one concludes that 56:9–57:2

56: 9 All you beasts of the field,
come to devour,
all you beasts of the forest.
10 My watchmen are all blind,
they have no understanding,
they are dumb dogs,
they cannot bark;
the seers are reclining,
they love to slumber,
11 they are greedy dogs,
they cannot be sated;
the shepherds are evil,
they have no understanding,
they all go their own way,
each one to his gain.
12 "Come, let me fetch wine,
and let us guzzle beer;
tomorrow will be like today,
even far more glorious."
57: 1 Alas, the righteous man perishes
and no one takes it to heart,
men of faith are removed
and no one gives it a thought.
Because of evil the righteous is removed,
2 the upright enters (the grave) in peace,
they rest upon their biers.
3 But as for you, come here,
you sons of a witch,
offspring of the adulterer and the whore;

was originally an independent composition, representing an attack on the leaders of the community by the prophetic group, and that someone within that same group later expanded that composition with the addition of 57:3–13.

The movement of the resulting unit is dramatic and consonant with that found in Isaiah 65 and 66: the community leaders are indicted (56:9–12); the innocent victims are lamented (57:1–2); in the archaizing language of the traditional lawsuit, the cult of the community leaders is bitterly attacked by equating it with paganism (57:3–11); the apostates are threatened with judgment (57:12–13a); the faithful are promised salvation (57:13b).

	Text	Structure				Meter	Prosodic Units
56:9	כל חיתו שדי	a	b	c		6	b:b:b
	אתיו לאכל		d	e		5	
	כל חיתו ביער	a	b	c_1		6	
10	צפי [a] עורים כלם	a	b	c		6	b:b:b:b::b:b:b:b::
	לא ידעו [הבין] [b]		d	e	f	6	b:b:b:b
	כלבים אלמים		B			6	
	לא יוכלו לנבח		d	e_1	f_1	6	
	[ח]זים [c] שכבים	a_1	b_1			5	
	אהבי[ם] לנום			e_2	f_2	5	
11	כלבים עזי נפש		B_1			6	
	לא ידעו שבעה		d	e	f_3	6	
	[רעים] המה רעים [d]	a_2	b_2			6	
	לא ידעו הבין		d	e	f	6	
	כלם לדרכם פנו		c	g	h	7	
	איש לבצעו[ ] [e]		c_1	g_1		4	
12	אתיו [f] אקחה יין	a	b	c		6	b:b::b:b
	ונסבאה שכר		B	c_1		6	
	יהיה כזה יום מחר		d	e	f	7	
	גדול יתר מאד		g	h	i	5	
57:1	[הן] [g] צדיק אבד	a	b			6	b:b::b:b
	ואין איש שם על לב		d	e	f	6	
	אנשי חסד נאספים	a_1	b			6	
	באין [איש] [h] מבין		d	e_1		5	
	[i] [ ] [j] מפני רעה נאסף צדיק	a	b	c		9	1:1:1
2	יבוא שלום [k] 'הלך נכחו' [l]		b_1	a_1	c_1	9	
	ינוחו על משכבותם		b_2	A		8	
3	ואתם קרבו הנה	a	b	c		7	1:b:1:b:b:b:1:b
	בני עננה		a_1	d		5	
	זרע מנאף ו[ ]זנה [m]		a_2	d_1	d_2	7	

4 against whom are you jeering,
against whom are you sneering
and wagging your tongue;
are you not children of sin,
offspring of lies and treachery,
5 growing passionate with the Els
under every leafy tree,
slaughtering children in the valley
among the rocky crags?
6 Among slippery wadi-stones is your portion,
these, these are your allotment;
to them you pour out libations,
you bring up offerings to them;
will these things appease me?
7 Upon a mountain high and lofty
you have placed your bed;
to that place you go up
and you offer your sacrifices;
8 behind door and doorpost
you have placed your symbol;
for having departed from me
you have spread out your bed,
you have made yourself a treaty
with those whose lying you love;
9 you lavish oil on the king,
you multiply your perfumes,
you send your envoys afar,
you send them as far as Sheol.
10 With the length of your travel you were weary,
but you did not say, it is hopeless;
you rediscovered your strength
so that you did not weaken.
11 Whom did you dread and fear
when you were false to me,
and did not remember me
or cherish me within your heart?
Have I not kept silent even for a long time
though you had no fear of me?
12 but I will declare your "righteousness,"
your deeds which will not help you.
13 When you cry, let your idol-clusters deliver you,
the wind will carry all of them away,
but he who seeks refuge in me will inherit the land,
he will take possession of my holy mountain.

4	על מי תתענגו			e	f		6	
	על מי תרחיבו פה			e	f_1	g	6	
	תאריכו לשון				f_2	g_1	5	
	הלוא אתם ילדי פשע	a	a_3	d_3			7	
	זרע שקר [ורמיה] [n]		a_2	d_4	d_5		6	
5	הנחמים באלים [o]	a	b				7	1:b:1:b
	תחת כל עץ רענן		c	D			5	
	שחטי ילדים בנחל[ ] [p]	a	b_1				9	
	תחת סעפי סלע[ ] [p]		c	D			5	
6	בחלקי נחל חלקך	A	b				7	1:b::1:b:1
	הם הם גורלך		c	c	b_1		5	
	גם להם שפכת נסך		c	d	e		7	
	העלית מנחה [להם] [q]			d_1	e_1	c	6	
	העל אלה אנחם [r]	f	c	g			7	
7	על הר גבה ונשא	a	b	b_1			7	1:b:b:b::b:b:b:b:
	שמת משכבך		c	d			5	:b:b::1:b:1:b
	גם שם עלית		e	f			4	
	[ות]זבח [s] זבח		c_1	d_1			4	
8	אחר דלת ומזוזה	a_1	b_2	b_3			6	
	שמת זכרונך		c	d_2			5	
	כי מאתי גלית[ ] [t]		e_1	f_1			6	
	הרחבת משכבך		c_2	d_3			6	
	ותכרת לך מהם [tt]		c_3	d_4	e_2		6	
	אהבת משכבם[ ] [u]		c_4	d_5			6	
9	ותשרי [v] למלך בשמן		c_5	e_3	d_6		8	
	ותרבי רקחיך		c_6	d_7			7	
	תשלחי ציריך עד מרחק		c_7	d_8	g		10	
	ותשפילי עד שאול		c_8		g_1		7	
10	ברב דרכך יגעת	a	b	c			7	b:b::b:b
	לא אמרת נואש		d	e	f		5	
	חית ידך מצאת	a_1	b_1	c_1			6	
	על כן לא חלית		g	e_1	f_1		5	
11	מי דאגת ותיראי	a	b	b_1			7	b:b::b:b
	כי תכזבי		c	d			5	
	ואותי לא זכרת	a_1	B				6	
	לא שמת על לבך		B_1	e			5	
	הלא אני מחשה [w] ומעלם	a	b	c			10	1:b::1:b
	ואותי לא תיראי	a_1	B				7	
12	[x] [ו]אני אגיד צדקתך	a	b_1	d			8	
	מעשיך לא יועילוך		d_1	B_1			7	
13	בזעקך יצילך קבוציך [y]	a	b	c			9	1:b
	כלם ישא רוח [z] [ ]		c_1	b_1	d		5	
	והחוסה בי ינחל ארץ	a	b	c			8	1:b
	יירש הר קדשי		b_1	C			5	

TEXTUAL NOTES

a) The MT reading צפו is problematical, since the suffix lacks an antecedent. The versions vary, Vg agreeing with MT, Pesh reading צפים, LXX צפו. Either צפים or צפי would suit the sense of the passage.

b) LXX preserves the word missing in the MT.

c) The MT results from the confusion of *hē* for *ḥêt.* Not only does the MT reading introduce a *hapax legomenon,* but the reading with the *ḥêt* is supported by 1QIsa[a], many Hebrew mss, and Pesh.

d) All the versions are reading the consonants המה רעים. LXX, Tg, and Pesh read רָעִים, MT, Vg, and 1QIsa[a] read רֹעִים. We propose that both preserve an element of the original reading רצים המה רָעים (a very effective paramonasia) and that one רעים was lost by haplography.

e) מקצהו seems to be a gloss. It is not in the LXX.

f) The first person plural in Vg, Tg, Pesh, and 1QIsa[a] is a secondary harmonization to the next colon. This entire verse is missing in LXX.

g) Supplying הֵן on the basis of meter, rhetorical form, and the presence of equivalents in Pesh (ܗܐ) and LXX (Ἴδετε). 1QIsa[a] has a *wāw.*

h) איש could easily have been lost after אין by a simple haplography.

i) The metric structure of vv. 1c–2 is badly disrupted in the MT. LXX is very paraphrastic, and offers little help. Our reconstruction is conservative, but must nevertheless be considered tentative, given the state of the text.

j) Omitting כי with LXX.

k) יבוא שלם is very unclear by itself. The context, however, suggests a plausible meaning, that context being a lament over the righteous man who dies because of the negligence of the leaders. The next colon refers to the righteous resting in their graves (for משכב = grave, see Ezek 32:25; 2 Chr 16:14; and the tomb inscription from the Mount of Olives in G. A. Cooke, *A Textbook of North-Semitic Inscriptions* [Oxford: Clarendon, 1903], p. 341. For אסף = taken away for burial, see Jer 8:2; 25:33; Ezek 29:5; 2 Kgs 22:2). It is likely that יבוא שלום is a parallel thought, and thus elliptical for the full prose phrase, בא אל אבתיך בשלום (cf. Gen 15:15).

l) Displaced in the MT.

m) Emending the MT on the basis of LXX, Vg, Tg, and Pesh.

n) We should expect two elements after זרע as in 3c. For the parallel שֶׁקֶר//רְמִיָּה, cf. Ps 101:7; 120:2; Mi 6:12.

o) אלים in this verse is usually rendered "oaks" or "terebinths" in the translations. However, LXX, Tg, Pesh, and Vg all read it as "gods." Moreover, the same word is attested at Ras Shamra in this sense, as pointed out by J. W. Jack, *The Ras Shamra Tablets: Their Bearing on the O.T.*, Old Testament Series no. 1 (Edinburgh: T. and T. Clark, 1935).

p) The plural of these nouns could be the result of harmonization with באלים in v. 5a.

q) With LXX.

r) Either this colon is extrametrical or a colon has been lost.

s) The infinitive form of the verb appears only here, and the resulting line is very short (three syllables).

t) The MT's reading yields very poor poetic structure. Good structure is restored by regarding ותעלי as a secondary addition introduced by analogy to v. 7b.

tt) כרת, "to make a treaty," without the object ברית is common (cf. 1 Sam 11:2; 20:16; 22:8; 1 Kgs 8:9, 21; Neh 10:1; 2 Chr 5:10; 7:18).

u) A gloss, or the vestige of a disintegrated third colon.

v) For the etymology of שרה. "to be abundant," hip'il, "lavish," cf. P. Wernberg-Møller, "Short Notes," *VT* 8 (1958): 307-308. The parallel between מלך and צירים makes "king," rather than Moleck, the more likely translation of מלך.

w) We retain the MT reading rather than resorting to the usual emendation, ומֵעָלם. This use of *wāw*, found also in Ugaritic, "has the effect of calling special attention to the word to which it is attached." (M. Pope, " 'Pleonastic' Waw in Classical Hebrew," *JAOS* 73 [1953]: 98).

x) Reading the conjunction with LXX. The original parallel structure, lost in MT, is preserved in Vg and Pesh.

y) Within the context, this interpretation of the *hapax legomenon* seems preferable to emendations.

z) יקח הבל is too short to be a third colon (three syllables). It may be a variant to ישא רוח which was noted in the margin by a scribe, and later found its way into the text.

Even after the conclusion is drawn that 56:9-57:13 is a unified composition (resulting from the organic growth from 56:9-57:2 to the larger unit), the problem of dating remains a very perplexing one; indeed, this oracle perhaps is the most difficult of the entire Third Isaiah corpus to date with confidence, the reason being that both the attack on the unfaithful leaders in 56:9-12 and the diatribe against the defiled cult in 57:3-11 are couched in phrases which could date anywhere from the pre-exilic to the post-exilic period. It is therefore not surprising to find a bewildering range of dates offered by the critics.[122] The difficulty naturally stems from the fact that one finds Hosea, Amos, Isaiah, Jeremiah, Ezekiel, and Ezra all facing the problems of corrupt leaders and defiled cults similar to those depicted in this oracle. Hence not one of the attempts to date the material on the basis of the individual abuses being attacked has been widely accepted.

The one tool which has not been utilized may be the one holding greatest promise for casting light on the perplexing problem of dating this oracle, namely, that based on the typology of prophetic genres. We observed that in the oracles discussed in sections D through F above a new hybrid form of prophetic genre was emerging, the salvation-judgment oracle. Since Isaiah 66 can be dated circa 520, it seems likely that this new genre emerged during the third quarter of the sixth century. The oracle in 57:3–13, like those in chapters 65 and 66, represents the salvation-judgment oracle in its fully developed stage. This typological consideration suggests a setting for 57:3–13 in the same period as chapters 65 and 66, namely, in the last quarter of the sixth century. Since 56:9–57:2 contains the same dichotomy between the wicked leaders of the community and the oppressed minority of faithful which is at the base of the new salvation-judgment genre, its origin and transmission prior to its being fused with 57:3–13 probably belongs to the earlier phase of this same period.

This dating receives corroboration of a sort from another typological consideration, that concerning the meter and prosodic structure. Although 56:9–57:2 upholds a regular meter (again suggesting an origin in the earlier phase of the general period in question), the breakdown of a consistent meter is again in evidence in 57:3–13. Moreover, both 56:9–57:2 and 57:3–13 contain examples of the

122. Duhm, Marti, and Skinner identify the idolaters with the Samaritans of Ezra's time; Ewald and Volz recognize the setting to be that of the pre-exilic community; Feldmann believes the godless in exile are the object of attack; Glahn and Kessler recognize the conditions immediately after the return from exile; Elliger and Jones the time preceding the rebuilding of the temple.

long, baroque prosodic unit which has by the time of these oracles all but replaced the classical structure based on the bicolon. The prosodic unit in 56:10–11 is worthy of note, developing as it does the basic scheme *a b c: d e f* through ten lines, and concluding with a repetition of the *c* element from line one plus two new elements. The long, complex prosodic unit in 57:7–9 is especially noteworthy, beginning with the scheme *a b b: c d: e f: c d,* then repeating that same scheme, and finally concluding with an extension of the *c* element through six more lines in a list-like fashion. Within the typology of meter and prosodic structure, 56:9–57:13 falls at a point close to Isaiah 65 and 66.

We shall now look more closely at this oracle, interpreting it against the background of our proposed date circa 515–510. This we do in the full knowledge that the results must be considered more tentative than usual, in light of the ambiguity of much of the material. By attempting to account for the oracle as a unit, we still feel that the method we are applying, though tentative, results in a more adequate understanding than does the commonly applied method of trying to date isolated, individual abuses mentioned in the oracle. Once again our approach is based upon the recognition that the same prophetic genre and underlying polemical community setting found in the other oracles of Third Isaiah characterize this present composition as well.

In many respects, the attack on the leaders of the community in 56:9–57:2 resembles the oracle in Jer 12:7–13. Comparison of the two oracles, however, reveals a very basic difference: while the Jeremiah oracle, dating from the end of the seventh century, summons the beasts of the field to devour because of the guilt of the nation taken as a whole, the Third Isaiah oracle places the guilt upon the leaders of the people, whereas the righteous men of faith are separated out as the innocent victims who will finally be delivered. That is to say, the new post-exilic situation in which the community had become divided into two contending parties seems to be reflected.

But who are the guilty watchmen, seers, and shepherds

that are being attacked? In the historical books, the *ṣōphîm* ("watchmen") are sentinels who stand watch over the city to warn of enemy attack (1 Sam 14:16; 2 Sam 18:24ff; 2 Kgs 9:17ff). In the prophets the term is applied to Israel's religious leaders in their role of warning the people of impending threats (Jer 6:17; Ezek 3:17; 33:3ff; Is 52:8). Since the *ḥōzîm* ("seers") were prophetic figures, the term *ṣōphîm* may here designate the priests of the people. The *rō'eh* ("shepherd") is the classical designation of the king, and appears in this sense in the Old Testament (Jer 6:3; 12:10; 25:34ff; Is 44:28).[123] Similarly, Yahweh, as Israel's king, can be so designated (Jer 31:10; Is 40:11). In the later periods of Israel's history, especially in the exilic and post-exilic periods, *rō'îm* came to designate the civil leaders of the people in general (Jer 2:9; 10:21; 22:22; 23:1f, 25:34ff; 50:6; Ezek 34, etc.). This appears to be the usage reflected in our oracle. This first indictment of the oracle thus applies to Israel's religious and civil leaders: to priests, prophets, and political heads. The religious leaders have failed in their duty to warn and admonish the people. They are blind and dumb, they cannot even bark,[124] even though it is their responsibility to "cry out aloud" (58:1). They are a sleepy, greedy group. Nor are the civil leaders any better; they are without understanding, seeking not the welfare of the people, but only their own gain. Pictured is the complete collapse of order and justice which was portrayed earlier in Isaiah 59. The underlying cause of their laxity and greed is portrayed exquisitely in the drinking song in verse 12: they live in the illusion that they may satisfy their lust and greed with impunity. There will be no day of judgment, no reckoning with Yahweh; every day will be glorious like today. Their attitude can best be described as anti-eschatological, the same attitude manifested by the jeering remark of the brethren who cast those who feared

123. Cf. John W. Waters, "The Political Development and Significance of the Shepherd-King Symbol in the Ancient Near East and the Old Testament" (Ph.D. dissertation, Boston University, 1970).

124. For the very ancient use of *keleb* to designate civil and religious officials, see D. Winton Thomas, "Kelebh 'Dog'; Its Origin and Some Usages of It in the O.T.," *VT* 10 (1960): 410–427.

Yahweh from the cult: "Let Yahweh display his glory that we may see!" (66:5). Here we receive a hint at how the oppressed minority was interpreting the life attitudes of the community's leaders: they were betrayers of the prophetic tradition! This basic accusation makes more intelligible the other bitter charges which they hurl at their opponents.

The indictment against the faithless leaders is immediately followed by a lament depicting the fate of the faithful man, the innocent victim of a fallen society. In the use of the appellative *ṣaddîq* ("righteous") it seems that conscious reference is being made to the righteous one of Isaiah 53, even as *'ebed* ("servant") is used in Isaiah 63, 65, and 66. The oppressed prophetic group apparently identified itself closely with the righteous Suffering Servant of Second Isaiah, a fact made all the more apparent by the emphasis in 57:1 that no one gives a thought to the passing of the righteous man (cf. 53:8), and by the reference in 57:2 to his burial (cf. 53:9). It was probably also the conscious attempt to identify the suffering prophetic group of the late sixth century with the Suffering Servant of Second Isaiah which prompted the use of the singular noun *ṣaddîq* to be construed collectively as indicated by the following parallel term in the plural: *'anšê ḥesed* ("men of faith"). The latter also strikes one as a technical designation for a distinct group, the men of *ḥesed* whose zeal for the prophetic faith anticipates the later *ḥăsîdîm.*

In the oracle which elaborates the attack on the leaders in 56:9–57:2, the sharpest possible contrast is drawn between the men of faith just described and the apostates by the emphatic formula characteristic of the salvation-judgment oracle: "But as for you" (*wᵊ'attem*). Although they presume to jeer and deride others (that is, the oppressed prophetic group), their true nature is revealed by tracing their progenitors: the witch, the adulterer, and the whore. Their shameful ancestry is further underscored by the titles, "children of sin," "offspring of lies and treachery," and then the manner of life stemming from such an ancestry is described through a list of stereotyped phrases describing Israel's apostasy and drawn from the traditional language of earlier prophecy (v. 5f).[125] The intention behind this acrimonious use of traditional language is clear: even as the prophetic group constantly identifies its ancestry with those faithful to Yahweh in the past, they identify their foes with those in Israel's past history who forsook Yahweh and turned to foreign gods. This means that the description of their activity in verses 5–10 is to be taken no more literally than is the designation "sons of a witch, offspring of the adulterer and the whore." As in 59:5f ("they hatch adders' eggs, they weave the spider's web") and 65:11 ("who set a table for Gad, who fill cups of mixed drink for Meni"), various types of symbols are being used to support their accusation that those being attacked are unclean, and their cult is defiled. The metaphorical use of language found here is illustrated clearly by verse 6. Various attempts have been made to identify the pagan cultic practice being attacked here. But note the roots being used: *ḥlq* ("apportion" – "be slippery"); *nḥl* ("inherit" – "wadi"); *grl* ("allotment" – "stony place"). Although the exact translation of this colon must remain uncertain, one thing is clear: this is no objective description of a cultic practice, but rather a highly sardonical paronomasia used to ridicule the cult of those being attacked.

The author of this oracle departs from traditional language in verses 7–10 to create an ingenious and sarcastic image of his own to carry further his attack on the defiled cult. The switch to the third feminine singular, far from being an indication of a new unit,[126] is dictated by the new image being developed, that of the prostitute (= the apostates) and her bed (= their temple). To be sure, the metaphor of Israel as the faithless harlot was borrowed from tradition,[127] but the manner in which it is developed is shockingly new.

125. It is readily apparent that these verses incorporate verbatim the phrases used in earlier prophecy to describe Canaanizing activities, e.g., "under every leafy tree": Jer 2:20; 3:6, 13; 17:2; Ezek 6:13; 2 Kgs 16:4; "slaughtering children": Jer 7:31, 19:6, 32:35; Ezek 20:31; 23:39; Ps 106:37f.

126. Contra Volz, p. 208.

127. E.g., Hosea 1 and 3; Is 1:21; Jer 2:1f, 20ff; 3:6–10; Ezekiel 16 and 23.

The question of the identity of the referent of the image of the *miškāb* ("bed") is a most perplexing one. Most scholars, interpreting all of the images in verses 5-10 literally, believe that the *miškāb* refers to a pagan high place. But several considerations call this interpretation into question: first, in the prophetic literature, it is generally the pagan *bāmôt* that are attacked, and not one individual *bāmāh*.[128] Yet here one single bed on one particular mountain is under attack. Secondly, the great height of that mountain is emphasized; it is no normal hillock, but "a mountain, high and lofty," that is, a mountain with a special significance. It is difficult not to be reminded of Zion (cf. Mi 4:1; Is 2:2; Ezek 40:3). Finally, reference is made to the door and doorpost, features not found in the open-air *bāmôt*. Rather, reference is being made to a structure with doors and doorposts like the temple (cf. 1 Kgs 6:33f).

But what then is this structure on a high and lofty mountain to which Israel goes up to sacrifice and which the prophet calls a *miškāb*? That one cannot take the image literally is clear, for one does not go up to a bed to sacrifice! However, once we recognize the skillful use of paronomastic surrogates in this oracle (cf. v. 6) and consider that the main thrust of the oracle has been to liken the defiled cult to ancient fertility practices, it no longer seems preposterous to conjecture that the object of attack is the *miškān* on Zion which, according to Isaiah 66, the priestly group was building. The prophetic circle, bitterly opposed this temple since it was being built by a group whose hands allegedly were defiled with blood, a group which mixed legitimate practices with all sorts of moral and cultic abominations (66:3).[129] Maintaining the tack followed from verse 3 on, that of tracing the ancestry of the defiled group back

128. For example, in the passage upon which much of 57:5-13 is patterned, Jer 2:20-37, the whore Israel is active upon every high hill (v. 20).

129. H. L. Ginsberg, "Some Emendations in Isaiah," *JBL* 69 (1950): 59-60, wants to emend the text to read *mizbᵉăh miškān*, but this is to overlook the image developed throughout vv. 7-10 of the harlot and her activities centered around the bed of shame. Brownlee, *Meaning*, pp. 190-191, argues that the reference is to an idolatrous cultic *bāmāh*, and the prophet, rather than calling it a *miškān*, identifies it with what it really is, a *miškāb*.

to adulterers and whores, and of equating their activity with the paganizing fertility practices of their forefathers, the oracle, in a most vivid manner, now compares the temple which they have built to a gigantic bed of prostitution, a brothel upon Mt. Zion. To be sure, the image is a shocking one, but no more shocking than the attack found in other parts of Third Isaiah (e.g., 59:5–8; 65:2–7; 66:3).

The symbol (*zkrwn*, suggesting a sexual image, since *zkr* = "male") which she places behind door and doorpost is perhaps one of the accouterments of her trade. Having departed from Yahweh (cf. 65:11) she makes her bed wide, that is, accommodating all sorts of non-Yahwistic elements. This is further explained by the reference to a treaty she has made with those lying with her. Reference in verse 9 to gifts sent to the king and envoys sent afar indicates that this treaty refers to a pact between the whore (the defiled normative party of Israel!) and a foreign land. In keeping with the resistance of the prophets to treaties not ordained by Yahweh, the prophetic group here is apparently opposing the collaboration of the hierocratic party with some foreign country. When it is recalled that the priestly group returned under the aegis of the Persian government (Ezr 1:1–4) and that the temple was built practically as a shrine for the Persian emperor with funds from the royal treasury (Ezr 1:2; 6:3–10), the inference seems plausible that the alliance being opposed here is that between the temple hierocracy and the Persian government. The sending of envoys afar would then refer to the feverish diplomatic activity going on between Jerusalem and Persia, reminiscent of the similar relations between Jerusalem and Egypt which in the eighth century were attacked by Isaiah (Isaiah 30; the parallel "as far as Sheol" is a hyperbolic restatement of the previous colon to emphasize the extremes to which the whore Israel is willing to go to please the foreign sovereign).

The image of the untiring whore is sustained without a break through verse 11, where it is climaxed by a powerful complaint by Yahweh which clarifies the background of the whore: she is originally Yahweh's (cf. Hosea 1–3; Ezekiel

16 and 22; Is 62:4–5), but she is false to him, does not remember him, does not cherish him, even though he is very patient with her. In verse 12 the oracle returns from the metaphorical to the literal plain, as Yahweh pronounces the sentence upon the indicted party. Acting for a moment in the guise of defense attorney, he announces that he will declare their righteousness, their deeds, those credentials upon which the self-righteous priestly party prides itself and which it feels imbue it with a holiness not shared by other men (cf. 58:2-3; 65:6; 57:4). But the very defense which would normally acquit the accused here becomes a further indictment, for these purported deeds of righteousness are in fact abominations. The very essence of the polemic throughout the Third Isaiah oracles is thereby given shocking expression: what the priestly party considers righteousness the prophetic group claims is defilement to Yahweh. We find here a harsh testimony to the extreme polarization of the post-exilic community; how vastly divergent are the perspectives of the opposing factions! As in 65:5f, where those busily engaged in cultic activities look down their noses and say, "Keep your distance, approach me not, or I will communicate holiness to you," but Yahweh declares, "Such men are a smoke in my nostrils. . . .I will not remain silent, but I will repay"; as in 66:5, where those controlling the cult cast out the prophetic group, but the prophet declares, "But . . . *they* shall be confounded"; as in 57:4, where those oppressing the righteous jeer at them, but are told, "Are *you* not children of sin?" so too here the tables are turned. Their very acts of "righteousness" become an indictment against them, for as 58:2 indicated, though they revel in holy observances, they are not a righteous nation, but only delude themselves into thinking so.

But according to this oracle, their cult will be unable to save them in the impending day of judgment awaited by the prophetic group, for it is a cult of abominations: "When you cry, let your idol-clusters deliver you, the wind will carry all of them away." Then the concomitant theme of promise concludes the oracle, since the judgment of the apostates, and their removal from Zion will prepare the way for the return of the faithful and their reconquest of Zion: "But he who takes refuge in me will inherit the land, he will take possession of my holy mountain." As in chapters 65 and 66, once again the promise of salvation to the faithful takes the form of an unmediated act of Yahweh, unrelated to the pragmatic concerns of human agents or favorable historical conditions. On that day of Yahweh's intervention, the plan of restoration which had been frustrated by the oppression of the powerful priestly party would be delayed further by no human power; the promise would be fulfilled: "Your people shall all be righteous, they shall possess the land forever" (60:21). Thus we are again reminded that while the *form* of the future hope was altered by the harsh experiences of the prophetic group, its content remained essentially unchanged throughout the development we have followed through Third Isaiah.

63: 1 Who is this coming from Edom,
in crimsoned garment from Bozrah,
he that is so gloriously appareled
marching in his mighty strength?
It is I announcing victory,
it is I powerful to save.
2 Why is your apparel red,
your garment like the grape treader?
3 I have trodden the winepress alone,
and from the peoples no one was with me.
I trod them in my anger,
I trampled them in my wrath.
Their blood spattered my garment,
I have stained all my apparel.
4 For the day of deliverance was in my heart,
my year of redemption had come.
5 I looked but there was no helper,
I was appalled, there was no one to support.
So my own arm delivered me,
my wrath supported me.
6 I trod down the peoples in my fury,
I made them drunk in my wrath,
I poured out their blood on the earth.

H. THE OTHER EDGE OF THE SWORD: JUDGMENT AGAINST THE NATIONS (63:1-6)

63:1-6 is a tightly knit unit, clearly independent from what precedes and follows it. It is a fine example of a Divine Warrior Hymn as that form was taken up into the proto-apocalyptic and apocalyptic literature, replete with shocking images of blood and gore as Yahweh is portrayed executing judgment upon the peoples of the earth on the Day of Yahweh.

The hymn is similar in many respects to 59:15b-20. While the latter is in the third person singular, the present hymn presents Yahweh speaking in the first person. In the vision the observer and Yahweh are engaged in a dialogue: lab = question, 1c = answer, 2 = question, 3-6 = answer. This dialogue format is very dramatic in its effect.

	Text	Structure	Meter	Prosodic Units
63:1	מי זה בא מאדום	a b c	6	b:b::b:b
	חמוץ בגד[ ][a]מבצרה	d e c_1	6	
	זה הדור בלבשו	a d_1 e_1	6	
	צע[ד][b] ברב כחו	d_3 E	6	
	אני מדבר בצדק	a b c	7	b:b
	[אני][c] רב להושיע	a_1 b_1 c_1	6	
2	מדוע אדם[ ][d]לבושך	a b c	8	1:1::1:1
	בגדך כדרך בגת	c_1 d e	8	
3	פורה דרכתי לבדי	e_1 d f	8	
	ומעמים אין איש אתי	g h i	8	
	ואדרכם באפי	a b	7	1:1
	ארמסם בחמתי	a_1 b_1	7	
	ויז נצחם על בגדי	a b c	7	1:1
	כל מלבושי [ ]גאלתי[e]	C a_1	7	
4	כי יום נקם[f] בלבי	a b c	7	1:1
	שנת גאולי באה	a_1 b_1 c_1	7	
5	ואביט ואין עזר	a b c	7	1:1
	אשתומם ואין סומך	a_1 b c_1	7	
	ותושע לי זרעי	a b c	7	1:1
	חמתי סמכתני	c_1 a_1 b_1	7	
6	אבום עמים באפי	a b c	7	1:1:1
	אשכרם בחמתי	A c_1	7	
	ואוריד לארץ נצחם	c_1 d b_1	7	

TEXTUAL NOTES

a) Regarding the emendation to singular, cf. בגדך and לבש in verses 1, 2, and 3.

b) This is an emendation, supported by Vg, which is made by most scholars.

c) As it stands in the MT, this colon is short (four syllables). That an אני has dropped from the text is only a conjecture.

d) Dittography.

e) אגאלתי is a mixed form combining two variants.

f) נקם, as first recognized through comparison of biblical material with the extra-biblical sources, can mean either vengeance against an enemy or deliverance of an ally or vassal. In this passage the parallel suggests the former connotation.

At the outset, the question must be asked whether this Divine Warrior Hymn is pertinent to the present discussion of the visionary tradition. A conspicuous difference marks this oracle off from the preceding: the inner-community polemic which could be seen developing before between two factions within the post-exilic community is not reflected in this oracle; instead, its focus is upon Yahweh's judgment against the nations. The contrast is not indicative of a different tradition, however, but points toward a twin theme solidly at home in the prophetic tradition stemming from Second Isaiah, the theme of Yahweh's judgment in the end-time upon the nations. It is thus comparable in many respects to Isaiah 34. The visionary group, uncompromising in its insistence upon the purity of the national cult, was just as uncompromising in its claim of Yahweh's lordship over the nations of the world. They believed Yahweh's restoration would establish the defeat of Israel's foreign enemies as well as those within the nation (Is 60:12, 14). Throughout the program in 60–62 the nations are portrayed as subservient to Israel; no longer would the restored people of Yahweh suffer shame, but would instead be honored by the nations; as for those nations which refused to serve, they would be utterly destroyed. But as the next chapter will indicate, the rival hierocratic tradition maintained its control over the cult precisely on the basis of a close alliance with the Persian crown. To the visionary group this type of alliance implied a blasphemous compromise of Yahweh's exclusive claim upon Israel (cf. 57:9f). Though the post-exilic oracles of the visionary group directed against the nations are more difficult to date than the oracles stemming from the polemic within the community, they are nevertheless an essential element within the total eschatological message of that group. They are found scattered throughout the collections of oracles against the nations.

That the foreign nation oracles represent a twin theme to the oracles in which the visionary group battled against their enemies within the community is seen through a comparison of 59:16b–20 and 63:1–6. In both the archaic Divine Warrior tradition is applied, in the former case to the inner Israelite polemic, in the latter to the international sphere:

	59:15b–20	63:1–6
Yahweh acts alone:	וירא יהוה כי אין איש	ומעמים אין איש אתי
He is appalled, for there is no other:	וישתומם כי אין מפגיע	ואשתומם ואין סומך
His own arm delivers:	ותושע לו זרעו	ותושע לי זרעי
His glorious apparel:	וילבש צדקה כשרין	הדור בלבוש

Whereas it is possible to place 63:1–6 with confidence within the visionary tradition, the problem of determining its date is difficult. The very nature of the vision of this group, being utopian and relying solely upon an unflinching faith in Yahweh's intervention, makes their foreign nation oracles very timeless in nature and difficult to date. A clue to the historical background similar to that found in the oracles dealing with the inner-community polemic is absent from the composition in 63:1–6. We are therefore dependent exclusively on typological considerations.

The evidence from the typology of prosodic structure and meter is unambiguous. We have here a poetic composition closely resembling the archaizing quality of Second Isaiah. The meter is remarkably regular throughout, and the poem preserves the parallel bicolon structure in exemplary fashion. The tricolon at the conclusion of the poem is also a fine archaic feature. Thus the poem would fit in the typology either within the poetry of Second Isaiah or very closely thereafter.

This conclusion is corroborated by consideration of the typology of prophetic eschatology, for the poem falls within the phase introduced by Second Isaiah, the phase during which mythic material from the league ritual conquest and the royal procession traditions was being introduced into prophecy. The effect which myth had upon the prophetic eschatology was controlled carefully by Second Isaiah, who skillfully maintained the dialectic between mythic embellishment and the relation of divine action to the historical realm. Whereas he allowed myth to add a cosmic dimension to Yahweh's acts, those acts were always anchored in mundane events. As we have already seen, the development toward apocalyptic involved the weakening of that tie to the realm of history and politics. Where does the present oracle fall in this typology?

Although the poem is too short to allow confident judgments, it seems that it reflects the period when the attempt to translate the eschatological hope into the terms of plain history is beginning to weaken. Yahweh is portrayed acting alone; both human instruments and identifiable historical foes are absent. Edom is mentioned but, as in Isaiah 34, a specific historical event involving that nation is not the focus of the oracle; rather Edom has become a symbol of Yahweh's foes throughout the earth who attempt to oppose him in the eschaton.[130] Bozrah, the capital of Edom, is intended, it would seem, to suggest the vintage (*bōṣrāh*/*bāṣîr*) which is about to be gathered and trampled. Moreover, Edom is but the starting point of Yahweh's march (similar to his marching forth from Sinai in Dtn 33:2), for in verse

130. In contrast, Obadiah 1-14 seems to reflect directly Edom's involvement in the catastrophe of 587. The reason why Edom was chosen to symbolize opposition to Yahweh is readily discernible. After a period of rivalry dating back to the early years of Israel's history, the Edomites committed an act of treachery which paled all earlier acts of aggression when they overran southern Judah as far as Hebron in the wake of the catastrophe of 587 (cf. Jer 44:7-22; Obadiah; Ezek 35:1-15; Isaiah 34). The history of the enmity between Edom and Judah-Israel has been studied most recently by B. C. Cresson, "The Condemnation of Edom in Post-Exilic Judaism," in *The Use of the Old Testament in the New and Other Essays*, ed. J. M. Efird [Durham: Duke University, 1972], pp. 125-148).

6 he treads down "the peoples," pouring their blood upon the earth. The picture of universal carnage resembles that in 66:16:

For Yahweh will execute judgment with fire, and with his sword, against all flesh, and those slain by Yahweh will be many. (66:16)	I trod down the peoples in my fury, I made them drunk in my wrath, I poured out their blood on the earth. (63:6)

It would thus seem that in 63:1-6, as in 59:15b-20 and 66:15-16, the influence of myth on prophetic eschatology is becoming apparent in a loosening of ties with plain history, and in a universalizing of the end-time judgment which in late apocalyptic eschatology would become a judgment cosmic in scope, encompassing the entire created order, even the stars of the heavens. The influence of myth, with its dualistic imagery of a conflict between the warrior god and the insurgent foe, ultimately would lead to a picture of judgment in apocalyptic eschatology which construed the enemy increasingly in terms of absolute evil. All the nations of the world would be portrayed as one monolithic force confronting the Divine Warrior Yahweh in the final cosmic battle. Their overthrow would take place in a cataclysmic event which would destroy the old order of evil and usher in the new order of shalom.[131]

It is obvious that a long distance separates the full-blown apocalyptic picture of the final judgment from the picture given in 63:1-6. Myth in this composition has only begun to make the judgment scene cosmic, and the dualism is still inchoate.

On the basis of these typological considerations we would propose that the Divine Warrior Hymn in 63:1-6 stems either from a late point in the life of Second Isaiah, or from a disciple in the period immediately thereafter. Any attempt to come to more precision would necessitate a thorough study of Isaiah 34-35 and the other post-exilic

131. Cf. Wright, pp. 151-152.

oracles against Edom.[132] On the basis of both the prosodic typology and the typology of prophetic eschatology, the poem, however, seems to belong to the same approximate period as Isaiah 60–62. Isaiah 60:12 and 14 indicate the position which an oracle against the nations assumes in the total restoration program of the visionary group. Whether faced by forces within the nation which threatened to profane their cult and deprive them of their eschatological hope, or by international powers which threatened to interfere with Yahweh's sovereignty over his people, that visionary group found its source of comfort in the same myth-inspired cosmic vision of Yahweh the Warrior intervening on their behalf to deliver them from their foes and to grant them victory.

132. Obadiah; Jer 49:7–22; Ezekiel 36; Sam 4:21–22; Psalm 137 and Mal 1:2–5.

CHAPTER III

The Origins of the Post-Exilic Hierocracy

A. THE SECOND GROUP COMPETING FOR CONTROL OF THE RESTORATION CULT

In Chapter II the matrix within which apocalyptic eschatology arose was located within the early post-exilic community in the bitter struggle between two groups for control of the restoration cult. It was possible to trace the successive stages in this struggle from the point of view of the prophetic group which finally was defeated and excluded, at least for a time, from the mainstream of post-exilic Judaism, a group whose spiritual ancestry went back through the prophets to the time of the league. They regarded themselves, like the Israel of the time of Moses (cf. Is 61:6 with Ex 19:5–6), as a nation of priests ruled directly by the Divine Warrior and King, Yahweh. Their immediate spiritual ancestor was Second Isaiah, though their circle probably came to encompass various dissident elements, including disenfranchised Levites.

In their struggle with the other group in question, a priestly group which we have tentatively identified with the Zadokites, the visionaries developed an eschatology which moved further and further from the politically oriented eschatology of the classical prophetic period toward the otherwordly orientation of apocalyptic. The steady takeover of control of the cult by the rival group obliged those insisting that Yahweh would yet vindicate them to view the final restoration in terms moving away from the traditional prophetic hope which anticipated the reconstitution of the whole political entity, Israel. That national hope was denied the prophetic group from the time when they were removed from a position of control, and even of membership, in the nation and its cult by a rival priestly group which they considered defiled and illegitimate. A new situation necessitated revision of the traditional prophetic hope, and thus served as a powerful impetus toward apocalyptic eschatology.

The task of the present chapter will be to trace the history of that struggle for control of the cult in the early post-exilic period from the point of view of the second party in the struggle, the hierocratic party dominated by the Zadokite priests which controlled the high priesthood from the first years of the Solomonic temple down to the second century B.C.[1]

It is difficult to overemphasize the significance of this struggle in the sixth century, for contending were the two vital forces constituting the heart of the religion of Israel, what we have come to designate as the "visionary" element on the one hand and the "realistic" or "pragmatic" element on the other. The tragedy of that struggle was that it threatened to dissolve the prophetic dialectic of faith which the classical prophets had maintained within the field of tension between vision and reality. The specter arose of a polarization in which the pragmatic program of the hierocracy would become devoid of the visionary element of prophecy, while the vision of prophecy would cut its moorings with the real world and take flight into the realm of apocalyptic dreams. In fact this polarization did develop in the sixth and fifth centuries, with very serious effects on post-exilic Judaism: the demise of prophecy, the diminution of a genuine eschatological dimension in the normative post-exilic legal and historical literature, and the forcing underground of the eschatological hope with the con-

1. The late sixth-century literature from the hierocratic side of the struggle reflects the inner-community tensions as unmistakably as did the material examined in the previous chapter. For example, "For before those days [i.e., before the temple foundation had been laid] there was no wage for man or any wage for beast, neither was there any safety from the foe for him who went out or came in; for I set every man against his fellow" (Zech 8:10).

sequent transformation of prophetic eschatology into apocalyptic eschatology.

Even when the immediate struggle was ended by the victory of the hierocratic group, the tension between the visionary and the realistic, the prophetic and the priestly elements within Israelite religion was not permanently resolved. For not only were there periods when the dialectic was at least partially revived (cf. the books of the Chronicler), as well as times when the visionary element became embodied in a fresh new outburst of literary activity (e.g., the early second century), but even rabbinic writings, from the time of the amorim to the epoch of the gaonim, incorporate apocalyptic themes,[2] and at no point in the history of Jewish apocalyptic was all contact with the historical realm abandoned. In order to resolve completely the tension between the visionary and the realistic elements of its religion, post-exilic Judaism would have been obliged not only to renounce its pre-exilic prophetic roots, but to overcome a tension inherent in all ethical religious systems. For the struggle between these two elements goes far beyond the history of Israel's religious experience. It is a struggle basic to all ethical religions. For this reason, a brief consideration of several sociological works from the first third of our century will provide useful conceptual tools for the historical analysis of this chapter.

B. THE SOCIOLOGICAL BACKGROUND OF THE POST-EXILIC STRUGGLE

The events of 597 and 587 B.C. represent a type of crisis which is of decisive importance in the history of social institutions. Through the trauma of national disaster, the traditional community structures which supported the social life of the people suddenly collapse. A profound need

2. For example, see Sanh. 97b. To the writer's knowledge, the most comprehensive discussion of apocalyptic in the writings of the rabbis is found in J. Bloch, *On the Apocalyptic in Judaism, JQR* Monograph Series II (Philadelphia: Dropsie College, 1952). Bloch repeatedly marshals evidence against G. F. Moore's and H. L. Ginsberg's views that Rabbinical Judaism ignored and was uninfluenced by apocalyptic writers (pp. 60, 122, and *passim*).

is created to find models upon which to pattern the reconstruction of the community, but the result is often a bitter struggle between groups each claiming that its particular model offers the legitimate basis for reconstruction. The reason for that struggle is clear; the catastrophe has not created the divergent views but has merely destroyed the hegemony of the controlling party thereby releasing latent dissent. The disaster has suddenly made peers of ruler and subject, *clerus major* and *clerus minor,* and an abrupt end comes to the peace imposed by the dominant party, for its loss of power undermines its ability to minimize the tension between the divergent forces in the society. The result is rivalry and struggle which tend to polarize and throw into bold relief the divergent forces lying at the heart of the society in question.[3]

In the realm of religious institutions, as in the realm of politics, the polarization tends to develop primarily between two forces, the one embodied in the ruling classes and devoted to preservation of the former institutional structures, the other found among the alienated and oppressed and bent on revolution leading to change of the status quo. The models to which each turns in the search for a basis for restoration is intimately related to the social status of each group. The ruling classes, because of their vested interest in the institutional structures of the immediate past, construct a program for restoration on the basis of those recently disrupted structures so as to preserve their position of supremacy. The alienated and oppressed classes look to the more distant past for models which call into question the position of power claimed by the ruling classes, and readily adhere to prophetic figures calling for revolutionary change on the basis of such archaic models.[4]

3. As will be argued below, the struggle appears to have been ended by the time of the composition of the Chronicler (ca. 400), for the element of polemic is there replaced by a spirit of conciliation, and by what appears to be an active attempt to bring alienated elements back into the mainstream.

4. See Max Weber, *The Sociology of Religion,* tr. E. Fischoff (Boston: Beacon, 1963; first German edition, 1922), pp. 80 ff, 106–107; and T. Parsons, "Introduction" to the above work, pp. xxix–xxx and xxxv.

Karl Mannheim, in a work first published in 1929,[5] designates the two mentalities which we are here contrasting as "ideological" and "utopian." The proponents of ideology, the ruling groups, are so interest-bound to existing structures that they posit these structures as "absolute and eternal," and are blind to all facts which would call into question either these structures or their own positions.[6] They resort to all sorts of romantic notions and myths to support their claims.[7] The opposite mentality is the "utopian," characteristic of "certain oppressed groups" which are "so strongly interested in the destruction and transformation of a given condition of society that they unwittingly see only those elements in the situation which tend to negate it."[8] Utopian thinking is marked by a harsh incongruity between the vision and the actual state of reality. Therefore, when the utopian thinking becomes a direction for action, as it always threatens to become, it leads to the destruction of existing structures in the attempt to realize the utopia.[9] It is thus understandable why representatives of the given order try to render the utopian notions socially innocuous by confining them to a realm beyond history and society, where they are unable to disturb the status quo.[10] But as we noted above, in a period of national disaster, such control of the utopian impulse is no longer possible, and therefore it bursts forth in new vigor.

Max Weber is another sociologist who studied carefully these two mentalities and their socio-economic roots. As pointed out by Talcott Parsons, at critical periods (such as the early sixth century B.C. in Israel) the concept of "breakthrough" is a crucial one in Weber's analysis where "the alternative is between a direction which makes for a source of evolutionary change in the 'established' order . . . , and

5. Karl Mannheim, *Ideology and Utopia, an Introduction to the Sociology of Knowledge*, tr. L. Wirth and E. Shils (New York: Harcourt, Brace and Co., 1936; first German edition, 1929).

6. Ibid, p. 40.

7. Ibid, p. 87.

8. Ibid, p. 40.

9. Ibid, p. 192.

10. Ibid, p. 193.

another direction which tends either to reinforce the established order or at least not to change it drastically."[11] The former mentality Weber finds characteristic of prophetic religion, for the essential criterion of prophecy he finds to be "whether or not the message is a call to break with established order."[12] In opposition to this is the mentality of the various groups dedicated to the preservation of the status quo, the nobility,[13] the priests,[14] and other religious types such as the Hindu *guru*.[15] In describing the elements within society which readily adhere to the prophetic impulse, Weber, like Mannheim, points to the alienated, the disprivileged social groups who gain their identity from a "promise for the future which implies the assignment of some function, mission, or vocation to them. What they cannot claim to be, they replace by the worth of that which they will one day become. . . ." In a world fallen to evil, they long for a worthiness which has been denied them, and derive comfort from the belief in a "divine authority possessing a scale of values different from the one operating in the world of man."[16]

When prophets come proclaiming the advent of the longed for transformation, they readily find a following among these alienated elements, and when that transformation is delayed and the oppressing classes remain in power, "it was inevitable that consolation should be sought in genuine otherwordly hopes."[17] In contrast, the privileged classes assign to religion a totally different function, that "of legitimizing their own life pattern and situation in the world."[18] Their superior status in the existing established order is an expression of "their underived, ultimate, and qualitatively distinctive being."[19] With such a vested

11. Parsons, "Introduction," p. xxix, to Weber, *Sociology of Religion.*
12. Ibid., p. xxx; also Weber, *Sociology*, pp. 46 ff., 65 ff.
13. Weber, *Sociology*, p. 106.
14. Ibid., pp. 66–67.
15 Ibid., pp. 189–190; cf. Parsons, "Introduction," p. xxxv.
16 Weber, *Sociology*, p. 106.
17. Ibid., p. 140.
18. Ibid., p. 107.
19. Ibid., p. 106.

interest in the status quo, it is obvious why the leading classes are dedicated to continuity and bitterly opposed to the revolutionary change called for by prophetic religion.

Finally, we turn to another very important sociological work, Ernst Troeltsch's *The Social Teaching of the Christian Churches,*[20] for a description of the two types of religious organization resulting from the two mentalities we have been considering. Though his study concentrates on a period centuries later than that concerning us, the sociological types apply admirably to those emerging in the struggle of the sixth century B.C. The institution of the ruling classes, the Church, is "overwhelmingly conservative," and accepting of "the secular order"; she "dominates the masses," "she is universal, i.e., she desires to cover the whole life of humanity." In keeping with her attitude of toleration, the Church "utilizes the state and the ruling classes, and weaves these elements into her own life; she then becomes an integral part of the existing social order; . . . the Church both stabilizes and determines the social order; in so doing, however, she becomes dependent upon the upper classes, and upon their development."[21] Her dealings with the social and political orders are marked by toleration and compromise[22] and by the awareness that all members cannot be expected to attain to the same level of sanctity;[23] the holiness of the Church is preserved in its priestly hierarchy, whereas practical standards are made relative. In a spirit of compromise, the institutions of state and society are accepted, as is the "world" as a whole.[24] This compromise does not prevent the Church, however, from viewing herself as identical with the Kingdom of God. This identification means, moreover, that redemption is viewed as a finished work, and eschatological teachings are kept at a minimum.[25]

20. Ernest Troeltsch, *The Social Teaching of the Christian Churches*, 2 vols., tr. O. Wyon (New York: Harper Torchbooks, 1960; first German edition, 1911).

21. Ibid., p. 336.

22. Ibid., p. 337.

23. Ibid., p. 339.

24. Ibid., p. 379.

25. Ibid., p. 995.

In stark contrast to the Church as the institution of the leading classes, with her identification of self with both the secular order and the Kingdom, is the sect-type, drawing its members from "the oppressed and idealistic groups within the lower classes."[26] Having no worldly power, the sect understandably denounces the idea of world domination. Indeed, the attitude toward the world is usually one of hostility, and an insistence on radical and literal obedience to moral demands makes any form of compromise impossible; this stubborn idealism is supported by "a complete ignorance of the complicated conditions of life."[27] Accompanying this idealism is a strict individualism whereby each member must aspire after personal holiness, rather than allow the holiness of the priestly hierarchy to cover for him.[28] Because of the Church's compromise with the world, the members of the sect "felt obliged to consider the Church as degenerate, and they did not believe that the world could be conquered by human power and effort; that is why they were always forced to adopt eschatological views."[29] The attitude of the sect toward the Church varies with the conditions of the time:

> At first men hoped that this ideal would be realized naturally, as soon as the relatively corrupt Church was reformed; then arose the hope of a miraculous Divine intervention and the Chiliastic dream; then, with the appeal to the Old Testament, men took to violence and brought in a Christian communism by force; ultimately these idealists withdrew once more from the world as a religious community and tolerated secular institutions as the results of sin and as an alien environment, waiting for their hour of doom to strike.[30]

This changing attitude of the sect toward the Church reveals striking parallels to the relation between the hierocratic and visionary elements during the post-exilic peri-

26. Ibid., p. 337.
27. Ibid., pp. 336–337.
28. Ibid., p. 380.
29. Ibid.
30. Ibid.

od, for after a period of open resistance the latter, having lost all effective control, went underground, giving expression to their persevering hope only in anonymous and later pseudononymous compositions which became increasingly cryptic in character.

The characteristics of these two mentalities, the ideological and the utopian, together with the features of the corresponding organizational types, the Church and the sect, illumine significantly the nature of the struggle occurring in the exilic and post-exilic community. For in that struggle the lines were drawn between the Zadokite-dominated priestly party which had controlled the Jerusalem temple hierarchy prior to the Babylonian defeat and an alliance of dissident, alienated elements, especially those holding to the eschatological message of the prophets. The latter were likely driven to silence in the years immediately prior to the destruction of Jerusalem, but the crisis of 587 created a vacuum receptive of their minority views as well as of the views of the temple priests. In keeping with the sociological analyses delineated above, the social position of each group determined the models upon which they drew in setting forth their restoration programs. Dedicated to the preservation of the pre-exilic structures which would guarantee their continued superiority in the restored national cult, the temple priests patterned their restoration program on the model of those pre-exilic institutions, making accommodations to the changed political situation where necessary.[31] The literary genres and motifs which they adopted were placed in the service of legitimating the institutions and structures upon which their positions of power depended. The development of their program, and its intention as a guarantee of the

31. The conservative position of the Zadokite temple priests was of course one which had grown over the centuries of the pre-exilic period during which they supplied the leadership for the temple cult. Roland de Vaux describes them thus: "It seems that the descendants of Sadoq were a conservative-minded family, with little liking for innovations which might change their ways of life. We know, for example, that the religious reforms were initiated by the kings, not by the priests." R. de Vaux, *Ancient Israel. Its Life and Institutions*, tr. J. McHugh (New York: McGraw-Hill, 1961), p. 375.

supremacy of the Zadokite ruling class, will be the subject of study in the discussion which follows. In contrast, the alientated and oppressed elements which were left out of the temple organization once it had come into the firm control of the Zadokite priesthood turned to models which undermined the claims of the leading class, models from a more archaic period when different social structures characterized the institutions of Israel, models which stressed discontinuity with the structures of the immediate past,[32] and emphasized Yahweh's personal intervention to inaugurate "new things."[33] Adapted to the eschatological message of the pre-exilic prophets, and given new life through the infusion of various mythical motifs by the great prophet of the exile, Second Isaiah, these models became the basis of a prophetic program for restoration which was revolutionary in character and which called into serious question the exclusive claims of the Zadokite temple party. Thus not long after the exile had taken place, the polarization had widened between the two elements in Israelite religion which ideally belonged together in closest union, the ideological and utopian, the realistic and the visionary. In the previous chapters we traced that struggle through its various stages from the point of view of the prophetic group.

We now turn to retrace those stages from the perspective of the hierocratic party, the party which returned from exile under the leadership of the Zadokite priests and which stood in unbroken continuity with the ruling classes of the temple prior to the exile. True to the sociological types we have described above, they were devoted to preservation of as much of the pre-exilic structures as possible,

32. For the prophetic group, the events of 597 and 587 represented Yahweh's judgment upon the institutions of the preceding period and thus added strong support to their claim that those institutions offered an inadequate model for restoration. For the new era which was about to be inaugurated, purer models were necessary, and these the prophetic group found in following the lead of their teacher, Second Isaiah, by turning to the archaic traditions of the league. At that archaic period Yahweh led Israel directly, and all the nation was holy (Ex. 19:5-6).

33. These alienated elements could turn to the prophecies of Jeremiah and Second Isaiah who announced that Yahweh would effect new things—a new covenant, a new exodus, a new Moses.

were willing to compromise with the ruling Persian powers so as to preserve their own position of relative supremacy within the nation and its cult, and were eager to adapt their program to the existing political conditions so as to become a secure part of the existing world order. In their effort to guard against any threat to the internal peace which was essential to their strategy of collaboration with the Persians, they found it necessary to silence the revolutionary and disruptive voices of the dissident prophetic group. This led to the bitter struggle already traced in Chapter II which finally rendered the prophetic group impotent as a political power, forcing them to remove their vision from the historical realm of political realities, and thereby leaving the leadership of the nation and its cult exclusively in the control of the hierocratic group. The only realm left to the visionary group after that period of struggle was the realm of apocalyptic, a realm not yet emancipated from this world in the manner of the gnostic realm of salvation, but yet one quite indifferent to any real contact with political realities and aloof to all questions of how, in historical terms, the restoration would be accomplished.

Once defeated in the political arena, the visionary group in the era of the Second Temple sublimated that defeat by a growing indifference to the world of politics and by a single-hearted devotion to the belief that Yahweh would one day intervene to bring them their salvation. The events of political history were of interest to them only as they pertained to predictions concerning the nearness of that day of fulfillment. The realm of politics was left to the domination of the hierocratic party. The point was thus reached where prophecy had died, for once the message of the prophets was no longer carefully related to the concrete events of the political process, once the word of Yahweh was no longer cited to change the character of the present order, the period of prophetic eschatology was past. By the same token, once the prophetic tradition turned its attention toward a realm aloof from political realities, the era of apocalyptic eschatology had arrived. This landmark in the history of prophecy marked the victory of the hierocracy, for it demonstrated its ability to defuse the revolutionary element of the prophetic tradition by denying its applicability to the political realm, thus making good the hierocratic claim to sole authority over the people and their cult.[34]

C. THE RISE OF THE HIEROCRATIC PARTY OF THE ZADOKITES

When we speak of the hierocratic party, we refer to the leading priestly group of the post-exilic period whose center of power was the Second Temple in Jerusalem; we also include under this designation the tradition reaching back into the exilic period upon which the ruling priestly party of the Second Temple builds. By the period of the Chronicler, it came to include more than one priestly family, gathered under the general designation "sons of Aaron." As the more exclusive designation "sons of Zadok" in earlier sources (e.g., the book of Ezekiel) indicates, however, the situation in the time of the Chronicler was characterized by a far more tolerant spirit than was present at an earlier period. In fact, the history of the priestly families in Israel is marked by bitter feuds and struggles for power which flared up at frequent intervals in bitter invective and perhaps open conflict.

The crisis in the post-exilic community in the decades immediately after the return cannot be fully comprehended apart from an understanding of this history of priestly conflict. Coming to the problem without this understanding could lead to an oversimplistic interpretation of the struggles of the post-exilic period as struggles dividing the community between priestly leaders and their followers on the one hand and protagonists of a prophetic position on the other. Coming to the problem with this

34. This final phase of the cycle in the struggle between the two vital forces is described thus by Mannheim: "Consequently representatives of a given order have not in all cases taken a hostile attitude toward orientations transcending the existing order. Rather they have always aimed to control those situationally transcendent ideas and interests which are not realizable within the bounds of the present order, and thereby to render them socially impotent, so that such ideas would be confined to a world beyond history and society, where they could not affect the status quo." Mannheim, *Ideology*, p. 193.

understanding, however, leads one to recognize a highly volatile situation within the priestly families which would lead to bitter strife as soon as the unquestioned power of the ruling Zadokite party was undermined by national catastrophe. Stated simply, adequate understanding of the pre-exilic history of the priestly houses will lead one to discern the presence, in the struggles of the sixth century, of disenfranchised Levites smarting from a long history of defeats at the hands of the Zadokites and welcoming any alliance which might give them an opportunity to reestablish themselves as a priestly power of significance in the religion of Israel.

The history of the conflict between the priestly houses begins at least as early as the reigns of David and Solomon, involving Zadok, a priest whose lineage is not established with certainty by biblical sources, but who most plausibly can be regarded as a descendant of a Hebronite clan tracing back to Aaron,[35] and Abiathar, whose ancient Levitical lineage is virtually certain. These two individuals served together as David's chief priests, a partnership which was rudely terminated at the end of David's reign when the two priests sided with opposite aspirants in the struggles for the Davidic throne. As a result, Abiathar, who supported Solomon's opponent Adonijah, was banished to Anathoth by Solomon immediately upon his securing the throne. Anathoth was a Levitical town, and it is thus no surprise that Abiathar became the patron of all those Levites who in subsequent centuries fell victim to the ever increasing power of the Zadokites.

Once Abiathar had been eliminated, Zadok became the sole incumbent of the priestly office (1 Kgs 2:35), a position held by his descendants until Onias III was murdered in 175 B.C. Thus began a long and woeful history for the Levites throughout the course of which they witnessed the gradual erosion of their priestly powers. As late as the

35. Cf. de Vaux, *Israel*, pp. 373–374, for a discussion of the various hypotheses concerning Zadok's origin. Most recently, see Cross, *Myth*, pp. 206–215, for a defense of the Aaronic lineage of Zadok.

time of formulation of the Deuteronomic Law, however, all the Levites retained the privilege of performing the priestly duties (Dtn 18:6–7), *de jura*, that is. For the repeated Deuteronomic legislation designating "the Levite that is within your towns," alongside the sojourners, the fatherless, and the widow, as objects of special charity (e.g., Dtn 14:25–29) bespeaks a *de facto* situation which falls far short of full participation by the Levites in the temple cult. Even before the reformation under Josiah it would seem that the chief cult centers in Jerusalem and Bethel competed so strenuously with the outlying cultic places that many Levites were denied a priestly livelihood and reduced to poverty.[36]

The nadir of Levite fortune soon followed in connection with Josiah's thoroughgoing reform, in which the law of centralization of worship in Jerusalem was vigorously enforced. This move played directly into the hands of the Zadokite priests in the Jerusalem temple, for through Josiah's reform they gained control over all legitimate priestly functions in Israel. Deuteronomic legislation (Dtn 18:6–7) was ignored as the Zadokites, no doubt anxious to protect their unique status in the face of an influx of Levites from outlying districts into the Jerusalem cult, denied the sons of Levi access to Yahweh's altar: "However, the priests of the high places [i.e., the Levites] did not come up to the altar of the Lord in Jerusalem, but they ate unleavened bread among their brethren" (2 Kgs 23:9).

The Zadokites apparently wasted little time in translating the new exclusive hold on the priestly office which Josiah's reform placed in their hands into new laws which superseded the older Deuteronomic legislation. For the priestly laws in Numbers, likely based upon Zadokite formulations shortly before the exile, legalized the distinction between priests and Levites, restricting full priestly privileges before the altar of Yahweh to the Zadokites, and leaving an inferior position as temple servants to the Levites (*nᵊtunîm layhwh*):

> I have taken your brethren the Levites from among the people of Israel; they are a gift to you, given to the Lord, to

36. Cf. de Vaux, *Israel*, p. 364.

> do the service of the tent of meeting. And you and your sons with you shall attend to your priesthood for all that concerns the altar and that is within the veil; and you shall serve. I give you the priesthood as a gift, and any one else who comes near shall be put to death." (Nu 18:6-7; cf. 3:6-9; 8:19).

There are a number of texts at various points in the Bible which indicate that the Zadokite takeover of the cult was resisted strenuously by the Levitical descendants of Abiathar. Whereas we shall deal with the most significant of these later, we mention several at this point. One is the polemical narrative concerning Aaron's idolatry in connection with the molten calf (Exodus 32). Here the sons of Levi are singled out as faithful to Yahweh in contrast to the faithlessness of Aaron: "And all the sons of Levi gathered themselves together to him . . . and the sons of Levi did according to the word of Moses . . . . and Moses said, 'Today you have ordained yourselves for the service of the Lord, each one at the cost of his son and of his brother, that he may bestow a blessing upon you this day' " (Ex 32:26-29). To this should be contrasted the numerous statements coming from the Zadokite side, which single out one tribe from the house of Levi to receive the promise of a perpetual priesthood: "and the priesthood shall be theirs by a perpetual statute. Thus you shall ordain Aaron and his sons" (Ex 29:9; cf. 29:44 and 40:12-15). The concomitant of that statute was of course the subordination of the other Levites to the status of minor clergy.

Another series of texts which reflect the controversy between the disenfranchised Levites and the powerful Zadokites are the priestly genealogies scattered throughout the historical writings. Without examining these intriguing—but difficult to date—pieces of evidence, we shall note one feature: up to the time of Ezra, the Zadokites remained content to trace their ancestry back to Zadok. But at a later period their genealogies move further into the ancient past by connecting Zadok with Phinehas, son of Eleazer, son of Aaron. This archaizing tendency on the part of the post-exilic Zadokite group was perhaps prompted by their struggles with the Levitical Ithamarides, who by their genealogy were able to claim a more ancient ancestry than the Zadokites, thereby no doubt making the exclusive claim of the latter very precarious. How much better to be able to claim Phinehas as their patron (cf. 1 Chr 5:30–34; 6:35–38).

Before thus altering their genealogy, however, the Zadokites had attempted to discredit the lineage of their Levitical opponents, as a Zadokite addition to the history of Eli in 1 Sam 2:27–36 indicates.[37] The Eliide ancestry of Abiathar was a vulnerable point for the disenfranchised Levites, in one respect, and the Zadokites capitalized on this vulnerability: the fall of Shiloh had been a pronouncement of divine judgment upon Eli and his descendants: "The man of you whom I shall not cut off from my altar shall be spared to weep out *his* eyes and grieve *his* heart; and all the increase of your house shall die *by the sword* of men." But Eli's bane was Zadokite gain:

> And I will raise up for myself a faithful priest, who shall do according to what is in my heart and in my mind; and I will build him a sure house, and he shall go in and out before my anointed for ever. And everyone who is left in your house shall come to implore him for a piece of silver or a loaf of bread, and shall say, "Put me, I pray you, in one of the priest's places, that I may eat a morsel of bread." (1 Sam 2:35–36)

The late Roland de Vaux was likely correct when he connected the utterances of Jeremiah against the temple to this same history of struggle between the Zadokites and the disenfranchised Levites who claimed Abiathar as their ancestor.[38] For Jeremiah came from the Levitical refuge city of Anathoth, and his attack on the idolatrous attitude of his opponents toward the temple was harsh. Moreover, his diatribe in 7:14 and 26:6 seems to be a direct answer to the Zadokite attempt to discredit the descendants of Abiathar by connecting them with the destruction of Shiloh:

> And now, because you have done all these things, says the Lord, and when I spoke to you persistently you did not listen,

37. Cf. ibid., p. 376.
38. Ibid.

> and when I called you, you did not answer, therefore I will do to the house which is called by my name, and in which you trust, and to the place which I gave to you and to your fathers, as I did to Shiloh. (Jer 7:13–14)

Do not boast prematurely, sons of Zadok, for the same fate awaits you which befell the luckless sons of Eli!

Thus the polemic was already bitter between the Zadokites and their Levitical opponents even before the exile. That the latter would seize upon every opportunity offered them by the events of the early sixth century to regain their place in the temple cult is to be expected. Our brief overview of the struggles between the priestly houses of the pre-exilic period thus lends credence to our suggestion that disenfranchised Levites allied themselves with the visionary followers of Second Isaiah in a coalition dedicated to a restoration of the Jerusalem cult along non-Zadokite lines. This picture, moreover, matches at every essential point the sociological descriptions given by Weber, Mannheim, and Troeltsch of the two basic types of religious parties.

We return now to our inquiry into the origins of the post-exilic hierocratic party. Since the Zadokites occupied the preeminent offices in the temple hierarchy during the period when the Babylonians exiled the top echelons of the Jewish population, it follows that the priestly element exiled would have been dominated by the Zadokites. In exile they likely renewed their control over the community, and set to work planning for the restoration of that institution with which their power was so closely identified, the temple cult. With them they had doubtlessly brought the basic legislation now codified in the Holiness Code and parts of the priestly laws of Exodus and Numbers. Above all, it is clear that they brought with them an ideal of a temple cult in which the full priestly functions were exclusively in the possession of the Zadokites.

This Zadokite ideal was transformed into a program of restoration by a very unusual priest named Ezekiel, a priest who combined with the sacerdotal office the call of a prophet of Yahweh. Whether Ezekiel was a Zadokite himself is a moot question; what is clear is that the Zadokite temple theology profoundly influenced his thinking. The study of the post-exilic history of the hierocratic tradition thus begins with Ezekiel, even as the study of the post-exilic visionary tradition begins with Second Isaiah.

As the recognized spiritual leadership in the exile, the hierocratic party led by the Zadokite priests would have been the group having access to the royal court, and thus they would have been the ones consulted by the Persians after Cyrus fell heir to the Babylonian Empire.[39] In accord with their strategy of consolidating the newly won empire by a policy of clemency, the Persians offered to lend their support to the hierocratic program of restoration of the temple and cult, naturally in return for unrelenting fidelity on the part of the Jewish leaders. The fact that the Zadokite high priests throughout the Persian era assumed a posture of collaboration with the Persians verifies this interpretation of conditions in the late exilic period.

Thus it was that the hierocratic party, led by the Zadokite priests and authorized by a Persian mandate, returned to Palestine to build Yahweh a house and to restore the land, a situation attested by Ezra 1-6, Haggai, and Zechariah 1-8. The priestly leadership of that group was very exclusive, since in the exile the hierocratic party maintained its firm hold on the leadership of the community which it had gained before the exile. This fact is illustrated by the list in Ezra 2, which most authorities now agree is a genuine list of those returning from exile in the period after Cyrus' decree,[40] for the Levites are very thinly represented, amounting to a mere 74 in contrast to a total of 4289 priests! Already at that time, the hierocratic tenor of the *gôlāh* group had been set, and we can speculate that most Levites who had participated in the exile saw no future in returning with a group so dominated by the Zadokites that

39. Unlike many prophetic elements, who bore with them into exile a traditional critical attitude toward existing civil authorities, the temple priests carried a different attitude nourished over the centuries of time in which they had served in a state sanctuary as civil servants, appointed by and answerable to the king: they would have found it most natural to cooperate with the royal authorities in making plans for the eventual restoration of their cult.

40. See W. Rudoph, *Esra und Nehemiah*, HAT (Tübingen: J. C. B. Mohr [Paul Siebeck], 1949), pp. 11-16.

they would be accorded no part in the leadership of the restored cult but would be faced instead with a discriminatory policy which would relegate them to the class of "servants of the temple" (Ezr 8:17). In addition, many Levites had never been exiled, since they were not among the upper priestly echelons at the time of the exile, and we have suggested in connection with Is 63:7–64:11 that the group which clashed with the exclusive hierocratic group upon the latter's return to the land included a significant number of Levites. We will find corroboration of that hypothesis in Ezekiel 44, a Zadokite addition to the prophecy of Ezekiel. A further narrowing of the hierocratic party is suggested by a second list, also to be regarded as a genuine document,[41] that listing those returning with Ezra. Among the returnees of that time *no* Levites were found, and it was only after a special delegation was sent to a certain Iddo of Casiphia that a tiny group of thirty-eight Levites were mustered. Only at a considerably later period, attested by the books of Chronicles, Ezra, and Nehemiah, were Levites reintegrated into the temple cult.[42]

Thus a very exclusive, and even intolerant, Zadokite-led hierocratic group returned to reestablish the structures which had given them exclusive control of the temple priesthood after the reform of Josiah had cut the ground from under their Levitical opponents. This they sought to do on the basis of a program of restoration legitimized by the prestigious name of Ezekiel and authorized by the official decree of the Persian emperor. Not long after the return the dual offices of the hierocratic program found claimants in the Davidide Zerubbabel and the priest Joshua. Then around the year 520 the prophets Haggai and Zechariah threw their powerful support toward the realization of the central institution of the hierocratic program, the temple. It was in connection with the building of that temple that the ever increasing resistance to the hierocratic program of the *gôlāh* came to a head. Leaders of that

41. Ibid., pp. 81 ff.
42. Cf. 1 Chr 24:1–3.

resistance were elements identifying themselves with the prophecy of Second Isaiah and joined, as we have suggested, by the traditional priestly adversaries of the Zadokites, the Ithamaride Levites. That side of the conflict we have traced in Isaiah 56–66. The other side we shall see reflected in the history of the hierocratic tradition which is our present object of study, the most bitter stage of the conflict being recorded in the Zadokite additions to the book of Ezekiel. The book of Chronicles is the last document of the hierocratic tradition which we shall consider, for it reflects the return to a more tolerant spirit within the hierocratic tradition, a spirit which then characterizes the remaining Persian period. In this period the active resistance of the visionary tradition had been broken, forcing them either to assimilate or to go underground, leaving the hierocratic party in unchallenged control of the temple cult and central religious community.

D. EZEKIEL: THE PRE-EXILIC ZADOKITE TEMPLE STRUCTURES TRANSFORMED INTO A HIEROCRATIC PROGRAM OF RESTORATION

The fact that in tracing the development of the hierocratic tradition in the exilic and post-exilic period we are obliged to recognize the prophet-priest Ezekiel as the fountainhead of that entire tradition should call into serious question the frequent attempts in the literature to account for apocalyptic as a unilinear development within one party or school. Eschatological and, indeed, apocalyptic eschatological hopes permeated the total religious environment of the Jews after the crushing defeats of the early sixth century, affecting all parties, all traditions, whether in Babylon or in Palestine. We are able to account for the complexities of the sixth-century literature only if we are perfectly aware of the fact that apocalyptic symbols and categories of thought are not the possession of one particular party in any age.[43] They are rather forms of con-

43. See Bloch, *Apocalyptic,* p. 136. We applaud Joshua Bloch's rejection of the "party" model as a means of explaining the history of Jewish apocalyptic. What is

ceptualizing future expectations which recommend themselves to men and women whose hopes and plans have been belied by the events of history, men and women who are prompted by despair to maintain their plans and hopes by looking to fulfillment on a plane which is indifferent to the contingencies and limitations of mundane realities.

It is our contention that particular groups utilizing the idiom of apocalyptic eschatology will continue to do so only so long as political and historical circumstances deny them the opportunity to give expression to their hopes within the political structures and historical events. To be sure, the apocalyptic outlook itself can so implant itself in the mentality of a group that that group becomes less and less capable of seizing positions of control in relation to existing structures. This self-perpetuation of the apocalyptic mentality of certain groups, even in our contemporary society, is further abetted by the continual influx of the socially powerless and disenfranchised into their ranks.

Thus it is that the otherworldly orientation of apocalyptic eschatology can become so deeply engrained into the fiber of a specific group that it in fact becomes an apocalyptic sect with a long continuous history; that is to say, there are examples of sectarian groups whose chief characteristic over decades or even centuries is their apocalyptic eschatology. This seems to be the case of the circle of disciples of Second Isaiah which, together with the other disenfranchised elements which came to associate with it, perpetuated a tradition through the last half of the sixth century and on into the fifth which moved further and further in the direction of full-blown apocalyptic.

The picture was otherwise with the post-exilic tradition which derives from Ezekiel and traces ultimately to the Zadokite temple structures of the pre-exilic period. Arising

---

lacking in his discussion, however, is an adequate explanation of the factors guiding specific groups in certain periods to embrace apocalyptic forms as the means of expressing their hopes concerning Yahweh's final saving acts. Bloch is not to be singled out in this lack, for studies in the apocalyptic literature in general have failed to supply the explanation. Apocalyptic thinking is the product of a mentality which has specifiable characteristics, and is born of historical and sociological circumstances which must be investigated if the nature and function of apocalyptic eschatology are ever to be adequately understood.

amidst the same climate of despair and shattered hopes in the face of the Babylonian conquest and the resulting disintegration of political and religious structures, this tradition—like that stemming from Second Isaiah—drew on visionary (and mythical) motifs to maintain future hopes of restoration. But two chief differences distinguish this group from that developing out of the prophecy of Second Isaiah. With regard to the question of the carrier of apocalyptic eschatology in the post-exilic period, these differences are crucial: (1) During the early period of Israel's exile, the hierocratic tradition was developed by those Zadokite priests who had controlled the Jerusalem temple cult up to the time of its destruction; thus as leaders of the exilic community they symbolized continuity and stability amidst disintegration and change. (2) After the return from exile, those same leaders of the hierocratic tradition, supported by the Persian government, were able to assert their authority over rival claimants, and thus to reconstruct the Jewish community along the lines of their restoration program. Thus the "apocalyptic" forms and motifs which were a visible part of their early literature outlived their meaningfulness and utility after the completion of the temple in 515.

The visionary phase in the history of the hierocratic tradition thus was short-lived. Following the realization of the restoration program of the Zadokite priests, this group, now charged with the responsibilities of overseeing a religious community integrated into the political structures of the Persian Empire, adopted a pragmatic approach to the everyday affairs of temple and state which was uneschatological in nature. For this reason we must disagree with those (most recently Hartmut Gese)[44] who would claim that within the tradition reaching from Ezekiel to Zechariah one can trace the rise of apocalyptic in Israel. Ezekiel, Zechariah, and Haggai, like Second and "Third" Isaiah, utilized some of the forms and motifs which would become a part

44. H. Gese, "Anfang und Ende der Apokalyptik, dargestellt am Sacharjabuch," *Theologie und Kirche* 70 (1973):20–49. Our disagreement with Gese rests in part on methodological considerations. First, he defines apocalyptic on the basis of a list of

of later apocalyptic writings to maintain the hopes of their community amidst crushing disappointment and defeat. But in contrast to the tradition building upon the prophecy of Second Isaiah, which continued to move in the direction of full-blown apocalyptic on into the fifth century, the tradition developing out of the program of Ezekiel discarded the apocalyptic idiom after 515 B.C. In this fact we see evidenced the divergent functions which apocalyptic (mythic) motifs served in the hierocratic and visionary segments of the early post-exilic community. True to the observation of Karl Mannheim, the members of the ruling hierocratic group were interest-bound to their own positions and structures which they regarded as absolute and eternal and utilized the apocalyptic motifs to legitimize and sanctify their claims. Once those claims were no longer seriously threatened, such motifs were no longer essential to their purposes and therefore disappear from their writings. In contrast, the oppressed and disenfranchised within the community utilized apocalyptic (mythic) motifs to call into question the validity of existing structures by pointing out the incongruity between their apocalyptic vision of a perfect realm and the actual state of reality. Their apocalyptic eschatology persevered and developed so long as their status of inferiority continued,[45] on into the fifth century and beyond.

Remembering that the hierocratic tradition which built upon the thought of Ezekiel was carried by the Zadokite priests, that is, by the group in control of the temple before its destruction in 587 and charged with leadership of the *gôlāh* both during and after the exile, we therefore must

characteristics (such as those in J. Schreiner, *Altestamentlich-jüdische Apokalyptik* [München: Koesel, 1969], pp. 73–110 and 111–164, to which he makes reference). We feel that such a list, mixing literary and substantive features gleaned from widely diverse compositions, and never all found in a single work, fails to define the phenomenon of Jewish apocalyptic (see Chapter I above). Secondly, he restricts his examination too narrowly to the book of Zechariah, thereby failing to place the visions of that book in their larger sixth-century context and giving inadequate attention to the inner-community struggles of that century within which apocalyptic eschatology developed. Thirdly, he fails to distinguish between different functions which the same symbols and genres can serve in different settings. Finally, he uncritically accepts an organic connection between Zechariah 1–8 and 9–14.

45. See Mannheim, *Ideology*, pp. 87 and 192.

take care in discerning the precise function played by "apocalyptic" forms and motifs in this literature. Do these forms and motifs become an essential part of the beliefs of this tradition (as was found increasingly to be the case in the history of the visionary group), or are they forms which never become significant in themselves, but even before being discarded entirely serve merely as carriers of a very pragmatic program of rebuilding a historical community? In this connection, it would be well to heed a warning of James Luther Adams: "The 'use' made of a symbol may vary according to the social status or frustration or demands of a particular social group; the 'use' made of a symbol by a ruling group will be different from the 'use' made by a deprived group."[46] If our understanding of the fully developed apocalyptic writings is correct, the idiom of apocalyptic eschatology functions in those writings to maintain the future hope of a community in the face of circumstances in the political and historical realm which call into serious question the possibility of that hope being realized within the existing order of things. Precisely because historical realities seem to belie divine promises, the community of believers adopts the idiom of apocalyptic eschatology to portray divine intervention and fulfillment of the community's hope on a level unaffected by the limitations of historical events. Existing powers, political and religious structures become matters of indifference. This function of the apocalyptic idiom we found developing in the oracles of Isaiah 56–66. We turn now to trace the development of the hierocratic tradition from Ezekiel to Haggai and Zechariah, and shall ask whether this "use" or function of full-blown apocalyptic can be recognized there as well.

Modern sociologists like Mannheim and Weber have demonstrated convincingly that powerful officials ruling over the religious or political structures of a society do not dream apocalyptic visions of the revolutionary overthrow of the existing order of things. Temple priests are not

46. "The Pragmatic Theory of Meaning," Presidential Address, American Society of Christian Ethics, Washington D.C., January 24, 1969.

likely candidates for apocalyptic seers, not, that is, so long as they are in control of their temples. We are not surprised, therefore, to find no eschatological writings from the Zadokite leadership in pre-exilic times. But what of the period after the destruction of the temple and the disruption of the cult over which they presided? The post-exilic period presents us with two very interesting bodies of literature from priests turned prophets. In Ezekiel and Zechariah we receive the messages of priests who have been denied their temple. It is not surprising that these priests draw upon visionary forms to maintain their hopes for restoration. But do these visionary forms affect the substance of their beliefs, or are they forms which are utilized for a time only to be discarded once the earlier structures have been reestablished and the old positions of control have been regained?

Although the answer to this question will be quite straightforward in the case of Haggai and Zechariah, the matter is much more complex in the book of Ezekiel. Here the genuine qualities of the classical prophet blend into the interests of the priest in an unusual way. It is quite clear that the book of Ezekiel as it has come down to us has been recast along the official lines of the hierocratic tradition. It seems that there were prophetic elements in Ezekiel's prophecy which ill-suited their program, leading to the additions and alterations which we shall discuss below. But even within those parts of the book which can with reasonable confidence be attributed to Ezekiel, we find a message basically consonant with the aims of the later hierocracy, a message drawing upon the norms of prophecy to prepare for and describe a restoration program continuous with the Zadokite structures of the pre-exilic temple cult. It is not accidental, therefore, that the hierocratic group which gained control over the post-exilic community, which rebuilt the temple and then presided over the reconstituted cult, was able to adopt Ezekiel as its patron saint. For Ezekiel was one of their spiritual forefathers, and his message contained the blueprint for a restoration which would restore them to their original power. Ezekiel 40–48 served the purpose of the Zadokite priests of the last third of the sixth century as well as Isaiah 40–55 and 60–62 served the visionary followers of Second Isaiah. Thus it was that both parties in the struggle of the restoration period were able to claim the authority of one of the great prophets of the first half of their century.

This comparison leads to an important question: if the prophecies of Second Isaiah can be called proto-apocalyptic, can the same be maintained for the message of Ezekiel? The connections between the book of Ezekiel and later apocalyptic writings are unmistakable: the bizarre imagery, the form of the vision, and the device of divine interpretation (later developing into the figure of the *angelus interpres*) live on in later apocalyptic compositions. Such features in themselves, however, do not constitute the eschatology of apocalyptic, for they are literary devices which can be found in earlier compositions as well. Nevertheless, because the connections between Ezekiel and later apocalyptic writings are many, we must consider the nature of the relation between Ezekiel and apocalyptic eschatology.[47]

In this consideration it may be useful to contrast Ezekiel and Second Isaiah in several respects. In describing the restoration plans, Ezekiel stresses continuity with pre-exilic structures and institutions, Second Isaiah discontinuity; Ezekiel describes the restored community with great attention to the officialdom, Second Isaiah's attention is almost exclusively on Yahweh's role in the restoration; central to the concern of Ezekiel is the rebuilding of the temple, while in Second Isaiah the temple barely receives mention. In many other respects as well the contrast could be drawn between the pragmatic priest Ezekiel concerned with laying

47. Cf. L. Dürr, *Die Stellung des Propheten Ezekiel in der israelitisch-jüdischen Apokalyptik* (Münster: 1923). In a discussion of the relation of the prophet Ezekiel to apocalyptic, chapters 38–39 do not enter the picture, being products of a later period when the attempt was being made to answer why the glorious promises of Ezekiel 36–37 were not fulfilled as expected once the program outlined in chapters 40–48 had been completed. In a sense, Ezekiel 38–39 serves to reinterpret Ezekiel 1–37, 40–48, even as Isaiah 56–66 seeks to interpret Isaiah 40–55. Why have the dazzling promises of the prophets not taken place? Because the evil remaining in the land necessitates further destruction and judgment, after which the restoration will finally occur.

the basis for the continuation of pre-exilic structures in the post-exilic era and the visionary prophet Second Isaiah boldly announcing Yahweh's creation of a new order which would supplant the structures of the past; between the priest Ezekiel drawing on models from the immediate past so as to guarantee continuation of the former institutions and the prophet Second Isaiah summoning archaic, even primeval images to announce the dramatic turn from old things to things which are radically new.[48] These contrasts strongly suggest that, while the book of Ezekiel utilizes a number of forms and symbols which are later adopted by apocalyptic writings, one must be careful to discern whether the "use" or function of these forms and symbols in Ezekiel is that found in later apocalyptic compositions like Daniel, Revelation, and 4 Ezra.

First it must be recognized that, unlike the visions of Zechariah which we shall discuss below, the visions of Ezekiel do emerge from a time when existing political and historical structures do not permit the prophet's community to effect the envisioned restoration program by their own efforts. There is a genuine element of waiting for Yahweh's intervention which is more than a literary device for legitimating a program already being constructed by the community leaders (as in the case of Haggai and Zechariah). While this element brings the prophecy of Ezekiel close to the orientation of apocalyptic, it is another aspect of the book, and indeed *the* aspect which was accentuated by later hierocratic editors of the book to the neglect of the future thrust, that causes us to refrain from applying the designation *proto-apocalyptic* to the message of Ezekiel. That aspect is manifested in the contrasts we drew above between Second Isaiah and Ezekiel, and can be characterized as a strong pragmatic orientation in Ezekiel which always

48. Even in those pre-exilic sections where Ezekiel reveals his solidarity with the earlier prophets by announcing judgment on Israel because of the nation's sin, he betrays his priestly background, for sin to him is primarily construed as violation of sacral orders. When Ezekiel spells out the reasons for the imminent destruction, he finds Israel's failures in the cultic realm (Ezek 5:11; 8:7ff; 14:3ff). Israel has "defiled herself with all the idols. . ." (23:7). Even the *Unheilsgeschichte* reflects Ezekiel's priestly point of view, for that history is seen as a steady decline of the cult (see Ezekiel 16, 20, 23). Cf. von Rad, *Theology* II, pp. 225 ff.

construes the restoration of the community on the basis of specific temple structures and priestly offices drawn from the temple cult of the pre-destruction period, structures and offices which would be reconstituted by the Zadokite priests once the community had returned to the land. This pragmatic orientation, enhanced by the consciousness of Ezekiel and his fellow priests that they were still the leaders of the people and thus in a favorable position to one day effect their restoration plans, supplied the basis upon which the visions of Ezekiel could be integrated into the realities of the historical and political order, once the opportunity presented itself. Thus a tenacious apocalyptic thrust is lacking in the prophecy of Ezekiel; the visionary forms are used primarily as literary devices for outlining a program of restoration along the lines of the Zadokite-led temple cult of the period immediately before the Babylonian conquest, and describing the conditions within the Jewish community prerequisite for this restoration.

As we trace the beginnings of the hierocratic tradition of the post-exilic period back to the prophecy of Ezekiel and contrast this with the origins of the visionary tradition in the prophecy of Second Isaiah and the programmatic summary of Second Isaiah's restoration hope in Isaiah 60–62, we must take care to sort out the similarities from the differences between these two programs. In both the visionary form is pronounced, in both the future orientation toward a restoration to be inaugurated by Yahweh is apparent, in both images and symbols are applied to Israel's situation which would later be adopted by apocalyptic writers. These similarities could lead one to conclude that both the Zadokite-led hierocratic group and the visionary followers of Second Isaiah take their point of departure from the same future-oriented, visionary, or even apocalyptic view of Yahweh's relation to his defeated community, a view replete with forms and motifs which could easily develop into full-blown apocalyptic, given the right circumstances. One could go on to observe that in the writings of Haggai and Zechariah on the hierocratic side, and in the writings of "Third Isaiah" on the visionary side, these forms and motifs move further in the direction of apocalyptic.

This reconstruction of sixth-century developments would finally be confronted with the task of accounting for the sudden disappearance of the apocalyptic thrust in the hierocratic tradition after 515, in contrast to the further development of that thrust on the visionary side. This task could be accomplished by noting that the proponents of the hierocratic tradition gained control of the post-exilic community in the last third of the sixth century, translated their visionary program into a rebuilt temple and a reconstituted Zadokite priesthood, and thereby were able to discard the visionary form of their program. On the other hand visionaries, defeated and removed from any participation in the leadership of the community and the cult, were driven to accentuate the visionary aspect of their program even further, thus moving them closer to a full apocalyptic outlook. This reconstruction of the parallel nature of the two rival traditions of the sixth century has much to recommend itself: (1) It is a healthful antidote to simplistic theories of the origins of apocalyptic which would trace one single line of development within a particular party of the post-exilic community. (2) It takes into account the visionary elements on both sides of the sixth-century controversies. (3) It recognizes the importance of sociological factors in determining which segments of the community cling to apocalyptic forms, and which adopt pragmatic views instead. It stands in need of qualification, however, at two points: (1) It does not carefully distinguish between the different "uses" to which visionary or proto-apocalyptic forms and symbols are put on different sides of those controversies (e.g., in the oracles of Third Isaiah and the visions of Zechariah). (2) It fails to recognize that already at the earliest stage of the development of the two traditions, a distinct pragmatic *Tendenz* is present in the program of Ezekiel, in contrast to a pronounced visionary and, indeed, proto-apocalyptic thrust in Second Isaiah and the program in Isaiah 60–62.

Thus we are obliged to eschew this reconstruction as

oversimplistic as well and are thrust back on examination of the actual writings in question. As we now move on from Ezekiel to the later writings of the hierocratic tradition, we thus bring from our study of Ezekiel a recognition of that book as a hybrid composition, serving as the fountainhead of the hierocratic tradition, and yet utilizing forms and symbols which live on in later apocalyptic writings. When viewed as a whole, however, the pragmatic aspect of the book seems more dominant than the visionary dimension inherent in the forms and symbols. The ultimate goal of Ezekiel's prophecy seems to be the promulgation of a program of restoration which is dedicated to the preservation of the institutions of the immediate past and which thus stands in marked contrast to the themes of later apocalyptic such as the absolute break with structures of the past and the imminent judgment followed by a new creation. The priestly interests of Ezekiel are thus very visible beneath the visionary forms, and they determine the use to which those forms are put: the temple would be rebuilt according to the traditional patterns of the era immediately preceding the Babylonian destruction, and the Glory of Yahweh would then return to a cultic setting emulating that which existed prior to the exile.

In Ezekiel 40–48 the post-exilic Zadokite leaders thus found a suitable blueprint for their restoration efforts. Moreover, the central theological theme running throughout Ezekiel's prophecies was embraced by the hierocratic leaders as most compatible with their own interests, that theme being the reestablishment within the nation Israel of a state of holiness conducive to the return of Yahweh to the midst of his people. In contrast to the view of many visionaries, the catastrophe of 587 was not interpreted by Ezekiel as a judgment on the Zadokite temple theology; only as a result of the defilement of the temple through idolatrous rites was Yahweh forced to withdraw from Zion. What Ezekiel therefore called for was the restoration of the proper cult, and the reorganization of the legitimate priesthood to safeguard the sanctity of that cult. It is not difficult to see how this central theme served well the purposes of the hierocratic group, especially since it was united with the view that reform legitimately could stem only from leaders of the *gôlāh* (Ezek 11:14ff; 33:23ff), i.e., from the Zadokite-dominated hierocratic party.

But in Ezekiel's program of restoration, attention was not given exclusively to the temple institution, but was turned also to the other pre-exilic institution, the Davidic monarchy (e.g., 34:23f; 37:24ff), for in the restored community leadership was to be shared by priest and king, although the powers of the latter were to be strictly defined and limited.[49] Ezekiel thus advances a program standing in continuity with pre-exilic structures, as a result of which Yahweh's "everlasting covenant with them" would be reestablished, and Yahweh would set his "sanctuary in the midst of them forever" (37:25–27).

As background to later developments within the hierocratic tradition, it is also important to notice in the basic work of Ezekiel the absence of the bitter polemic against the Levites which came to characterize the Zadokite writings later in the sixth century. When judgment is proclaimed upon the priests by Ezekiel (22:23ff; 8:5ff), no distinction is made between one priestly group which is guilty and another which is innocent (cf. 44:9–16!). Whether or not Ezekiel 40:45–46a and Ezekiel 48 (minus the gloss in v. 11) come from the prophet himself, they do belong to a level of tradition close to the time and spirit of Ezekiel, and it is therefore very significant that while a distinction between Levites and Zadokites is made, they are both designated "priests" (*kōhănîm*) (40:45f; cf. 44:13!). The superiority of the Zadokites which resulted from Josiah's reform is taken for granted without discrediting the priestly status of the Levites. Only by means of late glosses in 40:46b and 48:11 is the degrading of the Levites accentuated.[50] Thus the basic stratum of Ezekiel gives the ap-

49. Tending to avoid the designation *melek* ("king"), Ezekiel favors the term *nagîd* ("prince"). Moreover, he assigns only a very modest role to this functionary (Ezek 47:7–8, 17, 21–25; cf. 43:7–9; 37:22–24).

50. Cf. W. Zimmerli, *Ezekiel*, BK (Neukirchen: Neukirchen, 1956), p. 1133. On the levels of tradition in Ezekiel, see also H. Gese, *Der Verfassungsentwurf des Ezekiel* (Tübingen: J. C. B. Mohr [Paul Siebeck], 1957), and A. H. J. Gunneweg, *Leviten und Priester* (Göttingen: Vandenhoeck und Ruprecht, 1965), pp. 188 ff.

pearance of an ideal program yet untarnished by the struggles of history; it assumes, in this respect, a position in the hierocratic tradition similar to that occupied by Isaiah 40–55 and 60–62 in the prophetic tradition stemming from Second Isaiah. And the parallel continues through the further history of the two traditions, with the polemical element increasing in both until the acrimony manifested by Isaiah 66 and 56:9–57:13 is equivalent to that permeating Ezekiel 44. It is our contention that this parallel development occurring within the hierocratic tradition and the prophetic tradition reflects two sides of a single post-exilic struggle. We now turn to trace the hierocratic tradition in its development beyond the original Ezekiel program.

E. HAGGAI AND ZECHARIAH: THE HIEROCRATIC TEMPLE PROGRAM RECEIVES PROPHETIC LEGITIMATION

The biblical records leave considerable gaps in our understanding of the history of the hierocratic group in the period between the prophetic careers of Ezekiel and Zechariah. What evidence does exist points to a period of struggle between rival groups for control of community leadership, especially as that leadership related to the temple cult. This struggle centering around rival temple rebuilding programs involved more than religious considerations, narrowly construed, as can best be understood by reference to the law regulating land tenure in Lev 25:23: "The land shall not be sold in perpetuity, for the land is mine; for you are strangers and sojourners with me." Yahweh is the land owner, which translated into the realities of economics would read thus: those having a part in the rebuilding of Yahweh's temple, and thereby establishing their membership in his temple community, would be entitled to share in Yahweh's land; those excluded from the rebuilding and from the temple community would forfeit that claim.[51] Ezek 11:14–21 indicates that struggles involving these claims already caused dissension between

51. Morton Smith, *Palestinian Parties and Politics that Shaped the Old Testament* (New York: Columbia University, 1971), p. 108.

Jews in exile and those remaining in the land during Ezekiel's lifetime:

> And the word of the Lord came to me: "Son of man, your brethren, even your brethren, your fellow exiles, the whole house of Israel, all of them, are those of whom the inhabitants of Jerusalem have said, 'They have gone far from the Lord; to us this land is given for a possession.' Therefore say, 'Thus says the Lord God: Though I removed them far off among the nations, and though I scattered them among the countries, yet I have been a sanctuary to them for a while in the countries where they have gone.' Therefore say, 'Thus says the Lord: I will gather you from the peoples, and assemble you out of the countries where you have been scattered, and I will give you the land of Israel.' " (Ezek 11:14–17)

For those remaining in Jerusalem, the catastrophes of the time had proven Yahweh's judgment upon those now in exile, that is, especially upon the Zadokite priesthood and their temple cult. The deed to the land had thus been transferred to those escaping the exile, who had thereby been singled out as recipients of Yahweh's blessing. In this controversy, Ezekiel takes his stand squarely against this Palestinian position, arguing on behalf of the exiles and their Zadokite leaders: the disasters of the temple destruction and the exile only gave the appearance of judging the exilic group and favoring those remaining in the land. In fact Yahweh did not remain among the latter, but he rather became a sanctuary *(miqdāš)* for the exiles in the countries where they had been scattered. The legitimate line of succession within the people of Yahweh was thus to be traced in the exile and not among those who were able to stay in Jerusalem.

This apology underlies the entire vision sequence dealing with the departure of Yahweh's Glory from the temple, of which the passage 11:14–21 is a part. The prophet Ezekiel is lifted up in a vision from his place among the elders of Judah in Babylon and transported to the temple area in Jerusalem (Ezek 8:1ff). There he sees the Glory of the God of Israel, like the vision he had received earlier in connection with his call. That earlier vision had established

Yahweh's presence among the exiles along the river Chebar. The present vision addresses the question of the relation of Yahweh's Glory to those inhabiting Jerusalem and making the claim that they were the rightful heirs to the land: "Son of man, do you see what they are doing, the great abominations that the house of Israel are committing to drive me from my sanctuary?" And from there the heavenly guide proceeds to show Ezekiel even greater abominations, the net result of which is the withdrawal of Yahweh's Glory from the midst of the city, and his departure in an eastward direction (11:22–23). This direction of departure, Ezekiel's vision of the Glory of Yahweh in Babylon (1:1ff), Yahweh's declaration that he has been a sanctuary for the exiles in their places of exile (11:16), and finally the notation in connection with the return of the Glory in the restoration program that "the Glory of the God of Israel came from the East" (43:2), all state the argument in no uncertain terms: Yahweh's Glory has departed from those remaining in the land, has moved to the east to watch over those in exile, and would return to Jerusalem only in company with the returning exiles and in connection with their temple rebuilding program.[52]

These polemical confrontations between the conflicting claims of the *gôlāh* and the inhabitants of Jerusalem before the return of the exiles to Palestine made even more acrimonious confrontation inevitable once the return had taken place. We know from the book of Ezra, as indicated in the previous chapter, that the returnees, carrying with them a program for restoration which was bound to an exclusive claim to being Yahweh's chosen community, refused to permit "the people of the land" to cooperate with them in the rebuilding efforts. The temple cult was their exclusive right. When we recall that this cultic claim was tied up with the legal right to land tenure, we are not surprised to observe the bitter struggle which ensued be-

52. Ezekiel's pro-*gôlah* position is stated just as clearly in 33:29: "Son of man, the inhabitants of these waste places in the land of Israel keep saying, 'Abraham was only one man, yet he got possession of the land; but we are many; the land is surely given us to possess.' " Ezekiel denies the claim with a harsh imprecation in the name of Yahweh.

tween rival claimants. The books of Ezra and Haggai report that in the years immediately after the return of the Zadokite-led *gôlāh* the restoration efforts of the hierocratic group were met only with failure and frustration, because of the strenuous opposition with which they were met.

The investigation of the oracles of Isaiah 56–66 in the previous chapter has brought to light the activity of one opposition group which, it seems, claimed to have held possession of the temple area for a time and continued to press its claim to be the rightful heir to that holy precinct even after being overpowered by the leaders of the returned *gôlāh*. Thus our interpretation of the early oracles of the Third Isaiah group accords well with evidence just examined in Ezekiel regarding the contending claims for possession of the land. It adds plausibility to the theory that the restoration program of Isaiah 60–62 had the support of various groups (including disenfranchised Levites) which had remained in the land of Palestine during the exile. In the prophecy of Second Isaiah they would have recognized prophetic support for their leadership claims once the return of the exiles—coming perhaps in a number of waves rather than in one influx—had greatly complicated the hopes and plans of those who, during the years of the exile, had remained faithful to Yahweh around the temple site in Jerusalem. On the basis of Second Isaiah's promise of Yahweh's glorious return to deliver his people, this Yahwistic group resisted the Ezekielian program of the Zadokites. The minority status of this group, and the setbacks which it apparently suffered already at the early stages of the confrontation, likely prompted its members to cling with ever greater tenacity to the most visionary parts of Second Isaiah's prophecy.

Looking back upon the first decade or two of the return of the *gôlāh,* one of the spokesmen of the hierocratic group could therefore describe that period as a time when "there was no wage for man or any wage for beast, neither was there any safety from the foe for him who went out or came in; for I set every man against his fellow" (Zech 8:10). This verse serves as a terse summary of the inner-community tension and struggle which we have been describing. It also explains why the first Jewish prince *(nāsî'*, Ezr 1:8) to be designated governor of Judah by the Persians, Sheshbazzar (Akkadian, Sin-ab-uṣur) was unsuccessful in rebuilding the temple or restoring order to the community.

The turning point in the struggles of the contending groups came around the year 520. The book of Haggai suggests that the hierocratic group had become dispirited as the result of repeated setbacks in its attempts to rebuild the temple. Conditions in the land were not good, with bitter strife tearing at the fabric of the community and with uncertainity on the international scene. The hierocrats laid the blame for this curse upon the fact that their temple restoration plan had not been effected, thereby leaving conditions in the land which were unsuitable for the return of Yahweh's Glory. It seems obvious, however, that they would be unsuccessful in mustering sufficient support for their temple program so long as masses of people in the land were captivated by the vision of a rival group, which portrayed in brilliant colors a restoration which would be inaugurated not by efforts of the Zadokite priests, but by Yahweh himself as he returned to Zion as Warrior and Judge (cf. Is 59:15b–20 and 66:6–16).

The standoff between the rival parties came to an end as the result of a remarkable turn of events which temporarily transformed the pragmatic, pro-Persian hierocratic party into a zealous nationalistic group of reformers bent on inaugurating the eschatological reign of peace prophesied by Ezekiel in their own day. The international situation created the background for that transformation, for upon the accession of Darius Hystaspes (December 522 or January 521) the Persian Empire appeared to be crumbling. A spirit of awakened nationalism swept over the subject people of the Empire. Into this potentially volatile situation stepped two prophetic figures, Haggai and Zechariah, announcing that the long awaited eschaton was about to arrive. But these two figures did not throw in their lot with the visionary followers of Second Isaiah, who had been announcing Yahweh's return to deliver his faithful followers for years. For Haggai and Zechariah did not cast their prophecies in the elevated language of the visionaries; they did not portray a cosmic redemption by Yahweh alone unrelated to the particulars of historical events. Instead they tied their eschatological predictions to the specific details of the hierocratic program. Theirs was no dream limited to a vision of Yahweh's coming to redeem his remnant amidst the trembling of the foundations of the earth and clamor of the thunderstorm, but above all a detailed plan of rebuilding the temple community: a specific high priest, Joshua, a specific David prince, Zerubbabel, a specific temple plan, that delineated in the book of Ezekiel.[53]

The strategy of the prophets Haggai and Zechariah was masterful; to the priestly tradition of the Zadokites they welded the eschatological fervor which was the hallmark of the prophetic group. Thus the detailed, pragmatic plans representing the interests of the hierocrats were cast into the visionary forms of the prophets, orchestrating the impulses of the visionaries and the realists into one passionate message, a message whose appeal was enhanced by an international situation which fanned the burning embers of nationalistic hope into the brilliant flames of an allegedly attainable eschatological plan: build the temple and the kingdom of blessedness would arrive.

The effect of their message on a populace torn between two rival programs of restoration seems to have been immediate and pronounced: many people who had been attracted to the visionary message of the prophetic group now found the message of Haggai and Zechariah even more appealing, for it offered the wonders of the eschaton

53. The dependence of Haggai and Zechariah's prophetic movement upon the program of Ezekiel is manifested even in the architectural plan of the new temple, for as Joachim Jeremias has demonstrated by a comparison of the Ezekiel plan with all the existing information about the Zerubbabel temple, "the agreements between the temple plan of Ezekiel and the rebuilding of the temple after the exile are so extensive that it is most probable that the new temple was erected on the basis of the plan which is expressly so designated in Ezek 43:11" ("Hezekieltempel und Serubbabeltempel," *ZAW* 52 [1934]: 112).

now, if only the people rallied behind the hierocratic program. That the appeal was made to a very broad spectrum of the community is indicated by Haggai 2:4, where the prophet encourages "all the people of the land" to join Zerubbabel and Joshua in the temple rebuilding program, a position vastly more latitudinarian and conciliatory than that taken by the hierocratic party at an earlier period according to Ezr 4:1–5. It would seem that such a liberal-minded attitude could have become a part of the hierocratic party only as the result of a concerted effort to muster enough popular support to overpower the rival claims of the opponents. The defection of many people from the prophetic to the hierocratic cause is perhaps attested in the note in Ezr 6:21 concerning the passover celebration at the dedication of the newly built temple, a note which obviously expresses the partisan view of the hierocratic party that every Jew, until such time that he joined their ranks, was given to "the pollutions of the peoples of the land": "it was eaten by the people of Israel who had returned from exile, and also by every one who had joined them and separated himself from the pollutions of the peoples of the land to worship Yahweh, the God of Israel." Haggai and Zechariah, by injecting prophetic fervor into the hierocratic program, made that program appealing to the masses, and their accomplishments played no mean role in the ultimate victory of the hierocratic tradition over rival claimants to community leadership.

It can therefore be maintained that the hierocratic party entered the last two decades of the sixth century as the dominant power in the Jewish community largely due to the infusion of the prophetic spirit into their languishing cause by the prophets Haggai and Zechariah. Though the effects of this last outburst of prophetic activity in Israel cannot be discussed at length here, a number of points can be made. First, it is evident that although the impact of this prophetic activity on the hierocratic tradition was pronounced, since it reaffirmed the eschatological element which had been introduced by Ezekiel, it was also very transient. Once the hierocratic temple program had been accomplished, a temple theology evolved which was centered on the Torah and which was weighted heavily away from the eschatological themes of late prophecy. Secondly, it is apparent that their tying the prophetic word to a particular political officialdom and a specific political program contributed to the further discrediting and final demise of the prophetic office. Although the historical particulars are not known, disruptions in the text of Zechariah and the sudden, mysterious disappearance of Zerubbabel and his royal office from the historical narrative indicate that the hierocratic program ran into serious difficulties, difficulties perhaps involving the intervention of the Persians due to the pretentious nationalistic claims which accompanied the enthusiam of temple reconstruction.

Zech 13:2–6 suggests the ignominious path upon which the prophetic office was sent by Haggai and Zechariah. Prophecy had arisen in Israel as an independent, spiritual check on kingship. Haggai and Zechariah, though using the forms and phrases of prophetic eschatology and exercising the prophetic functions of appointing the king and sanctifying the priesthood, placed prophecy in the uncritical service of a specific political system. In giving Yahweh's unquestioned sanction to a particular human institution, and to particular priestly and royal officials, they were wedding their fate to the fate of that institution and those officials, and were giving up the independent stance always maintained by the classical prophets vis à vis the institutions of the temple and royal court. They were giving up the revolutionary element which was always an essential ingredient in genuine prophecy, an element stemming from a vision of Yahweh's order of mercy and justice which called into question every human institution and every human officebearer. Instead they dedicated themselves to continuity, to preservation of the pre-exilic structures, to maintenance of the status quo. Theirs was the characteristic stance of the prophets of weal, and hence the bitter resistance they met from the minority group which looked upon itself as the carrier of the true prophetic tradition.

Turning first to the prophecy of Haggai, we find that he,

like Ezekiel, was centrally concerned with the restoration of the temple as the essential means of preserving the covenant. Once that house had been built, the curse would be ended, and the blessings of the covenant would return to the land. Along with the temple, the other essential element in the covenant was the Davidic dynasty which also would be restored "on that day" in the person of Zerubbabel. Thus it is that he applies to the latter such loaded terms as "servant" *('ebed)*, "signet ring" *(ḥôtām)*, "chosen" *(bḥr)* (2:23).[54] In contrast to Jeremiah, who applied the term *'ebed* to Nebuchadnezzar; to Second Isaiah, who described the *'ebed* as a Suffering Servant; and to Third Isaiah, who identified the *'ebed* with the oppressed prophetic community, Haggai announces that Yahweh has chosen a living, contemporary Israelite, Zerubbabel, as his *'ebed.*[55] What Haggai did was thus to take the program of Ezekiel and to announce that it was being effected in contemporary events and persons. The eschaton had arrived. Accompanying the eschaton were the extravagant wonders of unheard of prosperity and spectacular fertility of the land which had long been a part of the eschatological hope. Figures which in the eschatological promises of Ezekiel (e.g., chapter 47) added vivid color to the future hope seem magical and excessive when applied by Haggai to the contemporary events. The human endeavor of rebuilding the temple becomes the condition for the arrival of the messianic kingdom, a belief which apparently seemed pagan to some opponents of the hierocratic program as they contrasted it with the classical prophetic view that only an act of Yahweh accompanying the repentance of the people could usher in the eschaton.

To be sure, once Israel had adopted the Canaanite prototype of the temple, such an abuse became a recurrent threat, since the mythological belief that the temple was the

54. Haggai here makes very clear that Jeremiah's message that Coniah and his sons would no longer sit upon the throne of David has been abrogated by a new divine word. See. G. Sauer, "Serubbabel in der Sicht Haggais und Sacharjas," in *Das Ferne und Nahe Wort Gottes*, Festschrift L. Rost, ed. F. Maass (Berlin: Töpelmann, 1967), p. 204.

55. Cf. Ezek 34:23f and 37:24f.

supernatural source of all prosperity and fertility could never be totally suppressed. It is this resurgent mythical equation of temple structure and prosperity, and this inability to conceive of the presence of Yahweh apart from the temple edifice, which sets Haggai apart from the pre-exilic prophets and explains the bitter opposition which his message met from groups regarding themselves as carriers of the prophetic tradition. By the same token, it is the exalted position attributed to the temple in his prophecy and the emphasis upon continuity with pre-exilic cultic structures (in contrast to the prophetic group's stress on "new things") which made Haggai's message completely compatible with the interests of the hierocratic leaders.

In Zechariah's prophecy a more complete picture is preserved of the restoration program championed by these two prophets. It is the original plan of the prophet Ezekiel which is being promulgated by this prophet, who like Ezekiel seems to be a descendant of a priestly family (Zech 1:1; cf. Ezek 5:1; 6:14; Neh 12:16).[56] Zechariah sees his nation at the point in history prophesied by Ezekiel when Yahweh would return to Zion to dwell in the midst of his people (1:16; 2:15ff); the tangible sign of that return was the rebuilding of the temple (1:16); the tangible results would

56. Supporting the evidence which will be given in this chapter for the unity of tradition binding Zechariah to Ezekiel are two key concepts shared by these books. The key term used in the hierocratic tradition to express the mode by which Yahweh was present in the midst of his people is the qal of the verb *škn*. Related to this is the designation of the temple as the *miškān*. Behind these words is an archaic root in Northwest Semitic with the basic meaning "to tent." This meaning was probably derived denominatively from the noun *miškān*, "tent" (see F. M. Cross, "The Priestly Tabernacle," in *The Biblical Archaeoligist Reader,* eds. G. E. Wright and D. N. Freedman [New York: Doubleday, Anchor Books, 1961], pp. 225–226. This terminology is applied by Ezekiel in key passages which express the covenant conditions under which Yahweh will be present with his people (37:24–27; 43:7–9). It is then adopted by Zechariah in the same sense to express the restoration hope of Yahweh's tenting in the midst of his People: "I come and I tent in the midst of you" (Zech 2:14 [10]): "I will return to Zion, and will tent in the midst of Jerusalem" (Zech 8:3; see also 1 Chr 23:25).

Closely related to the *škn* terminology is another concept which is central to the literature of the hierocratic tradition, namely, *kābôd yhwh*. Originally borrowed from the Yahwist, the priestly tradition infused it with new theological content to designate the tabernacling presence. It is in this sense that it is used in Ezekiel's visions (e.g., Chapters 1–3; 8–11). The rich theological content of the term is seen in especial clarity in the descriptions of the departure of the *kābôd* tied to the destruction of the city (11:23), and of the return of the *kābôd* which was the basis for material and spiritual restoration (43:4; 44:4). The term is then used in the same technical sense in Zech 2:9 and 12 (cf. 2 Chr 7:1c–3).

be the prosperity which would come to the land (1:17).[57] The structures of the restored community would be those outlined in detail by Ezekiel (chapters 40–48), with the leadership invested in the offices of high priest and Davidic prince. These two figures would thus reestablish and preside over the two institutions, priestly and royal, of the pre-exilic period.

There can be no question that Zechariah, like Haggai, was a forceful spokesman for the Zadokite temple program. Nor can it be disputed that he utilized a genre which later was adopted by apocalyptic writers—the vision with the *angelus interpres*—to communicate his message to the people. The crucial question, however, is that raised by Hartmut Gese when he proceeds one step beyond the latter point with the thesis that "the nocturnal visions of Zechariah are the oldest and best known apocalypse."[58] We are here thrust upon the difficult problem of definitions. It is very true that the visions of Zechariah 1–8 have formal characteristics in common with parts of later apocalyptic books. If apocalyptic is to be defined strictly on the basis of literary types one can grant a degree of truth to Gese's thesis: Zechariah's visions would be an early example of one type of apocalyptic composition. But can justice be done to the multifarious literary characteristics of full-blown apocalyptic works on the basis of so narrow a definition? So complex is the nature of late apocalyptic that we eschew the attempt to give a simple literary definition of that phenomenon.[59] Apocalyptic writings utilize virtually all of the old literary genres of biblical literature: judgment and salvation oracles, hymns, testaments, laments, visions, etc. It would seem advisable, therefore, to alter the form of the question concerning apocalpytic origins. First, it seems imperative to clarify which aspect of fully developed apocalyptic we are addressing. In drawing connections with

57. Cf. Chary, *Prophètes*, pp. 139 ff.

58. Gese, "Anfang." Unlike Stone, "Lists," Gese does not draw a clear distinction between "apocalyptic" and "apocalypse."

59. See the author's "Jewish Apocalyptic," pp. 31–35.

biblical prophecy, Gese seems to be interested in the eschatology of apocalyptic. This is our concern as well.

The next task must be that of defining apocalyptic eschatology and distinguishing it from the earlier eschatology of classical prophecy. The essential difference between the two is found in the otherwordly orientation of apocalyptic eschatology; the prophetic vocation of integrating the vision of divine activity into the structures, figures, and events of the historical realm is in large measure abdicated. Because conditions in the political arena and the relations of the apocalyptic circle in question to those conditions do not offer realistic means by which the fulfillment of the divine promises can be accomplished within existing structures, the vision of fulfillment is described in a manner of indifference to those structures. The sociological position of the proponent of apocalyptic eschatology is therefore that of powerlessness and disenfranchisement vis-à-vis the controlling powers of his community and world. His vision of the future, portraying Yahweh's intervention, thus has a genuine future orientation, intended to sustain hope in the midst of events which would deny any earthly basis for hope. What we have here described was the position of the community that produced the oracles of Isaiah 56–66, and hence we detected an important impulse toward apocalyptic eschatology in that collection of writings.

Can the visions of Zechariah similarly be described as a primary source of apocalyptic eschatology? Hardly. In this prophet we find anything but a spokesman for a group denied a position of power in relation to controlling forces within the community. Rather, we find a representative of the group which has emerged in control of the offices of community and cult and which enjoys the support of the world power of the day, the Persians. Nor is the vision the product of the fervent longing of the oppressed for an intervening act of Yahweh which will overthrow existing powers so as to elevate them from their powerlessness. It is rather the idiom of the vision applied as *post factum* legitimation of a pragmatic political program over which the spokesman's group has control and which, moreover, already is well on its way toward completion. In a word, Zechariah represents not the use of visionary forms as a means of sustaining the hope of the disenfranchised and powerless in the face of historical realities which belie all basis for hope, but rather the use of the vision to establish divine legitimation for the very group which is in power and to win popular support for its pragmatic cultic and political program. The relation between the nocturnal visions of Zechariah and the temple program of the Zadokites is thus similar in function to the relation between the cosmogonic myth and the typical ancient Near Eastern royal dynasty: the visions like the myth function as the cosmic legitimization of the existing power structures and institutions.

How vastly different this is from the use of mythopoeic (cosmic) motifs in the early apocalyptic oracles of Third Isaiah or in the fully developed apocalyptic writings of later centuries where the Divine Warrior is summoned to overturn existing powers and structures, supplanting them with a totally new order of reality. Because of this vastly different relation to existing powers and the status quo, another chief feature of apocalyptic eschatology is absent in Zechariah, the anonymity or pseudonymity whereby the writer hid his identity for fear of retaliation by the authorities. Zechariah, like Haggai, had no need for disguise, for his relation to the authorities was cordial. Hence his use of the vision functions in a manner contrasting sharply with the use of the vision in genuine apocalyptic compositions. It is possible, however, that Zechariah's use of forms resembling those used in apocalyptic did result from a distinct relation to the apocalyptic eschatology of the visionary group in Third Isaiah, but a relation of a very particular nature. In the period of struggle for temple control, with the visionary group making rival claims and contesting the legitimacy of the Zadokites in the name of the word of Yahweh and in the idiom of the apocalyptic vision, it is very possible that Zechariah's use of the form of the vision arose as a conscious attempt to redirect the enthusiasm aroused by the apocalyptic vision away from the disenfranchised protesters and toward the official temple program. We are again reminded of James Luther Adams's trenchant observation that "the 'use' made of a symbol may vary according to the social status or frustration or demands of particular social groups: the 'use' made of a symbol by a ruling group will be different from the 'use' made by a deprived group."[60] In the case of Zechariah, the forms and symbols utilized on behalf of the ruling group bear a *prima facie* resemblance to the forms and symbols of deprived apocalyptic groups. But the "use" made of them in one case is that of underpinning existing structures, in the other case that of undermining those same structures.

We turn now to the visions of Zechariah to indicate how they functioned as propaganda for the Zadokite temple program by announcing that Yahweh was actively engaged in the events of the time to bring about the fulfillment of the restoration plans of Ezekiel 40–48. In the first vision (1:8–17) the prophet sees four horses which the *angelus interpres* explains were sent out by Yahweh to patrol the earth. Their report is: "All the earth remains at rest." The angel then inquires how long Yahweh would continue to withhold his mercy from Jerusalem, and in the phrase, "against which thou hast had indignation these seventy years" the answer is already implied (cf. Jer 25:11). That answer is then given expressly in verses 13–17 (which may include some expansionary material): the restoration period is at hand.

The second vision (2:1–4 [1:18–21]) elaborates further: that restoration is now possible because Yahweh is eliminating the powers which had scattered his people. In the third vision (2:5–9) the restoration of the city and the return of Yahweh's Glory is heralded, thereby announcing the fulfillment of Ezekiel's prophecy (cf. Ezek 40:5; 42:20).

The fourth vision (3:1–10), excluded by Gese and ill fitting his reconstruction,[61] is a further elaboration of the programmatic sequence, for as the first three visions fo-

60. Adams, "Theory."
61. Gese, "Anfang."

cused on the restoration of the temple and the land this one deals with the leaders of the restored temple and land, the priest and the Branch. The words concerning the latter in this vision are related to the promise in 4:6a–10a, for both deal with Zerubabbel's role in rebuilding the temple. Mention of a very unusual stone (likely the cornerstone) in both suggests that these passages stem from the critical period when the temple construction was beginning; attention is directed by Zechariah upon Zerubbabel by heralding him as the messianic builder of the temple. A. Petitjean has demonstrated that the vision in chapter 3 contains striking parallels to Mesopotamian texts dealing with cornerstone ceremonies in new temples, those parallels involving the cornerstone and inscription (v. 9), the rites of purification (vv. 4–5, 9), and the resulting fertility of the land (v. 10).[62] If such a ceremony was in fact the background of this vision, its various sections become clear. Verses 1–7 deal with the purification of the high priest and his consecration into the priesthood of the new temple. Isaiah 66 has indicated how strenuously the new temple and its priesthood were resisted by the visionary group, and other oracles in Third Isaiah attested to the shocking accusations of defilement which the latter leveled against the Zadokite priesthood. It therefore seems reasonable that the accusations by Satan and the reference to the filthy garments stem from the growing conflict between temple and prophetic parties: the latter have accused the Zadokite candidate for high priest of being defiled, a charge which could hardly go unchallenged if the people were to be expected to accept Joshua. But Joshua is exonerated completely; the accuser is identified as Satan, and Yahweh rebukes Satan (and by implication anyone else would challenge Joshua's legitimacy!). Then in accord with the ordinance of the Priestly Document, he is subjected to ritual purification by the changing of his clothes (cf. Ex 29:6; Lev. 16:4). Comparison of this passage with the oracles of Third Isaiah

62. A. Petitjean, "La Mission de Zorobabel et la Reconstruction du Temple. Zach. III, 8–10," *Ephemerides Theologicae Lovanienses* 42 (1966): 54 ff.

discloses the perplexing situation within a religious community where opposing sides both claim divine legitimation.

Verses 6-7 are considered a later addition by W. A. M. Beuken, supposedly coming from a period when the high priest's prestige had grown considerably at the expense of the *nāsî'*.[63] His argument is not convincing inasmuch as verses 1-5 already accord Joshua a lofty place of honor, and Beuken's attempt to argue that Joshua's presence in the "original" oracle 1-5, 8-10 was only to announce the coming of the Branch is untenable. As chapter 4 will indicate, Joshua and Zerubbabel are both accorded positions of honor as sacral and royal leaders at the head of the community, and thus it seems best to regard verses 6-7 as original. In them Yahweh promises Joshua the right of access among "those who are standing here." The reference seems to be to those standing before the angel in verse 4, that is, the divine assembly present at the trial of Joshua. Verse 7 therefore seems to promise the high priest that, if he is obedient to his duties, he, as mediator between Yahweh and the people, will be given access to the divine assembly.

Verses 8-10 then announce the coming of the Branch, refer to the temple construction, and promise the purification of the land and the prosperity of the people. They explicitly tie together the appearance of the Branch and the building of the temple with arrival of the new era.

The vision in chapter 4 (verses 6a-10 and 12 are secondary) combines the themes of the preceding visions: Yahweh's eyes are watching over the restoration from the temple, and he has provided the two leaders for the newly reconstituted community. The commitment of Yahweh to the Zadokite program is powerfully symbolized. The gold lampstand with the seven lamps represents Yahweh's world dominion, and the two olive trees flanking the lampstand are the two "sons of oil," that is, the Davidic Messiah (Zerubbabel) and the high priest (Joshua), who are thus

63. W. A. M. Beuken, *Haggai-Sacharja 1-8* (Assen: Van Gorcum, 1967), pp. 282-303.

represented as the guardians of Yahweh's dominion in the restored community.

The sixth and seventh visions (5:1–4 and 5:5–11) revolve around the priestly concern so central to Ezekiel's program and the necessary prerequisite for Yahweh's dwelling among his people—that the purification of the land from iniquity be accomplished. Finally, the last vision (6:1–8), forming an inclusio with the first, returns to the theme of Yahweh's preparations for the restoration in the four corners of the earth.

Our argument that the visions of Zechariah do not constitute genuine apocalyptic eschatology but represent instead the use of the genre of the vision to promote and legitimate a specific pragmatic program of restoration is corroborated by the sign-act called for by a divine word immediately after the last vision (6:9–14). This text deals with the same themes as the fourth and fifth visions, indicating that the specific genres used are incidental, interchangeable, and adopted only insofar as they are suitable carriers of the propagandistic message of the hierocracy. Unfortunately, the text is marred by corruption, and in places it is impossible to be certain of the original reading. In light of the plural "crowns" (*ʿaṭārôt*) in verses 11 and 14, the view that the prophecy originally referred to crowns worn by both Joshua and Zerubbabel seems correct, especially since the hierocratic tradition of this period so consistently refers to the dual offices of the Branch and the priest. In any case, this oracle too is concerned with the diarchy of the hierocratic restoration program, and with the peace which would exist between the two rulers (v. 13); thus it develops further the central theme of this tradition, that the building of the temple under the sponsorship of the Davidic Branch was inaugurating the new era.

As we have seen earlier, the prophecy of Zechariah, together with that of Haggai, was successful in mustering popular support for the hierocratic temple program. That success may have been in part due to his skillful use of the genre of the vision in announcing Yahweh's endorsement of the institutions of the hierocratic group as the fulfillment of the eschatological promises. Once that support had been won, and once the temple program of Ezekiel had been accomplished, it is no wonder that the visionary forms had served their purpose and could be discarded by the hierocratic group. Although the aneschatological orientation of the hierocratic tradition would not be firmly established until late in the fifth century in the Chronicler, we receive hints in the additions to the book of Ezekiel and in alterations in the text of Zechariah (e.g., chapter 3) of the unvisionary posture assumed by that normative group.[64] Once their victory over rival restoration programs had been accomplished, and their reestablished institutions could be viewed as fulfillment of the eschatological promises, the major impulse toward an apocalyptic orientation had been lost. Efforts were turned instead to the day-to-day affairs of cult, to codification of the laws regulating the life of the community, and to development of tradition aiding in the interpretation of those laws.

Our dissatisfaction with purely literary definitions of apocalyptic and our effort to distinguish between possible divergent uses to which visionary forms and motifs were put in different traditions has led us to the following conclusions: Although a genuine eschatological thrust is not lacking in Ezekiel, already in that prophecy a pragmatic orientation is discernible which places the form of the vision in the service of outlining a program of restoration which stands in continuity with the structures of the pre-exilic temple cult, and which looks to the future restoration with an eye to specific institutional details and concrete historical carriers. This pragmatic orientation is discernible beneath the literary forms of Zechariah's prophecy as well, for the genre of the vision and the genre of the oracle alike are pressed into the service of the temple rebuilding program of the Zadokite priests. At no point in the hierocratic tradition do restoration hopes threaten to

64. Comparison of Hag 2:23; Zech 3:8 and 4:6aβ-10a with the alterations in the text of Zech 6:9-14 indicate how the incipient messianism of the hierocratic tradition was brought to an end, although it is impossible to determine the relative roles played by accident and design in this result.

break ties with mundane contingencies, for those restoration hopes were always firmly bound to a specific program which was viewed by its protagonists as basically capable of being effected within the historical realities of the sixth century and which, moreover, represented the most dependable path toward reestablishment of their positions of leadership. Indeed, the pragmatic orientation of the hierocratic tradition is seen even at those points where full realization of specific plans could not be realized within the unfolding historical realities, for like the "Church" of Troeltsch's typology, the hierocratic temple group, viewing its destiny as bound up with historical contingencies, was capable of adaptation, compromise, and adjustment, even in the face of adverse circumstances. This capability placed it in a position even to seize upon adverse developments and bend them toward enhancement of their own interests. A noticeable example of this is the manner in which the downfall of Zerubbabel was used to increase the power and prestige of the high priest, leading to the exclusive rule of the Zadokites over the post-exilic Jewish community.

Our conclusions that the genre of the vision was used by Zechariah as a literary device in a campaign to win popular support for the hierocratic temple program and that his eschatology was inseparably bound to the reestablishment of the Zadokite temple structures make one important fact intelligible which remained a riddle in the reconstructions of those who viewed Zechariah as the father of apocalyptic: the tradition of which Zechariah was a part moved into the last decade of the sixth and into the fifth century free of any significant eschatological, much less apocalyptic, dimension. This is seen clearly when one observes the pragmatic orientation of the Chronicler, as well as when one studies the material of the earlier strata of Ezra and Nehemiah, or the late additions and editorial alterations in Ezekiel and Zechariah 1–8. It is a most intelligible development when one realizes how any genuine otherworldly (apocalyptic) impulse was lacking in the pragmatic hierocratic tradition of the sixth century, and how unessential to the heart of the hierocratic program was the genre of the vision once the temple program had been implemented and the old positions of leadership had been restored.

Since the application of visionary forms was short-lived in the hierocratic tradition and confined to the period during which it was deprived of a temple, it seems futile to look within that tradition for the carrier of the impulse which would give rise to apocalyptic eschatology.[65] By virtue of its relations to the institutions of the period immediately preceding the fall of Jerusalem, and by virtue of its relation to the leadership of the community, the Zadokite-dominated hierocratic group was incapable of sustaining and developing an apocalyptic eschatology. Fulfillment of the plans came within the structures of this world, and the divine realm was summoned not to disrupt those structures but to sanctify and maintain them.

While refusing to tie the rise and development of apocalyptic by definition to one party within post-exilic Judaism (after all, in the second century B.C.E., the Zadokites become the disenfranchised priests who dream apocalyptic dreams!), we recognize that within the specific conditions of the sixth century the group which carried the orientation of apocalyptic eschatology into the fifth century was not the hierocratic group controlling the Jerusalem temple cult, but the elements studied in Chapter III which were denied a part in that cult as a result of the inner-community struggles of the sixth century. In Chapter IV we shall trace the further development of apocalyptic eschatology among those disenfranchised elements.

Inner-community strife is never benign. The weak, both individually and in groups, inevitably are hurt, and as the contending sides harden in their respective positions, the essential elements of the dialectic of faith polarize; the visionary elements (which focus on a transcendent order

65. The relation between the hierocratic tradition of the sixth century and apocalyptic forms and motifs is the same as that visible throughout the history of the rabbinic writings. Apocalyptic forms and motifs are utilized (with restraint, to be sure) during certain periods (usually periods of stress), whereas at other times (times of greater security) apocalyptic themes are purged from the literature (e.g., under R. Judah ha-nasi).

calling under divine judgment all existing mundane structures) part company from the pragmatic elements (which concentrate on the embodiment of the divine in human institutions). The Old Testament is not immune to such strife. Indeed, in all periods of the religion of Israel tensions are visible between men with differing notions of what it meant to be God's people, although, at times of crisis like the sixth and second centuries, those tensions are exacerbated to the point of breaking the community into hostile factions. For the modern individual or group which confesses that the Old Testament records the self-disclosure of divine will within Israel's history as a nation, either such inner-community strife and polarization must be ignored, or God's self-disclosure must be discerned precisely within the field of tension between the vision of the transcendent divine order and the Israelite's sense of solidarity with his community's institutions and practices. While the latter alternative raises many questions which must be addressed anew by thoughtful persons of faith (e.g., the meaning of canon, the sense in which a unity of scripture can be ascertained), it does resonate with certain aspects of the modern religious person's experience: God is the unconditioned and is beyond facile comprehension by the human mind; the religious life therefore involves struggle, and can even be characterized as a dialectic of faith.[66]

In studying the biblical documents of the sixth century, we thus face two traditions emphasizing different facets of Israel's religious experience and, in a period of crisis, diverging increasingly from each other amidst bitter polemic. It is understandable that the group which gains ascendancy increasingly emphasizes continuity with existing structures and the pragmatic application of traditional teachings to the affairs of community and cult, whereas the oppressed group appeals to a vision of divine intervention which will supplant existing structures with a radically new order, an order within which its aspirations can be actualized. More

66. See Chapter V for further discussion of the implications of our study for contemporary theology.

difficult to discern is the degree of accuracy in the accusation made by one group against the other. Perhaps all that can be said with confidence is that hyperbole and distortion enter into the arguments of both parties, a fact which must be remembered as we seek to interpret the meaning of the literature produced by each group and to reconstruct the community setting within which that literature arose. In pursuing this investigation we have traced the development of the hierocratic tradition from Ezekiel through Zechariah, and have noticed how visionary forms were used to promote a particular restoration plan. Before tracing the hierocratic tradition further, we shall pause to recall, on the basis of our observations in the preceding chapter, how the visionary followers of Second Isaiah were responding to the temple restoration of the Zadokites.

Stated tersely, what were heralded as signs of the fulfillment of Yahweh's promises to his people by the hierocrats were condemned as defilements of true religion by the visionaries. Coming at the climax of a bitter struggle for control of the temple, the identification of the accession of two representatives of the hierocratic party and of the completion of their cultic shrine with the arrival of the eschaton appeared to the visionaries as a blatant instance of blasphemy which they compared with the most crass of pagan cultic practices. Far from representing the realization of the prophetic hope, the hierocrats were adversaries of Yahweh, according to the visionaries. Their claims were illegitimate, and they and their temple would be objects of Yahweh's wrath in the imminent judgment.[67]

The visionaries found themselves in a situation similar to the one experienced by Jeremiah, where opposite claims were being made in the name of the same God. For in the figures of Haggai and Zechariah the hierocratic party found prophetic legitimation of their restoration program. Those two prophets announced that the eschaton was being realized in the contemporary event of the rebuilding of the temple, and in the contemporary persons Zerubba-

67. See, for example, the oracle in Is 66:1–16.

bel and Joshua. Once that temple was completed, it is obvious how useful the prophecy which connected the eschaton with the temple rebuilding would be to the priestly hierarchy in charge of the temple: it provided prophetic legitimation for the claim that Yahweh's purposes in Israel's history were fullfilled in that temple institution, and that the glorious new era envisioned by the prophets had now been realized in the priestly hierocracy.

Like Jeremiah, the visionary group could only await Yahweh's day of wrath as the verification of their message and as the vindication of their claim, and hence the apocalyptic dimension of their oracles deepened. But as is so often the case, history proved to be an ambivalent principle of verification, and both sides in the struggle found evidence for the vindication of their cause in the events of history. The hierocrats saw their position of power established, and, in fact, after the disappearance of Zerubbabel, the position of their leader, the high priest, was increasingly enhanced until the time when the Davidic line of governors was ended and effective internal power fell solely to the high priest, who was answerable alone to the Persian governor.

The visionaries viewed these circumstances in another manner and interpreted the history of the rise to power of the temple hierarchy as the last phase of the reign of evil which was soon to be ended by a dramatic judgment upon the old era. In the conditions of the late sixth century and after, as delineated, for example, by Malachi and Nehemiah, the visionaries also found ample support for their interpretation: corruption of the priests and civil authorities, economic distress, defiled cultic practices, waywardness of the people, the continued yoke of the Persians. As we shall see in Chapter IV, they therefore remained constant in their hope of ultimate victory, and continued to pronounce Yahweh's judgment upon the illegitimate leaders and the whole fallen order and Yahweh's salvation to the remnant which remained faithful. In this persistent clinging to hope despite repeated defeats, the orientation of the visionaries became increasingly the otherworldly orientation of apocalyptic eschatology.

F. BITTER CONTROVERSY AND THE ZADOKITE MOVE TO REFORM THE HIEROCRATIC TRADITION ALONG NARROWLY EXCLUSIVE LINES

The polemic of the visionary group became most acrimonious around the time of the building of the Second Temple, as indicated by Isaiah 57 and 66. There is evidence that from the hierocratic side the battle was fought just as bitterly, as the Zadokite leadership of the hierocratic party stepped forward to revise the Ezekielian program of restoration along narrowly exclusive lines. After the appeal for popular support had been made by Haggai and Zechariah and the temple reconstruction had been completed, the Zadokites seemed to return to the exclusive view that in the new temple there was room only for their own priestly party. Therefore, they tolerated no other priestly elements in their revised program of restoration and moved to take over the entire priesthood. It is the task of this section to consider several parts of Ezekiel where this attempted Zadokite takeover is reflected.[68]

This inquiry necessarily follows the method of the study of the history of tradition and thus cannot be immediately translated into an absolute chronology. Yet the general period in which such a takeover could have been attempted is quite apparent, namely, in the decades following the rebuilding of the temple. This conclusion is based on several observations. First, the study of Third Isaiah indicated that the period of the temple building inaugurated the period of the most bitter polemic between contending sides.[69] From the other side, the Chronicler, writing at about the year 400, exudes a tolerant and conciliatory spirit free from any of the polemic found in Third Isaiah and the Zadokite sections of Ezekiel. Within this general context, and considering the conditions of the first half of the fifth century as recorded by Malachi, we are led to speculate

68. The Zadokite revision of Ezekiel is found in 44:6–31; 45:13–15; 40:46b; 43:19a; 48:11. Cf. Gese, *Verfassungsentwurf*, pp. 85 ff., and Zimmerli, *Ezekiel*, pp. 979 ff.

69. Zech 8:10 indicates that the other side viewed this same period as one of bitter inner-community struggle.

whether Ezra, equipped with the law of God in his hand, was not sent by the Persians precisely because of the internal tension and conflict which was afflicting the Jewish community, thereby threatening to render it useless as a buffer against Egypt. Ezra indeed seems to have achieved the type of internal peace which is the background of the Chronicler's work. These factors would set the date of the attempted takeover of the Zadokites between the last quarter of the sixth and middle of the fifth century.

The Zadokite revision reflects a polemic operating on two fronts, both based on the attempt to enhance the position of the Zadokite priests. Though the polemic on the first front is not nearly so conclusive as that on the second, there seems to be evidence of a Zadokite attempt to deemphasize the importance of the *nāśîʾ*. In Ezekiel, Haggai, and Zechariah, the *nāśîʾ* enjoyed a position of prestige at least equal to that of the priest. But in contrast to the active participation of the *nāśîʾ* in the cult in Ezekiel (e.g., 45:16–17), the Zadokite revision reserves the cultic duties for the priest (45:18f; 46:2).[70] In Ezekiel the prince was allowed to enter the sanctuary to eat bread before Yahweh (44:1–3), while in the Zadokite revision he is not allowed to approach the holy area too closely (46:2). A marked contrast is also apparent between Ezekiel's plan whereby the prince was to occupy a most hallowed portion on both sides of the "holy portion" (48:21), and the Zadokite plan of keeping the temple and palace completely separate, lest the temple be defiled by the sepulchers of the idolatrous kings (43:7–9). This Zadokite attempt to degrade the role of the *nāśîʾ* in favor of the Zadokite priesthood may underlie the textual disruption in Zech 6:9–14, where the crowning of Zerubbabel seems to have been deleted from the account.

The second and certainly the most unambivalent front upon which the Zadokites were advancing their exclusive claim was in the attempt to eliminate all non-Zadokite elements from the central priesthood. In Ezekiel's program,

70. Cf. E. Hammerschaimb, "Ezekiel's View of the Monarchy," in *Some Aspects of Old Testament Prophecy from Isaiah to Malachi* (Copenhagen: Rosenkilde og Bagger, 1966), pp. 61–62.

priests and Levites are both *kōhănîm*. How different the situation has become in the Zadokite revision, as indicated especially by the passage we shall now examine, Ezek 44:4–31.

The polemic thrust of the claim to authority being made by this passage is already felt in verses 4–5, for it places the passage in the context of a direct revelation from Yahweh upon his return to the temple. This literary feature already betrays the secondary character of the section, inasmuch as verse 2 thus repeats the event already reported in 43:1–6.

The form of the oracle which follows is intriguing, and adds a very significant dimension to our understanding of the forms, as well as the underlying situations, of this period, for it follows that form of the salvation-judgment oracle whose rise we traced in the struggles of the prophetic group in Third Isaiah. Only here the sides are reversed: the side being threatened with judgment in the oracles of Third Isaiah here is promised salvation, and vice versa, pointing to the perplexing community crisis where antagonistic claims are being made in the name of the same God. Hence from the side of the opposite party in the conflict we again find the form which grew out of a new situation within the community of Israel, a situation where a rift was growing between two parties, thus no longer allowing the same pronouncement of salvation or doom to apply to the entire people, and leading to a transformation of the basic form of the oracle.

Verse 6 is in the form of the commission to address the rebellious house of Israel. The indictment against the apostate people comes in verses 6b–8, followed in verse 9 by "therefore" *(lākēn,* cf. LXX); but instead of the sentence of judgment which normally follows upon this introduction, a cultic ordinance follows, which is a unique element in this priestly adaptation of the salvation-judgment oracle. Then in verses 10–14 the awaited sentence appears, being a sentence of judgment against the Levites for having gone astray after idols. Two features of this sentence are very noteworthy: (1) the offense for which the sentenced party is being indicted is construed in the vaguest of terms, in the terms of idolatry in general,[71] an idolatry which moreover is applied indiscriminately to all elements in Israel which are non-Zadokite. This language, so reminiscent of the vague and generalizing changes of idolatry in Third Isaiah, is not cast in the language of historical description, but rather in the language of heated polemic where the sole object is to malign the opposing party so as to support the accuser's claim to sole legitimacy. (2) The incredible degree to which the status of the Levites has been degraded is expressed by the fact that their duties are assigned to them as the substance of their sentence of judgment. Whereas their duties in the basic work of Ezekiel were given them because they were the honored possession of Yahweh, here these duties are *their punishment for idolatry!* These are the terms of temple slaves, not of members of the priesthood, and the description of their duties bears this out: theirs are the most menial types of tasks, watching the gates and preparing the sacrificial animals (v. 11). Whereas the Zadokites are to serve Yahweh (v. 16), the Levites are to serve the people (v. 11). Whereas the Zadokites are to draw near to Yahweh to serve him as priests (v. 16), this is strictly forbidden the Levites, who must bear their shame: "They shall not come near to me, to serve me as priest, nor come near any of my sacred things and the things that are most sacred; but they shall bear their shame, because of the abominations which they have committed" (v. 13).

Immediately upon the sentence of judgment against the Levites follows the promise of salvation to the Zadokites. Even as the Levites are handed a blanket comdemnation for their apostasy, the Zadokites are left blameless, because in contrast to the Levites, they "kept the charge of my sanctuary when the people of Israel went astray from me" (v. 15). Again the terms are stereotyped, generalized, undifferentiated, i.e., the terms of polemic. Following this

71. They "went far from me, going astray from me after their idols when Israel went astray" (v. 10); "they ministered to them before their idols and became a stumbling block of iniquity to the house of Israel" (v. 12); "because of the abominations which they have committed" (v. 13). Similar in tone is the reference to the territory allotted to the Zadokites in 48:11: "This shall be for the consecrated priests, the sons of Zadok, who kept my charge, who did not go astray when the people of Israel went astray, as the Levites did."

exoneration, the duties of the Zadokites are given as the terms of their salvation. As the Levites' duties are narrowed to the menial duties of temple slaves, the Zadokites' duties are correspondingly broadened: in 40:46 they were given charge of the altar; in 44:16 their sphere of control is broadened to the entire sanctuary.

This polemical passage, with its exclusive claim by the Zadokites combined with a most bitter attack on all non-Zadokite elements, is unique in the biblical literature. It moves far from the tolerant spirit of the original Ezekiel, where the people as a whole are held accountable for the national disaster (22:23ff). There is simply no room in the prophecy of Ezekiel for the exoneration of one particular priestly family alongside the condemnation of all elements not belonging to that family.

From this central passage of the Zadokite revision the sharp division between priests with the accompanying reduction of the Levites to the level of temple servants found its way into other parts of Ezekiel. In each case the gloss clearly betrays the concern to transform an original program which obliged the Zadokites to share the priestly rights with non-Zadokite elements into a program which gave the Zadokites sole access to the actual priesthood. Such glosses are found in 40:46b; 43:19; and 48:11. Longer sections from this same stratum are found in 45:1–8a and 46:19–24.[72]

The question arises whether the Zadokites' aggressive move toward exclusive control of the cult led to revision of other parts of the canon. The question is especially pertinent with regard to Numbers 16–17,[73] a section combining several layers of tradition which tell of various priestly struggles dating back to the ancient feud between the Mushites and the Aaronides found in the J stratum

72. Cf. Gese, *Verfassungsentwurf*, p. 67.

73. Also worthy of study in this connection are Nu 4:1–20 (where the duties originally assigned to the Levitical Qohath group are removed and given instead to Aaron and his sons), Nu 17:16–28 (EVV: 17:1–12) (where Aaron's rod takes its place among the rods of the twelve tribes as the sole representative of the tribe of the Levites—that there are other Levites is ignored completely), and Numbers 18 (where the subordination of the Levites is stated in unambiguous terms—note the threefold warning of death to violators; vv. 3, 5, 7).

(16:1ba, 2aa, 12–15, and 25–34). On top of this stratum are two others usually assigned to P, one recounting the rebellion of Korah and two hundred and fifty leaders against Moses and Aaron, the other telling of the demand of Korah and other Levites for priestly rights equal to those claimed by Aaron for himself.[74] It is possible that the Zadokites were behind the final redaction of this section, since in it an attack on the Levites is found which is unparalleled anywhere else in P (16:8–11), but which is very reminiscent of Ezekiel 44. That final redaction lumps all of the various dissident elements under the blanket designation *Levites,* and connects with this rebellious congregation the claim that "all the congregation are holy."

Against this democratizing viewpoint is set the hierocratic claim that cultic holiness was reserved for the Aaronide priests. The polarity thus emerging is remarkably similar to that already recognized within the community on the basis of Third Isaiah, Ezekiel, Haggai, and Zechariah, the polarity between a visionary group viewing an Israel like that of Moses' time (Ex 19:6) within which all the people are righteous and are priests of Yahweh (e.g., Is 60:21; 61:6) and a realistic program aimed at creating a holy nation by means of the temple cult and strict separation between the holy priests and the profane people. It thus seems possible that the Zadokites edited the Priestly Writing, as they did Ezekiel and Haggai-Zechariah, in conformity with their ambitions to gain control over the temple cult. To all those challenging their exclusive claim they would thereby be promising the same fate which met the rebels of antiquity who challenged Aaron and Moses.

Support for our hypothesis that the Levites are allied with the followers of Second Isaiah in this post-exilic struggle against the Zadokite-dominated hierocratic party is found in the claim of the group associated with Korah, the Levite: "You have gone too far! For all the congregation is holy, every one of them *(kol hā'ēdāh kullām qᵊdōšîm)*, and the Lord is among them; why then do you exalt yourselves

74. Cf. M. Noth, *Numbers*, tr. James D. Martin (Philadelphia: Westminster, 1968).

above the assembly of the Lord?" For this claim, as pointed out by Gerhard von Rad, is reminiscent of the basic doctrine of Deuteronomy that the people as a whole represent the *'am qādôš* (Dtn 7:6; 14:2, 21; 26:19; 28:9).[75] The Levitical proclivities of Deuteronomy are well known, as is the fact that Deuteronomy harks back to many old amphictyonic traditions which had been preserved in the Northern Kingdom. Thus much of the democratizing impulse and appeal to archaic, amphictyonic traditions which we have found within the visionary group and which they use in the bitter polemic against the exclusive claims of the hierocratic party can be connected with ancient Levitical traditions. From various sides tantalizing evidence accumulates suggesting that, in the struggle for control of the restoration cult, the Levites are allied with the followers of Second Isaiah against the official Zadokite-led *gôlāh* group.

As we have already noted, the attempted takeover of the entire temple cult by the Zadokites represents a relatively short phase in the history of the hierocratic tradition, for as we shall see shortly, the Chronicler records a return to a more tolerant spirit within that tradition. Nevertheless, that phase was a critical one, for in it visionary and pragmatic elements reached their most extreme polarization, producing a rift within the congregation of Israel which would never again be completely closed. From this period on the historian must speak of the congregations of Israel, though the congregation characterized by a vision of a whole nation of priests was suppressed, removed from a position of effective power, and thus almost lost to the ken of the historian.

G. THE CHRONICLER: THE VICTORIOUS HIEROCRATIC PARTY RETURNS TO A MORE CONCILIATORY POSITION

The Zadokite revision of Ezekiel represents a watershed in the history of the hierocratic tradition, for in that revision the claim of the Zadokite party reaches its most ex-

75. G. von Rad, *Die Priesterschrift im Hexateuch* (Berlin: W. Kohlhammer, 1934), pp. 109–110

clusive point, and the polemic against non-Zadokite priestly elements becomes most bitter. On either side of that watershed the hierocratic program is couched in a more tolerant spirit. We have already noticed this in the original Ezekiel and have seen as well how Haggai and Zechariah make an appeal for wide popular support of the hierocratic temple program. In turning to the Chronicler we find a return to a more tolerant and conciliatory mood. The reason for the pacific mood of Ezekiel is clear: it is in the form of a theoretical program, largely unblemished by the harsh realities of opposition from rival programs. The tolerant and conciliatory spirit of the Chronicler is of a different order: it is the spirit of conciliation made possible for the hierocratic party because of its ultimate victory over rival claimants in the struggle for control of the cult. By the time of the Chronicler's activity (ca. 400),[76] the most bitter struggles of the temple rebuilding period were long past, and the deplorable conditions of the early fifth century as indicated by Malachi were vastly improved as a result of the missions of Ezra and Nehemiah. As is seen in the mission of the Zadokite Priest Ezra (cf. Ezr 7:1f), who was sent as an official of the Persian government to unite the Jewish community under "the law of the God of heaven,"[77] the one hundred years from the middle of the fifth century was a period of healing the wounds of past strife and of uniting the community under the now authoritative hierocratic program. The narrow extremes of the attempted Zadokite takeover were ameliorated, and the hierocracy was brought back to the ideal set forward by the prophet Ezekiel.

This means that the diarchy of priest and king was upheld by the Chronicler. The tendency observable in the Zadokite revision of Ezekiel to deemphasize the role of the Davidic ruler is replaced in Chronicles by a vivid interest in the kingship of David. In his genealogical lists, the Chroni-

76. The evidence for this date, together with the relevant bibliography, is gathered in John Bright, *A History of Israel* (Philadelphia: Westminster, 1972²), pp. 398-399.

77. The law which Ezra carried as his decretal was likely the Pentateuch in some form (see W. F. Albright, *The Biblical Period from Abraham to Ezra* [New York: Harper Torchbook, 1963; first edition, 1949], pp. 94-95.

cler traces the Davidic line down to his own time (2 Chr 3).

To be sure, one could argue that his homage paid to the Davidic line was token, inasmuch as the Davidic governor was gradually being eclipsed by the high priest as the native ruler and would finally be replaced by a Persian governor, thus leaving the high priest the sole effective native power. There is some truth to this argument, as shown by the absence of a real messianic interest in the Chronicler. Nevertheless, the picture of David is too lively to be merely a device for supporting the institutions of the hierarchy. The Chronicler shows a genuine interest in the Davidic dynasty and seems to be respectful of the royal office.

The Chronicler is seen to return to the program of Ezekiel also in his treatment of the priesthood, for the exclusive claim of the Zadokites to sole possession of the priesthood is nowhere in evidence. While the Zadokites (Eleazarides) remain the dominant priesthood, alongside them is another Aaronide priesthood, the Ithamarides, who are recognized as full priests in spite of their non-Zadokite ancestry.

Whereas this more tolerant spirit was in large part the result of the new self-confidence characterizing the Zadokite priesthood once they had successfully eliminated rivals to their leadership, there are hints of other factors abetting this development. For one thing, there were more Levites present in Jerusalem in the last half of the fifth century than in the century before, thereby representing a larger power group: according to the census taken by Nehemiah, 284 Levites lived in the city (Neh 11:18). Another factor may have aided in this development toward tolerance of the Levites: In the struggles of the early post-exilic period, it seems that Levitical opponents of the Zadokites emphasized their lineage tracing back to Ithamar, a close relative of Aaron the Levite, Moses' brother. Not to be out-archaized by their rivals, the Zadokites no longer contented themselves with tracing their ancestry back to the relative late-comer, Zadok, but pointed back to Phinehas and ultimately to Aaron. As a further move, they at some point sought to deprecate their rivals by tying their destiny to the curse on the house of Eli (cf. 1 Sam 2:27-36). But this deprecation was finally abandoned in favor of a new genealogy worked out by the Chronicler, in which the Aaronide ancestry of both the Zadokites and Levites was recognized (1 Chr. 24:1-6). Thus in the Chronicler all of Israel's priests are called "sons of Aaron." It is important to note, however, that this move toward tolerance does not go so far as to equalize the status of all the "sons of Aaron": the Zadokites remain ascendant; their past is described as more noble than that of their fellow priests, since Eleazar, and not Ithamar, is the priest of Israel in the stories at the end of the period of wandering in the desert (e.g., Nu 25:11; 26:1; 31). Also, the Zadokites fill twice as many classes as the Ithamarides. Ezra, the great hero of the Jewish community of the Chronicler's time, is claimed to be a Zadokite (Ezr 7:1-5). Finally, from the Zadokites come the high priests from Joshua in the late sixth century to Onias III in the second.

This primacy of the Zadokite priesthood does not deny the fact that all traces of the bitter polemic staged by the Zadokites against the Levites have disappeared in the Chronicler's work. Instead the Levites are treated with honor and respect, although not all Levites may have been satisfied with the fact that their status as *clerus minor* was maintained. Among their duties of honor were the carrying of the ark (1 Chr 15:2, 11-15, 16:4ff), singing praises to Yahweh (1 Chr. 6:31-32; 16:4-37; 2 Chr 8:14), and taking care of the sanctuary and holy vessels (1 Chr 23:28). Indeed, in one connection the Chronicler maintains that "the Levites were more upright in heart than the priests in sanctifying themselves" (2 Chr 29:34). It is obvious that the bitter polemic between priestly factions has ended by the time of the Chronicler.[78] The Zadokites retain the top

78. Another illustration that the attitude toward the Levites has returned to that of the original hierocratic program is seen by comparing 2 Chr. 36:14 (cf. 2 Kgs 24:18-20), where all the priests are blamed for the disaster of 587, and Ezekiel 8 and 22:23ff (Stratum I), where all officials, including all the priests, are likewise blamed, with Ezek 44:9-16 (Zadokite Stratum), where the Levites are accused of going astray from Yahweh and the Zadokites are exonerated.

priestly offices, but the Ithamarides and Levites have been restored to the hierocratic cult in good favor.

The concilatory spirit of the Chronicler is also seen in his drawing upon divergent traditions in his history. For example, he brings together the southern P tradition and the originally northern Deuteronomic tradition. This fusing of tradition is apparent even in details such as the designations used for priestly groups. For instance, he uses both the phrase "the priests and the Levites" used by P and the Deuteronomic phrase "the Levitical priests." The reason for this tolerance toward what was formerly a rival tradition is related to the tolerance toward the Levites mentioned above: after the struggle between the rival traditions resulted in the victory of the hierocratic tradition, the latter was able to absorb into it aspects of those rival traditions. Similarly, the numerous elements of holy war tradition in the Chronicler (1 5:22; 14:15; 18:6; 2 13:12; 14:10-14; 20:15-17, 29; 24:24; 25:8; 26:7) may stem from the effort to attract the dissident prophetic elements which held to the visionary concept of the Divine Warrior.

In spite of the effort made by the hierocratic tradition to heal the wounds of past controversy by presenting their program in a more conciliatory guise, the Chronicler's work also betrays the elements remaining constant throughout the Persian period which would have continued to alienate and offend those remaining faithful to the visionary tradition. Certain of these elements are in need of no explanation, like the temple theology which the visionaries had opposed so strenuously in the sixth century, and the Zadokite stamp upon the hierocratic tradition as preserved by the Chronicler which continued as a reminder to all priestly families that one family had been victorious in the struggle for control of the cult. Two further elements, however, do deserve closer attention, the pro-Persian proclivities of the Chronicler and his uneschatological perspective. A visionary group which derived its vitality from the hope of Yahweh's final intervention to restore his holy people would find great difficulty in making peace with a hierocratic group which established its position squarely within the present order and maintained its security by means of a coalition with a foreign pagan power. Their determination to resist such a compromise of true Yahwism would only be increased when pressure was applied to force them to conform. Such pressure to subscribe to the hierocratic program was probably great, and we get a glimpse of it in connection with the account of Ezra's mission. When he was commissioned by the Persians to return to Palestine to enforce the "law of God" throughout the land, he was able to do so under the authority of the Persian emperor, and was even authorized to appoint magistrates to enforce it (Ezr 7:25f). In the matter of obedience to this law, leniency was eschewed: "Whoever will not obey the law of your God and the law of the king, let judgment be strictly executed upon him . . . . " The offense taken by the visionary group must have been great: what they regarded as an illegitimate interpretation of Israel's faith was now being enforced upon them with the authority of a pagan emperor, under the threat of punishment by death. The overtures made by the more conciliatory spirit exhibited by the Chronicler were likely powerless to prompt many visionaries to abandon their eschatological program in favor of the hierocratic plan, nor would coercion have had an effect on the persistent.

We turn now to examine more closely the first major element which continued to characterize the hierocratic tradition, and which likely remained grossly offensive to the visionaries, the policy of collaboration with the Persians. We have observed that the hierocratic party returned from exile as the group recognized by the Persians as the leaders of the Jewish community. The price paid for this Persian support was absolute fidelity to the Persian emperor, with the resulting necessity that hopes for regained national autonomy be eschewed. The Chronicler stands in wholehearted support of this Persian-Israelite alliance.

The first indication of the Chronicler's pro-Persian proclivities is his attaching the edict of Cyrus directly onto the end of his history of Judah in order to show that no real break exists in the movement of history from the period of Judean statehood to the era of Persian control. Then he goes on in his work to relate how the post-exilic restoration would have been impossible without the active and generous support of the Persian emperor. It is Yahweh who has stirred up the spirit of Cyrus, and who has given him the kingdom of the earth (Ezr 1:1f), "and he has charged me to build him a house at Jerusalem. . . ." Both in the decrees which likely stem from the Persian emperor himself and in the sections from the Chronicler, this Persian sponsorship of the temple building is gratefully acknowledged. The hierocratic party answers "the adversaries" who would join them in the building: " . . . we alone will build to Yahweh, the God of Israel, as King Cyrus the king of Persia has commanded us" (Ezr 4:3). The Aramaic decree lists both dimensions and materials and orders that the costs "be paid from the royal treasury" (6:4). Then follow words which clearly establish the Persian emperor as patron of the temple: "that they may offer pleasing sacrifices to the God of heaven, and pray for the life of the king and his sons" (6:10). Anyone violating the decree would be guilty of transgressing against the emperor himself (6:11f). The Chronicler adds the note: "And the elders of the Jews built and prospered, through the prophesying of Haggai . . . and Zechariah . . . .They finished their building by the command of the God of Israel and by the decree of Cyrus and Darius and Artaxerxes king of Persia" (6:14).

Completely absent from the Chronicler's work is the element of judgment against the nations so prominent in the prophets, that element jealously guarding Yahweh's exclusive claim on his people. The Chronicler reflects the mentality of a people which has worked out a satisfactory *modus vivendi* with the Persian overlords. As the high priest was satisfied to share the power of leadership with the Persian monarch, so Yahweh was obliged to share his claim with a pagan emperor; hence the situation which could only appear syncretizing to the visionaries: "They finished their building by the command of the God of Israel *and by the decree of Cyrus and Darius and Artaxerxes king of Persia*" (6:14).

The contrast between the hierocratic party's willingness to accommodate itself to an environment dominated by a secular power and the visionary group's stubborn insistence to give neither themselves, nor their foes, nor Yahweh any rest until Yahweh came to inaugurate the new era would find its exact parallel in the second century. There the hierocracy centered around the temple quickly accepted the secular environment of the Maccabean state, leaving no genuine eschatological dimension in their religious system. The Essene community which fled to Qumran found this environment hostile to their eschatological faith, and as the War Scroll indicates, they described in apocalyptic terms the imminent Day of Yahweh when the military leaders of this world, as the agents of evil, would be eliminated, thus making way for the establishment of Yahweh's Holy People.

This comparison leads to the second major element which would have alienated the visionary group, the absence of an eschatological dimension in the Chronicler's History.[79] The affirmation of existing structures as "absolute and eternal" implies a strong negation of the eschatological element of classical prophecy, for the element calls for judgment on the status quo, and for the supplanting of old structures by a new order.[80] Thus it is not surprising to find that, while the Chronicler dwells at length in the first part of his work on the glories of the Davidic era, and on the importance of David in establishing the temple cult, the eschatological element implicit in the Davidic covenant is neglected. Whatever his hopes for the future were, he does not express them. For the fulfillment of history is not envisioned in an event of the future which would supersede and even negate past hisory, but is recognized in the

79. Cf. W. Rudolph, *Chronikbücher*, HAT (Tübingen: J. C. B. Mohr [Paul Siebeck] 1955), p. xxiii: "That in a work as long as that of the Chronicles it is difficult to find one passage clearly expressing the old prophetic, eschatological hope proves to what level of unimportance this hope had sunk for him and, we can assume, for the community of which he was spokesman." Noth also emphasizes that this uneschatological attitude is not a peculiarity of the Chronicler but the position of his community, since no individual *Tendenz* is recognizable. The document he has written is "party line" (M. Noth, *Überlieferungsgeschichtliche Studien I* [Tübingen: J. C. B. Mohr (Paul Siebeck), 1957²], p. 204.

80. Cf. Mannheim, *Ideology*, p. 192

present order. It would not be out of place to speak of "realized eschatology" when describing the historical view of the Chronicler. Haggai and Zechariah had declared that once the temple was rebuilt, the long awaited eschaton would arrive. The Chronicler, living at a time when the temple was erected and standing at the very center of the life of the community, sees in the present order the fulfillment of history; past history is used not to point beyond the present to a future fulfillment, but to prove that the present represents the culmination toward which past history has been moving.[81] The overall structure of the Chronicler's work bears this out: 1 and 2 Chronicles narrate first the glorious establishment of Israel's sacred institutions under David followed by the tragic loss of those institutions due to Israel's sin. The goal of the Chronicler's work is then reached in the original sections of Ezra-Nehemiah[82] as the result of two very important events involving a gracious act of the Persian emperor and a great cultic celebration: (1) After the conquest of Babylon, Cyrus issues his edict allowing the return of the *gôlāh*; the temple is rebuilt and dedicated (Ezra 1-6). (2) Ezra is commissioned by the Persian emperor to introduce the law of God entrusted to him; the people confess their sin and renew the covenant (Ezra 7-8; Nehemiah 8, Ezra 9-10, Nehemiah 9-10). The result of this restoration and covenant renewal is the reestablishment of the people around the temple cult which is for the Chronicler the fulfillment of the historical process he has been describing. The work does not look for a further eschaton, for Israel's eschaton has been realized in the restoration of the institutions long ago established by David but lost. This culmination is also seen in a series of notes attached to the descriptions of the passovers under Hezekiah and Josiah and the celebration

81. Ibid., p. 233: "The utopia in this case (i.e., in the case of conservativism) is, from the beginning, embedded in existing reality. To this, obviously, there corresponds the fact that reality, the 'here and now,' is no longer experienced as an 'evil' reality but as the embodiment of the highest values and meanings."

82. Cf. W. Rudolph, *Esra und Nehemiah,* HAT (Tübingen: J. C. B. Mohr]Paul Siebeck], 1949), pp. xxii-xxiii, who includes the Nehemiah material in the original Chronicler's work.

of Tabernacles under Ezra. As for Hezekiah's celebration, there had been nothing like it in Jerusalem "since the time of Solomon" (2 Chr 30:26). As for Josiah's, nothing like it "since the days of Samuel" (2 Chr 35:18). As for Ezra's, "from the days of Jeshua the son of Nun to that day the people of Israel had not done so" (Neh 8:17). Thus the institutions of the Chronicler's own time mark the culmination of the entire history of Israel from the time of Joshua to the time of Ezra.

This "realized eschatology" of the Chronicler is manifested in yet another way: the prophecy of Jeremiah (25:11f) that the exile would last seventy years became important in the literature of the post-exilic period. Zechariah (1:12) refers to it in his announcement of the arrival of the eschaton. The Chronicler connects it with the Cyrus edict, and thus implies that the new era had begun with that event which marked the beginning of the post-exilic hierocracy (2 Chr 36:21).[83]

While the fact remains that the Chronicler presents the hierocratic program in a conciliatory form which may have attracted some of the dissidents back into the mainstream of post-exilic orthodoxy, the community which he described still fell far short of the vision of restoration tenaciously held by some of the members of the prophetic group. For them, restoration remained a future event, and the orthodox party which found the prophetic dream of God's Kingdom on earth realized in a community led by an illegitimate priesthood, centered around a corrupt temple

83. This interpretation which implied that the eschaton had arrived with the birth of the post-exilic hierocracy is refuted by Daniel 9 by means of reinterpretation of the number 70. See O. Plöger, *Theocracy and Eschatology*, tr. S. Rudman (Richmond: John Knox, 1968), p. 43

When the Chronicler's position in relation to Persian rule and his lack of interest in the eschatological themes of earlier prophecy are contrasted with the teachings of the post-exilic visionary group which we have described earlier, the sociological dimension of apocalyptic eschatology again becomes apparent. That is, apocalpytic eschatology rises and flourishes among those whose oppressive environment denies them all means of realizing their eschatological faith within this world's structures. Conversely, apocalyptic eschatology is given no room within the religious thought of a community which believes that it has entered into its fulfillment within the realities of the historico-political realm, which believes in effect that its institutions have come to embody the qualities of the Kingdom of God.

dedicated to a foreign monarch and supported by the funds and military might of a pagan empire, could only be the object of their derision.[84] Contrary to the prophecy of Haggai and Zechariah and the interpretation of history by the Chronicler, the visionaries continued to maintain that the eschaton had not arrived; rather, the old era was still very much with them, which meant that restoration could come only on the other side of a mightly judgment by Yahweh upon his foes, foes both within Israel and without.

The oracles which we shall examine in the next chapter indicate that certain visionaries, though forced from any effective power in the real politics of the nation and cult and largely silenced by the victorious hierocratic group, remained faithful to the vision they had inherited from their teacher Second Isaiah, and their faithfulness implied continued resistance to the hierocratic program. To be sure, in the face of frustration and defeat they made alterations in their vision: salvation was limited to a small segment within Israel, further judgment was foreseen preceding deliverance of the faithful, and Yahweh's saving acts were envisioned increasingly in the idiom of myth which made the restoration hope ever more indifferent to the contingencies of plain history. While these alterations hastened the prophetic hope of the followers of Second Isaiah along the road to apocalyptic eschatology, in an important sense their basic vision remained constant, the vision of a day inaugurated by Yahweh when his holy people would be restored in their land as a nation of priests. What underwent drastic change was the relation of that vision to the historical realities within which they lived out their daily lives.

84. The visionary tradition could conceive of a foreign monarch as a tool in Yahweh's hand, as indicated by the prophecies of Jeremiah and Second Isaiah, but it viewed the permanent alliance of the hierocratic party with the Persian king and his use of the temple cult only as a repetition of the idolatry of Manasseh, that is, as a wanton neglect of Yahweh's exclusive claim upon his people.

CHAPTER IV

Zechariah 9–14 and the Development of the Apocalyptic Eschatology of the Visionaries

A. THE HISTORICAL AND SOCIOLOGICAL BACKGROUND OF THE CONTINUED STRUGGLE

In the previous two chapters the examination of Third Isaiah and the hierocratic tradition revealed a hard-fought struggle for control of the central cult which issued in victory for the hierocratic party and in defeat for the visionary elements that had resisted the Zadokite temple program. Thus the Zadokite priesthood, supported by the other Aaronide elements allied with it, was able to establish itself as the sole custodian of the central cult for the remainder of the Persian period, and was in a position to mold the character of post-exilic Judaism along the lines of its temple theology. While victory led to a somewhat more conciliatory attitude toward rival factions on the part of the Zadokite-dominated temple party, many of the prophetic and Levitical elements which had rallied behind Second Isaiah's vision of restoration found themselves disenfranchised from, and at times even persecuted by, the central cult. The rift between realist and visionary which we traced through various stages of development was partly based on rivalry between contending priestly houses, but on a deeper level it stemmed from two attitudes toward the restoration: the realists promoted a pragmatic restoration program of cultic orthopraxy based on the temple structures of the pre-exilic Zadokite cult, while the visionaries espoused an eschatological belief which insisted that restoration would be initiated and effected by a miraculous act of Yahweh, as a result of which the old structures would be supplanted by a new sacral order.

This polarization between two elements within Yahwism which occurred in the latter half of the sixth century B.C. had roots in pre-exilic times, as a study of antitheses such as the following would bear out: Aaronide/Mushite; Southern/Northern; P/Deuteronomy; Temple Theology/ Prophetism; Zadokite/Levite. During and immediately after the exile the latter two sets of antitheses played a key role in the conflict, and to these were added others: *gôlāh/'am hā'āreṣ;* hierocratic/prophetic; rulers/alienated elements; realized eschatology futuristic eschatology; continuity/change. As we go beyond the sixth century and beyond the Third Isaiah and hierocratic material to later post-exilic literature, we shall not be surprised to find this polarization between realist and visionary drawn out even further, involving contrasts such as halakah/apocalypse; temple/synagogue; Maccabees/Qumran Covenanters; Sadducees/Pharisees; Judaism/Primitive Christianity. These contrasts are not intended to imply diametric opposites, for the polarities characterizing the period of the Second Temple are very complex. Nor are they intended to convey value judgments; to the contrary, it is our opinion that at each point in time these antitheses represent a rending asunder of that which belongs together, the realistic and visionary aspects of faith. That is, the aspect of faith which takes with utter seriousness the real events of history and politics and interprets faith within the context of those events, and the aspect of faith which maintains a perspective above any political order and acts as a check on existing structures so as to prevent any blurring of the line between human and divine or any absolutizing and eternalizing of the status quo.

The polarization of which we speak began in struggles within the pre-exilic, exilic, and early post-exilic communities which were all too human, involving rivalries and self-interest, and this human factor has continued to drive a wedge between realistic and visionary elements of faith ever since. For example, the early Christian community had a new vision of what God was intending for humanity, but human factors on both sides of the struggle led to the severing of that vision from the political sphere which led to consequences within Christianity which still plague the Church. In no way is the suggestion being made that these polarizing struggles were superficial, involving only the baser passions in humanity. For in the field of tension between vision and reality men and women were struggling with two elements forming the warp and woof of the deepest level of human existence. Though very unworthy human motives always diluted the noble ingredients of the conflict, the conflict itself has been very basic to the spiritual development of mankind. Indeed, persons of faith confess that within the field of tension between vision and reality *God* was the primary actor, struggling with his historical community.

The conflict of the sixth century which was investigated in the last two chapters thus provides the background for our continued study of the development of apocalyptic eschatology, for the history of that development is the history of the further polarization of realistic and visionary elements in the prophetic tradition. As mentioned earlier, classical prophecy stubbornly insisted upon translating the vision received from Yahweh into the categories of politics and plain history, and thus resisted the temptation of escape from the real world to the cosmic realm offered by myth and ecstasy. But in the post-exilic period developments in the political realm made such translation increasingly difficult, as little within plain history could be identified with divine action and the political realm took on the appearance of unmitigated evil. A sudden resurgence of myth began to offer the possibility of escape rejected by early prophecy, and the result of this development was the death of prophecy and the birth of apocalyptic eschatology.

It is impossible to determine with any degree of exactitude the identity of the group or groups which embraced and further developed the idiom of apocalyptic eschatology in their continued resistence to a form of Yahwism which they considered illegitimate. Since specific points of contact can be demonstrated between the material to be examined in this chapter and the oracles of Isaiah 56–66, we feel reasonably sure that the dissident visionaries still can be identified as followers of the tradition of the classical prophets, especially of Second Isaiah. Moreover, the attacks against the dominant temple cult in Zechariah 10, 11, 12, and 14 strongly suggest that up to the time of the composition of these oracles not all Levites had been lured back into the hierocratic tradition by the more tolerant overtures of the Zadokite priesthood, overtures which finally were given written form by the Chronicler. As is so often the case in polemical literature of this nature, the dissident group can be defined more sharply in terms of the party and structures which it opposed than in terms of its own positive attributes. Regarding the latter, we can only suggest that we again are dealing with an alliance of visionary followers of Second Isaiah and disenfranchised Levites who carry forth the struggle which we traced in Isaiah 56–66. Against the unambiguous message of historical developments they cling tenaciously to their hope for ultimate victory, and seek to reconcile the incongruity between historical realities and their vision of the ideal in their oracles. These oracles are comprised primarily of pronouncements of judgment upon the leaders of the community, whom they declare are illegitimate, and cultic practices of the temple, which they declare are defiled, and announcements of salvation to the remnant which, in their view, has remained faithful to the prophetic vision of Yahweh's final vindication of his people. But the very attempt to reconcile the vision and historical realities under historical circumstances which are increasingly hostile to their aspirations leads to disappointments and frustrations which have been the birthplace of apocalyptic in many periods of history.

This rather vague characterization of the visionary tradition with which we will be dealing stands in contrast to the more specific description which we were able to give in the last chapter of their opponents, the Zadokite leaders of the hierocratic party. It may be well to recall here the main features of the victorious hierocratic party which would be the chief source of irritation and alienation for the visionaries during the period of the Second Temple. The first is the central importance of the temple in Jerusalem, built under Persian sponsorship and thereby symbolizing vividly for the visionaries the Persian-Israelite coalition. Opposition to the temple of course drew on an ancient tradition which was very critical of the temple theology, a tradition tracing back as far as Nathan's oracle, and appearing also in Jeremiah and the Isaianic school. But in the post-exilic period, opposition went far beyond rivalry between divergent traditions as the visionaries looked upon the temple and the policy of collaboration with the Persians as a threat to the very autonomy and lordship of Yahweh, the supreme God who needed no sponsor beside himself. The memory of what had happened under the Zimride dynasty in the North and under Manasseh was too much alive in the tradition to permit some Yahwists to acquiesce to foreign control of the central unit.

A second point of offense closely related to the first was the corruption of cultic and civic leaders which the visionaries probably felt resulted from the Persian alliance, and which represents the "tolerance and compromise"[1] which is characteristically the mark of the established national cult. The books of Ezra, Nehemiah, and Malachi suggest that the nobles and religious leaders were quick to stray from the way of holiness after pleasure and gain. Moreover, the fact that all the officials, from the Davidic *nāśî* on down to the temple priests and lesser civic officers, belonged to a party of which the visionaries were bitter rivals made harsh criticism of their corruption particularly inviting.[2]

The third, and perhaps most important point of opposition was the virtual indifference of the hierocratic party toward eschatology and their tendency to regard as eternal, absolute, and immune to judgment a temple and priesthood, supported by a foreign alliance, in which the opponents were able to recognize nothing of what they believed

1. Troeltsch, *Teaching* I, p. 337.

2. Troeltsch (ibid, p. 339) points out that the Church-type organization is aware that not all members can be expected to attain to the same level of holiness. Naturally the sect bitterly opposes this view, demanding holiness of each individual member. This eliminates the necessity of a priesthood which vicariously represents the holiness of the entire group (cf. Zech 14:20–21).

were the signs of the eschaton. Ultimately, we believe, this was the most basic reason for their rejection of the temple, the cult, and the cultic personnel, upon which they proceeded to announce the imminent judgment of Yahweh. For the eschaton, in their opinion, had not been realized by the hierocracy, nor was the day of Yahweh's wrathful judgment past. The prophetic opponents of the hierocratic party thus continued to insist that the fulfillment of Israel's history remained a future event, and that the eschaton would arrive only after the present structures which the hierocrats had absolutized had been destroyed and supplanted by a new, more glorious order. To explain how this judgment and final restoration would occur the visionaries drew upon the archaic Divine Warrior material; restoration would not come by human efforts, but by a new conquest of the land by the Divine Warrior. On the basis of this faith in Yahweh's future intervention, all identification of present phenomena with the eschatological kingdom was rejected, whether it be identification of Zerubbabel with the Messiah, the temple with the New Jerusalem, or the Zadokite priesthood with the end-time rulers. Behind such radical opposition one recognizes alienated elements which drew upon archaic models calling into question the status quo as they longed for Yahweh to upset the hierocratic order, an order preserving the pre-exilic Zadokite priestly structures which contained a built-in prejudice against the non-Zadokite families.

Opposition along these three fronts—the Persian-sponsored temple, the civic and spiritual leaders of the hierocratic party, and the virtually uneschatological stand of post-exilic orthodoxy, together with the borrowing of the mythic Divine Warrior motifs, fusing the ritual conquest tradition of the league with the ritual procession of the royal cult—permits us to identify the literature of the visionary group in the remainder of this study. The examination of this literature will bring us a step further along the path leading from prophetic to apocalyptic eschatology.

The situation within which the visionaries continued to find themselves increasingly vitiated the attempt to translate their visionary program into the terms of plain history. In control over the temple and in coalition with the Persians the hierocratic party introduced abominations into the community such as prayers for the Persian emperor in the temple[3] and perhaps even the sale of Jewish slaves into the royal army.[4] Hierocratic control and the Persian coalition appeared to be permanent elements of the political order. Hence the deep borrowing upon the mythic Divine Warrior material to explain the bleak situation and to provide a means of preserving the promise that Yahweh yet one day would save his people in spite of the seemingly unambivalent message of history that the adversaries of the visionary group had emerged as victors.

B. IN DEFENSE OF A NEW APPROACH TO THE ORACLES OF ZECHARIAH 9-14

Although it is intended that the investigation begun here will later be carried through the pseudepigrapha and the literature of the Essene community at Qumran, the present study will conclude with this chapter on Zechariah 9-14. None of the oracles in these six chapters contains historical allusions on the basis of which the material might be dated, but typological considerations as well as the community situation reflected allow us to attach approximate dates to most of the oracles. That this section belongs to the same visionary tradition which we have found in Third Isaiah is demonstrated by the following considerations: (1) The vision of Israel's restoration is the eschatological one of Yahweh coming to save his faithful and establishing them as a people. (2) The leaders of the people come under harsh condemnation. (3) The marks of apocalyptic eschatology are present in the indifference to the actual events of the political realm and in the lack of any sense of vocation within the present political order. (4) The mythical motifs of ritual conquest and royal procession, which can be

3. Cf. Ezr 6:10.

4. Cf. Zech 11:4 ff, and E. E. Urbach, "The Laws Regarding Slavery as a Source for Social History of the Period of the Second Temple, the Mishnah and Talmud," in *Papers of the Institute of Jewish Studies, London* (Jerusalem: Magnes, 1964), pp. 1-94.

traced throughout the visionary tradition from the proto-apocalyptic of Second Isaiah to the late apocalyptic of the pseudepigrapha and Qumran, are of central importance in Zechariah 9-14.[5]

Even a cursory glance at the commentaries suggests the need for a fresh approach to the material of Zechariah 9-14 (often called Deutero-Zechariah or Second Zechariah). For in those commentaries the text is tortuously forced to serve one historical hypothesis after the other (the "interpolations" removed in some cases add up to three-fourths of the received text), with Assyrian and Persian sources carelessly being used as support. Using methodologies very similar to one another, Kraemer, for example, argues that Second Zechariah comes from the reign of Hezekiah, while Marti is just as confident that it dates from the Maccabean period.

EXCURSUS: PAST BIBLICAL RESEARCH ON ZECHARIAH 9-14

We shall here offer only a broad sketch of the history of criticism of Zechariah 9-14.[6] It is interesting to note that we have before us one instance where the orthodox attitude toward the inerrancy of Scripture prompted biblical criticism. A real problem was posed in the seventeenth century by the fact that the New Testament tradition (Mt 27:9f) attributed to Jeremiah words which were found in Zechariah 11:13. This problem exercised pious scholars for a century and a half, leading to solutions which

5. We stress again that the continuity of tradition with which we are dealing in tracing the development of apocalyptic eschatology involves a continuity in the manner of relating the vision of divine intervention and restoration to historical realities rather than a continuity of specific religious parties. This continuity can be accounted for on the basis of similar sociological circumstances to which visionaries of widely divergent periods were all reacting. Thus the Qumran community lived amidst circumstances which permitted them to relive the experience of the community addressed by Second Isaiah and which led them to adapt the forms and images of that earlier proto-apocalyptic figure to their own apocalyptic message. Similarly, the communities that produced Daniel, the Assumption of Moses, and Jubilees stand in continuity with the visionary tradition of the sixth and fifth centuries. For the reuse of the visionary material of the Second and Third Isaiah by these later communities see George W. E. Nickelsburg, Jr., *Resurrection, Immortality, and Eternal Life in Intertestamental Judaism*, Harvard Theological Studies XXVI (Cambridge: Harvard University Press, 1972), pp. 11-42.

6. For a detailed survey, one can consult B. Otzen, *Studien über Deuterosacharja* (Copenhagen: Prostant Apud Munksgaard, 1964), pp. 11-34, and O. Eissfeldt, *The Old Testament: An Introduction*, tr. P. R. Ackroyd (New York: Harper & Row, 1965), pp. 434-440.

in many cases are very ludicrous. For example, Joseph Mede in 1664 accused the Jews of having falsified Holy Writ, adding: "And if one of the Apostles of our Lord play here [Mt 27:9f] the Critick, it is no sin to follow him, say the Masorites what they will" (*The Works of Joseph Mede* [London: 1664[2]], p. 963).

The study of Zechariah entered a new phase in 1785 with the appearance of William Newcome's *An Attempt towards an Improved Version, a Metrical Arrangement and an Explanation of the Twelve Minor Prophets.* First he demonstrated the differences in content and style which divided the first eight chapters from the remainder of the book. Then he went on to separate chapters 9-11 from 12-14, dating the former ca. 722 and the latter ca. 600. This solution dominated the scene for a century, not only in England but in Germany, where Leonhard Bertholdt became its chief protagonist (L. Bertholdt, *Historischkritische Einleitung in saemmtliche kanonische und apokryphische Schriften des alten und neuen Testaments,* vol. 4 [Erlangen, 1814], 1697-1728).

A notable dissenting voice was that of J. G. Eichhorn, who after a period of vacillating, came out in the fourth edition (1824) of his *Einleitung* with a careful argument for placing chapters 9-10 in the period after Alexander's conquest, with 11-13:6 probably coming from the same period and 13:7-14:21 perhaps stemming from the Maccabean era (J. G. Eichhorn, *Einleitung in das alte Testament* [Göttingen: C. E. Rosenbusch, 1824[4]], pp. 455 ff.).

Eichhorn's thesis gained little popularity until more than a half a century later when it was developed by Bernhard Stade, after whom it remained the most popular solution for decades, continuing to find many supporters until today. If a student wants to win a good understanding of the history of research of Zechariah 9-14, Stade's work must be read; indeed, it would be a good place to begin. His remarks on methodology are very insightful; he criticizes his predecessors for having been preoccupied with attaching dates to isolated historical references, and proposes instead that the work be seen in the line of development of prophetism as a whole. Behind Second Zechariah he sees a line running from Jeremiah (31:15-22) to Ezekiel (33-39). But that Second Zechariah represents a further step after Ezekiel is seen in the fact that, while in the latter Yahweh is restoring both Judah and Joseph, in the former Ephraim is being freed by Judah, indicating that Judah has already returned from exile (B. Stade, "Deuterozacharja. Eine kritische Studie," *ZAW* I [1881]: 1-96; 2 [1882]: 151-172, 275-309).

Stade perhaps provides the best work that has been done on Second Zechariah, and he thus represents a notable exception to the criticism of previous scholarship expressed above. This makes it all the more regrettable that even he falls from the excellent methodology sketched in the first pages of his work. When he comes to give a more precise date to the material (his method of studying where Second Zechariah fits into the development of prophecy showed him that it came somewhere after the exile), he succumbs to precisely the method of his predecessors which he has criticized: he bears down on the reference to the Sons of Greece in 9:13, to Assur and Egypt in 10:10f, and to military conflict in 9:1-8 and 11:1-3, and decides they reflect the era immediately following the period of Alexander.

Generalizations such as the following can be as dangerous as they can be helpful in organizing a bulk of literature too large to review in detail here: All of scholarship since Stade has been built upon his epoch-making study, but it has completely missed the best in Stade, drawing instead upon what represents Stade's fall from his excellent approach. It has concentrated almost exclusively on isolated historical allusions scattered especially in chapters 9-10 in the effort of attaching dates to them, while his excellent method of seeing where Second Zechariah fits into the stream of prophetism has been regrettably forgotten. One author after the other has taken the place names in 9:1-8 and, by forcing tne text and extra-biblical sources in this direction or that, has sought to prove his solution of what is reflected: the era of Hezekiah (E. G. H. Kraeling, "The Historical Situation in Zechariah 9:1-10," *AJSLL* 14 [1924-25]: 24-33) or the reign of Josiah (Otzen, *Studien,* 69, n. 25) or the first campaign (738) of Tiglath-Pileser (T. H. Robinson and F. Horst, *Die zwölf kleinen Propheten,* HAT 14 [Tübingen: J. C. B. Mohr (Paul Siebeck) 1964²]) or his second campaign (734-32) (Aku Masing, *Die Proklamation des Tab'alsohnes,* Piam Memoriam Alexander von Bulmerincq [Riga, 1938], pp. 117-126) or the attack of Sargon against the West in 720 (A. Malamat, "The Historical Setting of Two Biblical Prophecies on the Nations," *IEJ* 1 [1950]: 149-159) or the Maccabean period (K. Marti, *Das Dodekaprophetenbuch erklärt* KH-CAT 13 [Tübingen: J. C. B. Mohr (Paul Siebeck); 1904]); B. Duhm, "Anmerkungen zu den zwölf Propheten," *ZAW* 31 [1911]: 189 ff.; E. Sellin, *Das Zwölfprophetenbuch,* KAT 12 [Leipzig: Deichert, 1929²]; J. A. Bewer, *The Literature of the Old Testament* [New York: Columbia University, 1922]; W. O. E. Oesterley-T. H. Robinson, *An Introduction to the Books of the Old Testament* [New York: Macmillan, 1934]).

If any one solution, however, were singled out as representing majority opinion today, it would be the solution connecting 9:1-8 with Alexander's conquest, since many exegetes continue to work and rework text and sources to strengthen Stade's conclusion (Eissfeldt, *Introduction,* p. 437; K. Elliger, *Das Buch der zwölf kleinen Propheten,* ATD 24/5 [Göttingen: Vandenhoeck und Ruprecht,

1949-51]; and "Ein Zeugnis aus der jüdischen Gemeinde im Alexanderjahr 332 vor Christi," *ZAW* 62 [1950]: 63-115; J. M. P. Smith, *Zechariah,* ICC [New York: Charles Scribner's Sons, 1912]; R. C. Dentan, *Zechariah* 9-14, IB 6 [New York: Abingdon, 1956]; M. Delcor, "Les Allusions à Alexandre le Grande dans Zach. 9, 1-8," *VT* 1 [1951]: 110-124).

If one were to survey the research on other passages, say 9:12-13; 11:4-17; or 10:6-10, one would find an equally bewildering picture. In the case of 9:13, those arguing for a Hellenistic date of the corpus make much of the mention of the Sons of Greece; in turn, those supporting the earlier dates will dwell on the reference to the Northern and Southern Kingdoms in 9:10, 13 and 10:6, and to the mention of Egypt and Assyria in 10:11.

One final line of criticism attempts to do justice to both those verses apparently reflecting a pre-exilic situation and those seemingly stemming from a later period by uncovering behind Zechariah 9-11 a document from ca. 730 which was then reworked in the post-exilic era (S. R. Driver, *An Introduction to the Literature of the Old Testament* [New York: Charles Scribner's Sons, 1913]; W. W. Baudissin, *Einleitung in die Bücher des alten Testamentes* [Leipzig: S. Hirzel, 1901]). Neither this solution nor a similar one by A. Jepsen ("Kleine Beiträge zum Zwölfprophetenbuch" II, *ZAW* 57 [1939]: 242-255) have proven to be very influential, for they too resort to a very mechanical way of eliminating difficulties.

Naturally, the fact that this collection of oracles contains some of the most obscure and textually corrupt material in the entire Old Testament has something to do with the problem. But the major difficulty lies deeper, involving the methodology usually used in treating this material, that of evaluating the historical allusions in the text in the effort to connect them with an absolute date in history. For example, the cities and districts in 9:1-7 are plotted on the map so as to determine which conquest was being described, whether that of Sargon, Tiglath-Pileser or Alexander, just to mention three of the most popular solutions. In fact, each of these solutions can be argued as persuasively as the others, granting the necessary emendations of the text, since none of those conquests matches the text perfectly. Nor does the reference to the return of exiles from Assur and Egypt (10:10-11), the mention of the Sons of Greece (9:13), or the allusions to the Northern and Southern Kingdoms (9:13; 10:6) offer anything more gratifying by way of an historical peg for the material.

The difficulty lies in the fact that one very important characteristic of the material in Second Zechariah generally has been overlooked, namely, its relation to history is different from that found in the prophecy of a classical prophet like Isaiah. For as Chapter II indicated, the stubborn insistence of the classical prophets in translating their vision of Yahweh's acts into the terms of politics and plain history was increasingly abandoned by the visionaries of the post-exilic period. The divine act stands in a much looser relation to historical processes, meaning that the conqueror acting to effect Yahweh's intentions in history in Zech 9:1-7 is not Tiglath-Pileser, Nebuchadnezzar, or Cyrus, but the Divine Warrior Yahweh himself. The use of historical allusions has undergone a great change since the time of the pre-exilic prophets, and the failure to recognize this has led to the chaotic state of the scholarhip of Zechariah 9-14.

This failure to recognize the relation of this early apocalyptic literature to actual historical events is accompanied by a second methodological flaw shared by many exegetes, the application of a grossly inaccurate typology of the development of apocalyptic. Still laboring under the false view that the basic ideas of apocalyptic entered Israel from Persian dualism at a late point in the post-exilic period, they assign passages which include apocalyptic notions generally to a period which is much too late. As indicated in the introduction, the entire typology of apocalyptic must be revised on the basis of new evidence ranging from Ugarit in the fourteenth century B.C. to Qumran in the second and first.

In an attempt to avoid the pitfalls mentioned above, we shall apply the contextual-typological method utilized earlier in connection with Third Isaiah. Inquiry will be made into the tradition or traditions to which the material belongs and into the situation within the community which seems to be reflected. Stylistic and metric features will be observed. Careful note will be made of the types of traditional material which are borrowed, and of the influence these materials have had in shaping these chapters. Finally the important question will be posed, where in the continuum extending from prophetic to apocalyptic eschatology does the material belong?

While not ignoring historical allusions, we will take care to determine the use being made of such references, and the connection which they have to actual historical events will be investigated. This investigation will be carried out with the awareness that in the early apocalyptic literature the relation of the visionary community to history is undergoing a change. As the visionaries utilize myth to explain their situation, history is not dissolved into a mythological worldview, but neither is the prophetic message any longer translated directly into the terms of plain history. Their message is gradually becoming emancipated from the restraints of political realities, as primordial events and eschatological events, while not merging, are at least being drawn more closely together.

C. A DIVINE WARRIOR HYMN DRAWING ON THE RITUAL PATTERN OF THE CONFLICT MYTH (9:1–17)[7]

The problem of determining the divisions between units of tradition in Second Zechariah arises immedately, and in proposing that our first unit extends from 9:1–17, we are not stating the obvious. The Hebrew text places dividers at Zech 9:1; 12:1; and Mal 1:1 with the words *massā̆' dəbar yhwh;* since the *mal'ākî* of the superscription in the last mentioned is derived from the "my messenger" referred to in Mal 3:1, it seems likely that in Zech 9:1–11:17; 12:1–14:21; and Mal 1:1–3:24 we have three anonymous blocks of tradition which were added to the end of the minor prophets, each being given the title "oracle of the word of Yahweh." At some point the first two blocks were considered part of the book of Zechariah while the last was

7. For a fuller treatment of this composition, see the author's "Zechariah 9 and the Recapitulation of an Ancient Ritual Pattern," *JBL* 92 (1973): 37–59.

given independent status so as to expand the minor prophets to the holy number twelve; a name was supplied for this last block by interpreting *mal'ākî* as the proper name of the prophet uttering the words.

The divisions made by this thrice-appearing formula are significant, and the resulting three blocks each have unique characteristics binding them from within and distinguishing them from each other. However, even behind these blocks, a history of tradition must be recognized. First, it is obvious that 11:4ff is an independent unit, whether from the same prophet as the rest of 9-11 is another question. Most of the exegetes recognize that a new unit begins in 10:1, another in 11:1, and from there on divisions vary a great deal. Regarding the first composition, most scholars do not treat 9:1-17 as a unity. For example, Kraeling, who is followed by Dentan,[8] holds that the original oracle comprised only the first ten verses, since "the resumption of war after the coming of the king of peace is unbearable" (may one ask "to whom?" to the prophet, or to Kraeling?).[9] Sellin maintains that the oracle extends through verse 17, but only after deleting verses 9-10,[10] since he also finds it impossible to reconcile the juxtaposition of war and peace within one unit. Elliger uses both this argument and a metrical one in insisting that the original unit extends through the first eight verses. He recognizes three stress tricola throughout 1-8, whereas in 9-10 bicola are obviously found. But this insistence that a unit of tradition must utilize but one metrical scheme is simplistic and false,[11] and in our instance for two reasons: (1) The stepped-up tempo in verses 9-10 is completely consonant with the crescendo of excitement at this point in the unit. (2) Verses 9-10 likely comprise an old traditional poem from royal ritual, a poem drawn into our song with-

8. Dentan, *Zechariah,* n. 5, p. 1092.

9. Kraeling, "Situation," n. 5, p. 24.

10. Sellin, n. 5, p. 496.

11. Mixed meter is not uncommon in Ugaritic epic style, and continues to be found in early Yahwistic poetry. It is utilized as well by compositions which attempt to imitate archaic canons of poetry. Cf. F. M. Cross, "Notes on a Canaanite Psalm in the Old Testament," *BASOR* 117 (1950): 20.

out alteration of meter, since its meter was firmly set by tradition. Furthermore, bicola appear also in verses 1–2. But these negative reasons for rejecting the various divisions of the chapter proposed by the exegetes are a minor factor in the total argument, for when the chapter is seen

---

9: 1 The oracle of Yahweh's word:
Yahweh is against Hadrach,
Damascus is his throne dais;
to Yahweh belong the people of Aram,
and all the tribes of Israel,
2 even Hamath, which borders thereon,
Sidon, which is so wise.
3 Tyre has built herself a rampart,
has heaped up silver like dust,
gold like the dirt of the streets.
4 The Lord will capture her,
he will hurl her wealth into the sea,
she will be consumed by fire.
5 Seeing this, Askelon will be terrified,
Gaza will be struck by anguish,
Ekron's plans will be shattered.
The king will perish from Gaza,
Askelon will be depopulated,
6 a usurper will sit (enthroned) in Ashdod.
I will destroy the arrogance of Philistia,
7 I will remove the blood from its mouth,
and the abominations from between its teeth.
He will be a remnant for our God,
he will be like a clan in Judah,
and Ekron will be like the Jebusite.
8 I will stand guard near my house,
the oppressor will not overrun them again;
for now I see with my own eyes.
9 Rejoice heartily, daughter of Zion!
shout gladly, daughter of Jerusalem!
Your king now comes to you,
triumphant and victorious is he,

against the background of the ritual conquest and royal procession traditions upon which the early apocalyptic literature drew so heavily, a beautifully developed poetic unit is recognized which allows no divisions. Demonstration of this fact will be made below.

	Text	Structure	Meter	Prosodic Units
9:1	משא דבר יהוה	rubric	6	
	[יהוה] [a] בארץ חדרך	a b c	6	1:1::1:1:1:1
	ודמשק מנחתו [b]	c_1 D	7	
	ליהוה ע[ם] א[ר]ם [c]	a b_1 c_2	6	
	וכל שבטי ישראל	B c_3	7	
2	גם חמת תגבל בה	c_4 e f	6	
	[ ][d]צידון חכמה מאד	c_5 e_1 f_1	7	
3	תבן צר מצור לה	a b c	6	1:1:1
	ותצבר כסף כעפר	a_1 c_1 d	7	
	חרוץ כטיט חוצות	c_2 D	6	
4	אדני יורשנה	a b c	7	1:1:1
	והכה בים חילה	b_1 d c_1	7	
	והיא באש תאכל	c_2 d_1 b_2	7	
5	תרא אשקלון ותירא	a b a_1	7	1:1:1
	ועזה תחיל מאד	b_1 A	7	
	עקרון הביש מבטה	b_2 a_2 c	7	
	ואבד מלך מעזה	a b c	7	1:1:1
	אשקלון לא תשב	c_1 A	6	
6	ישב ממזר באשדוד	a_1 d c_2	7	
	אכרת גאון פלשתים	a b c	7	1:1:1
7	אסר דמיו מפיו	a_1 b_1 c_1	6	
	שקציו מבין שניו	b_2 C	7	
	ישאר [ ] לאלהינו	a b c	8	1:1:1
	יהיה כאלף ביהודה	a_1 D	8	
	ועקרון כיבוסי	b d	7	
8	אחנה לביתי מצבה [e] [ ] [f]	a b c	8	1:1:1
	לא יעבר עליהם עוד נגש	d e f	9	
	כי עתה ראיתי בעיני	g a_1 b_1	9	
9	גילי מאד בת ציון	a b c	7	1:1
	הריעי בת ירושלם	a_1 C	8	
	הנה מלכך יבוא לך	a b c	7	1:1:1:1
	צדיק ונושע הוא[ה]	d d_1 a_1	7	

humble and riding on an ass,
on a colt, the foal of an ass.
10 He will banish chariotry from Ephraim
and horses from Jerusalem,
the bow of war will be banished
and he will proclaim peace for the nations.
His dominion will stretch from sea to sea,
from the River to the ends of the Earth.
11 As for you, because of the blood of your covenant,
I have released your captives from the pit;
12 return to the stronghold, prisoners of hope,
for today I will repay you double.
13 I have bent Judah as my bow,
I have made Ephraim its arrow.
I wield your sons, Zion,
I have made you like a warrior's sword.
14 Yahweh will appear above them,
his arrow will flash forth like lightning,
Yahweh will sound the trumpet,
he will advance on the southern stormwinds.
15 Yahweh will protect them,
they will tread (the enemy) *like slingstones,*
they will drink their blood like wine,
they will be filled like an altar bowl.
16 Yahweh will save them like sheep,
his people like stones for a crown,
they will glisten upon his land.
17 How great their prosperity and beauty!
Corn *will make fat* the young men,
wine will make the maidens fruitful.

TEXTUAL NOTES

a) In agreement with LXX, Vg, and Tg, we read משא דבר יהוה as a construct chain. The conjunctive accent *mehuppak* under משא in the MT indicates the Masoretes also understood the construction thus. The oracle would then begin after this superscription, and if a second יהוה is restored (lost by haplography), the metric structure of the first bicolon is regained.

b) The common meaning of מנוחה is "resting place," especially in reference to a land dwelling peaceably, and in contrast to a state of wandering without a home (e.g., Dtn 12:9); it can also mean the condition of "rest" (Jer 45:3). A less commonly recog-

Verse	Text	Scansion	Count	Pattern
	עני ורכב []חמור	d_2 d_3 e	7	
	ועל עיר בן אתנות	E	7	
10	יכרית [g] רכב מאפרים	a b c	7	1:1::1:1
	וסום מירושלם	b_1 C	7	
	תנכר קשת מלחמה	a_1 B	7	
	ודבר שלום לגוים	a_2 b_2 c_1	7	
	משלו מים עד ים	a b c	7	1:1
	מנהר עד אפסי ארץ	b_1 C	7	
11	גם את בדם בריתך	a b c	7	1:1:1:1
	שלחתי אסיריך מבור[ ] [h]	d a_1 e	8	
12	שובו[ ] בצרון אסירי[ ]תקוה	f g a_2	9	
	גם היום[ ]משנה אשיב לך [i]	h i d_1	8	
13	אדרך לי יהודה	a b c	6	1:1:1:1
	קשת מלאתי אפרים	d a_1 c_1	6	
	עוררתי בניך ציון[ ] [j]	a_2 e c_2	7	
	שמתיך כחרב גבור	A_3 D	6	
14	יהוה עליהם יראה	a b c	8	1:1:1:1
	יצא כברק חצו	c_1 d a_1	7	
	[ ] [k] יהוה בשופר יתקע	a d_1 c_2	7	
	יהלך בסערות תימן	c_3 D	7	
15	יהוה[ ] [k] יגן עליהם	a b c	7	1:1::1:1
	[ ]יכבשו [כ]אבני קלע	d E	7	
	ישתו [ד]מ[ם] כמו יין	d_1 e f	7	
	ימלאו כמזרק [ ]מזבח [l]	d_2 F	8	
16	יושיעם יהוה [m] [ ]כצאן	a b c	7	1:1:1
	עמו ב[ ]אבני נזר	a_1 C	6	
	יתנוססו[ ]על אדמתו [n]	d e	8	
17	כי מה טובו מה יפיו	a b a b_1	8	
	דגן [דשן] [o] בחורים	c d e	7	
	תירוש ינובב בתלות	c_1 d_1 e_1	8	

nized meaning is found here: "throne dais," as the place where the king rests. To it can be compared *nḫt* in the Ugaritic texts, especially 4.1.34 (51) where Hayyin-Khasis is seen casting *il nḫt* in response to Baal's complaint to El that he has no temple like the gods (cf. 22.1.18 [123] and 16.6.24 [127]). Besides our verse, it is used in this sense in 1 Chr 28:2 (מנחה בית = a shelter for Yahweh's throne dais, as indicated by the parallel להדם רגלי אלהינו), Is 66:1 (note the parallels מקום מנוחתי, בית, הדם רגלי, כסאי), Ps 132:7 (again parallel to הדם רגליו), Ps 132:8 and 14, and Is 11:10.

c) A conjectural emendation for the difficult עין אדם. M.

Dahood (*CBQ* 25 [1963]: 123–124) proposes a masc. *'ādam* with the same meaning as *'ădāmâ*. Thus the phrase would be equivalent to *'ên hā'āreṣ*, "the surface of the earth." But this vague phrase ill fits the context, where every other colon refers to a very specific city or people. Moreover, the claim in the preceding colon that Damascus is Yahweh's throne dais leads naturally to the conclusion, "to Yahweh belong the people of Aram."

d) As the singular verb and the meter suggest, one of the city names is secondary (the plural verb in LXX and Vg is a later correction). Since צר forms the heart of the next verse (the recurrent *ṣādê* and *rêš* in v. 3 are obviously playing on צר), the redundancy may be removed only by regarding צר as a secondary intrusion into v. 2b. Such intrusion is not surprising in light of the frequent mention in prophetic literature of Sidon and Tyre as comprising an inseparable unit.

e) Deriving מצבה from the root *nṣb* (supported by LXX and Pesh).

f) מערב ומשב seems to be an explanatory gloss. Verse 8 presents a number of difficult problems; our emendations are tentative.

g) As indicated by LXX, Pesh, and the context, a third person singular verb seems original here.

h) אין מים בו is a gloss, probably stemming from Gen 37:24 and attempting to draw a typological connection between the exile and Joseph's captivity (cf. Jer 38:6).

i) The sense of the first colon of v. 12 fits the context well, but as it appears in MT it is metrically long. There is no versional evidence to support drastic change. Since שוב can appear without a preposition, the ל may be secondary, and the noun may have been pronounced with two syllables. Definite articles are usually later additions in poetry. With these changes the meter is normal. In the second colon, the מגיד is probably intrusive. Given the corrupt nature of the text, our reconstruction of v. 12 must remain tentative.

j) על בניך יון is shown by meter and parallel structure to be intrusive. It is a clear example of an error stemming from dittography (בניך יון/בניך ציון).

k) As commonly, the divine name has been expanded.

l) The meter and the prosodic structure of the poem suggest that one of the verbs in this colon is superfluous. כבש gives the appearance of originality by producing a fine image with the adverbial phrase "like slingstones," whereas אכל could have come into the text under the influence of the common parallel pair, שתה//אכל (note especially Is 22:13 and Ezek 39:17); an alternative interpretation is that it could be what remains of a variant colon, originally reading יאכלו בשרם כלחם, or the like. Once the second verb entered the text, the syntactical force of the adverbial phrase would have been lost, with the *kap* being lost and "slingstones" becoming the direct object (resulting in a bizarre image!). Added plausibility adheres to our reading on the basis of the syntactical structure of the next four cola with their repetitive comparisons constructed with adverbial phrases. In v. 15b דמם is supported by the Greek uncials A and Q (*το αιμα αυτων*); BS and W have *αυτους* as object followed by *ως οινον*. The Targum also includes the notion of blood. MT and Vg give the appearance of the suppression of a crude image.

m) We regard אלהיהם as an expansion of the divine name, and ביום ההוא as a gloss.

n) Inasmuch as the latter two cola of v. 16 present many difficulties, we offer our reconstruction only as a reasonable conjecture.

o) The prosodic and syntactic problems of the last two cola of the poem are solved if one restores a verb which would have been lost by haplography: דגן/דשן.

Except in those sections where textual corruption has taken its toll, the meter and poetic structure of the hymn are quite regular, although the skillful blending of various metrical schemes has begun to yield to a rather monotonous repetition of 1:1 bicola. The contrast offered by the shorter six-syllable lines is not enough to create b:b or l:b bicola. The feel for archaic metric structures is thus being lost. The next step in the typology will be the wholesale breakdown of metric structure. Although the quality of the prosody is thus not equal to the poetry of Second Isaiah—who truly marks the final flourishing of classical Hebrew poetry—and although several features of the later decay of Hebrew prosody are foreshadowed in the prosaic tricolon of verse 8, or in the list-like structure of verses 13 and 15, nevertheless the poet is able to imitate some of the features of archaic poetry. Note, for example, the parallelism, frequent chiasm, and fairly regular meter. On the metric typology, the poem falls later than Second Isaiah, but before the disintegration of metric structure that occurs in the latest oracles of Third Isaiah.

Viewed as a whole, the poem represents one of the purest examples of a genre which becomes extremely important within the visionary tradition in the exilic and post-exilic period, the Divine Warrior Hymn.[12] It was already met in Third Isaiah (59:15b–20; 66:15–16; 63:1–6; 63:19b–64:2), in which connection it was noted that this genre was introduced to the prophetic tradition by Second Isaiah, who fused the league tradition of ritual conquest with various features of the royal festival to create an eschatological poem celebrating Yahweh's new act of delivering his people.

To understand with a degree of clarity the background of the Divine Warrior Hymn it becomes necessary to consider in some detail the nature of the two Israelite traditions—the conquest tradition of the league and the enthronement tradition of the royal cult—from which it was derived, and even to move behind them to the ancient ritual pattern of the conflict myth in Canaan and Mesopotamia, which is the ultimate source of the genre in question. The common element running throughout the history of the Divine Warrior Hymn, from its point of origin in ancient myth to its late application in apocalyptic compositions, is a scenario depicting the cosmic battle of the Divine Warrior (originally the storm god) and his subsequent temple building, banquet, and glorious reign. On Israelite soil the variable is the extent to which the cosmic matrix of the scenario has been impregnated with a new historical perspective, a phenomenon which vastly altered the thrust of the genre once it was adopted to celebrate Israel's faith in Yahweh. Nevertheless, even in Israel the mythic potency of the Divine Warrior Hymn was never completely sterilized, and thus it represented throughout Israelite history a potential source of recrudescent mythic thinking, especially during several phases of the royal cult in Jerusalem and in the early post-exilic period which is the object of our present study.

Within the literature of the league, the finest example of

12. The Divine Warrior Hymn belongs to the hymnic literature of the Bible in a specialized sense. The dominant tone of this type of composition is hymnic, that is, it celebrates an anticipated future act of Yahweh the Warrior. Yet it functions in a special way within its late setting: besides being a paean of praise, it serves as an announcement of restoration to the faithful, offering comfort and hope in troubled times.

the Divine Warrior Hymn is found in Exodus 15.[13] This early poem betrays Israel's intimate acquaintance with the ritual pattern of the conflict myth, and suggests that the most natural means of expressing her faith at the earliest period of her history was in the idiom of this mythic pattern.[14] Nevertheless, already at that early time, Israel's perception of her religious experiences was quite distinct from the perception recorded in the conflict myths of her ancient neighbors. In the latter attention was centered on the cosmic activities of conflicting deities; in Israel Yahweh's saving acts were recognized chiefly in historical events. Thus from the beginning of the history of the Divine Warrior Hymn on Israelite soil tension was introduced between the literary form and the religious substance. Specifically in Exodus 15 this is apparent in the way the hymn is suspended precariously between the cosmic and mundane. The cosmic dimension is present in the unmistakable traces of the primeval battle between the Divine Warrior and the inimical sea. But the impact of the new historical perspective is seen in the sea's loss of his vitality as an adversary seriously threatening the natural order. Rather he is delineated as a passive instrument in Yahweh's battle against an enemy of a different order, Pharaoh, king of the Egyptians. In spite of this impregnation of the conflict myth with a new historical substance, however, the essential structural elements of the ritual pattern of the conflict myth are present.

Combat-victory (1-12)
Theophany of Divine Warrior (8)
Salvation of the Israelites (13-16a)
Building of the temple and procession (16b-17)
Manifestation of Yahweh's universal reign (18)

The present study is not the place to offer an extended discussion of the backgroud of this ritual pattern which the earliest singers of Israel adopted. We shall merely cite two

13. See F. M. Cross, "The Song of the Sea and Canaanite Myth," *JThCh* 5 (1968): 1-25.

14. See the author's "Jewish Apocalyptic," pp. 31-58.

examples of that pattern from the cultic rituals celebrating the victory of the god of the thunderstorm in Canaan and Mesopotamia. The Canaanite version is preserved in the Ugaritic literature discovered at Ras Shamra; in fact, variants of the conflict myth are found there, but since both the Yamm and Mot episodes follow the same basic pattern, we need not be concerned with the fact that the precise division between the two is still a matter of scholarly debate. We follow the most common reconstruction of the Baal-Yamm conflict:

Threat (2.1 [137])
Combat—victory (2.4 [68])
Temple built (4 [51])
Banquet (4.6.39 ff [51])
Manifestation of Baal's universal reign (anticipated: 2.4.9-10 [68]; manifested: 4.7.9-12 [51])
Theophany of Divine Warrior (4.7.27-39 [51])
Fertility of restored order (anticipated: 4.5.68-71 [51]; effected: 4.7.18-30 [51]; cf. 6.3.6-7, 12-13 [49])

As argued convincingly by Thorkild Jacobsen, the second example which we cite of the ritual pattern behind Exodus 15 is a reflex of the West Semitic myth of Baal's battle with Yamm.[15] It finds its classical formulation within the Mesopotamian realm in the *Enūma eliš:*

Threat (I:109-II:91)
Combat-victory (IV:33-122)
Theophany of Divine Warrior (IV:39-60)
Salvation of the Gods (IV:123-146; VI:1-44; cf. VI:126-127, 149-151)
Fertility of the restored order (V:1-66; cf. VII:1-2, 59-83)
Procession and victory shout (V:67-89)
Temple built for Marduk (V:117-156; VI:45-68)
Banquet (VI:69-94)
Manifestation of Marduk's universal reign (anticipated: IV:3-18; manifested: VI:95-VII:144)

This ritual pattern in shorter compass is found also in the Apsû-Ea conflict of tablet I:

15. T. Jacobsen, "The Battle Between Marduk and Tiamat," *JAOS* 88 (1968): 104-108.

Threat (37–58)
Combat-victory (59–70)
Temple built (71–77)

Although the ritual pattern of the conflict myth likely continued throughout the league period to influence the form of Israel's confession, the Song of Deborah in Judges 5 indicates that the incongruity between the old form and the new substance had reached the breaking point in Israel by the eleventh century. The skeleton of the pattern is still visible, with the Divine Warrior marching forth from his holy habitation amidst earthquakes, the dripping of the heavens, and the shaking of the mountains. The battle is briefly described in verse 20: "From the heavens the stars fought, from their stations they fought with Sisera." The Warrior is victorious, and he saves his people. Seen schematically, the ritual structure is this:

Combat of Divine Warrior (4a, 20)
Theophany (4b–5)
Victory (21)
Salvation of Israel (31)

While the skeleton of the ritual pattern of the conflict myth thus remains, the flesh of the poem is supplied from a new source, namely, from a drama experienced within the historical realm. The drama of the Divine Warrior and his hosts pales in significance before the deeds of a daring woman whose heroism is described in realistic detail. Yahweh recedes into the background; he relies upon human agents (v. 23), and the ritual pattern of the conflict myth seems to be retained as a stylistic device and as a gentle reminder that somehow Yahweh is active in Israel's historical adventures.

Within one segment of Yahwism, that coming to expression in the classical prophets, the ritual pattern finally was discarded entirely in favor of a new vehicle more adequate as a carrier of Israel's historical faith. Rather than as a storm god, Yahweh was seen by the prophets as a king presiding over a divine assembly, which was also a very ancient way of conceptualizing the divine realm in the ancient Near East. But this model received a particular character in the prophets for the following reasons: it largely excluded other ways of conceptualizing divine governance, it relegated all other members of the divine realm to the one god with absolute power, Yahweh, and it introduced, in the form of the *nābî*, a human agent charged with translating the activities of the divine council into the categories of the historico-political realm. Thus the prophets not only discarded the formal pattern of the conflict myth; they tied the new model for conceptualizing divine activity so inextricably to the historical realm that the substance of mythopoeic religion was broken. No longer was the deity a guarantor of the status quo embodied in the royal dynasty; the God of Israel had associated himself with a realm which was incompatible with the gods of Israel's neighbors, the profane realm of historical change.

Within another segment of the religion of Israel, however, the ritual pattern of the conflict myth not only survived, but flourished, for present in the royal cult in Jerusalem was an ideology which welcomed the sacralization which the conflict myth lent to the Davidic dynasty. The efforts of the prophets to integrate divine activity into the events of history introduced a revolutionary dimension into the nation's religion which could only be a threat to the perpetual structures of the monarchy. The conditional character of prophetic Yahwism was eschewed in favor of the royal myth with its promise of conveyance in perpetuity.[16] Zion was the new divine mountain, the Davidic king was the new son of the high god, and both were established parts of the static order of myth. The ritual pattern, which had served the Mesopotamian and Canaanite royal cults for

16. As suggested by comparison of the Davidic covenant with the Mesopotamian "covenant of grant," the term *unconditional* may not be the proper one to describe the difference between the Davidic covenant with its promise of extension into perpetuity and the Mosaic covenant, with its highly conditional nature which the prophets found so useful in their polemic against king and nation. It has been suggested that the quality of "conveyance in perpetuity" making the covenant available forever, but not guaranteed forever, more adequately defines the nature of the Davidic covenant (according to an unpublished paper written at Harvard by Richard E. Friedman, who builds upon the study of M. Weinfield, "The Covenant of Grant in the Old Testament and in the Ancient Near East," *JAOS* 90 (1970): 184–203).

over a millennium, became a useful vehicle for the ideology of the royal cult in Jerusalem as well. It can be recognized in numerous psalms from various periods in the biblical psalter:

Psalm 2	
1-3	Threat: Conspiring of the nations
4-5	Combat—victory over enemy
8-11b	Manifestation of universal reign of Messiah
11c	Victory shout
Psalm 9	
6-7	Combat—victory over enemy
8-9	Manifestation of Yahweh's universal reign
10-11	Salvation of his people
12-13	Victory shout
Psalm 24	
1	Manifestation of Yahweh's universal reign
2	Combat vs. seas/rivers-victory
(3-6	Entrance Torah)
7-10	Victory shout
	Procession after victory to temple
Psalm 29	
3-9a	Combat vs. waters-victory
9b	Victory shout
10	Manifestation of Yahweh's universal reign
11	Shalom (abundance) of the restored order
Psalm 46	
2-7	Threat: Chaos and nations
	Combat—victory over enemy
8	Salvation of his people
9-12	Manifestation of Yahweh's universal reign
Psalm 47	
2-4	Combat—victory over enemy
5	Salvation of his people
6	Procession
7-8	Victory shout
9-10	Manifestation of Yahweh's universal reign
Psalm 48	
5	Threat: Kings assemble vs. Zion
6-8	Combat—victory over enemy
9	Salvation of Zion
10-12	Victory shout
13-14	Procession around the city
15	Yahweh's universal reign
Psalm 65	
6	Salvation of his people

7-8 Combat vs. seas and nations—victory
9 Manifestation of Yahweh's universal reign
10-13 Shalom (return to fertility—new creation)

Psalm 68
a)
1-2 Combat—victory
3 Victory shout
b)
7-8 Combat of Divine Warrior (ritual conquest)
9-10 Salvation of his people
11-14 Victory over enemy
15-18 Procession to Zion
19-20 Victory shout
c)
21 Combat—victory over enemies
22-23 Salvation of his people
24-27 Procession to sanctuary—victory shout
28-35 Manifestation of Yahweh's universal reign

Psalm 76
4-8 Combat—victory
9-10 Salvation of oppressed
11-12 Procession to bring gifts to Yahweh
13 Manifestation of Yahweh's universal reign

Psalm 77:17-21
17-19 Combat vs. sea—victory
20 Procession
21 Salvation of his people

Psalm 89b
6-9 Yahweh's universal reign
10-13 Victory over enemies
11-19 Procession—victory shout

Psalm 97
1-2 Yahweh reigns
3-5 Combat—victory over enemies
6-7 Manifestation of Yahweh's universal reign
8-9 Victory shout

Psalm 98
1-2 Combat—victory
3a Salvation of his people
3b Manifestation of Yahweh's universal reign
4-9 Procession—victory shout

Psalm 104
1-9 Combat—victory (creation myth)
10-30 Shalom (return to ferility—new creation)
31-35 Victory shout

Psalm 106:9-13
9-10a Combat vs. sea—victory

10b Procession
11-13 Salvation of his people

Psalm 110
1.4 Yahweh establishes his king
2 Manifestation of king's universal reign
3 Procession to Zion
5-7 Combat—victory

Isaiah 11:1-9
1-3 Royal shoot promised, equipped
4-5 Combat—victory
6-8 Shalom
9 Manifestation of Yahweh's universal reign

We shall consider three of the psalms by way of illustration. Psalm 29 is an early example which stems originally from an ancient Canaanite hymn.[17] It opens with a summons to the *bənê 'ēlîm* to glorify Yahweh (vv. 1-2), who appears in the theophany of the storm god. Accompanied by the flashing of lightning and earthquakes, the Divine Warrior defeats his enemies in terrifying combat (vv. 3-9a), including the most inimical enemy of them all, the *mayîm rabbîm* (v. 3b). The scene then shifts to the temple of the warrior god, before whom the victory shout rings out (v. 9b). Yahweh's universal reign is next manifested in a description of his sitting enthroned over the flood as eternal king (v. 10). Finally entreaty is made for shalom, the abundance of the restored order established by the Divine Warrior's victory (v. 11).

In Psalm 47 the conflict and victory of the warrior god is recounted, amidst a call to praise *yhwh 'elyôn* (vv. 2-5). There follows the victory procession: "Elohim has gone up with a shout, Yahweh with the blast of the trumpet" (v. 6). Verses 7 and 8 resound with the victory shout, greeting the victorious Divine Warrior: "Sing forth to Elohim, sing forth, sing to our king, sing! For Elohim is king of the whole earth, sing forth with a *mdskîl.*" Verses 9-10 manifest Yahweh's universal reign.

In Psalm 48 Zion is identified with the locus of the ritual pattern, becoming the glorious cosmic mountain of the far North (vv. 2-5).[18] The threat is in the form of a coalition of

17. H. L. Ginsberg, *Kitvê Ugarīt* (Heb.) (Jerusalem, 1956), pp. 129 ff; F. M. Cross, "Notes on a Canaanite Psalm in the Old Testament," *BASOR* 117 (1950): 19-21.

18. See Richard J. Clifford, *The Cosmic Mountain in Canaan and the Old Testament*

kings assembling against the divine mountain; the storm god defeats them straightway (vv. 6–9). Verse 10 shifts to the temple after the conflict; the victory shout goes forth in verses 11 and 12. This is followed by the royal procession around the city, and finally by the announcement of Yahweh's universal reign.

There is no need to enter into the much debated question of the annual festival(s) of the royal cult in Jerusalem. The ubiquity and regularity in structure of the ritual pattern of the conflict myth in the royal psalms document the point which is essential here:[19] the conflict myth was reintroduced into the religion of Israel and given a prominent position in the central cult by the priests of Jerusalem. The contrast between this literature and the austere language of the classical prophets is striking. Two very different views of Israel's covenant and Yahweh's mode of action on behalf of his covenant people are embodied in these psalms and in the oracles of judgment and salvation in prophets like Hosea and Jeremiah. As the inclusion of Is 11:1–9 in our list of royal psalms with the ritual pattern serves to remind us, the prophetic literature is not completely lacking in a royal dimension. In large part, however, the typical attitude of the prophets is one of severe criticism of the royal cult and the excessive claims made by Israel's kings on the basis of the ideology of that cult. The absence of a profound mythic dimension in the prophetic tradition

---

(Cambridge: Harvard University, 1972), pp. 131–160 for the religio-historical background of this and a number of other royal psalms.

19. The following chart indicates how regularly the elements of the ritual pattern appear in the royal psalms. The structure of Isaiah 11, the Ugaritic Baal cycle (Ug) and the *Enūma eliš* (EE) is also indicated.

Psalms	2	9	24	29	46	47	48	65	68ª	68ᵇ	68ᶜ	76	77	89	97	98	104	106	110	Is, 11	Ug	EE
Threat	x				x		x														x	x
Combat	x	x	x	x	x	x	x	x_2	x	x	x	x	x		x	x	x	x	x_3	x	x	x
Victory	x	x	x	x	x	x	x	x_3	x	x_3	x	x	x	x_2	x	x	x	x	x_4	x	x	x
Salvation		x_5			x	x	x	x_1		x_2	x	x	x_4		x_4	x		x_4		x		x
Victory Shout	x_5	x_4	x	x		x_5	x		x	x_5	x					x_5	x_4					
Procession			x			x_4	x			x_4		x	x_3	x_3		x_6		x_3	x_2		x	
Manifestation of reign	x_4	x_3	x_1	x	x	x_6	x	x				x		x_1	x_3	x_4			x_1	x_1	x	x
Banquet																					x	x
Shalom				x				x									x_3			x_3	x	

may be due in part to a reaction against what the pre-exilic prophets considered an excessive use of elements hostile to Yahwism within the hymnody of the royal cult. The Deuteronomic History indicates the degree to which circles stemming from the pre-exilic prophetic tradition purged Yahwism of the cosmic ingredient of myth in the account of Yahweh's sovereignty over the history of the two kingdoms.

A picture emerges which requires explanation. In the centuries leading up to the exile the ritual pattern of the conflict myth enjoyed an important place in the hymnody of the royal cult, while at the same time the prophetic tradition seems to have avoided it entirely. Yet when we come to the prophetic literature of the exilic and post-exilic periods, we find numerous examples of that same ritual pattern incorporated into the oracles of the prophet Second Isaiah and his disciples of later decades. This reentry of the conflict myth into the prophetic tradition can perhaps best be explained on the basis of two observations. The polemic between prophetism and the royal cult, which contributed to the abrogation of the mythic ritual pattern by the prophets, came to an end with the demise of the royal cult in 587. Forms and motifs which had been identified with royal ideology were freed for use by other traditions. Added to this was the changed attitude toward the austere, mythless historicism of pre-exilic prophetism which culminated in the work of the Deuteronomic Historians. The events of the catastrophic last decade of the seventh century and the first two decades of the sixth century demanded explanations which the prophetic theologumenon of promise and fulfillment—by that time bound dogmatically to the cult center in Jerusalem—could not answer. Why did catastrophe follow on the heels of the event which should have inaugurated—according to the orthodox view—the era of fulfillment; that is, why did the *David redivivus* Josiah, the restorer of the cult to purity and the purger of defilement from the land, fall meaninglessly in battle, thereby setting the land on a sudden and violent path to destruction?

Even as the animating experiences of a vigorous emergent prophetism had led to the abandonment of the conflict myth in favor of a new, more adequate model, so the buffeting experiences of a weaker, declining prophetism led to its readoption. Once again tension had grown intolerably severe between forms of expression and beliefs (and doubts) born of experience. Could a theologumenon which taught that Yahweh's actions and intentions would be discerned directly and transparently within the events of history sustain faith in a period when contemporary historical events suggested Yahweh's indifference to Israel's fate, or even his impotence to save? This is one of the profound questions which underlies the prophecy of Second Isaiah. In reformulating a confession which had become so brittle as to threaten disintegration in the face of harsh historical experiences, he adopted mythic forms in order to explain the relation of Israel's God to the catastrophic events of the immediate past. It was thus this great prophet of the exile who for the first time placed the ritual pattern of the conflict myth at the center of the prophetic message. It was not necessary for him to hark back to foreign sources, however, for the liturgy of the then defunct royal cult of Jerusalem supplied numerous hymns based on the ritual combat of the divine king against the cosmic enemies threatening his sovereignty. To these he was able to fuse another, even more archaic, native tradition, stemming from the league and celebrating in ritual form the victories of the Divine Warrior Yahweh against the Egyptians and Canaanites.

These two traditions were possibly given new force by direct contact with late Babylonian ritual during the exile. Second Isaiah combined them into a powerful portrayal of a second exodus-conquest, universal and even cosmic in scope, by which the Israelites would be restored in their land. Is 51:9–11 is the finest example of this. Here Yahweh's saving activity is first described in the language of the conflict myth; the divine king [<Baal] slays the dragon of chaos [Rahab/Yamm] (v. 9). In this way a concept of God which had shriveled up to the point of transforming Yahweh into a patron of the royal house (now defunct) of Jerusalem is exploded by impregnation with the cosmic

metaphor of myth. But he does not stop at this recosmologizing of God-language, which would have destroyed the prophetic dialectic and returned Yahwism to the lap of a mythopoeic worldview. In the following verse the ritual conquest tradition of the league is recalled (cf. Ex 15), within which Yahweh's victory against the Pharaoh is celebrated in metaphors at once drawn from myth and at the same time filled with a persistent historical orientation. Finally in verse 11 the prophet moves one step further. The God who established order in the primordial battle and the God who saved Israel in the historical events of the past will save Israel in eschatological events of the future. In three verses he thereby recapitulates the entire development of prophetic Yahwism from the cosmic vision of myth, to the translation of that vision into the categories of history, to the future orientation of prophetic eschatalogy. This is made possible through the interpretation of the old combats, victories, processions, and banquets of the past as prototypes of the eschatological battle, victory, procession, and banquet of the future. Rather than go on to discuss other texts in which Second Isaiah incorporates the ritual pattern of the conflict myth, we merely list a number of them, with 51:9-11, in outline form:

Is 42:10-16
- 10-12 Victory shout
- 13-15 Combat—victory over enemy
- 16 Salvation of the "blind"
Procession

Is 43:16-21
- 16-17 Combat (vs. sea=Babylon)—victory
- 18-19a Victory shout
- 19b Procession (=Second Exodus-conquest)
- 20-21 Salvation of his people

Is 51:9-11
- 9-10a Combat (primordial>Exodus)
- 10b Salvation of his people
- 11 Procession to Zion (=Second Exodus-conquest)

Is 52:7-12
- 7-8 Herald announces Yahweh's return to Zion
- 9-10 Victory shout—manifestation of Yahweh's universal reign

11a Salvation: Release of captives
11b–12 Procession

Both in the ordering of the various elements and in the fusing of league and royal motifs a great degree of poetic license is manifested, a license made possible by the fact that Second Isaiah is utilizing material now freed from its original function in the life of the national cult. But the basic pattern of combat-victory-salvation-procession is still discernible in Second Isaiah.

To lift Yahwism from the fragile state to which it had fallen Second Isaiah adopted the old ritual pattern which we have traced through some two thousand years of history. His message was daring: Yahweh, the same God who was actively shaping the world in primordial times, was not now impotent to save; he was mighty and sovereign over all the nations, and even in Israel's defeats he was at work to prepare for more glorious acts of salvation. Those who saw historical events as evidence of Yahweh's weakness or unwillingness to save needed their visions raised to the heavens. Second Isaiah drew upon the elements of ancient myth to do just that.[20] Yet he achieved this without abrogating the historical perspective which the earlier prophets had struggled to develop and safeguard against repeated encroachments of Baalism, for in a delicate manner he was able to dovetail the motifs of myth and those of Israel's historical credo, reapplying both to the historical events of his time.

Though Second Isaiah was able to maintain the historical perspective of classical prophecy, we still find it appropriate to call his prophecy "proto-apocalyptic," inasmuch as it represents an important turning point in the development of the eschatology of prophecy into apocalyptic eschatology. His reintroduction of the ritual pattern of the conflict myth illustrates this with great clarity. For that pattern which he made subservient to an historical announcement

20. In reintroducing the cosmic element of myth into the Yahwistic tradition, Second Isaiah was not directing the faith of Israel in a direction alien to its spirit. Rather, he was enhancing a dimension of Yahwism with deep roots in Israel's earliest traditions, the future-orientation which can be found at the heart of the exodus, patriarchal and Davidic traditions alike, a fact demonstrated and well-documented by H. D. Preuss, *Jahweglaube und Zukunftserwartung* BWANT 87 (Stuttgart: W. Kohlhammer, 1968).

was one which, in the decaying community situation of the following decades, would offer a means of reinterpreting the prophetic message in terms indifferent to the events of plain history. One fine composition, stemming either from an early disciple of Second Isaiah or from the latest phase of Second Isaiah's own career, draws upon the same ritual pattern in a manner which betrays a loosening of the relation to plain history:

Is 34-35
- 34:1-4 Combat vs. nations and cosmic hosts—victory
- 5-7 Banquet with bloody sacrifice
- 8-17 *ḥerem* (=return to chaos)
- 35:1-7 Shalom—salvation of the weak
- 8-10 Procession to Zion

In a similar manner the Isaiah Apocalypse, probably written in the mid- or late-sixth century by a disciple of Second Isaiah, utilizes the same ritual pattern in an eschatological message which has advanced even further toward full-blown apocalyptic, thus best being designated as early apocalyptic:

24:1-13	Combat—*ḥerem* of whole earth
14-16a	Victory shout
(16b-18b	Lament)
18c-22	Combat—victory
23	Manifestation of Yahweh's universal reign
25:1-4b	Victory shout
6-8	Banquet

The mythic pattern is similar to that applied by Second Isaiah, but the ties to the actual political realm are weakened as the scene moves closer toward the cosmic realm of the Divine Warrior: the enemy is no longer a particular historical foe of Israel; rather, the entire world, including nature, is consigned to the *ḥerem.* Nor is a human instrument utilized by Yahweh, but Yahweh the Warrior battles directly against the nations and the cosmic hosts. Although the cleavage between the hierocratic leaders and the disenfranchised dissident elements is not yet pronounced, it may underlie the equation in 24:2 of priest with laity, slave with master, etc. If the city of chaos, the destruction of which is celebrated by the apocalypse, is the Jerusalem controlled and defiled (in the eyes of the visionists) by the hierocratic party, then the composition could stem from a point fairly late in the sixth century, perhaps from the period of the temple controversy ca. 520, but this hypothesis requires closer examination than can be given here, involving in particular a comparison of the Isaiah Apocalypse with compositions like Zechariah 12 and 14.

Little need be added concerning the utilization of the royal and league ritual traditions by the visionary group in Third Isaiah, for Chapter II has demonstrated how those traditions were adopted to reaffirm the eschatological message of Second Isaiah in a community situation where political conditions left little hope of restoration for the entire historical entity Israel. Thus the ritual pattern was fused to the prophetic *rîb* to indicate that the saving activity of the Divine Warrior had been redirected and limited so as to benefit only a minority group within Israel. The inevitable result was that the mythic background of these ritual traditions, combined with the disintegrating community situation, began eroding the tenacious mooring which prophetic eschatology had maintained with the events of plain history, thereby tugging the vision of the future in the direction of the cosmic realm of the Divine Warrior and his council.

Underlying both the Isaiah Apocalypse and Third Isaiah we recognize a visionary group of disciples of Second Isaiah for whom conditions involving the world empires as well as the situation within their own community seemed to belie the glorious announcement of Second Isaiah that events in the historical realm were about to inaugurate the restoration of the people of Yahweh. Given events which all seemed to increase the oppression of the faithful remnant at the hands of the ungodly, could the confession of the classical prophets that Yahweh acted within historical events to deliver his servants be upheld? The historical perspective which had established itself within the prophetic tradition, and which had effectively purged the ritual pattern of the conflict myth from the prophetic idiom, was now being seriously challenged. To visionaries smarting under the blows of historical events which seemed to verify the exclusive claims being made by their rivals and oppressors, the old gospel of the conflict myth grew increasingly attractive. That gospel was completely compatible with a pessimistic view of the existing order, for it spoke of a god who delivered the individual out of the flux of the fickle world into the eternal order of the gods. Although the visionary descendants of the prophets did not go so far as to abandon their confession in the sovereignty of Yahweh, and did not break their vision completely from an historical setting, they did set in motion a reversal of the earlier historical thrust of prophetism. The timeless element of myth assumes a new, vigorous role in their interpretation of history. To an increasing extent salvation is portrayed not in the terms of political events, but in the idiom of the cosmic victory of the Divine Warrior who delivers his faithful from, rather than through, historical events.

This history of Divine Warrior Hymns furnishes the background against which the hymns in Zechariah 9 and 10 finally become intelligible. Originating in the league and royal cults which in turn drew upon Canaanite mythic traditions, this hymnic form was later adopted into prophetic eschatology by Second Isaiah, finally being applied by the visionary followers of Second Isaiah to their polemic against the hierocratic leaders. Here, as in Third Isaiah, the visionary element within the post-exilic community is reaffirming its faith in the eschatological message of Second Isaiah through the adaptation of the league-royal cult ritual pattern. This thesis now requires elaboration, and we shall consider the Divine Warrior Hymns in Zechariah 9 and 10 in that order.

Zechariah 9 is a paradigm example of the prophetic adaptation of the league-royal cult ritual pattern. Its structure breaks down as follows:

Conflict—victory (1-7)
Temple secured (8)
Victory shout and procession (9)
Manifestation of Yahweh's universal reign (10)
Salvation: Captives released (11-13)

Theophany of Divine Warrior (14)
Sacrifice and banquet (15)
Fertility of restored order (16-17)

Comparison of this structure with the ritual conquest hymn in Exodus 15 and with the royal hymns analyzed above indicates how perfectly this hymn recapitulates the earlier rituals. Combined in one individual whole are elements from both the league tradition of ritual conquest and the royal hymn. Together, these elements are eschatologized to announce Yahweh's new act which is imminent.

The first section, describing the Divine Warrior's combat and victory, draws upon the league ritual-conquest tradition. It begins with Yahweh enthroned in his northern habitation, whence he, in keeping with the geography of the conflict myth, marches forth to battle the enemy and to reconquer the land which is rightfully his. This is the section which has misled the history of the interpretation of this chapter most sorely, for once the genre of the composition has been misconstrued, the attempt is made to discover the historical event underlying the description in verses 1-8. As indicated above, the results of such an approach confirm the inapplicability of the method, for an author like Otzen painfully works for sixty pages through the same eight verses and the same extra-biblical sources which Elliger struggled through, with the former arriving at the date 620, the latter 333. Once the genre is recognized as the Divine Warrior Hymn, the source of the problem is solved: no specific historical conquest by a specific historical conqueror is being described, nor is there anywhere in these verses so much as a hint that a foreign king is being used by Yahweh as his instrument. This is an essential difference between the early apocalyptic literature which we are interpreting here and the eschatological message of a prophet like Isaiah: no longer is the message translated directly into the terms of plain historical events and persons. Here Yahweh intervenes, and the question of how the restoration might be effected within the context of human contingencies is of fleeting concern.

If the path followed by the Divine Warrior is not the

path of an actual historical conquest, what is the significance of the area conquered? It is the area which the visionaries believed would be restored to the faithful on the day of Yahweh's conquest on behalf of his people. The borders of that area are not arbitrarily set, but outline what ancient Israelite tradition held to be the ideal kingdom of the Jews.[21] As evidence in favor of this thesis, we shall now point out how the place names circumscribe the ideal kingdom envisioned as the restored Israel, how the people mentioned are Israel's traditional enemies, attacked by the prophets for centuries, and how the judgment prophesied against each is stereotyped, not reflecting a specific historical event but being drawn from the repertory of stock prophetic formulae.

Hadrach, a district of Syria north of Hamath, is located at the northern limit of David's sphere of influence. Within a mythic context, it is appropriate that Yahweh begins his conquest at that northern point, for the home of Baal in ancient Canaanite myth was Zaphon (6.1.11; 4.4-5.19.85.117); from there the warrior god would advance to combat the foe (cf. Ps 48:3; Is 14:13; Jer 10:22). Damascus, capital of the Aramean state, Yahweh makes his throne dais, and since the king occupying that position controlled the people of Aram, and frequently extended his control over Israel as well, it follows that this conquest would bring the *'am 'ărām* under Yahweh's control, as well as "all the tribes of Israel." The sense of the parallel is this: just as obviouslv as all the tribes of Israel belong to Yahweh, so also will the people of Aram. That such a comparison between Israel and Aram is not inconceivable is illustrated by Isaiah 17:3b: "and the remnant of Syria will be like the glory of the children of Israel." Damascus, of course, was long considered an enemy by the prophets, and both Amos (1:3-5) and Isaiah (17:1-3) proclaimed oracles of judgment against her. Aram was attacked especially by Isaiah (7:1ff; 9:11; 17:3), and Amos (1:5) prophesied that Aram's people would be exiled.

21. See Nu 13:21-24; 34:1-12; Dtn 1:7, Josh 1:3-4; I Kgs 4:24; 5:1 [4:21]; 2 Kgs 14:25, 28. Cf. the author's "Zechariah 9," pp. 49-50.

Next mentioned is Hamath, condemned together with Damascus by Jeremiah (49:23ff). In Ezekiel's vision of the boundaries of the restored ideal kingdom (chapters 47–48), Damascus and Hamath play a prominent role. Again it is clear that these are traditional boundary marks and traditional enemies handed down by prophetic tradition.

The prophets commonly group together the cities of Phoenicia and Philistia in their judgment oracles, and here again this hymn follows the traditional pattern. Sidon is a common object of attack, as in Is 23:2–4; Jer 25:22; Ezek 28:20–23; and Joel 4:4–8. In keeping with the pattern of these oracles, here Sidon is closely connected to Tyre, judgment on the latter following in verses 3–4 in Zechariah 9.

A particularly great amount of time and energy has been devoted by the exegetes to verses 3 and 4 as they use the references to the building of a rampart, the accumulation of wealth, the loss of wealth, and the burning of the city as a basis for connecting the oracle to a particular period and a certain military campaign. But the results are bewildering, for the hymn again is utilizing for its eschatological purposes stereotyped phrases which the prophets of every age used in oracles of judgment, whether in describing Tyre, Ashkelon, Gaza, or some other city. Several illustrations of our point will suffice. First, far from being a peg to which an exact date could be attached, the reference to Tyre's might and riches was as timeless as reference in our day to Minnesota's lakes; it was found throughout the prophetic period (Am 1:9–10; Is 23:8; 13ff; Ezek 27:1–25; 28:5; Joel 4:4). Secondly, that Yahweh would strip her of her possessions was again a common theme (Is 23:18; Ezek 26:12, 19; 27:27; Joel 4:5). Thirdly, that her wealth would be hurled into the sea was a theme used especially by Ezekiel (26:19; 27:32, 34; 28:8). And finally, that she would be burned by fire was prophesied by Amos (1:19), Jeremiah (49:27), and Ezekiel (28:18), a fate pronounced by the prophets also against such cities as Damascus, Gaza, Teman, Rabbah, and Moab.

Similarly, the stereotyped nature of the prophecies against the Philistine cities could be demonstrated (e.g., Zeph 2:7), but the point is illustrated sufficiently that the hymn is using stock names and phrases throughout, and is not giving an historical account of a specific campaign. Even the list of place names circumscribing the ideal kingdom was apparently common property within the prophetic tradition, as is suggested by comparison of three other such lists from widely separated periods. Here the order is: Hadrach, Damascus, Hamath, Sidon, Tyre, Ashkelon, Gaza, Ekron, Ashdod, Philistia. In Am 1:3–9 the list includes Damascus, Gaza, Ashdod, Ashkelon, Ekron, Philistia, Tyre; in Zeph 2:4–5: Gaza, Ashkelon, Ashdod, Ekron, Philistia; in Jer 47:4f: Philistia, Tyre, Sidon, Gaza, Ashkelon. The hymn thus seems to have drawn not only upon stereotyped phrases describing the judgment, but even upon a list of Israel's traditional enemies.

The traditional pattern being followed in verses 1–7 is thus the pattern of ritual conquest, drawing upon the sacral literature of the league cult which described Yahweh's conquest of the land for Israel. To seek to discover a campaign by Tiglath-Pileser, Sargon, or Alexander is to misconstrue the relation of the hymn to history, for this hymn stems from a period when prophecy has begun its transformation into apocalyptic, and when divine activity no longer is translated directly into the events and figures of plain history. Even as the hymn itself proclaims, it is the Divine Warrior Yahweh himself who is on the march, moving from the north, taking Syria, Phoenicia, and Philistia, claiming them all for his possession. Therefore, the imagery throughout is that of holy war, with the enemy writhing in anguish, confounded and afraid, as Yahweh strips her of possessions, devours her by fire, and lays waste her cities (cf. this imagery with Ex 15:14–16).

Verse 7b has caused much difficulty to the commentators, the question again being asked: when in Israel's history did Philistia become a remnant for Israel's God, and when was Ekron grafted onto Judah? Different points in history then are suggested. But once more the answer is being sought in the wrong direction, for the oracle does not look to Israel's historical past but to the future Day of Yahweh, when Yahweh would possess the people of Aram (v. 1) and the remnant of Philistia and Ekron (v. 7). Israel's traditional enemies and rivals alike would be absorbed into a kingdom surpassing even that of David. The meta-historical dimension resounds throughout: Yahweh's throne will be in Damascus, the people of Aram, like the tribes of Israel will be Yahweh's, Philistia will be like a clan in Judah, Ekron will be like the Jebusite, that is, grafted into the nation of Yahweh. Here, as elsewhere in the poem (especially, v. 10b), the ancient Near Eastern ideal of universal kingship underlies the description: Yahweh is universal king; he even sits enthroned in Damascus!

After the description of the conquest in verses 1-7, the ritual-conquest pattern is continued in verse 8, for the march of Yahweh has a specific goal, the temple. It is the goal attained by the Divine Warrior after his combat throughout the history of that tradition, from the ancient mythic cycles of Marduk and Baal, to the account of the Divine Warrior of the league (Ex 15:17; Josh 4:19f), to the ritual of the monarchy (Psalm 24), and finally to the adaptation of the ritual pattern in late prophecy (Is 51:11; 35:8-10). It is thus totally unjustifiable to remove verse 8 as a later addition. After a successful conquest of the land, Yahweh will encamp at his temple and from that central point protect his people from the enemy, a theme developed further in verses 11-17 (cf. *Enūma eliš,* IV:10-12).

The conquest has been completed upon the victorious return of the Divine Warrior to his temple. In verse 9 that return is greeted with an exultant victory shout which likely derives from an old hymn of the royal cult. In keeping with the fluidity running throughout the royal literature of the Bible and other ancient Near Eastern sources, the anointed ruler here is celebrated alongside the divine king.[22] The background of our text in ancient kingship ideology is also seen in the close affinities with the Ugaritic Baal myth. Baal, after defeating Yamm, also directed his attention toward his temple. Once it was built, it became the center from which he provided the fructifying waters which blessed the earth. Once one's attention is freed from a preoccupation

22. Cf. Oppenheim, *ANET*², pp. 299-300 and 315-316 and H. Ringgren, "König und Messias," *ZAW* 64 (1952): 138-139.

with individual verses in isolation from one another, and sees the larger patterns, the fallacy of attempting to draw a separation on form-critical grounds between the battle and the ensuing restoration of shalom becomes evident. This is indicated as well by verse 10, where the newly established shalom is secured by destruction of the implements of war (cf. *Enūma eliš* IV: 111, Ps 46:10; 48:8; 76:4; Ezek 39:3, 9). Verse 10 closes with the manifestation of Yahweh's universal reign by incorporating the standard formulae of Babylonian and Assyrian royal literature. From sea to sea is from the Mediterranean to the Persian Gulf; from the river to the ends of the earth is from the Euphrates to the farthest known reaches of the Southwest (cf. Ps 72:8, *CTCA* 2.4.9-10[68], *Enūma eliš* VI:95ff).

The manifestation of the victor's royal power is followed, again in keeping with the ritual pattern, by the release of captives[23] and then by the theophany demonstrating the glory of the Divine Warrior. The theme of restoration seems to develop the message of Isaiah 60-62, as indicated especially by comparing verses 11-13 with Is 61:1-3. The captives are summoned to their stronghold, Zion, or in the imagery of the poem, to the house secured and protected by Yahweh in verse 8. In the final battle of the warrior god, divided Israel would be reunited in the hands of Yahweh, for he would use Judah as his bow and Ephraim as his arrow. Here one is reminded of the twin weapons fashioned for Baal by Kothar-Khasis,[24] although the restraints placed on the readopted myth are vividly apparent in this comparison; not weapons fashioned by a Canaanite Vulcan, but the historical kingdoms of Judah and Ephraim are in Yahweh's hands. At the center of the recapitulation of the ritual pattern the frayed mooring to the historical realm still prevents full flight into the mythopoeic.

As Baal, victorious over his foes, having established his universal reign and taken up residency in his temple (*CTCA* 4.7[51].9-14), proceeds to display his power in a mighty, earth-shaking theophany which scatters his enemies

23. Cf. Is 52:7-12; Ps 68:2-7 and Psalm 76.
24. Compare also. *Enūma eliš* IV: 35-36.

(27–39), so too we find the Divine Warrior of our hymn demonstrating his might. The theophany of Yahweh in verse 14 is described in language which is as archaic as it is plastic: arrows go forth like lightning as Yahweh blasts on his horn and marches on the southern stormwind. Here we are squarely within the conceptual world of myth, the cosmic realm of the god of the storm, of Marduk rushing forth to duel Tiamat with his arrows and his storm chariot, of Baal the cloud rider marching out to vanquish Yamm (cf. Psalms 29 and 68).

Finally the ritual pattern reaches its culminating point in the last three verses of the hymn. In celebration of the victory and in acknowledgment of the universal sovereignty of the Divine Warrior and King, a bloody sacrifice-banquet, is held. This is an essential element in the mythic pattern with which we are dealing, and betrays the original fertility function of the ancient cult. We are dealing with a *rite de passage,* where the victory alone does not restore the fertility of the earth; necessary in addition is a bloody sacrifice of the enemy's warriors, whereby the shedding of their blood has the effect of releasing the earth's fertility which had been suppressed during the enemy's reign: "How great their prosperity and beauty! Corn will make fat the young men, wine will make the maidens fruitful."

After analyzing the form and structure of Zechariah 9, we raise the question of its date and function. Having concluded that the attempt to date the hymn on the basis of supposed historical allusions is ill-fated, we seek now to apply the contextual-typological method developed in connection with the Third Isaiah material. The first task is to determine the tradition to which the hymn belongs, and there are several pieces of evidence which aid in this inquiry. First, the tradition is thoroughly eschatological in nature, proclaiming that Israel's fulfillment lay in a future event inaugurated by Yahweh. The picture of that restoration resembles the picture found in Second Isaiah and the program of restoration in Isaiah 60–62. Another feature that ties this hymn to the eschatological tradition stemming from Second Isaiah is the adaptation of the ritual pattern that fuses league and royal cultic material to announce the restoration which is to come. This adaptation of the ritual material was introduced into the prophetic tradition by Second Isaiah and was continued by his disciples in the post-exilic period, as indicated by the oracles in Isaiah 56-66. It therefore seems reasonable to see a close association between the hymn of Zechariah 9 and the visionary group which kept alive the eschatological hope of Second Isaiah in the period after the return.

Next, we turn to typological considerations in the effort to attach a relative date to the composition. The prosody indicates that the poem stems from a period before the breakdown of the classical canons of Hebrew poetry, suggesting a date relatively close to Second Isaiah and related compositions like Isaiah 34-35 and 60-62. This relative date is corroborated by the position assumed by the hymn in the prophetic eschatology-apocalyptic eschatology typology. It definitely represents an advance beyond Second Isaiah, for the connection to the events and persons of plain history is very loose. Yahweh himself is the conqueror, his enemies are practically all of Israel's traditional enemies, his kingdom extends from sea to sea, and it will incorporate features of a virtual paradise. Moreover, the sense of vocation on the part of the nation within the political order and to the nations of the world is completely abandoned in this hymn. The vision is narrowed to encompass Israelites alone, basking in a glorious restoration which frees them from responsibility to the political realm. On the other hand, all features of late apocalyptic are lacking, such as the sharp dualism and resulting division of history into aeons, and the cataclysmic disruption of the natural order heralding the eschaton in late apocalyptic. At most, the description of the final bloody struggle against the foe couched in the language of myth and the juxtapostion of passages like verses 4-9 and 10, and 14-15 and 16-17 adumbrate the dualism of later apocalyptic.

Finally, one further key to dating the literature of the visionary tradition, discussed in Chapter II, was based on the developing schism characteristic of the post-exilic period. Whereas Isaiah 60–62 reformulated Second Isaiah's restoration hope in brilliantly optimistic terms and in terms applying to the whole nation, the later oracles of Third Isaiah reflected an increasingly bleak situation where salvation was narrowed to a minority within Israel who were being oppressed by the nation's leaders. In this later period the Divine Warrior material was fused to the *rîb* oracle to condemn the majority of the nation and to promise salvation to the remnant of the faithful. No sign of this schism is visible in Zechariah 9, and the Divine Warrior motif is used to express the promise of salvation to the nation as a whole. This optimism and freedom from the polemic element which distinguished Isaiah 60–62 from the later oracles of Third Isaiah thus characterizes also the Divine Warrior Hymn in Zechariah 9, thereby corroborating the tentative dating of the hymn in the mid-sixth century, prior to the bitter conflict between visionary and hierocratic elements in the post-exilic community.

10:1 Ask Yahweh for rain
in the season of the early rain and the late;
Yahweh, who sends the lightning,
will give rain showers to them,
to each of the plants of the field.
2 For the teraphim utter wicked words,
the diviners have false visions,
they proclaim empty dreams,
they console with vain promises.
Therefore they withdraw like sheep,
they are afflicted for want of a shepherd.
3 My anger burns against the shepherds,
I will punish the he-goats.
For Yahweh cares for his flock,
he will make them his proud steed.
4 From them will come cornerstone and tent-peg,
from them the battle bow,
from them all the leaders.
5 Together they will be like heroes

D. THE DIVINE WARRIOR HYMN APPLIED TO THE INNER-COMMUNITY POLEMIC (10:1-12)

The only question which arises in the attempt to delimit the primary unit in Zechariah 10 concerns the relation of verses 1-2 to the rest of the composition. The theme of these verses is the fertility of the land, which thus stands in continuity with the last verse of chapter 9. But the thrust of this theme has shifted away from grateful acknowledgment to Yahweh for the fertility which issued forth from his successful battle against the forces of chaos, and has been transformed instead into an attack on unfaithful leaders of the people. Although these verses do not fit structurally into the normal scenario of the Divine Warrior Hymn (in contrast to verses 3-12 which do), they nevertheless can be understood best as an original part of Zechariah 10, which, as other characteristics of the composition will indicate, is no longer a pure example of the genre of the Divine Warrior Hymn, but is an adaptation of that genre to a new polemical setting. It thus seems advisable to treat Zechariah 10 as a unified composition.

	Text	Structure				Meter	Prosodic Units
10:1	שאלו מיהוה מטר	a	b	c		8	1:1
	בעתו [יורה] [a] ומלקוש	d	c_1	c_2		8	
	יהוה עשה חזיזים	a	b	c		7	1:1:b
	ומטר גשם יתן להם	c_1	b_1	d		8	
	לאיש עשב בשדה [b]	d_1	c_2	e		6	
2	כי תרפים דברו און	a	b	c		8	1:b::1:b
	קוסמים חזו שקר	a_1	b_1	c_1		6	
	חלמות שוא ידברו		C	b_2		8	
	[ו]הבל ינחמון		c_2	b_3		6	
	על כן נסעו כמו צאן	a	b	c		8	1:b
	יענו כי אין רעה		b_1	d	c_1	6	
3	על רעים חרה אפי	a	b	c		7	1:1
	על עתודים אפקוד	A		b		6	
	כי פקד יהוח[ ] [c] עדרו[ ] [d]	a	b	c		7	1:1
	ישמם כסום הודו[ ] [d]	a_1	c_1	d		7	
4	ממנו פנה ויתד	a	b	b_1		8	1:1:1
	ממנו קשת מלחמה	a	B			7	
	ממנו יצא כל נוגש	a	c	b_2		8	
5	יחדו יהיו כגברים	a	b	c		8	1:1

trampling the dirt of the streets.
They will fight, for Yahweh is with them,
they will confound those mounted on horses.
6 I will make mighty the house of Judah,
and the house of Joseph I will save.
I will restore them, for I love them,
they shall be as though I had not rejected them,
for I Yahweh will give them answer.
7 Ephraim will be like a warrior,
their hearts will be cheered as with wine;
their sons will see it and rejoice,
their hearts will exult in Yahweh.
8 I will whistle to them for I will redeem them,
they will be as numerous as formerly.
9 Though I scattered them among the nations,
in remote places they will remember me,
their children will survive and return.
10 I will restore them from the land of Egypt,
and from Assur I will gather them.
To the land of Gilead I will bring them
till there is no room for them.
11 They will pass through the sea of Egypt,
the waves of the sea will be smitten,
all the depths of the Nile will be dried up.
The pride of Assyria will be cast down,
and the scepter of Egypt will be removed.
12 I will make them mighty in Yahweh
and in his name they shall walk.

TEXTUAL NOTES

a) The formula with which this colon was constructed has become truncated through loss of one of the terms for rain. It is preserved in the LXX. Cf. Dtn 11:14; Jer 5:24; Joel 2:23; Hos 5:3.

b) The emendation of Duhm, which has found very wide acceptance, completely destroys the metric structure (ימטיר גשם ויתן לחם לאיש ועשב לבהמה). The MT reading seems preferable as it stands.

c) The familiar expansion of the divine epithet.

d) Gloss.

e) Gloss.

f) The MT conflates two variants, the hip'il of שוב (as in Tg, Pesh, and Vg) and the hip'il of ישב (as in some Heb. mss and LXX).

	בוסים בטיט חוצות[ ][e]			c_1	D	6	
	ילחמו כי יהוה עמם	a	b	c		9	1:1
	יבישו רככי סוסים	a_1		D		7	
6	אגבר בית יהודה	a	b	c		7	1:1
	ובית יוסף אושיע	b	c_1	a_1		6	
	וה[ ]ש[י]בותים[f] כי רחמתים	A	a			9	1:1:1
	יהיו כלא[g]זנחתים	b	A_1			7	
	כי אני יהוה[ ][h] אענם	C	a_1			7	
7	יהיו כגבור אפרים	a	b	c		7	1:1::1:1
	שמח לבם כמו יין	a_1	c_1	b_1		7	
	בניהם יראו ושמחו	c_2	a_2	a_3		9	
	יגל לבם ביהוה	a_4	c_1	d		7	
8	אשרקה להם[ ][i] כי פדיתים	a	b	a_1		9	1:1
	ורבו כמו רבו		c	d	c	7	
9	ואזרעם בעמים	a	b			7	1:1:1
	במרחקים יזכרוני		b_1	c		8	
	יחיו[ ]בניהם ושבו			c_1	d c_2	8	
10	והשיבותים מארץ מצרים	a	b			9	1:1
	ומאשור אקבצם	b_1	a_1			8	
	אל ארץ גלעד[ ][j]אביאם	a	b	c		7	1:1
	ולא ימצא להם			d	e f	7	
11	יעבר[ו][k] בים [מ]צר[ים][l]	a	b	c		7	1:1:1
	והכ[ו][m] בים גלים		d	b	e	7	
	יבישו מצולות יאר		d_1	e_1	b_1	8	
	יורד גאון אשור	a	b	c		6	1:1
	ושבט מצרים יסור	b_1	c_1	a_1		6	
12	וגברתים ביהוה	a	b			7	1:1
	ובשמו יתהלכו	b_1	a_1			7	

g) For the idiom יהיו כלא cf. Ob. v. 16.

h) Expansion of the divine epithet.

i) **אשרקה להם** and **אקבצם** appear to be ancient variants (each = five syllables) whereas the usual deletion of **כי פדיתים** seems ill advised. The former of the variants gives the more original appearance, delineating a rather unique picture. The resulting structure of the colon can be compared with v. 6b, and also vv. 2c and 5b.

j) לבנון is likely the intrusive element (cf. 11:1).

k) Reading plural with LXX.

l) Adopting Wellhausen's plausible conjecture.

m) Reading this verb as a hop'al results in a good parallel between this and the following colon.

Metrically, this poem bears distinct resemblances to Zechariah 9. Although there are numerous cases of conscious imitation of archaic prosody, the genuine feeling for archaic metric schemes (such as one finds in Second Isaiah) has been lost. Longer and shorter bicola do not fit together in meaningful patterns, and very prosaic verses disrupt the poetic effect of the poem (e.g., vv. 5,6,10b). The list in verse 4 is prosaic and repetitious. There are other unpoetic features which indicate clearly that the development away from archaic canons of poetry is more advanced than in Zechariah 9, for especially in those places where reapplication of themes of Zechariah 9 are found, this reapplication is made without a manifestation of sensitivity for poetic formulae and parallel pairs.[25] Typologically, therefore, this chapter falls somewhat later than Zechariah 9.

Also with regard to the history of genres, Zechariah 10 is later than Zechariah 9. Here the development from the one to the other is similar to the development which we traced in Chapter II from the oracles of Second Isaiah to those of his post-exilic disciples found in Isaiah 56-66. Earlier pure literary types have been transformed into new, complex, often hybrid types. Thus in Second Isaiah and in Zechariah 9 the Divine Warrior Hymn, in a pure form reminiscent of the original mythopoeic setting of the genre, serves to describe Yahweh's combat which would lead to the delivery of his whole nation. In Zechariah 10, as in Third Isaiah, the Divine Warrior Hymn is fused to a *rîb* against certain adversaries in Israel who, together with the foreign nations, will be objects of Yahweh's wrath in Yahweh's day of vindication. Those adversaries within Israel are in both cases the leaders of the nation, described in the present composition as the "shepherds" and "he-goats." The effect of this hybridization on the function of this genre is profound: no longer does the action of the Divine Warrior lead to the salvation of the entire nation; rather it leads to a division between the faithful "flock" which will be saved and the wicked "shepherds" and "he-goats" which will be punished. This use of the Divine Warrior Hymn as an adjunct to a *rîb*

25. E.g., cf. 10:3b-5 with 9:13-14.

oracle seems to be closely related to the parallel phenomenon in Third Isaiah (59:15b–20; 63:19b–64:2; 66:15–16). There we were able to connect this development of a new prophetic genre on the form-critical level with the community development of a growing rift between visionary and hierocratic groups. Whether a similar situation is reflected here must be considered later.

Aside from the prefixed *rîb* against the nation's leaders, the structure of this poem follows the ritual pattern of the conflict myth which we delineated earlier:

1–3	(*rîb* vs. leaders)
4–6a	Combat—victory
4	Yahweh equips himself with Israel as his host
5–6a	Ritual conquest
6b–10	Salvation: Restoration of the scattered people
11	Procession reenacting the victory of the Divine Warrior over Yamm (= Assyria-Egypt)
12	Victory shout

The *rîb* which begins the composition is against the "shepherds" and "he-goats." Within the visionary tradition, the attack on the *rō'îm* was already found in Is 56:11, and in the remainder of the Second Zechariah material the leaders so designated are attacked repeatedly. This raises the question of their identity. The contrast shepherd/flock was the classical designation in both ancient Mesopotamia and Egypt for the king and his people.[26] This usage is found also in the Old Testament (e.g., 1 Kgs 22:17; Is 44:28; Jer 6:3); nevertheless, especially in the plural, *rō'îm* can designate the civil officials as a whole (e.g., Jer 23:1f; Ezek 34:1ff). Ezek 37:24 indicates that the Davidic governor in the diarchy of the post-exilic period may have been called the "shepherd," thereby preserving the archaic royal title. In our investigation of Zech 11:4–17, we shall find evidence that this is so, and that the Davidic governor (*rō'eh*) and his officials (*rō'îm*) are those under attack by the visionary party. Such an understanding of the term suits the evidence of our present hymn as well. The contrast

26. Cf. John W. Waters, "The Political Development and Significance of the Shepherd-King Symbol in the Ancient Near East and the Old Testament" (Ph. D. dissertation, Boston University, 1970).

drawn is between the shepherds and the flock (the he-goats of course also designate the civil leaders).

The composition begins where the ritual pattern of Zechariah 9 ends, with the theme of the restoration of fertility by the waters spent upon the land by the storm god. But the thrust of this fertility theme has been abruptly altered, for it has been melded with an attack on an illegitimate cultic practice which substitutes supplication to Yahweh with fertility practices directed at teraphim and diviners. The blame for this degenerate cult rests upon the "shepherds" and "he-goats," the leaders charged with caring for Yahweh's flock; their neglect has led to the straying of Yahweh's people.

Here, as in numerous places in this poem, the writer seems to be developing the themes of his "text," Zechariah 9. That earlier hymn had promised salvation for Yahweh's people as a result of his victorious combat. That saving act would bring with it the fertility of the land. But this glorious picture does not describe the situation of the present writer. Not fertility, but drought; not Yahweh worship, but a defiled cult. The earlier hymn promised, "Yahweh will protect them, . . . Yahweh will save them like sheep" (9:15, 16), but instead ". . . they withdraw like sheep, they are afflicted for want of a shepherd" (10:2). The situation is clear. In the minds of the visionaries the promised restoration has been delayed and their hopes have been frustrated by the wantonness of their faithless leaders. The frustration of the visionaries finds expression in Yahweh's word of judgment: "My anger burns against the shepherds, I will punish the he-goats" (v. 3a).

Frustrated hopes thus have altered the form of the Divine Warrior Hymn, but they have not led to an abandonment of the promises. The main theme of Zechariah 9 is picked up anew: "For Yahweh cares for his flock . . . " (v. 3b). Then the writer moves to the scenario of the Divine Warrior Hymn proper. But no longer are the foreign nations alone the objects of Yahweh's wrath, for the unfaithful shepherds of the community are threatened with punishment. In the holy combat which is then announced in the hymn, new leaders will be placed over the people to replace the old unfaithful shepherds: these new leaders will be drawn from among the afflicted flock of faithful, as expressed in the terms of holy war: "he will make them his proud steed. From them will come cornerstone and tent-peg, from them the battle bow, from them all the leaders" (3b–4). These verses again appear to be a reapplication of the earlier text (cf. 9:13).

This combination of the *rîb* with the Divine Warrior Hymn involves the same revolutionary vision of a turning-of-the-tables which was found in Third Isaiah, combining a bitter attack on the present community leaders with a democratization of the nation's offices. Those who presently hold control over the flock will be eliminated, whereas the flock will be exalted as Yahweh's sacred host. The visionary, democratizing element is strikingly similar to that found in the program of restoration of the visionary tradition in Isaiah 60–62. No concern for the realistic details of running the day-to-day cult is evident; the vision is the cosmic one of the faithful being exalted to the position of being Yahweh's host in the final battle. This visionary, democratizing feature characterized the visionary tradition throughout its history, as is seen when one compares a hymn such as the present one with similar material in the pseudepigrapha and in the sectarian literature from Qumran.

The contrast between the *rîb* section in verse 3, which attacks the leaders of the community, and the combat section in verses 4–6a, which shows Yahweh forging his host out of the flock itself, vividly illustrates the dichotomy developing in the post-exilic period between the leading hierocratic party and the minority visionary group.[27] Though presently without power or control, the latter maintain that in the final conflict they will be elevated to Yahweh's side as his warriors. The institution which is here being invoked is the archaic league institution of holy war: "They will fight,

27. Similarities in theme as well as in form are so striking as to make close connections between the present composition and the Third Isaiah material hard to deny (for example, cf. Is 56:9–57:2).

for Yahweh is with them, they will confound those mounted on horses. . . ." The contribution of the league period to the ritual pattern of the conflict myth is evident in the form in which that pattern reached late prophetic circles.

The effect of the holy combat of the Divine Warrior Yahweh and his host is then described in verses 6b–10. Both Northern and Southern Kingdoms will be restored, and those scattered among the nations will return to the land. Verse 10 is another one of the references over which the critics have exhausted themselves, some insisting that it proves a seventh-century dating, others a sixth, still others a Hellenistic dating. But even as the place names in 9:1–8 did not reflect a specific historical conquest, but rather Israel's traditional neighborhood enemies, so too Egypt and Assyria here and in verse 11 refer not to enemies of one historical period but to Israel's traditional international enemies. Moreover, the second half of the verse indicates that the message with which we are dealing is eschatological through and through, for again with reference to Gilead we are given the northern boundary of the ideal kingdom which would be restored on the Day of Yahweh. Even that vast land will be filled till no room remains (cf. Is 60:22).

After the salvation effected by the Divine Warrior and his hosts is delineated (vv. 6–10), the ritual pattern is carried a step further with a description of the royal procession (vv. 11–12). This description is a beautiful example of the tendency in the early apocalyptic literature to combine royal processional imagery with the imagery of the league ritual-conquest tradition, and to hold in a dramatic dialectic elements from myth and allusions to historical events. For the procession following the combat is a reenactment of the central event of the exodus-conquest tradition, the event at the sea of Egypt; "They will pass through the sea of Egypt, the waves of the sea will be smitten, all the depths of the Nile will be dried up" (11a). While referring explicitly to the event recorded in Exodus 14–15, the echoes of the conflict between the storm god and the inimical sea are unmistakable. Thus *Urzeit, Zwischenzeit* and *Endzeit,* though still distinguished, are gravitating dangerously close to one another as the lines separating the primeval events, the historical events of Israel's past, and the future eschatological events begin to fade.

The evidence which the above analysis of the structure and form of Zechariah 10 offers with regard to the date and function of the hymn can be sketched very briefly, since the similarities between this hymn and the one in Zechariah 9 are obvious. First, we are led to identify it with the same visionary tradition, for the eschatological hope of restoration inaugurated by Yahweh's act is identical, and it is again expressed in the language of the ritual pattern derived from league conquest and royal processional traditions.

With regard to typological factors, the prosody belongs shortly after that of Zechariah 9, but perhaps still falls within the sixth century. The hymn belongs at approximately the same point in the typology of eschatological concepts as Zechariah 9, manifesting a looser relation to the political realm and the events of history than Second Isaiah and containing many unhistoricized cosmic elements, but not yet betraying the full-blown traits of late apocalyptic eschatology. Although these features indicate that this composition derives from a period close to that of Zechariah 9, one observation on the form-critical level demonstrates its posteriority, namely, the fusing of the *rîb* against the "shepherds" and "he-goats" with the Divine Warrior Hymn. Whereas Zechariah 9 maintains the Divine Warrior Hymn in the pure form announcing the deliverance of the nation, Zechariah 10 places it as an adjunct to a *rîb* against the leaders of the people, and thereby implies a division between those within Israel who will be punished by the Divine Warrior and those who will be delivered. We are led to connect this form-critical development with the sociological situation in Israel in the mid-sixth century within which hierocrats and visionaries found themselves locked in an increasingly bitter conflict.

This relation between form-critical and sociological developments was already found within Isaiah 56–66; moreover, in the chapters remaining to be considered below, we shall find ample evidence to make a strong case that in Third Isaiah and Second Zechariah the conflict between hierocratic leaders and a minority visionary group is being reflected. This conflict gives rise to new literary forms and abets the development of prophetic eschatology into apocalyptic eschatology. These considerations suggest that this hymn stems from the third quarter of the sixth century, i.e., slightly later than Zechariah 9 and Isaiah 60–62, but not so late as those oracles in Second Zechariah and Third Isaiah which manifest a complete breakdown of metric structure, include the unmistakable features of late apocalyptic eschatology, and fall at an advanced stage in the inner-community conflict.

E. A TAUNT AGAINST FOREIGN NATIONS REDIRECTED AGAINST ISRAEL'S LEADERS (11:1–3).

The language and style of this poem set it apart from the narrative which follows it in 11:4–17. Yet it originates in the same general community setting as the latter, and in the position in which it was placed by a redactor of Second Zechariah, it forms a suitable introduction to the commissioning narrative in 11:4ff. It is noteworthy that both compositions take older genres and give them an ironic twist in adapting them to their new polemical setting.

[*Text and translation below.*]

---

1 Open your gates, O Lebanon,
that fire may devour your cedars.
2 Wail, O cypress, for the cedars have fallen,
for the mighty trees are ruined;
wail, O oaks of Bashan,
for the thick forest is laid low.

3 Hark, the wail of the shepherds,
for their rich pasture is ruined;
hark, the roar of the lions,
for ruined are the majestic haunts of the Jordan.

By now we have become familiar with the manner in which the visionaries of the post-exilic period commonly adopted old genres from the prophetic tradition, but at the same time remolded them to function in their attack upon the hierocratic leaders of the community. In the present short unit, the prophetic genre of the taunt against the foreign nations [28] is adopted and given a double ironic twist to form a sharp barb directed against Israel's leaders. The first twist comes in the introductory bicolon which begins with a call to Lebanon to open its gates; the picture evoked in the minds of the hearers is that of the royal procession, where the gates are thrown open for the entry of the victorious king (cf. Ps 24:7-10). But the second half of the bicolon shifts the mood of festive celebration to one of woe; the one entering is not a savior-king, but consuming fire. When contrasted with the hymn in Zechariah 9, we find that an old royal hymnic motif has become radically transformed, a transformation which had begun in Zechariah 10. Consonant with the original thrust of the old ritual pattern of the conflict myth, Zechariah 9 pictures the entry of the Divine Warrior Yahweh into his royal city to inaugurate an era of peace and prosperity (vv. 9-10); and

28. Cf. H. W. Wolff, "Der Aufruf zur Volksklage," *ZAW* 76 (1964): 48-56.

	Text	Structure				Meter	Prosodic Units
11:1	פתח לבנון דלתיך	a	b	c		8	1:1
	ותאכל אש בארזיך	a_1	d	c_1		8	
2	הילל ברוש כי נפל ארז	a	b	c	b_1	8	1:1::1:1
	אשר אדרים שדדו		B	c_1		8	
	הילילו אלוני בשן	a	B_1			8	
	כי ירד יער הבצור		c_2	B_2		7	
3	קול יללת הרעים	a	b	c		7	1:1::1:1
	כי שדדה אדרתם		d	e		7	
	קול שאגת כפירים	a	b_1	c_1		7	
	כי שדד גאון הירדן		d	E		8	

also in the spirit of the ancient form, he is greeted with a joyous shout. The present procession is of a vastly different nature: fire enters through the gates to devour and destroy, and far from being greeted with a shout, the entering fire is met with wailing. Once again the visionary tradition has drawn upon the royal procession tradition, but this time in a bitterly ironic way.

The following lines develop the taunt itself. The phrases and images are taken from the common stock of prophetic formulae, as comparison with Jer 25:34–38; Is 2:3; 10:34; and Ezek 27:5–6 indicates. Together the images of the cedar,[29] the cypress,[30] and the oaks[31] form an image cluster connoting the quality of inordinate pride. To this cluster Lebanon fits most naturally, for its glorious cedars were coveted by kings throughout the ancient Mediterranean world.[32] Bashan represented for the prophets a most repulsive, idolatrous place.[33] In Canaanite tradition, it was the domain of 'Al'iyān-Ba'l, and thus may have been regarded by the prophets as a place particularly hostile to Yahweh. Placed in opposition to all these images of pride and defilement is fire, that fierce instrument of Yahweh the Warrior at home in the institution of holy war. Thus the meaning of the taunt is clear: although men of might may now be proud, a "royal procession" of fire was soon to enter which would bring destruction and woe. One could go on to assume that the taunt is directed against the kings of the foreign nations which threatened Israel. But verse 3 brings the second ironic twist. That which is being bewailed is not the destruction of some foreign capital, but rather the destruction of "the majestic haunts of the Jordan." The shepherds and lions are thus no other than Israel's own leaders, and the destruction of Yahweh which is to come will be directed at them.

Once again an overly literal interpretation can be mis-

29. Ezek 17:3, 22f; 31:3ff; Am 2:9; Ju 9:15.

30. 2 Kgs 19:23; Is 14:8; 37:24; 60:13.

31. Am 2:9; Is 2:13.

32. Cf. Is 2:13, where the parallel Lebanon//Bashan epitomizes all that is proud and lofty and therefore is the object of Yahweh's wrath.

33. Am 4:1; Is 2:13; Jer 22:20.

leading, for the idiom of the visionaries tends to be highly metaphorical and at times even cryptic, a feature which will continue on into full-blown apocalyptic. The standard arborous images connoting hubris commonly found in speeches against foreign powers have here been recast into a taunt leveled at the leaders of the post-exilic community. This short pericope thus is related intimately to similar attacks against Israel's shepherds elsewhere in the visionary literature of the post-exilic period (cf. Is 56:9-12 and Zech 10:3). Though probably originally independent of the next composition in 11:4-16, the redactor who placed it as an introduction to the latter arranged his material wisely, for while 11:4-16 is of a strikingly different nature, its underlying polemical function and setting is identical to that underlying the short taunt in 11:1-3. Naturally he was guided toward this arrangement by the catchword "shepherd(s)" in 11:3 and 4.

F. A COMMISSIONING NARRATIVE TRANSFORMED INTO A PROPHECY OF DOOM (11:4-17 and 13:7-9)

There seems to be little justification for questioning the unity of the narrative in 11:4–16. Attempts to remove parts as secondary (e.g., v. 6) stem from the desire to repristinate this composition so as to bring it into conformity with pre-exilic models. This attempt is futile here as in the case of many other post-exilic compositions, for as we shall see when we come to consider the genre in question, we are dealing with an ironic metamorphosis of an earlier genre which involves a conscious departure from earlier "pure" forms.

The short "woe" oracle in verse 17 appears to be an original part of the composition, for it forms a dramatic conclusion to the second commissioning of the prophet according to which he was to assume the role of the worthless shepherd. The harsh imprecation draws on earlier tradition, as seen by comparison with Jer 23:1-4 and Ezek 34:1-10. It is also closely related in theme and structure to other post-exilic material stemming from the visionary descendants of the prophets (e.g., Zech 10:2-3 and Is

56:9–11). Also closely related in theme to 11:4–16 is the poetic fragment in 13:7–9. The imagery and the underlying theme of this passage become intelligible only in relation to 11:4–17. Does it represent the original conclusion of the composition beginning in Zech 11:4? There is no basis upon which this question can be answered with certainty. 13:7–9 addresses a question which is left unresolved by 11:4–17, namely, what will be the fate of the remnant faithful to Yahweh after the calamity brought about by the worthless shepherd? This is a question which weighed heavily upon the visionaries, as the oracles of Isaiah 56–66 indicated. It is also the central concern in Zechariah 14. But in this case was this question addressed by the original composition, or by a later addition? Since we are less concerned with the question of individual authorship than with the experiences of a sociologically definable group, this question is not of great moment. If an addition, it would have arisen not long after the time of the original composition, and under similar circumstances.

All things considered, the meager evidence would perhaps favor the view that 13:7–9 is an early addition rather than an original part of the composition. For verse 7a seems to repeat the message of 11:17 rather than continue it, and 7b–8 seems to be a commentary on the phrase "flock doomed to be slain" (11:4 and 7). The addition could have developed as an elaboration on the catchword *ḥereb* ("sword"). It would have arisen from the sense that 11:4–17 had not finished the story by leaving unaddressed the specific question of the fate of the faithful. When the final redaction of the material in Zechariah 9–14 took place, this addition was relocated immediately before the oracle in chapter 14, since the latter also answers the question of the escape of the remnant, though in a somewhat different way.

> [11:4]Yahweh, my God, says this: Shepherd the flock for slaughter. [5]Those who buy them slaughter them and incur no guilt, and those who sell them say, "Blessed be Yahweh, I have become rich;" but their own shepherds have no pity on them.[a] [6]For I will no longer pity the inhabitants of the land (a saying of Yahweh), but I will put every man in the

hand of his neighbor [or shepherd][b] and his king, and as
they crush the earth I will deliver none from their power.
7So I shepherded the flock for slaughter for the sheep dealers.[c]
I took two staffs: one I named Grace, the other I named
Union, and I shepherded the flock. 8In one month I de-
stroyed the three shepherds. But I lost patience with them,
and they came to detest me. 9So I said, "I will not shepherd
you. Any that are to die, let them die; any that are to be
destroyed, let them be destroyed; and the rest can devour
each other." 10And I took my staff Grace and broke it, so as
to annul the covenant which [Yahweh] had made with all
the nations.[d] 11So it was annulled on that day, and the
sheep dealers[c] who were watching me knew that this was
the word of Yahweh. 12Then I said to them, "If it seems
right to you, give me my wages, but if not, keep them."
And they weighed out my wages, thirty pieces of silver.
13Then Yahweh said to me, "Cast it into the treasury"[e] (the
magnificent price at which I was paid off by them). Thus I
took the thirty pieces of silver and cast them into the
treasury[e] in the house of Yahweh. 14Then I broke my
second staff Union, so as to annul the brotherhood be-
tween Judah and Israel.
15Then Yahweh said to me, Take once again the equipment of
a shepherd, a worthless one. 16For I am about to raise up
in the land a shepherd who will neither attend to the
perishing, nor search for the lost,[f] nor heal the injured, nor
nourish the sound, but will devour the flesh of the fat and
even tear off their hoofs.

17Woe to the worthless shepherd who abandons the flock,
a sword against his arm and against his right eye!
Let his arm be shriveled,
and his right eye blinded.

13:7Awake, sword, against my shepherd,
against the man at my side.
(a saying of Yahweh of Hosts)
Strike[g] the shepherd, that the sheep may be scattered,
I will turn my hand against the little ones.

8In the whole land (a saying of Yahweh)
two-thirds shall be cut off and die,
[h]while one-third shall be left alive.

9Then I will send this third through the fire
and I will refine them as one refines silver,
and test them as one tests gold.
Then they will call on my name
and I will answer them.
I will say, "They are my people,"
and they will say, "Yahweh is our God."

TEXTUAL NOTES

a) In 11:5 the text seems to be caught midway between two different readings with regard to the gender of the pronominal suffixes and the number of the verbs. The versions have eliminated the difficulty, with the Targum making the suffixes masculine, the LXX, Vulgate, and Peshitta making them feminine. All have the verbs in the plural. These consistent readings probably stem from the attempt to smooth out difficulties. Therefore each problem in the MT must be considered individually: קניהן and יהרגן can be read either singular or plural. The next verb is plural, and the following participle must be plural, given its orthography (מכריהן), but the next verb is singular. With these data, it seems most natural to regard יהרגן as plural, and to emend יאמר to read plural. Whether the masculine suffix on רעיהם should be made feminine to agree with the other suffixes is harder to determine since, as it stands, it could refer to the buyers and sellers as an antecedent rather than to the sheep. Since in the early orthography of the passage *mêm* and *nûn* were very similar in appearance, the alteration is slight, and since the sense favors that change, we shall adopt it. רעיהן can be either singular or plural, and thus it is unnecessary to change יחמול to a plural. As verse 6 speaks of "king" in the singular, this verse speaks of one shepherd.

b) In verse 6 it is possible that רֵעֵהוּ should be read רֹעֵהוּ in light of the parallel term מלכו.

c) Several proposals have been made regarding the כן עניי in verses 7 and 11; the most likely solution follows LXX (εἰς τὴν Χαναανῖτιν) by reading לכנעניי, "dealers" (cf. 14:21).

d) In verse 10 the sense requires the following: את ברית אשר כרת יהוה

e) We adopt the emendation of יוצר to אוצר in verse 13, an emendation supported by Pesh.

f) In verse 16, הנער does not seem plausible; instead we would expect האבדת (cf. Ezek 34:4), הנעדרת, or the like.

g) In 13:7, read הַכֵּי.

h) In verse 8 יגועו may be a gloss, although the metric structure is so chaotic that no judgment can be made on the basis of meter or prosodic structure.

This cryptic narrative has been a virtual hotbed for wild interpretations as most exegetes have applied the historicizing method of identifying purported allusions to events in Israel's history, then dating the passage on that basis. The Maccabean period has supplied most of the persons and events used to interpret the narrative, but other periods have been used as well. Indeed, over forty sets of names have been proposed to explain the "historical" figures behind the three shepherds in verse 8 alone, ranging all the way from Moses, Aaron, and Miriam to the Tobiads driven out by Onias, namely, Simon, Menelaus, and Lysimachus. Once again we fear that this historicizing approach is based upon a failure to understand the genre to which the narrative belongs.

The question of the particular genre with which we are dealing is critical to the interpretation of the entire passage. The safest point of departure is from the formal features of the composition, that is, the formulae and the overall structure. The narrative begins with a formula of commissioning: "Shepherd the flock. . . ." This is followed by a report on the shepherd's discharging the duties of his commission. Then in verse 15 a second formula of commissioning occurs: "Take once again the equipment of a shepherd. . . ." We conclude, therefore, that the genre being applied is the commissioning narrative. However, as is so characteristic of the visionary literature of the early post-exilic period, the traditional genre is remolded in such a way as to give it an ironic thrust which was alien to the original genre in question. The nature and intent of this metamorphosis we shall consider below.

Regarding typological concerns, the composition in 11:4–17 (and 13:7–9) falls at the point where prophecy is moving away from the dominance of metric forms and toward an increased use of prose. The poetry which is preserved in this composition falls on the same point in our typology as the latest works in Third Isaiah, for the meter is chaotic and the internal structure is on the borderline between poetry and prose.[34] At points in the prose section this same type of borderline poetry can be discerned below the surface of the present text (e.g., in vv. 5, 6b, and 16). The narrative also reflects the late movement within the prophetic tradition toward more cryptic, allegorical forms

34. The prosody of 11:17 and 13:7–9 is so irregular that we have not attempted a reconstruction and analysis of the meter and prosodic structure.

of expression, which, along with anonymity and pseudonymity, probably arose in response to the opposition encountered by the visionaries from official circles.

It is not, however, the typological dimensions of our investigation, but the contextual ones which offer a key to the passage, if our basic supposition is correct. That supposition is that the narrative stems from the same general community situation as Zechariah 9 and 10 and Third Isaiah, involving the struggle between the visionary and hierocratic elements within post-exilic Israel. Especially germane to the present passage is the bitter polemic of the visionary group against the official leaders of the nation and its cult.

The narrative begins with Yahweh's word of commissioning to the one speaking in the first person, whom we would identify as a spokesman of the visionary descendants of the prophets. He is commissioned to shepherd Yahweh's flock; this shepherding is the actual responsibility of the nation's leaders.[35] This commissioning must be seen against the background of passages like Zech 10:2–3 and Is 56:9–11 where Yahweh's wrath is poured out upon the shepherds of the people because they have sought only their own desires and left the flock to its destruction. In a dramatic sign, filled with biting irony, Yahweh commissions this late descendant of the prophets to be shepherd of the flock. But the commissioning is a mockery, without serious intention, for the flock is described as a "flock for slaughter." The commissioning is thus pointless, except in one respect: it serves a purpose alien to the original function of the genre, but central to the message of the visionaries, that of announcing the doom of a community which is beyond the point where the prophetic servants of Yahweh can save them (cf. Is 6:9–13). Why this sorry state of affairs? Verse 5 supplies the answer: Ruthless men buy and sell the people like so many sheep for slaughter, and this they do with impunity, for "their own shepherds have no pity on them." The commissioning narrative thus has been transformed

35. The "shepherd" is an ancient Near Eastern metaphor for the king, and came in post-exilic times to designate the civil leaders of the people.

into a bitter attack on the nation's leaders. So bad is the situation that Yahweh has given his people up into the hands of their pitiless leaders (v. 6), and now he dramatically testifies to the impending doom by a mock commissioning of a new shepherd.

Then follows in verses 7-14 a report in which the shepherd renders account of his activities as shepherd. This report contains striking resemblances to the prophetic sign-act, though it departs from that genre in including elements which the shepherd would have been incapable of acting out, and in moving back and forth between sign and interpretation. Again an earlier genre is being used, but in its very use it is being transformed. This is seen clearly as soon as one recognizes that the writer is here engaged in a debate with earlier prophecies and prophetic acts from the prophet Ezekiel. In this debate he harshly modifies the future vision of that prophet, and thereby is criticizing the optimistic views of the hierocratic followers of Ezekiel.

The first prophecy of Ezekiel which is being alluded to is found in Ezek 37:15-28. Ezek 37:1-14 had envisioned Israel's restoration as a resuscitation of dry bones in response to Israel's prior complaint: "Our bones are dried up and our hope is lost" (v. 11). In 37:15-28 Ezekiel portrayed in the form of a sign-act the manner of the restoration. Yahweh commanded him to take two sticks, representing the Kingdoms of Judah and Israel, and to "join them together into one stick, that they may become one in your hand" (v. 17). In Zech 11:14 we read of the shepherd's sign-act, "Then I broke my second staff Union, so as to annul the brotherhood between Judah and Israel." Ezekiel's vision of the future here has been reversed!

Ezek 37:19-28 goes on to elaborate on the splendor of the restoration. Yahweh will gather them from the nations and make them one nation, not to be divided again. "They shall be my people, and I will be their God" (v. 23), which is the familiar covenant formula. They will have one king over them all: "My servant David shall be king over them; and they shall all have one shepherd" (v. 24). The land will be cleansed of sin, will live in perfect obedience, and will enjoy peace and prosperity as the result of Yahweh's dwelling in their midst. Zech 11:7–17 reverses every one of these promises in a manner which could only be the result of a conscious polemic against those building their leadership claims upon Ezekiel's vision. Instead of the broken staff being united, the united staff would be broken; instead of perfect peace and harmony, there would be total destruction; instead of an ingathering from the nations, the annulment of the covenant with the nations; instead of an ideal shepherd caring for his flock, a worthless shepherd who would lead his sheep to their destruction. Even as the promise of brilliant restoration in Ezekiel comes as the word of Yahweh, so too does the message of doom come as Yahweh's word to the visionary of Zechariah 11. In Zech 13:7–9 the unmitigated picture of doom is qualified, and whether from the original writer of Zech 11:4 ff or from a later hand, this passage again seems to continue the dialogue with Ezekiel. For in Ezek 37:23 the vision of the restoration of Yahweh's whole people is associated with the covenant formula: "they shall be my people, and I will be their God." In 13:7–9 that vision is altered rudely: not restoration of the whole people, but of a mere third which would be delivered from the impending destruction, and even they would be subjected to the refining fire. Only after that purging act is the covenant formula invoked: "I will say, 'They are my people,' and they will say, 'Yahweh is my God' " (v. 9).

The sharp contrast between the vision of the future in Ezekiel and in Zechariah 11 is seen also in relation to another passage from Ezekiel, 34:1–31. The two passages begin at the same point with a condemnation of the evil shepherds. And Ezek 34:20 adumbrates the division of the community into two parts which we find in the later oracles of Zechariah 9–14. But these similar points of departure only cast in bold relief the sharp contrast in the future vision. In Ezekiel Yahweh himself will save the sheep from the shepherds and gather them from the nations (34:9–16); in Zechariah Yahweh will deliver them into the hands of the shepherds and let them be scattered (11:6;

13:7). In Ezek 34:23 Yahweh promises to raise up (*qûm* in the hip 'il) a shepherd over them who will feed them; in Zech 11:16 Yahweh promises to raise up (again *qûm* in the hip 'il) over them a shepherd whose attributes are diametrically opposed to those of the good shepherd—indeed, they resemble the attributes of the *evil* shepherds condemned at the beginning of Ezekiel's oracle (34:2-4)! In Ezek 34:25 Yahweh promises to establish a covenant of peace with them; in Zechariah 11:10 and 14 his representative breaks the covenants of Grace and Union. In Ezek 34:26-31 spectacular blessings, peace and prosperity are promised; in Zech 11:16 and 13:8 incredible doom and desolation.

Why this polemical dialogue with the Ezekielian vision of the future? The answer is intimately related to the controversy between the hierocratic followers of Ezekiel and the visionary descendants of Second Isaiah which we have traced earlier. The prophet Ezekiel, while decrying the sinful conditions which had brought on calamity and national disgrace, nevertheless developed a vision of restoration which would occur upon the return of the *gôlāh* to the land, and which would stand in continuity with the priestly structures of the pre-exilic period. This vision was the one held by the Zadokite priests who led the exiles back to their land. As the prophecies of Haggai and Zechariah indicated, Ezekiel's vision of one nation restored under one Davidide living in the peace and prosperity of the covenant and with Yahweh in its midst was, according to the hierocrats, at the point of fulfillment. Indeed the Zadokite-led hierocracy and its priestly leaders represented the fulfillment of Ezekiel's vision. It is against this Ezekielian vision of the hierocrats that the visionary spokesman of Zechariah 11 is reacting. The eschatological timetable which he follows does not anticipate direct passage from the present situation into the glories of the eschaton.

Anticipated instead is a very grim period indeed, for ruling over Israel was not the ideal Davidic shepherd of Ezekiel's vision (34:23f; 37:24), but evil shepherds of the sort attacked by Ezekiel. A harsh contradiction thus separates the hierocratic leaders of the temple cult from the visionaries. In the eschatological timetable the controlling group sees the hourglass just a few grains short of the glorious fulfillment, while the oppressed visionaries argue that they stand at a point just moments before the horrors of Yahweh's judgment. Thus the hierocratic group embraces a picture of the prophet (as seen in the oracles of Haggai and Zechariah) as a harbinger of the glories of the eschaton, whereas the visionary group develops an ideal of the descendant of the prophets as an agent of Yahweh's wrath, an instrument hastening the destruction of a people doomed to slaughter.

Against the background of these contradictory views of the future the composition in 11:4–17 (and 13:7–9) must be interpreted. We have already noted how in a mock commissioning Yahweh has made his servant a shepherd over a flock already doomed to slaughter. The report of that shepherd's activities follows in verses 7–14. Verse 7 again reminds the reader that this is a flock destined to be slain, and it amplifies this by describing the ones for whom they are to be slain, "for the sheep dealers." The equipment of the shepherd includes two staffs, one named Grace, and symbolizing Yahweh's covenant with all the peoples, the other named Union, symbolizing the brotherhood between the two kingdoms. The significance of these staffs becomes clear when one recalls the twin missions of Ezekiel's future Davidic king, a mission of gathering in those scattered among the nations—an ingathering made possible by Yahweh's covenant of peace with the nations—and a mission of reuniting the Northern and Southern Kingdoms in a union of brotherhood and peace. But the shepherd's career is as brief as it is violent: he administers Yahweh's vengeful blow upon "the three shepherds," referring back to the pitiless shepherds of verse 5. But the flock responds only with loathing. Therefore, the shepherd renounces his office, and leaves the flock to its own destruction. This means that the last divinely commissioned shepherd has been rejected by the people.

The results of this abdication of the shepherd's office follow quickly. The staff representing the covenant with all the peoples is broken. Then a startling fact surfaces when the shepherd goes to collect his severance pay: he has been under the hire of the sheep dealers, i.e., of the *enemies* of the people! As an instrument of Yahweh's wrath the shepherd of Yahweh is actually allied with the enemy, is actually dedicated to hastening the day of judgment and wrath. Even more startling is the command of Yahweh in verse 13 in regard to the thirty pieces of silver which are his wages: "'Cast it into the treasury' . . . .Thus I took the thirty pieces of silver and cast them into the treasury in the house of Yahweh." The message is shocking but seems unmistakable: by this act the shepherd identifies the ultimate source of the corruption and the exploitation which are destroying the community: the temple and its leaders are to blame! If our interpretation is correct, this constitutes an incredibly harsh indictment of the hierocratic leaders. Because of this appalling state of affairs, all hope of union between the Northern and Southern Kingdoms is broken. The shepherd therefore breaks his second staff.

In verses 15 and 16 the shepherd is commissioned again. The veiled language of the first commissioning is laid aside, and the real situation is described openly. This time he is to take not the equipment of the good shepherd, Grace and Union, but the equipment of a worthless shepherd. The glorious hopes of Ezekiel which the hierocratic party claimed to embody are contradicted: "For I am about to raise up in the land a shepherd who will neither attend to the perishing. . . ." All of those healing, saving acts which the good shepherd was to perform are ridiculed by this shepherd, who instead "will devour the flesh of the fat, and even tear off their hoofs" (verse 16). And this too is an act of Yahweh! We are faced with a shocking pessimism which sees divine guidance in that which is bent on destruction, for the corruption is so complete that judgment is inevitable. Hence that which hastens the judgment is from Yahweh.

Little need be added concerning the imprecation in verse 17. Like the instrument of Yahweh's wrath, the king of Assyria, who was the chosen agent of Yahweh's wrath but who would not escape judgment himself (Is 10:5-19), so too the worthless shepherd would be smitten. The poetic section in 13:7-9, which is perhaps a later addition (see above), goes on to account for the faithful. The pattern is that underlying the salvation-judgment oracles which we have found earlier in Third Isaiah and Second Zechariah. Two-thirds would be cut off, one-third delivered and refined by fire. Only after these terrible acts would the covenant again be renewed, a startlingly different picture from that found in the exuberant prophecies of Haggai and Zechariah.

What are the community setting and function of the composition which we have now studied? This question is perhaps best approached by inquiry into the identity of the worthless shepherd commissioned by Yahweh in verses 15-16. The narrative to that point deals with the rejection of the last true shepherd of Yahweh (with whom the visionary group would have identified itself), and the abdication of his duties as shepherd over a people bent on its own destruction and fallen under pitiless and corrupt leaders.[36] Thus the rejection of the visionaries and their expulsion from positions of power in the community have been accounted for. But the commissioning in verses 15-16 involves the community leadership following the fall of the last true shepherd. Who is the worthless shepherd whom Yahweh is appointing over his flock? The term *shepherd* would most naturally apply to the post-exilic successor of the Davidic king, since the royal connotation of the metaphor *shepherd* is the primary one, and since the passage seems to be a direct polemic against Ezekiel's vision, where the shepherd whom Yahweh would establish was the *David redivivus.* But is it possible to speak of Davidides during the post-exilic period?

Unfortunately our knowledge of the fate of the Davidic house in the late sixth and fifth centuries is very in-

36. Verse 8 reflects the experience of rejection of the visionaries. They grew impatient with a disobedient people (a fact illustrated vividly by the oracles of judgment in both Isaiah 56-66 and Zechariah 9-14) and that people came to loathe them (obviously because of their unrelenting words of judgment). A similar reflection on the rejection of the visionary group is found in Zech 12:10-14.

complete. It has long been the assumption that, after the disappearance of Zerubbabel, the high priest inherited the royal prerogatives formerly held by the Davidide. But there are pieces of evidence which are not adequately explained by this assumption. One of these is the Davidic genealogy in the Chronicler (1 Chr 3:17-24) which extends through the fifth century. Would the Chronicler have included this genealogy through the seven generations after Jeconiah if the Davidic house no longer played a significant role in the Jewish community after Zerubbabel?[37] Nor can the great enthusiasm of the Chronicler for the Davidic house throughout his work be explained alone as a desire to legitimate post-exilic cultic practices by tracing them back to Davidic origins.[38] Moreover, whenever the hierocratic program finds clear formulation (namely, in Ezekiel 40–48, Haggai, and Zechariah), it always includes the Davidic figure prominently beside the high priest. That suddenly at the end of the sixth century this diarchic structure of the hierocratic program should be abolished is supported only by an assumption which has gained almost unquestioned universal acceptance, an assumption unfortunately based on not one scrap of evidence. Still another intriguing set of data unexplained by this assumption will be encountered later in this chapter in connection with Zechariah 12. There a spirited polemic is evidenced between "the house of David" and "the tents of Judah." The polemic in that chapter is much too vivid to be mere shadowboxing. Evidently, the house of David was still very much a reality in the Jewish community of that time, a fact most naturally accounted for if we assume that the governors during at least part of the fifth century were still of the house of David.

Because of evidence of this nature, the time is ripe for a whole new examination of the Davidic house in the period

37. Cf. W. F. Albright, "The Date and Personality of the Chronicler," *JBL* 40 (1921): 108 ff.

38. Although D. N. Freedman's thesis that the Chronicler wrote his work in defense of the royal aspirations of Zerubbabel is open to question, the force of his argument that the Chronicler has a very strong pro-Davidic bias cannot be denied. This bias can hardly be accounted for if the Davidic house had ceased to play a role in the fifth-century Jewish community ("The Chronicler's Purpose," *CBQ* 23 [1961]: 436-442).

of the Second Temple, but until such is completed, this writer feels that there is sufficient grounds tentatively to assume that the Judean governor, at least during part of the fifth century, was of the house of David. If this assumption is correct, the worthless shepherd in verses 15–16 is best interpreted as the Davidic governor.[39]

Verse 17 levels a scathing imprecation at the worthless shepherd, an imprecation which is continued in 13:7 where the sword is summoned against the shepherd. The parallel to shepherd is *geber ʿămîtî*, which is used only here in reference to an official. The intimacy between Yahweh and the official which is implied by that term seems to suggest a royal figure, though conceivably the high priest could be so designated.

The bitter polemic of this composition thus is directed against the Davidic governor and the hierocratic temple party with which he is associated. Together they are destroying Yahweh's people through their corruption, self-interest, and blatant disobedience. To this situation of cultic and community degeneration the visionary group no longer responds by attacking specific abuses in the hope of reforming the cult and regaining positions of leadership. They have felt directed by Yahweh toward a new course of action, that of accepting the inevitability of the impending doom, hastening its advent, and looking for deliverance as a refining act of Yahweh on behalf of the faithful remnant and on the other side of the judgment. The experiences of the first shepherd in the commissioning narrative reflect the experiences of the visionary group. The slaying of the three shepherds seems to reflect the first stage of their opposition to the hierocratic majority, involving an active

39. If the governors of the part of the fifth century which concerns this study were in fact Davidic, the total absence of a Davidic messianism in the eschatology of the visionary tradition of this period becomes understandable. The future hope crystallizes instead around a vastly different type of figure, one who suffers oppression, even martyrdom (e.g., Is 52:13–53:12; Zech 12:10–14). This figure is comprehensible sociologically only within a matrix of persecution. It was only at a later period, when the Davidic line had ceased and the oppression of the visionaries under a Davidic governor had come to an end, that the idea of a Davidide could again be idealized by the visionary tradition into the conception of a Davidic Messiah.

attempt to defeat the defiled leaders of the community so as to deliver the people.

But the response of the people bespeaks the disillusionment born of this stage: they respond with loathing, and the shepherd (i.e., the visionaries) responds with impatience. This disillusionment is also reflected in the designation of the flock; what more could be expected of a "flock for slaughter"? The result is the abdication by the shepherd of his leadership responsibilities, an abdication which implies judgment upon the nation, symbolized by the breaking of the two staffs. In this violent act auguring woeful things to come, the shepherd actually reveals himself allied to the enemies of the people; his wages come from the sheep dealers. But it would be ill-fitting a servant of Yahweh to retain such blood money, so in another powerful sign the shepherd is commanded to cast the money into the temple treasury, thereby identifying the ultimate source of the corruption afflicting the land.

If this interpretation of Zech 11:4-17 is correct, the background of the betrayal story of Judas comes into a new light (cf. Mt 26:15 and 27:3-10). The source of the thirty pieces of silver which bought the betrayal (of God's people in Zechariah, of Jesus in Matthew) is the temple treasury (does the "potter's field" shed light on the problem raised in Zech 11:13 by *yoṣēr* ["potter"]?). The indictment on a cult which had become defiled is clear. But the commissioning narrative in Zechariah 11 indicates that the role of Judas must have been interpreted as a part of God's redemptive purposes (cf. Jn 13:27). The end-time terrors would have to befall God's son before the final glorious events could be inaugurated (even as the apocalyptic circles of Second Zechariah and elsewhere believed that the apocalyptic woes would have to befall the people before the glorious eschaton could arrive). Thus, according to Zechariah 11, a worthless shepherd is commissioned over God's people who will hasten that time of terror by neglecting and even destroying the flock. Thus, according to Matthew 27, a betrayer is commissioned as a disciple so as to hasten the end-time terrors experienced by Jesus on the cross. Both manifest the left hand of God punishing so as to save. This comparison between Zechariah 11 and the Judas narrative reminds us anew that the eschatology of the New Testament Gospels is comprehensible only against the background of Jewish apocalyptic eschatology.

After this, only one sign remains for the shepherd to act out, that portraying for the people the kind of shepherd Yahweh is raising over them since they had rejected the true shepherd of the flock (the visionaries). He would be a worthless shepherd (the Davidic governor and his party) who would exploit and ultimately destroy the flock.

Thus interpreted, this passage reflects a critical juncture in the history of the post-exilic prophetic tradition. At this point attempts were abandoned to reform the nation through judgment oracles and words of admonition, and pessimism with the existing order of things grew so heavy that visionaries longed vindictively for total destruction of the existing community leaders and institutions. Destruction alone could prepare for the fulfillment of their salvation hopes. The bitterness permeating the composition indicates that the struggle is at a stage far advanced beyond the optimism manifested by the original program of the visionary tradition in Isaiah 60–62, or by the Divine Warrior Hymn in Zechariah 9. Though Zechariah 10 reflects a somewhat later period in that the Divine Warrior Hymn had been fused to a *rîb* against the leaders of the community, it still retains a basic optimism concerning the restoration of Israel (vv. 6–12). Whereas Zechariah 10 speaks of a gathering of the people from the nations, and of Yahweh's making them as many as of old, our present passage awaits a day of slaughter, which is interpreted in 13:7–9 as a scattering of the flock and the perishing of two-thirds of the nation. Thus the community struggle which we have traced in the oracles of Third Isaiah[40] and have recognized behind Zechariah 10[41] is at a very advanced stage in this

40. See, for example, the attack on the leaders in 56:9–12 and the lament over the righteous victim of their neglect in 57:1–12.
41. E.g., 10:1–3.

composition. For the entire composition exudes a very grim view of the restoration hope, suggesting a relatively late period. How late remains the question.

The degree of pessimism permeating the composition is further demonstrated by comparing it with the passage in Ezekiel which served as an inverted model, namely, Ezek 37:15–28. In contrast to the hope of uniting Judah and Israel into one kingdom (Ezek 37:19), this passage speaks of the breaking of the covenant which unites them; in contrast to the gathering of the peoples (Ezek 37:21), their scattering (Zech 13:7a); in contrast to a faithful Davidic shepherd over them all (Ezek 37:24), a worthless shepherd who has no pity for the perishing (Zech 11:15f); rather than God with them (Ezek 37:27), God deserting them (Zech 11:9); rather than blessing and salvation for all (Ezek 37:25ff), destruction for most, while only a third will be delivered (Zech 13:9). The conclusion of the Zechariah passage invokes the same covenant formula which concludes the Ezekiel passage, but how its significance has been altered! Only after two-thirds have perished and the remaining third has endured the apocalyptic trials can the covenant be renewed: "I will say, 'They are my people,' and they will say, 'The Lord is my God.'"

It is apparent that the passage stems from a period when the rift between the contending parties had become far advanced, that is, the very end of the sixth century or the early fifth. This date is suggested also by other considerations: (1) the poetic parts come at a very late point in the prosody typology; (2) the picture of the end-time, with the scattering of the people, the destruction of the majority, and the final eschatological trials falls at a point on the typology of eschatology more advanced than any previously studied composition; (3) all attempt has been abandoned to relate the events of the end-time to the historical context; (4) the restoration hope of the visionary group has become very grim, even vindictive, the utter pessimism of their worldview being seen in their designation of the nation as "the flock for slaughter." All things considered, it would seem that this passage stems from a period after the building of the temple, that is, after 515, when the defeat of the visionary group was sealed.

More important than such attempts at actual dates, however, is recognition of the way in which Zechariah 11:4–17 exposes a factor of critical significance in the development of apocalyptic eschatology out of earlier prophetic roots. The abdication of the political task of the classical prophets of integrating their vision of Yahweh's will into the events and structures of their historical community occurred as a result of the oppression and their ensuing disillusionment. The staffs of the twin covenants, those effecting the two spheres of political concern, domestic and international, with which the classical prophets concerned themselves were thereby broken. Israel was thus left without the covenantal foundation upon which her life as a people of God had been based, and left without the guardians of that covenantal foundation, the prophets.[42] We have seen the results of the abdication of the political aspects of the prophetic office in this composition as well: the vision of the future has loosened its ties with political realities, as the future salvation is awaited only on the other side of a disruption of existing realities and frightful destruction. The effect of this abdication will be seen vividly in the last three chapters of Zechariah to which we now turn, two of which give us vivid examples of the apocalyptic eschatology which was born of the bitter experiences of the visionaries (chapters 12 and 14), and one of which expresses their cynical attitude toward those who in this period of gloom would call themselves prophets (chapter 13).

G. AN APOCALYPSE MOLDED BY THE INNER-COMMUNITY STRUGGLE (12:1–13:6)

Zechariah 12:1 begins a new booklet. The two compositions in this collection, 12:1–13:6 and 14:1–21 (13:7–9 has been treated above as a part of 11:4–17) are clearly distinguishable from the two Divine Warrior Hymns in the

42. Contrast this with the earlier visionary formulation in Is 62:1–12 with its promise of a nation secure in Yahweh's covenant and guarded by faithful watchmen, the prophets.

previous booklet, Zechariah 9–11, in that they fall at a more advanced point on the typology of Jewish eschatology and are written from a perspective which has narrowed from the very broad international scope of the earlier Divine Warrior Hymns to a myopic concern with Judah and Jerusalem. The transition to this later stage was already begun, however, in the last composition in Zechariah 9–11, where the genre of the prophetic commissioning was used to express disillusionment over the prophetic vocation of being a shepherd of the entire people, and where the visionaries expressed a sense of Yahweh's will that they abdicate the political aspects of the prophetic office so as to hasten the impending doom. The oracles of Zechariah 12–14 are concerned with this impending doom—described with the archaic phrase from the institution of holy war, "the Day of Yahweh" or simply "that day."

Zech 12:1–13:6 is the first composition to which we turn. 12:1–9 portrays the end-time battle which would occur at Jerusalem, and describes the roles to be played by the clans of Judah and the house of David (Jerusalem) in that conflict. 12:10–14 describes a massive mourning rite of the latter over one "whom they have pierced." 13:1 and 2–6 (the latter may not be an original part of this composition) tell how the land would be purified. Taken together these sections construct a scenario which gives every appearance of originality. The additions (indicated by square brackets below) are quite minor, with the exception of 13:2–6 if that section is secondary.

> [12:1]The oracle of Yahweh's word concerning Israel (a saying of Yahweh, who stretched out the heavens and founded the earth and formed the spirit of man within him). [2]I am about to make Jerusalem a cup of reeling for all the surrounding nations. The seige against Jerusalem will also be against Judah.[a] [3]On that day I will make Jerusalem a heavy stone for all the peoples. All who attempt to lift it shall injure themselves. And then all the nations of the earth will gather together against her. [4]On that day (a saying of Yahweh) I will strike every horse with panic, and its rider with madness. But I will keep watch over the house of Judah [as I strike all the horses of the nations with blindness][b] [5]Then the clans[c] of Judah shall say to themselves, "If only the in-

habitants of Jerusalem would raise a shout for Yahweh of
Hosts, their God."[d]

6On that day I will make the clans of Judah like a fire-pot
among the trees and like a blazing torch among the sheaves.
And they shall devour all the surrounding peoples on the
right and on the left. Thus Jerusalem shall again be in-
habited in its place, that is, in Jerusalem.

7First Yahweh will give victory to the tents of Judah, so
that the glory of the house of David and the glory of the
inhabitants of Jerusalem may not be exalted over that of
Judah. [8On that day Yahweh will shield the inhabitants of
Jerusalem, so that the feeblest among them, on that day,
shall be like David, and the house of David shall be like God,
like the angel of Yahweh before them. 9On that day I will set
out to destroy all the nations coming against Jerusalem.]
10Then I will pour out a spirit of pity and compassion upon
the house of David and upon the inhabitants of Jerusalem,
so that they may look upon the one[e] whom they have
pierced and mourn over him as one mourns for an only
child, and grieve over him as one grieves for a first-born son.
11On that day the mourning in Jerusalem shall be as great as
the mourning over Hadad-rimmon in the plain of Megiddo.
12The land shall mourn, each family by itself; the family of
the house of David by itself, and their women by themselves;
the family of the house of Nathan by itself, and their women
by themselves: 13the family of the house of Levi by itself, and
their women by themselves; the family of the Shimeites by
itself, and their women by themselves.

13:1 On that day a fountain shall be opened for the house
of David and for the inhabitants of Jerusalem to remove sin
and impurity.

2On that day (a saying of Yahweh of Hosts) I will cut off
the names of the idols from the land, so that they shall no
longer be remembered. I will also remove the prophets and
the unclean spirit from the land. 3And if anyone again
prophesies, his father and his mother who bore him will say
to him, "You shall not live, for you have spoken lies in the
name of Yahweh." And his father and mother who bore him
shall pierce him when he prophesies. 4On that day every
prophet will be ashamed of his vision when he prophesies,
and he will not dress in a hairy robe in order to deceive. 5He
will say, "I am no prophet, I am a tiller of the soil, for the
land has been my possession[f] since my youth. 6When some-
one asks, "What are these wounds on your chest?" he will
answer, "I was struck in the house of my lovers."

TEXTUAL NOTES

a) In verse 2b the MT has a conflate reading combining features of one tradition preserved in Tg and Vg, and of another represented by Pesh and LXX. The former has no equivalent of על before יהודה, the latter has no preposition before מצור. Thus the former has Judah included in the siege against Jerusalem, whereas the latter has the siege against Judah as well as Jerusalem. It seems advisable to consider the parts of the passage which are not marred by textual corruption, namely, verses 6–7. They depict Judah and Jerusalem both pitted against the foreign hordes. This inclines us toward the reading of LXX and Pesh: "The siege against Jerusalem will also be against Judah." Certainty is not possible, however, and for this reason we also discuss below the meaning which the reading of Tg and Vg would have in this passage.

b) The phrase וכל סום העמים אכה בעורון is redundant and may not be original. This is suggested also by the fact that v. 5 follows smoothly after את עיני.

c) Reading אלפי.

d) 5b has elicited numerous proposals for emendations in the commentaries, and they are consistently unconvincing. We submit yet another which has the advantages of fitting smoothly into the context and involving emendation of a single consonant (י to ו, the consonants most commonly confused by the ancient scribes): אם צהל <ו> ישבי ירשלם ביהוה צבאות אלהיהם, "If only the inhabitants of Jerusalem would raise a shout for Yahweh of Hosts their God!" (for צהל + ב, cf. Is 24:14, Jer 31:7). The scene is very graphic: in vv. 2–4 the nations are shown rushing against Jerusalem and Judah. Yahweh the Holy Warrior enters the scene: he strikes the horses and riders with confusion and focuses his special attention upon the house of Judah. The clans of Judah then express the wish that the inhabitants of Jerusalem would raise a shout to Yahweh the Warrior, implying that they are being threatened thus because of their failure to trust Yahweh. Then in v. 6 Yahweh uses the clans of Judah to accomplish the victory over the enemy, with the result that Jerusalem is saved.

e) Again the ו/י confusion. We should read אלו. The את is superfluous.

f) Wellhausen's conjecture seems best here: אדמה קניני

The history of the criticism of 12:1–13:6 is as bewildering as that of 9:1–8. Here attention has been centered on the mention of the pierced one, for whom the mourning would be "as great as the mourning over Hadad-rimmon in the plain of Megiddo." Through most of the ninteenth century there was general agreement that the reference was to Josiah. Stade, however, said the pierced one was Onias III, and since then most interpreters have dated the text in the Maccabean period and have either accepted Stade's solution or suggested that Simon Maccabeus was the hero being mourned. It may seem surprising how the historicizing method of dating the anonymous post-exilic material almost invariably arrives at a Maccabean date. It is not surprising at all, however, when one considers that the Maccabean period (in contrast to the fourth and third centuries) is relatively well documented, thus providing ample persons and events to which the tantalizing "historical" allusions of the texts can be attached. Now that paleographic evidence from biblical manuscripts from the Judean Desert has proven the untenability of these dates, confidence in the historicizing method should be shaken. Just because many periods of post-exilic history are enshrouded in darkness does not mean that some of the anonymous biblical texts may not stem from those periods. We, therefore, again choose to approach our composition using the contextual-typological method.

An essential characteristic of the visionary tradition is its reapplication of older material, much of it drawn from the classical prophets, some of it appropriated from the traditions of the league and royal cult. The basic tradition upon which the author of the present composition drew is one stemming from the royal cult, being related to the royal theology and its doctrine of Yahweh's perpetual covenant with the house of David. It is the tradition of the unassailability of Jerusalem, the royal city of David (e.g., Psalms 2, 46, 48, 76). Isaiah, a prophet intimately acquainted with the royal court, draws heavily upon this tradition (e.g., 7:4–9; 8:9–10; 14:29, 32; 17:12–14; 28:14–18). Thus the tradition entered prophecy, there to be developed in new directions, and to be combined with other motifs.

One of the most basic points at which the visionary group disagreed with the hierocratic party was in connection with the concept of the Day of Yahweh. For the hierocratic group, that Day of Yahweh's judgment upon his people had occurred in the events of the early sixth century, after which Yahweh had again restored his people.[43] For the visionary group, the Day of Yahweh's wrath was still a future event, for the nation remained in a state of wickedness and defilement. It is this point of disagreement which accounts for the continued use and reapplication by the visionary group of the old league and royal traditions centering around the Divine Warrior.

We mentioned that the tradition underlying Zech 12:1ff is the royal tradition of the unassailability of Zion. Once that ultimate derivation has been clarified, the major exegetical task remains, that of seeing how the visionaries of the post-exilic era adapt that tradition to their situation and place it in the service of their eschatology. As a hymn like Psalm 48 indicates, the original royal tradition of the unassailability of Zion comes to expression in a special form of the Divine Warrior Hymn. It includes these basic themes:

1. Attack of the nations against Jerusalem.
2. Yahweh strikes them with panic.
3. Jerusalem is delivered.
4. Celebration of the king's victory.

In Zechariah 12 these major themes form the skeleton of the narrative:

1. In verses 1-3 the nations come against Jerusalem.
2. In verse 4 Yahweh strikes the enemy with panic.
3. In verses 5-9 Jerusalem is delivered.
4. In verses 10-14 a ceremony is described.

We have seen repeatedly how the visionaries drew upon older genres, and how, in their very act of reapplying them, they molded them into new forms which spoke to a radically altered setting and function. This distinctive metamorphosis is in the present composition as well, enabling us to discern the underlying situation most clearly where the alteration of the earlier genre is most pronounced. We turn

43. See pp. 247-62.

now to examine each of four themes of the royal tradition of the unassailability of Zion as they are remolded in this composition. In verses 2 and 3 two images are used to portray the attack of the nations against Jerusalem, "cup of reeling" and "heavy stone." What seems to be redundancy to the modern reader must not lead to surgery on the text to eliminate one of the images as secondary. Not only in poetry, with its use of *parallelismus membrorum*, but in Hebrew prose as well repetition of a basic thought with the use of parallel words or images represented good style. The image of the cup filled with a beverage which would bring staggering and ruin upon those imbibing it is taken over from tradition, where it was used in judgment contexts, both relating to Israel and the foreign nations.[44] Here the image is welded into the tradition of the unassailability of Zion by identifying Jerusalem with the woeful cup. The same is true of the second image, the heavy stone. By this identification the disastrous effect of the attack of the nations against Jerusalem is already suggested.

One alteration in the first theme is worthy of note: the siege will be not only against Jerusalem, but against Judah as well. Mention of the siege against Judah could have been motivated only by some special purpose, since in the original version of the theme the holy mountain of Jerusalem was the sole center of attention, and since a siege against a whole land seems rather awkward. That purpose becomes apparent in the remainder of the oracle: Jerusalem no longer can stand in the minds of the protagonists of this oracle as representative of the entire nation. Though still the holy city and held in special favor by Yahweh, it is presently under the control of a defiled priesthood. Hence

44. Is 51:17–23; Jer 25:15–29; Lam 4:21; Ezek 23:31–34; Obadiah 16; Na 3:11; Hab 2:15–16; Ps 60:5(3); 75:9(8). A. Weiser, *Das Buch des Propheten Jeremiah*, ATD 20/21 (Göttingen: Vandenhoeck und Ruprecht, 1960), pp. 223–224, refers to the oracular practice in Nu 5:11ff as the background of the image as it is used in Jeremiah 25. This connection seems unlikely in the Jeremiah passage, as it does in most of the above, since the image serves a vastly different purpose in them and likely arose from the wartime experience of the plundering and carousing of soldiers which led to reversal in an ensuing battle and finally defeat. The practice in the Numbers passage may be related at best to Ezek 23:31–34, though even there the martial use of the image has influenced the account, as seen in verse 33.

in the end-time battle described, a distinction must be introduced into the theme of the attack of the nations against Jerusalem: the siege will not be on Jerusalem alone, but also upon another segment of the population which is to be distinguished from the defiled inhabitants of Jerusalem, the clans of Judah. We will see that this distinction runs through the entire oracle.

EXCURSUS: THE TEXTUAL PROBLEM OF ZECHARIAH 12:2 AND AN ALTERNATE INTERPRETATION

Given the division among the textual traditions (cf. textual note "a" above), it is impossible to be certain of the emendations which we have adopted in the translation and notes above, assigning the preposition before Judah as original and that before siege as secondary. It seems wise to ask how the text would relate to our interpretation should the other alternative be original, that is, "Also Judah will be in the siege against Jerusalem." If that reading is the original one (cf. Zech 14:14), the passage supports the reconstruction which we shall be developing even more emphatically, inasmuch as it heightens the dichotomy between Jerusalem and Judah yet another degree. The picture in that case is one of Judah participating in the attack on Jerusalem, but then turning as Yahweh's ally against the foreign hosts so as to deliver Jerusalem at the last minute.

Such a picture of Yahweh leading foreign hosts against his city and then turning against the foreigners to punish them is a familiar one in the Old Testament (e.g., Is 10:5ff; Jer 25:8-14; Is 29:1-8; Ezek 38:1-23). That it would exalt the dignity and importance of the "clans of Judah" in relation to the safety of the holy city is obvious. Since we interpret "clans of Judah" as the designation used by the visionaries to distinguish themselves from the hierocratic group ("the inhabitants of Jerusalem"), the passage thus translated would be consonant with the message which the visionaries have proclaimed elsewhere (e.g., Zech 11:4-17): though they have abdicated their prophetic office of shepherding the people, and indeed through their oracles of judgment and their prayers for destruction of their adversaries have taken sides with the foreign nations bent on destroying Jerusalem, yet when the Day of Yahweh arrives and the apostates within Israel have been punished, Yahweh will use them as instruments of saving the people from total destruction. This will occur before the eyes of the entire nation, leading to their exaltation.

If the reading which we adopted in our translation is correct, the change in the text which pitted even Judah in the siege against Jerusalem could not be attributed merely to scribal error, but would have been a later intentional change intended to heighten the dichotomy between Judah and Jerusalem. This alteration in the text may have stemmed from the time of the composition of Zechariah 14, where we read in the description of the trials of the end-time: "even Judah will fight against Jerusalem" (though this clause may be a later addition to Zechariah 14; see below). This, in the last analysis, is the interpretation which we find most plausible.

We turn now to consider the way in which the second theme, Yahweh's striking the enemy with panic, is applied in the oracle. Here too the most noteworthy feature is the manner in which the sharp distinction is drawn between "the inhabitants of Jerusalem" and "the house" or "clans of Judah." In verse 4, a special note is added to the report that Yahweh will strike the enemy with panic: "but I will keep watch over the house of Judah." Verse 5 further develops the unique status of Judah: the clans of Judah express the wish that the inhabitants of Jerusalem would join the battle cry of their Warrior God, Yahweh, the implication being that the visionaries feel that the land is in dire straits because the leaders of Jerusalem have ignored the message of their only sure protector, Yahweh. In effect, this verse, if our interpretation is correct, is a plea that the Jerusalemites join the visionaries in the eschatological faith expressed in hymns like Zechariah 9 and 10.

The third theme is the deliverance of Jerusalem. This theme has been adapted to the interests of the visionary group by identifying the instrument which Yahweh would use in delivering his city with the clans of Judah (cf. 10:4–7). Yahweh's chosen host, devouring the enemies round about, would not be the leaders of Jerusalem, but the clans of Judah! What has been repeatedly implied in the special nuances given to the themes of the attack, panic, and deliverance in the preceding verses is stated explicitly in verse 7: in the end-time battle which will demonstrate Yahweh's power over his enemies, "First Yahweh will give victory to the tents of Judah, so that the glory of the house of David and the glory of the inhabitants of Jerusalem may not be exalted over that of Judah." Before going on to examine the remainder of this composition, we shall consider the question of the community background of verses 2-7.

The tradition of the unassailability of Zion has been adapted in our oracle in such a way as to produce a document which accentuates the special status of a group designated "the clans" or "tents of Judah" at the same time as it seems to disparage the position of "the house of David" or "the inhabitants of Jerusalem." When the problem is treated contextually, an explanation of the dichotomy running throughout this oracle begins to emerge.

In the previous two chapters we were able to gather evidence for the growing rift in the post-exilic community between the visionary and hierocratic elements, and to demonstrate that this community struggle formed the matrix within which the apocalyptic eschatology of the visionary group was developing. We noted that the hierocratic group was centered around the Jerusalem temple, and that in its program for the future it placed a scion of the house of David alongside a priestly figure as the leader of the community, a program which was temporarily effected in the diarchy of Zerubbabel and Jeshua. This Jerusalemite, Zadokite-led program was opposed by the visionary group, which harked back especially to archaic traditions of the league in maintaining that the true cult was open to all the people and not restricted to a narrow circle of priestly elite. In this visionary group we felt that we could recognize followers of Second Isaiah, together with disenfranchised priestly elements including a large segment of the Levites. These elements, many of which had remained in the land during the period of the exile, and all of which disassociated themselves from the Jerusalem temple, sought to identify themselves with archaic names recalling the pre-monarchic period when their model of a cult in which all the people were holy was a reality. Such an archaizing tendency can be recognized in "clans of Judah," "tents of Judah," and "house of Judah," the names of the group opposed to the "house of David" in the present composition.

This dichotomy is not encountered for the first time

here. In the third verse of the Divine Warrior Hymn in Zechariah 10, Yahweh expressed his burning anger against the shepherds and leaders, that is, the officials of the hierocratic party in Jerusalem, or in the terminology of Zechariah 12, against the "inhabitants of Jerusalem," and the "house of David." In contrast to these foes of Yahweh, Zech 10:3 goes on to explain that "Yahweh cares for his flock," and as a gloss (perhaps originating with a later redactor of the visionary group) correctly explains, the flock is "the house of Judah." The following verses then go on to explain that, in contrast to the shepherds and leaders, it is out of this flock that Yahweh will derive his host of warriors for the great battle of the end-time. It is very apparent how close this dichotomy is to that in Zechariah 12, where it is the house of Judah which fights as Yahweh's host to win the battle for Jerusalem. This same exaltation of Judah as Yahweh's end-time cosmic host is found in Zech 10:6, as well as in the thirteenth verse of the Divine Warrior Hymn in Zechariah 9. We are witnessing here the development of what would become a key notion in full-blown apocalyptic, that of Yahweh forging his fighting host out of the ranks of the righteous.[45] The notion has not yet reached the end of that development, for the true servants within Israel here fight only against the foreign hosts, not yet against all the wicked of the earth which would include many of their own brethren.

A number of passages thus corroborate our suggestion that behind the designations "tents of Judah" and "house of David" are to be discerned the visionary group and the hierocratic party, the two groups locked in the post-exilic struggle for control of Israel's cult. The phrase used here as a synonym of "Jerusalem" to designate the hierocratic party, namely, the "house of David," also corroborates the hypothesis mentioned in Section F above that the Davidic house retained an important position in the politics of the Zadokite party well into the period of the Second Temple.

Returning to an examination of Zech 12:1ff, we discover

45. Cf. 1QM, *passim,* and Zech 14:5.

that the rather garbled verse 8 revises the emphasis of verses 1-7 by exalting the inhabitants of Jerusalem. It and verse 9, which seeks to summarize the preceding, are likely from the hand of a later editor writing from the viewpoint of the hierocratic party, and seeking to blunt the edge of verses 1-7.

We turn finally to the fourth theme of the royal tradition underlying this composition, the celebration of the king's victory. Here the traditional material is altered more radically than at any other point, for the celebration of victory is replaced by a ceremony of a vastly different nature, representing the type of ironic twist given to the old genres which is the hallmark of the post-exilic visionary group: victory celebration is replaced by a gigantic mourning rite. In contrast to the scenario of the royal hymn, "the house of David" and "the inhabitants of Jerusalem" do not exult in their magnificent victory, but are brought to an awareness of a grievous sin which they have committed. We interpret this twist of the tradition as another indication of the conflict between the protagonists of the composition, the visionaries, and the hierocratic group. The latter, "the house of David," will become aware of its grievous sin only through an act of Yahweh in the end-time. In other words, only then will the visionaries, who have been defeated and removed from positions of honor in the cult, be vindicated, the same theme found in verses 2-7. The occasion of their atrocious offense is as obscure as it is tantalizing to the imaginations of the critics, having to do with one "whom they have pierced." Recognizing that this composition—like those in chapters 9, 10, and 11—concerns itself primarily with groups rather than individuals, and with broad movements toward the eschaton rather than with the concrete details of historical events, we shall eschew all speculative attempts to tie the allusion to an historical person, and shall instead remain within the limits set by our contextual-typological approach.

The dichotomy running throughout this composition and the others we have studied allows one to associate this mysterious "pierced one" with the visionary group, long the object of the oppression of the hierocratic party. When one recalls the intimate relation which the visionary group felt with the message of Second Isaiah, and their identification with the Suffering Servant,[46] this association becomes even more reasonable. Various factors make this a very natural conclusion: (1) The visionary group already had come to identify itself with the Suffering Servant of Second Isaiah (e.g., Is 65:8, 13f; 63:17; 61:1-3). (2) Long conscious of its oppression under the hierocratic leaders, it was unflinching in its assurance of vindication by Yahweh (e.g., Is 66:5-16; 57:13; Zech 11:4-17). (3) The narrative in Zech 11:4-17 indicates how the visionary group depicted itself as an afflicted body under the image of a loathed and rejected individual.

This collective image is found in related compositions. In Is 66:5-16 the visionary group expressed the belief that although they had been cast out of the community by their brethren, they yet would be restored by Yahweh. In Zechariah 11 they maintained that while they, like the prophets before them, had been rejected by the leaders and the people, they yet would be established as Yahweh's people (Zech 13:9). Similarly in the present passage they refer to themselves as those who have been slain by the house of David and the inhabitants of Jerusalem, that is, the ruling hierocratic party, but yet uphold the belief that on Yahweh's final day of battle they would be vindicated in the eyes of their oppressors, which would elicit the mourning rite described in verses 10-14. That mourning would be as great as the mourning for Hadad-rimmon, that is, Baal, an allusion intended to underscore the status of the victim and the magnitude of the sorrow of the official community. Prophecy and the prophetic (visionary) community may have been slain by the normative community, but they would rise again, and all Israel would look upon them with honor, and with sorrow for their sin against them. The rite itself is described in very archaic terms with the royal house of David, the prophetic house of Nathan, the two priestly

46. See pp. 66-67.

houses of Levi and Shimei, and all the other families each mourning by itself. We picture Israel projected back to the Golden Age of yore, divided into the various houses as in the wilderness period, positioned once again as Yahweh's host, an archaism again adopted and revivified by the community of Qumran in the second century.

Verse 13:1 continues the description of "that day"; not only will the house of David and the inhabitants of Jerusalem mourn over their sin against the visionary group, they will also have to be cleansed from their sin and impurity, for which purpose a fountain will be opened. Again the theme is traditional, but the reapplication to the post-exilic polemic is new. *niddā,* as the description of the sin, recalls the accusations of cultic impurity raised continually against the official cult of Jerusalem by the visionary group in the oracles of Third Isaiah (59:1-8; 65:1-7, 11-12; 66:3-4; cf. Zech 10:1-2).

13:2-6, which may or may not be an original part of the composition, tells of one further way in which the land would be cleansed "on that day," by the removal of idols and false prophets, again reminiscent of the polemical passages of Third Isaiah. The passage is intriguing as evidence that the age of the prophets had passed and that those who claimed to be prophets were in fact false prophets. This explains why the visionary group, though the true successors of the prophets, refused to designate themselves *nᵊbîʾîm.* As Zech 11:4-17 indicated, they had abdicated the duties of the classical prophetic office, for that office had fallen into the hands of false claimants, who are here associated with idols and the unclean spirit.

In Zech 12:1-13:6 we therefore find the members of the visionary group of the post-exilic community once again drawing upon archaic hymnic material associated with the Divine Warrior—this time in the form of the tradition of the unassailability of the divine mountain—to reaffirm their hope in the ultimate restoration of Zion and their vindication as the true members of Yahweh's people. In a manner characteristic of the visionary literature, antecedent tradition is consistently altered so as to serve the purpose of their polemic against the hierocratic party which controlled the Jerusalem temple cult.

The task remains of applying typological tools to determine the approximate date of the passage. The style of the narrative is of minimal help, serving only in the most general way to suggest that the composition came in that period when prose came to be the dominant mode of prophetic composition, the fifth century.

Indicative of the relatively late date of the composition is the degree to which the future hope is molded by the struggle within the community between the visionary and hierocratic factions. This places it well along the way toward the final battle in late apocalyptic where the division would be between the righteous and wicked throughout the world (and cosmos), with national divisions no longer playing a part. But "well along the way" is to be distinguished from arrival, since the old national line is still stubbornly maintained in Zechariah 12. Although it creates an inner tension in the oracle, this would be resolved once the national distinctions yielded completely to the spiritual dualism dividing good and evil.

Finally, the attempt of classical prophecy to relate the vision of the divine council to plain history has disappeared completely, and the vision is left largely on the cosmic level. The hordes of the nations are unidentified, and Yahweh as Cosmic Warrior fights directly against the foe. The only identification of parties involved, the house of David and the tents of Judah, stems from the polemical function of the composition. It is true that the tents of Judah represent human instruments used by Yahweh, but this is not the instrumentality of classical prophecy, where an actual historical monarch or army carries out Yahweh's purposes. It is rather the instrumentality of late apocalyptic where Yahweh musters his cosmic hosts and includes some drawn from the ranks of his earthly community. The struggle between the sons of light and darkness reflecting a dualistic worldview is being closely approached by this composition. We therefore designate it middle apocalyptic and date it in the first half of the fifth century.

H. AN APOCALYPSE STRUCTURED UPON THE RITUAL PATTERN OF THE CONFLICT MYTH AND REFLECTING BITTER INNER-COMMUNITY CONFLICT (14:1–21)

The last composition which we shall consider forms an appropriate conclusion to the study of the rise of apocalyptic, for it represents the most advanced example of apocalyptic in our study. With Zechariah 14 one enters the period of full-blown apocalyptic literature. The composition extends throughout the chapter in an unbroken development.

> 14:1 A day of Yahweh is coming when the spoil taken from you will be divided in your midst. 2 For I will gather all the nations against Jerusalem for battle, and the city shall be taken, the houses plundered, and the women raped. Half of the city shall go into exile, but the rest of the people shall not be cut off from the city. 3 Then Yahweh will go forth and fight against those nations as he fights on a day of battle. 4 On that day his feet will stand on the Mount of Olives which lies opposite Jerusalem to the east, and the Mount of Olives shall be split in two from east to west by an immense valley; half of the Mount shall move northward, half southward. 5 And my mountain valley[a] shall be blocked,[b] for the mountain gorge shall extend to its side;[c] [and you shall flee[b] as you fled from the earthquake in the days of Uzziah king of Judah].[d] Then Yahweh my God will come, and all the holy ones with him.[e]
>
> 6 On that day there shall be neither heat nor cold (?) nor frost (?).[f] 7 And it shall be all one day (it is known to Yahweh), with no distinction between day and night, and at evening time there shall be light. 8 On that day living waters shall flow forth from Jerusalem, half to the eastern sea and half to the western, in both summer and winter. 9 Then Yahweh will become king over all the earth; on that day Yahweh will be one and his name one. 10 The whole land shall be turned into a plain from Geba to Rimmon south of Jerusalem. But Jerusalem shall stand high in its place from the Benjamin Gate to the site of the former, gate, to the Corner Gate, and from[g] the Tower of Hananel to the king's wine vats. 11 And it shall be inhabited, and never again shall the ban of destruction be upon her; Jerusalem shall be inhabited in safety.

12 And the plague with which Yahweh will strike all the peoples who warred against Jerusalem will be this: their flesh shall rot while they are standing and their eyes shall rot in their sockets and their tongues shall rot in their mouths.[h] 13 On that day a great panic, sent by Yahweh, shall fall on them, so that each will seize the hand of his neighbor and the hand of the one will be raised against the hand of the other. 14 [Even Judah will fight against Jerusalem.][i] And the wealth of all the surrounding nations will be swept away; gold, silver, and garments in great abundance. 15 And such shall be the plague upon the horses, the mules, the camels, the asses, and every beast in those camps.

16 Then every survivor from all the nations which came against Jerusalem shall go up yearly to worship the King, Yahweh of Hosts, and to observe the feast of Tabernacles. 17 If any of the families of the earth do not go up to Jerusalem to worship the King, Yahweh of Hosts, no rain shall fall upon them. 18 If the family of Egypt does not go up and enter, then upon them[j] shall fall the plague with which Yahweh strikes the nations which do not go up to observe the feast of Tabernacles. 19 This shall be the punishment of Egypt and of all the nations which do not go up to observe the feast of Tabernacles.

20 On that day there shall be inscribed on the bells of the horses, "Holy to Yahweh," and the pots in the house of Yahweh shall be like the bowls before the altar. 21 Every pot in Jerusalem and Judah shall be holy to Yahweh of Hosts, so that all who sacrifice may come and take some of them, and boil sacrifices in them. No longer shall there be a dealer in the house of Yahweh of Hosts on that day.

TEXTUAL NOTES

a) Tg and Pesh, probably influenced by the next phrase, read הרים. LXX, with MT, appears to preserve the best reading, since the contrast is thereby maintained. The referent is the Kidron Valley, which is being blocked in the cataclysm by the Mount of Olives being split, with the northern mass pushing up into the Kidron.

b) The thrice recurring נסתם raises a textual problem. Pesh and Vg follow MT in reading a form of נוס, whereas LXX has, in all three cases, the equivalent of the nip'al of סתם. Tg translates the verb as a derivative of the root סתם in the first case, of נוס in the second and third. By presenting this contrast, Tg seems to preserve an original reading which was lost through leveling in the other versions.

c) MT would suggest a proper name, but it would be an unidentified location. Similarly LXX. We read אצלו, assuming that the suffix was lost by haplography because of the *wāw*-conjunction which follows.

d) This reference to the earthquake of Uzziah's time (Am 1:1) seems to be a later "scholarly" notation.

e) Reading עמו with Tg, Vg, Pesh, and LXX and a good number of Hebrew mss.

f) We read the Qere וקפאון, since it has the support of all the ancient translations, and since attempts to translate it as a verb have only led to further confusion. Similarly we follow LXX, Vg, and Pesh in reading וקרות. Contrasted with this pair, frost and cold, we should expect, in light of the paired opposites in vv. 7-8, a term for heat. This we find in the third term which should be read אור. Wellhausen, on the basis of Gen 8:22, suggested the emendation of אור to חום; though this too would express the annulment of the original polarities of the created order which seems to be the sense of this verse, the emendation does not give satisfactory explanation of how חום became אור.

g) A second *mêm* should be restored in וממגדל (haplography).

h) Read בפיהו, since the rest of the verse uses the singular collective.

i) Since vv. 12-19 are concerned with Jerusalem vis à vis the foreign nations, 14a may be an intrusive element stemming from further reflection on the relationship between Jerusalem and Judah in chapters 12 and 14.

j) The obvious difficulty in vv. 18-19 is best resolved by the deletion of the לא before עליהם, a correction supported by LXX and Pesh.

In this composition the visionary group again draws upon an archaic form as the vehicle with which to express its future hope. Following the common custom of the literature with which we have been dealing, that archaic form is not preserved in its original contours, but is molded, fused, and reinterpreted so as to apply to the new post-exilic setting. As in the case of Zechariah 9, the basic underlying structure of Zechariah 14 is derived from the ancient ritual pattern of the conflict myth, as that pattern was mediated on Israelite soil by the Jerusalem royal cult. Moreover, in a manner recalling Zechariah 10—but in a more radical way—that basic ritual pattern is altered by the fusing of two prophetic elements which redirect the original thrust of the genre significantly. The first (in vv. 1-2) is the embodiment of the motif of the "attack of the nations" in a salvation-judgment oracle (the oracle form which came to replace the separate classical judgment and salvation oracles of the pre-exilic period). It stands in the position of the threat in the early versions of the conflict myth. The second element fused to this ritual pattern is an adaptation of the "curses of the covenant" (in vv. 12-15). Tracing ultimately to the archaic traditions of the league, this element forms a sequel to the description of the shalom inaugurated by Yahweh's victory. It dramatizes the message of the salvation-judgment oracle that the shalom does not apply to all, but only to the righteous, for upon the enemies of Yahweh will fall the curses of the covenant.

We sketch here the structure of Zechariah 14 to indicate its basic conformity to the pattern of the conflict myth,[47] while observing in the footnotes the points where that pattern has been readapted to a new setting:

Threat: gathering of the nations against Jerusalem (1-2).[48]
Conflict and victory: Yahweh intervenes and fights (3).
Theophany and procession: Yahweh prepares a processional way in a mountain-rending cataclysm (4-5a) and enters with his holy ones (5b).
Shalom: A new creation supplants the polarities of the old order with the harmony of a new order and the fertility of living waters flowing forth from Jerusalem (6-8).
Manifestation of Yahweh's universal reign: Yahweh alone will reign (9), and his holy mountain will be lifted up over a land (10) which will dwell in security (11).
Covenant curses: The enemies of Yahweh and his people will be destroyed (12-15).[49]
Procession of the nations: Yahweh's universal reign will be recognized by the survivors of the nations (16-19).
Sacrifice and banquet: In a sanctified Jerusalem sacrifice and celebration will be renewed (20-21).

As we turn to consider the individual parts of this com-

47. See pp. 300-16.
48. This motif has been recast in the form of a salvation-judgment oracle.
49. Although the theme of the scattering and destruction of the enemy is well established in the ancient versions of the conflict myth, the unique adaption here takes the form of the "curses of the covenant."

position, the points at which the ancient liturgical pattern is altered most require closest attention. Such alteration occurs already in the first two verses. In the usual scenario of the conflict myth, the threat is described, followed by the conflict of the Divine Warrior in which he is victorious over the enemy. In the royal psalms based upon this pattern, the nations gather against Jerusalem, only to be warded off by Yahweh as he intervenes to save his city.[50] In prophecy, we find the theme of the attacking nations used in a vastly different way: Yahweh has gathered them to march against his people in order to inflict upon them a blow which will devastate the rebellious nation.[51]

In our passage neither the royal nor the prophetic adaptation of the motif of the attack of the nations is found, but instead a new hybrid form emerges as the salvation theme of the royal version of the conflict myth and the judgment theme of the prophetic *rîb* are fused. The result of the attack of the nations upon Jerusalem is neither the deliverance of the whole people nor the exile of the entire nation. Rather, "half of the city shall go into exile, but the rest of the people shall not be cut off from the city."[52] The underlying community situation that remolds the ritual pattern of the conflict myth is closely related to the situation identified earlier in Isaiah 56-66 and Zechariah 10-11 which gave rise to the hybrid salvation-judgment oracle. No longer could the whole community of Israel be addressed in a divine speech cast in one of the classical oracle forms, for the community was no longer viewed by the visionary group as a unified entity. Rather, a bitter conflict had torn a deep rift between hierocratic and visionary factions, implying for the latter that there were henceforth *two* Israels.

50. E.g., Psalms 2 and 48.

51. Hos 5:8-9; Is 5:26-30; 22:1-8; Jer 4:5-8.

52. The divergence of our passage from the usual prophetic use of the motif of the attack of the nations is illustrated by comparison with Am 7:17, which bears enough affinities in vocabulary and theme to suggest the possibility that the writer of our present oracle may have been influenced by it. In the Amos passage, the judgment involving the ravishing of women and division of booty by the enemy leads to the exile of Israel as a whole. Thus in contrast to Zech 14:1-2, there is no sign of a distinction within the nation between those to be delivered and those to be exiled. Cf. Ezek 38:12f and Is 13:16b.

To treat the new situation, the pure oracles of the classical period had to be fused into hybrid forms to account for both factions: in our case the ritual pattern of the royal hymn is adopted to promise salvation to the faithful, but to it is fused the threat of the prophetic judgment oracle to account for the fate of the rest of the nation. We witness here, as we did in Third Isaiah, a new complex community situation leading to new adaptations within the post-exilic genres. These genres become impregnated with internal strains bespeaking the tensions between the visionary and realistic elements within the post-exilic Jewish community.

Moving beyond the first two verses, we need to say little about the terse announcement of Yahweh's intervention to fight the attacking nations in verse 3. This verse makes it clear that we are dealing with a celebration of Yahweh as Divine Warrior. His fighting will be like that "on a day of battle." This reference evokes memories of the long history of the Divine Warrior's battles, beginning with battles described in Exodus 15, Judges 5, Josh 10:12–13 and Nu 21:27–30, that is, the battles of the league period, and then extending through the battles celebrated in the royal psalms and on down to those of the early apocalyptic writings which we have already studied.

In keeping with the ancient versions of the Divine Warrior Hymn, both in the Old Testament and in the conflict myths of the ancient Near East, Yahweh's arrival is marked by a mighty theophany which rocks the natural order. To illustrate this pattern comparison can be made with Ju 5:4f, where Yahweh's going forth is recorded with the verb *yṣ'* even as it is in Zech 14:3f. In the Judges passage, the mountains quake as Yahweh comes to fight, as they do in Hab 3:6–10, Na 1:5, Mi 1:3–4, Is 64:1–3 and Ezek 38:20.[53] But here the function of the theophany in the ritual pattern has developed beyond the theophanies in the early hymns of the Old Testament and the ancient myths.[54] The

53. Note the use of the root *r'š* in the passages in Judges 5 and Nahum 1 as well as in our passage, and the use of the root *bq'* in Mi 1:4 and our passage.

54. Cf. J. Jeremias, *Theophanie* (Neukirchen: Neukirchener, 1965).

mountains do not merely quake in response to the Divine Warrior's epiphany; they are rearranged by Yahweh in a particular way: the Mount of Olives is split in half creating an immense valley running from east to west. Half of the mountain moves southward, and the other half moves northward until it blocks the Kidron Valley. The result is an immense processional way coming from the desert reaches of the southeast, whither Yahweh was known to march according to ancient Divine Warrior tradition (Ju 5:4; Dtn 33:2; Hab 3:3). The theophany thus has taken on a specialized function in the ritual pattern of the conflict myth as it comes to expression in this composition; the theophany effects a processional way making possible Yahweh's triumphal entry into the temple precincts of the holy city Jerusalem.[55]

That this is the correct interpretation of our passage is assured by the note which follows the theophany: "Then Yahweh my God will come, and all the holy ones with him." Thus, in keeping with the scenario of the ritual pattern of the conflict myth, the warrior god enters his temple area in triumphant splendor, accompanied by his holy ones, i.e., those who had been consecrated for holy war. The question of the identity of the holy ones (*qᵊdōšîm*) is moot; in the original cosmic setting of the conflict myth, they are the heavenly warriors of the divine host (cf. Dtn 33:2; Ps 68:18). It is not surprising that biblical writers made various attempts to deny divine status to these warriors, considering them stars (Ju 5:20), or identifying them with the congregation of Yahweh's people (Dan 7:18, 27). Later apocalyptic writings tend to combine the saints of Yahweh's congregation with the divine participants in the end-time battle.

This altered function of the theophany is best explained in terms of influence from the portrayals of the divine theophany found in the prophet whom we have repeatedly recognized behind the imagery of the post-exilic visionary writers, Second Isaiah. To the exiles that prophet had

55. Cf. Ps 24:7-10.

announced the preparation of a processional way back to Zion: "And I will make all my mountains a way, and my highways shall be raised up" (Is 49:11; cf. 40:3-5). In Zechariah 14 the promise of Yahweh's making a processional way for his return to deliver his people is reiterated to a later generation of Second Isaiah's disciples who have grown disillusioned in the face of the nagging question of whether the deliverer would ever come. Verse 10 of our composition also belongs to this reiteration of Second Isaiah's message of the leveling of mountainous paths and the exaltation of Zion.

But the rearrangement of the mountains to prepare a processional way is not the only effect which Yahweh's epiphany has upon the natural order. In Zechariah 14 another theme originating with Second Isaiah and developed further by his late sixth-century disciples is elaborated, the theme of the new creation which would supplant the old. Second Isaiah delivers Yahweh's word about "new things, hidden things which you have not known. They are created now, not long ago. . . ." (48:7). A disciple of Second Isaiah also speaks of forgetting the former troubles in anticipation of Yahweh's new act: "For now I create new heavens, and a new earth" (Is 65:17). In both collections of oracles which we have studied from the visionaries of the sixth and fifth centuries we have traced a growing pessimism vis à vis existing structures. Evil had so permeated the present order that nothing seemed to be untainted; the question even arose whether the existing order could be cleansed to provide a home for the redeemed. This deepening pessimism was the cradle of the growing speculation regarding a new creation, or more accurately in light of ancient Hebrew thought,[56] a radical reordering of the earth and the heavens.

Against this background verses 6-9 of Zechariah 14 become intelligible. In Yahweh's intervention to deliver the faithful segment of the nation from foreign hordes and wicked brethren alike, deliverance does not stop at the

56. D. J. McCarthy, "'Creation' Motifs in Ancient Hebrew Poetry," *CBQ* 29 (1967): 393-406.

point of military victory, but embraces the drama of renewal of the natural order which is at the center of the ancient fertility myths. The dominion of evil has established itself so thoroughly that a reordering of the natural realm itself is called for. What is the nature of the change which would occur "on that day" *(bayyôm hahû')*?

Essentially, what is promised is the abrogation of the polarities of the natural order which were, according to early tradition, established by Yahweh in the earliest times. According to the priestly creation account, creation of the world was accomplished by Yahweh's separating a series of binary opposites from each other: light from darkness, heaven from earth, dry land from sea, sun from moon (= day from night). After the order thereby established had been threatened by a return to chaos in the great flood, the Yahwist records Yahweh's promise never again to destroy his creation: "While the earth remains, seedtime and harvest, cold (*qōr*) and heat (*ḥōm*), summer (*q́ayiṣ*) and winter (*ḥ́ōrep*), day(*yôm*) and night (*laylāh*), shall not cease" (Gen 8:22; cf. Ps 74:16-17).

This age-old order—founded upon the old divine pairs which formed the basis of the most ancient Near Eastern theogonies—had to be changed according to our composition, for it was an order which had fallen under the curse of a defiled people. We examine first verses 7 and 8, and then turn to the corrupt verse 6. Verse 7 addresses the basic division into day and night. It announces a secret ("it is known to Yahweh") which is now shared with the elect, first positively: "it shall be all one day," then negatively: "with no distinction between day (*yôm*) and night (*laylāh*)." The ancient division of Genesis 1 is thereby resolved into a new unity.

Verse 8 also begins positively with the ancient symbol of the perennial life-stream flowing from the temple to revivify the earth. Represented in ancient art as early as the early second millennium B.C. in Mesopotamia,[57] and deriv-

57. Cf. W. F. Albright, *Yahweh and the Gods of Canaan* (New York: Doubleday, 1968), pp. 91-100; E. D. van Buren, *The Flowing Vase and the God with Streams* (Berlin: 1933); and R. J. Clifford, *Mountain*, pp. 98-103.

ing its meaning from the cosmogonic myth of the storm god which is the source of the ritual pattern of the conflict myth, this symbol lived on in the royal cult (Ps 46:5; 36:9f; 65:10–14) and was elaborated by Ezekiel in his vision of the restored temple (Ezek 47:1–12). Once again the ancient divisions are resolved, for the living waters will flow forth "in both summer (*qáyiṣ*) and winter (*ḥṓrep*)." The seasons of Gen 8:22 are annulled.

We proceed from the clarity of verses 7 and 8 to the obscurity of verse 6. If the reading adopted in our translation is correct, yet another of the pairs of Gen 8:22 is annulled, that of heat and cold. Another possible reading first suggested by Gesenius in his *Thesaurus Linguae Hebraeae* (under *qp'*) would be: "the sun shall be no more, the glorious stars shall be removed."[58] If this reading should be original, it negates another of the pairs of Genesis, the luminaries governing the day and the night (Gen 1:18–19; cf. Ps 74:16–17). The state of the text does not allow one to choose confidently between these two alternatives (or others?), but this troubles us little since the basic theme of the resolution of the ancient pairs of opposites seems certain in this verse as in verses 7 and 8.

Finally, the theme of the resolution of the ancient pairs into a higher unity is brought to a climax in verse 9: "Then Yahweh will become king over all the earth; on that day Yahweh will be one and his name one." The purpose of the "cosmic speculation" of verses 6–8 is brought to clarity by this formulation. Defeat following in the train of defeat has led to such depths of pessimism that a social order fallen to the point of unmitigated evil (cf. Isaiah 59 and 66; Zechariah 10 and 11) has been seen to pollute even the realm of nature (cf. Is 65:15–25). The order established for man by Yahweh in earliest times has collapsed. A view of time introduced into prophetism by Second Isaiah (48:6–7) which divided salvation history into two distinct eras has developed in Zechariah 14 far beyond the point of embellishing an eschatology firmly moored to the realm of his-

58. *'ôr* = sun as in Job 31:26; the meaning of the nip'al of *qp'* is derived from the common Syriac meaning of "collect." On *qp'*, cf. Cross *Myth*, pp. 128–129, n. 59.

tory. The raw force of the mythopoeic view of time lying far in the background of Second Isaiah's division reasserts itself powerfully in our composition, for that view of time, distinguishing between a present evil order and a future order of salvation has begun to apply extremely well to the bleak situation in which the visionary group found itself.

Restoration of Yahweh's true followers could no longer be envisioned within the present evil social and natural order. Therefore that day of restoration had to be preceded by a cosmic battle which would eliminate the enemies of wickedness who caused the fall of the world to evil, and then by a new creation intended to restore the world to a paradisiacal purity suitable as a context for the restoration. The dualism and the related doctrine of the two eras (seasons) of Near Eastern myth are here revitalized in the visionary tradition. This reconstruction does not strain phenomenological plausibility; when all of the assured structures of the past epoch have collapsed, to whom do the defeated and weary visionaries turn? To Yahweh who will intervene to engage in battle with all of the hostile forces of the world, to Yahweh who will enter his holy city in a victorious procession accompanied by his holy ones, to Yahweh who will reorder the fallen creation into a new harmony free from the divided structures which no longer could support life, to Yahweh who "will become king over all the earth, . . .who will be one and his name one." The resolution of the pairs of opposites into a higher unity is based ultimately on one ingredient alone, the conviction that despite the ubiquitous defeat, division, and decay, yet Yahweh remains the One, the Sovereign over all. Thus in verse 9 the ancient formula of divine sovereignty from the enthronement festival takes on rich new meaning in the apocalyptic eschatology of a later period.[59]

Closely related to Zech 14:6–9 is a passage (Is 60:19–20) which was added at a later time to the mid-sixth-century program of restoration of the visionaries found in Isaiah 60–62.[60] According to that interpolation the polarities of

59. The ambivalence of the phrase *yhwh mālak* in the royal psalms is removed in this verse by the unambiguous formulation, *wəhāyāh yhwh lə melek.*

60. See p. 63, n. 33.

day and night, sun and moon would be abrogated in the day of restoration, for they would be gathered up into a higher eternal order: "Yahweh will be your everlasting light." This revealing of secrets of the universe is akin in spirit to our present passage, and likely stems from the same visionary circles and from the same period as Zechariah 14.

EXCURSUS: REVEALED SECRETS

Verses 6–9 raise questions regarding the history of later apocalyptic writings which cannot be penetrated here, but should at least be mentioned. It is well known that the lists of secrets of the universe in various pseudepigraphic writings have defied explanation for decades.[61] There seems little doubt that these lists originate outside of the stream of development of apocalyptic eschatology which we have been tracing. Although the question of whether they originate in "wisdom," Hellenistic speculation, or some other source may never be answered, the question of the function they assume once they have been adopted by Jewish visionaries must be addressed. Zech 14:6–9 may offer a pointer in the direction of a solution to this latter question, for here too the secrets of the universe (albeit on a much more modest scale than the later lists) are revealed. As in those later lists, they are secrets originally known only to Yahweh (v. 7), but they are revealed to the seer who in turn communicates them to the elect. Within the context of this oracle, it is quite clear how this revelation of secrets involving the order of the universe functions, and hence the possibility that the oracle may shed light on the later lists arises. As the culmination of the speculation in the declaration of Yahweh's universal reign indicates, the revelation of secrets is aimed at giving assurance to the elect of Yahweh's sovereign control over all of reality, and this sovereignty is the guarantee of the final victory which he will hand to the faithful. At the same time, because they are secrets known only to Yahweh, and now to the seer, this esoteric knowledge establishes the credentials of the seer to disclose the saving events of the end-time.

Do the lists of secrets in the pseudepigrapha function in a similar way? Only further study can answer this question, although a number of preliminary observations may be in order. It is first apparent that the lists are assimilated in differing degrees by the specific writings, ranging all the way from cases where outside lists seem to have been adopted virtually unchanged from their source to cases where they have been strongly altered to function in the new setting. An example of the former is 1 En

61. E.g., 1 Enoch 17–19, 41, 60; 2 Enoch 23, 40; 2 Baruch 59. Cf. Stone, "Lists."

60:11–24, a scientific-sounding enumeration of the winds, luminaries, etc., and their relations to each other. A list like this seems to stress the immutability of the natural order (cf. 1 En 41:5). To this may be contrasted the list in 1 En 52:1–9: the seven metals, each represented by a mountain, are listed. But far from emphasizing the immutability of the present order, the list is applied to an oracle: "All these shall be in the presence of the Elect One as wax before the fire. . . ." (v. 6). The list here functions in a manner similar to Zechariah 14, to praise the sovereignty of the Lord, which becomes the basis for confidence that ultimately he will save his people.

This contrast invites us to consider the lists of secrets as raw material—analogous to the raw material offered by various mythic sources—which is drawn into the apocalyptic writings to enhance the message of the seer. The specific applications may vary, but it can be suggested that the underlying common element is this: they always magnify the sovereign Lord who is the source of these secrets and whose sovereignty lays the foundation for hopes of deliverance; at the same time they establish the credentials of the seer as one having access to special knowledge, thereby adding validity to his promises of salvation to the elect, an important consideration in an era when opponents of the visionaries were pronouncing the demise of the prophetic spirit and the heretical status of the apocalyptic predictions.

The acclamation of Yahweh as universal king is followed in verses 10–11 by attention to the temple mount of Jerusalem. Since the actual topography of Jerusalem does not conform to the stature of the divine mountain in the mythic complex underlying Zechariah 14, it is not surprising that more alterations in the relief of the land occur at this point. Already the Mount of Olives (which actually towers over the temple mount!) has been split to prepare a processional way to the temple (vv. 4–5). Now in verse 10 the countryside around Jerusalem is leveled into a plain, so that Jerusalem in contrast stands prominently above the surrounding area. Once again roots in the Isaianic tradition are apparent. In Is 2:2 we read: "It shall come to pass in the latter days that the mountain of the house of Yahweh shall be established as the highest of the mountains, and shall be raised above the hills." The writer of Zechariah 14 may well be identifying his time with the "latter days" of Is 2:2. Affinities with the proclamation of Second Isaiah are also prominent. The leveling of the mountains and valleys which was a sign of Yahweh's victorious return to Zion in Is 40:4 is described again here: "The whole land shall be turned into a plain. . . ." In the boundaries of the land which follow we find the concrete type of detail which proves that in spite of the profound influence of myth, the vision of the future restoration has not extricated itself completely from the mundane in this composition. "From Geba to Rimmon" gives the northern and southern border points of Judah.[62] The gates and towers which follow delimit the four sides of historical Jerusalem. These details are preserved amidst the overarching mythic pattern of the chapter as so many vestiges of a past era. For Jerusalem has been elevated above the strict limitations of history in this chapter, and has been assimilated to the pattern of the divine mountain of the conflict myth.[63] Following a pattern already visible in the royal literature (cf. Ps 48:1–3), Zion has taken on the features of Mount Zaphon and the surrounding mountains have become a plain.

Thus exalted and located at the source of the life-giving stream which turns the surrounding area into a paradisiacal garden, the earthly Jerusalem has begun to be transformed into the heavenly Jerusalem located at the *axis mundi* where heaven and earth are conjoined. The transformation represents a powerful thrust in the direction of a mythopoeic view of salvation. The deliverance which the Divine Warrior brings according to this composition is not mediated by earthly events or human agents, but is accomplished by a divine *tour de force* which breaks all resistance amidst a cataclysm which disrupts and thoroughly transforms the order established at the creation of the earth. Even as the deliverance is not contingent upon earthly events, neither is the shalom which that deliverance inaugurates, as the unconditional promises of verse 11 indicate: "never again shall the ban of destruction be upon her; Jerusalem shall be inhabited in safety." Though ele-

62. Cf. 2 Kgs 23:8 and J. M. P. Smith, *Zechariah,* ICC (New York: Charles Scribner's Sons, 1912), p. 348.

63. Clifford, *Mountain,* p. 131.

vated to cosmic heights unprecedented in earlier Israelite tradition, this promise nevertheless builds upon the age-old blessings of the covenant (Lev 25:18–19; cf. Jer 33:16). Again we recognize the development of apocalyptic eschatology as the reformulation of the substance of earlier tradition within new modes of expression. Although this development does not leave that substance unaffected, the degree of continuity characterizing the development from prophetic to apocalyptic eschatology is quite remarkable.

This continuity with early tradition is manifested also in the next section, verses 12–15. An old theme stemming from the league is introduced into the scenario of the conflict myth to qualify the shalom established by the warrior god. It is the theme of the curses of the covenant, and is introduced to underline the fact that the shalom does not apply indiscriminately to all. In keeping with the bifurcation of the salvation-judgment oracle, it expresses the concomitant of the blessings promised to the elect, namely, the plague which will fall upon the damned. This theme fits smoothly into the context of holy war, for as Hab 3:5 and Ezek 38:22 indicate, the Divine Warrior could use the plague as one of his weapons. The general development of the curses as well as particular details reveal close affinities with Dtn 28:20–22:

> Yahweh will send upon you curses, panic, and frustration, in all that you set out to do, until you are destroyed and perish quickly for your evil acts, because you have forsaken me. Yahweh will cause pestilence to cleave to you until he has consumed you off the land which you are entering to occupy. Yahweh will afflict you with consumption, fever, inflammation, eruptions, drought, blight, and mildew; they shall pursue you until you perish.

In this passage, as in Zechariah 14, the curses are construed in terms of a great panic (*məhûmāh*) inflicted by Yahweh upon the accursed.[64] In verse 17 the curse of the drought occurs, which is also in the Deuteronomy passage.

64. Cf. also Lev 16:16; Dtn 28:27–28; Is 22:5; Ezek 38:21; 1 Sam 14:20.

We encountered the theme of the great panic inflicted by Yahweh in the trials of the end-time earlier in Zech 11:6. The same theme becomes an established element in later apocalyptic writings as well, taking the form of the gruesome descriptions of the apocalyptic woes. Although the connections with earlier pre-exilic traditions are apparent in those later writings, the theme of the curses which shall fall upon the wicked in the end-time has been universalized to include the wicked of all the earth, a tendency nascent in the visionary literature of Isaiah 56–66 (e.g., 66:16) and already quite developed in Zechariah 14. This universalizing tendency accompanied the breakdown of the close ties between the prophetic office and the political structures of the Israelite nation. Increasingly other traditions originally at home in the covenant between Yahweh and Israel were recast so as to apply to all the nations of the world. In the case of the covenant curses, a theme which in pre-biblical sources was at home in a universal (or even cosmic) setting thus began to move back to that setting as old mythic motifs increasingly reasserted their original intention.[65] In these curses as in the description of the conflict in verses 1–3, the political orientation of classical prophecy with its integration of divine activity into the events of history has been supplanted by a new perspective. Throughout, the Divine Warrior acts alone without the mediation or assistance of human agents. He fights alone, he sends panic upon the enemy alone, he delivers alone. Having abdicated the political office of the classical prophets and having focused on a lofty vision lifted above the limits of historical contingency, the proponents of the apocalyptic eschatology in Zechariah 14 and related writings found that the traditional materials most useful to them were the materials of the league and royal cult, that is, the materials which still preserved the cosmic orientation of their ancient mythic sources.

In keeping with the universalism of our passage is the following section describing the procession of the nations to Jerusalem (vv. 16–19). This section is a part of the theme

65. Cf. Goetze, *ANET*², p. 206.

of the manifestation of Yahweh's universal reign, for the purpose of their yearly pilgrimage is "to worship the King, Yahweh of Hosts."[66] Once again we recognize the close connections between Zechariah 14 and the restoration hopes of Second Isaiah and his disciples, as earlier promises, long having been deferred, are now reiterated. In Second Isaiah Yahweh addresses his servant, Israel: I will give you as a light to the nations, that my salvation may reach to the end of the earth" (49:6b). In Is 60:3 the glorious promise is made: "Nations will come to your light and kings to your rising brightness."[67] The universalism inchoate in those early formulations is stated boldly in what is perhaps one of the latest parts of Third Isaiah (56:1–8). In that passage we read about the part which foreigners will have in the worship in Yahweh's house:

> And to foreigners who pledge themselves to Yahweh to minister to him,
> to love the name of Yahweh,
> and to become his servants,
> all who keep the sabbath undefiled
> and hold fast to my covenant:
> them will I bring to my holy mountain
> and make them joyful in my house of prayer.
> Their burnt offerings and their sacrifices
> will be acceptable on my altar,
> for my house shall be called a house of prayer
> for all peoples.

This temple policy stands in sharp contrast to the narrow exclusiveness which we have found to be characteristic of the Zadokite-led hierocratic group. It is a tolerant policy which developed organically out of the open attitude toward temple worship and the priesthood and formed an essential part of the visionary program of restoration: "Your people shall all be righteous. . . ." (60:21a); "You will be named the priests of Yahweh, ministers of our God" (61:6a). To be sure, the openness in that sixth-century document was primarily inner-Israelite. Since that time,

66. Cf. Is 66:23.
67. Cf. Is 2:3.

however, the powerful impetus of nationalism had been driven out of the visionary group by the schism which tore the community assunder, and led to the salvation-judgment oracle which defined the division between those to be delivered and those to be damned not along national boundaries but on the basis of the distinction between the righteous and wicked "of all flesh." This new ethical (in contrast to national) definition of the righteous, coupled with the tolerant attitude toward those admitted to the temple priesthood found in the visionary restoration program, explains the formulation of temple participation found in Is 56:6–7. These two ingredients of the developing visionary tradition also account for the procession of the nations to worship Yahweh in Zech 14:16–19. This procession will take place after the attacking hordes have destroyed the wicked within the people of Israel from the land (14:1–2), and after Yahweh has destroyed the wicked from among the nations of the earth through his combat (14:3) and the curses of the covenant (14:12–15). With the families of the earth thereby purged of the wicked, "every survivor from all the nations which came against Jerusalem shall go up yearly to worship the King, Yahweh of Hosts, and to observe the feast of Tabernacles."[68]

The feast of Tabernacles (*ḥag hassūkôt*) became in the period of the monarchy the chief of the three pilgrimages to the temple.[69] Involving an entire week of sacrifice and fasting, it celebrated the enthronement of Yahweh as universal king. The royal psalms indicate that a central part of the celebration was a festive procession to the temple. If our connecting Zechariah with the ritual pattern of the conflict myth is correct (the pattern which is also the basis of the royal psalms), this setting of the procession of the nations within the feast of Tabernacles is most appropriate. In keeping with the emphasis of the ritual pattern on the

68. A related document from the visionary tradition, the last booklet attached to the original collection of the minor prophets (Hosea through Zechariah 1–8) called Malachi, combines attack on contemporary temple abuses with the universalistic spirit thus: "For from the rising of the sun to its setting my name is great among the nations, and in every place incense is offered to my name, and a pure offering; for my name is great among the nations, says Yahweh of Hosts" (1:11).

69. Cf. de Vaux, *Israel*, pp. 495–496.

universal reign of the warrior god (both in the ancient myths and in the royal psalms), the "survivors from all the nations" join the faithful of Israel "to worship the King, Yahweh of Hosts, and to observe the feast of Tabernacles," i.e., the primary royal festival.

The close connection of this composition with the ritual pattern of the conflict myth is evident also in the effect which neglect of this observance would have upon the disobedient nation: "no rain shall fall upon them" (v. 17). This connection of the ritual pattern with the fertility motif accords with that found in Zech 9:17 and all of the parallels cited in connection with that passage. It is another reminder that the ultimate origin of the underlying myth is the ancient Near Eastern fertility cult centering around the storm god, the sender of the fructifying rains. Throughout the history of the Israelite cult this connection was maintained, as seen in the fact that the feast of Tabernacles was a festival of thanksgiving for the harvest.

The final section (vv. 20-21) describes the conditions surrounding the banquet and sacrifices of the great festival in Jerusalem. The former beasts of war, the horses, will bear the same inscription upon their bells as that borne by the high priest on his turban, "Holy to Yahweh" (Exod 28:36; 39:30). And because of the great multitudes coming to worship the King, "every pot in Jerusalem and Judah shall be holy to Yahweh of Hosts, so that all who sacrifice may come and take some of them, and boil sacrifices in them."

This democratizing and universalizing of participation in temple sacrifice and celebration again stand in marked contrast to the narrow exclusiveness of the hierocratic group, even as it accords well with the tolerant spirit of the visionary program of restoration, according to which "your people shall all be righteous," and "you will be named the priests of Yahweh, ministers of our God" (60:21a; 61:6a). In our passage the gates of the temple are thrown open to participation by all who have passed through the trials of the apocalyptic woes. Distinctions dividing men into priests and laity, and vessels into consecrated and profane are eliminated (cf. Is 24:2). An ancient dream would thereby be fulfilled on that day: "and you shall be to me a kingdom of priests and a holy nation" (Ex 19:6; cf. Dtn 7:6; 14:2, 21; 26:19). Again we recognize the line of continuity with ancient tradition, even as the development toward a redefinition of "holy nation" as including families of all the earth represents the new dimension carrying apocalyptic eschatology beyond its prophetic roots.

EXCURSUS: THE REDACTIONAL FRAMEWORK OF THIRD ISAIAH (56:1-8 AND 66:17-24)

In our discussion of the visionary oracles of Third Isaiah, the verses (56:1-8 and 66:17-24) supplying the redactional framework of that collection were left out of the discussion, since they reflected a later period than that represented by the other oracles in Isaiah 56-66. The close thematic affinities which those verses have with Zechariah 14 suggest that the visionary material in Third Isaiah was collected and given its redactional framework at about the time of the composition of Zechariah 14 and within the same visionary group. We here shall draw attention only to the most salient points.

Is 66:18-24 is an addition to the Divine Warrior Hymn in 66:15-16 which supplies a number of the elements of the ritual pattern of the conflict myth not present in the original oracle (verse 17 is merely a reformulation of 65:3b-5, the time of origin of which cannot be determined). Both in this overall form-critical structural feature as well as in details which we shall mention, close kinship with Zechariah 14 is evident.

Verses 18-20 develop the theme of the manifestation of the universal reign of Yahweh, while displaying the same indifference to the particulars of history as found in Zechariah 14. The list of nations bears no relation to the particular events and conditions of the time of writing, but is taken from earlier prophetic writings (especially Ezekiel) to establish the universal fact of Yahweh's kingship. The part played by the survivors of the final day of wrath expresses a universalism comparable to that informing Zech 14:16, 20-21. In verse 20 the royal theme of the procession to the temple site of the triumphant warrior god is incorporated, thereby reiterating a theme (already found in the visionary program of restoration [60:4-9]), which was expressed as well in Zech 14:20-21.

Verse 21 reflects the democratization ot temple worship which we have traced through the various stages of the visionary tradition, and which bears close resemblance to the tolerant spirit of Zech 14:20-21. Once again this formulation would have been utter heresy to the hierocratic leaders of the temple, and can be explained only within the context of a bitter attack on the Zadokite priesthood.

Verse 22 renews the promise at the center of visionary thinking throughout the sixth and fifth centuries, the promise of being Yahweh's possession. Originating in the program of restoration of the visionaries (e.g., 60:21-22), this promise was reiterated in the recurrent crises which undermined it. In verse 23 we find the new universalism of apocalyptic eschatology (Zech 14:16; Mal 1:1), followed in verse 24 with the harshly vindictive condemnation of the wicked which reminds one of Zech 14:12-15 and lives on in later apocalyptic (e.g., Dan 12:2).[70]

Since the universalism of the other half of the framework (Is 56:1-8) was already discussed in connection with Zech 14:16, we shall limit ourselves to those observations which connect this section to the same period and tradition. In the authoritative form of an oracle of Yahweh, the orthodox position regarding foreigners (and eunuchs) is challenged (cf. Dtn 23:2-9; Ezr 9:1-2; Neh 9:2). The oracle again is a frontal attack on the narrow exclusiveness of the hierocratic tradition with its teaching that the temple priesthood was limited to the sons of Zadok, and that membership in the community was limited to the sons of Israel. The new universalism is summarized in verse 8.

The framework represented by these two passages ties the final form of Third Isaiah closely to Second Zechariah, and corroborates our argument that these two collections of material come from the same visionary tradition. The connection with Zechariah 14 also allows us to hypothesize that the oracles of Isaiah 56-66 were redacted within visionary circles in the mid-fifth century (the date which we suggest below for Zechariah 14).

Our analysis of Zechariah 14 leaves much interesting evidence untouched in a composition which deserves full,

70. Westermann (pp. 423-429) attributes Is 66:18, 19, and 21 to a different source than that which produced 66:20, 22-24. In this way he is able to discover a theological statement in verses 18, 19, and 21 which exudes a missionary spirit universal in breadth and filled with a most generous attitude toward foreigners. It is free from any trace of vindictiveness or gruesomeness. 66:20, 22-24, on the other hand, was added by a later editor who could not tolerate such generosity, and who therefore accentuated the subservient role of the foreigners and their eternal perdition. This type of "cleansing" of a prophetic oracle for the sake of producing respectable theology is indefensible, especially since Zechariah 14, which bears striking resemblances to Is 66:18-24, combines a sweeping universalism with a rigid vindictiveness against the wicked among the nations, and a generous inclusion of foreigners in the pilgrimage to Zion with interest in the temple cult and its chief festival (these contrasts are found even in Second Isaiah and Isaiah 60-62). Such "cleansing" is the result of the failure to recognize the community polemic which produced this late biblical literature, a polemic which, to be sure, broke the particularism of the national cult, but which, at the same time, hardened the vindictiveness felt toward the wicked within the community as well as among the nations.

individual treatment elsewhere. Our purposes have been served, however, in demonstrating that the basic underlying structure of this chapter conforms closely to the ritual pattern of the conflict myth, with several significant modifications, however, which record the influence of a new setting. Throughout our examination of Zechariah 14 twin characteristics kept reappearing (as they had indeed in all of the material studied in this book): (1) continuity with older Israelite (especially prophetic) traditions, and (2) important points of development beyond those antecedent traditions. This double edge is the cardinal feature that distinguishes the development of apocalyptic eschatology out of earlier prophetic roots.

The continuity with earlier tradition is especially apparent in the repeated affinities with the prophecies of Second Isaiah and with the program of restoration in Isaiah 60-62. As can be seen readily in comparing Zechariah 14 with Isaiah 60, we are dealing in this composition with a reformulation of the eschatological promises of the visionary program in a later period:

	Isaiah 60:	*Zechariah* 14:
Wealth of the nations is gathered	5	14
Nations will come to Jerusalem, bearing sacrificial offerings	6-7	16
Curse upon the nation not joining in the service of Yahweh	12	17-19
Eternal majesty of Jerusalem is established	15	10
Destruction eliminated and safety established	18	11
Sanctity of all the people	21	20-21
[Polarities of the old order supplanted by the new harmony of Yahweh's reign	19-20	6-9][71]

This comparison corroborates our argument that Isaiah

71. As observed earlier, Is 60:19-20 is a later addition. It may well have been added at the period in which Zechariah 14 was composed.

60–62 enjoyed a programmatic status within the visionary group of the post-exilic period. It continued to express the eschatological hopes of the disciples of Second Isaiah, hopes which they embraced even in the face of repeated defeats at the hands of their rivals. Since Zechariah 14 is the latest composition in our study of the post-exilic visionary tradition, it demonstrates the tenacity of the eschatological faith of the visionary elements within the Jewish community.

But the other edge of Zechariah 14 is equally incisive: conditions have changed for the visionaries in the years between Isaiah 60–62 and Zechariah 14, and the eschatological message of salvation had been obliged to assume new modes of expression. (1) In the sixth-century program of restoration, the object of hope was still the united nation of Israel: "They will be called 'The Holy People'" (62:12). In Zechariah 14 that united nation has been divided, only one segment of it being designated the holy people of God, the remainder being damned to destruction. (2) In the program of restoration, salvation was expected imminently and with great excitement "here comes your salvation!" (62:11). A grim alteration occurs in Zechariah 14, where salvation is deferred, being expected only after a period of apocalyptic woes inflicted by the attacking hordes of the nations. (3) The program of restoration exuded an optimistic attitude which foresaw no further judgment: "I will not give your grain as food for your enemies" (62:8). In Zechariah 14 enemies break into the land and plunder and divide the spoils. (4) On the form-critical level, the program of restoration is a pure oracle of salvation, balanced with traces of the oracle of judgment against the nations (60:12). Zechariah 14 is cast in the form of the new hybrid salvation-judgment oracle, which levels salvation and judgment words simultaneously against two different segments within a divided nation.

What conclusions can be reached regarding the sociological setting of Zechariah 14 on the basis of the above observations? The horror written into verses 1–2 bespeaks a feverish degree of polemical wrath on the part of the visionaries against their hierocratic opponents. The holy Jerusalem not only will be attacked as in Zechariah 12, but will be breached and decimated. This destruction of Jerusalem, home of the temple and the Zadokite cult, could be predicted as a part of Yahweh's salvation act only by a group bitterly opposed to the leaders of the Jerusalem cult. The division which we discussed in connection with Zechariah 12 between the "tents of Judah" and the "inhabitants of Jerusalem" and which is underscored by the gloss (?) in 14:14, lies at the heart of Zechariah 14. The post-exilic community within which this composition was written was split into two warring factions.

The grim character of the apocalyptic woes and the radical nature of the change required in political and natural structures alike point to a deepening of the pessimism found throughout the later compositions of the visionary literature. No attempt is made to relate existing realities, whether historical persons and events or institutional structures, to the events ushering in the restoration. The group represented by this oracle is obviously without power in a world which has turned completely against it. Restoration faith therefore comes to expression only in bald statements of Yahweh's violent overthrow of all enemies and his radical transformation of an evil order of creation into a paradisiacal realm of salvation.

Our identification of this composition with the visionary elements disenfranchised from the official Jerusalem cult is supported by verses 20–21. The democratization of worship envisioned in those verses is a harsh repudiation of the exclusive claims to priestly privileges made by the Zadokite priests. After the wicked (a group naturally including the priestly oppressors of the visionaries) had been purged from the people in Yahweh's destruction of the city (vv. 1–2), the faithful would all exercise priestly functions in a resanctified Jerusalem.

The polemical barb is directed against the temple priesthood which the visionaries allege to be defiled once again in the sentence which concludes the description of the new, democratized sacrificial cult: "No longer shall there be a dealer in the house of Yahweh of Hosts on that day" (21b). In our study of Zech 11:4–12 we encountered an incredibly harsh indictment leveled by the visionaries against the temple hierocracy: the heart of the corruption which was symbolized by the sheep dealers and was dooming the land to destruction was located within the temple itself! The deep pessimism of apocalyptic eschatology went even further in that composition by identifying Yahweh as directing and hastening the entire drive toward destruction. The appalling corruption of the land necessitated this destruction before the deliverance of the remnant could occur. Zechariah 14 describes fully the destruction foreseen by Zechariah 11 even as Zechariah 14 describes fully the deliverance of the remnant of the faithful prophesied in the sequel to Zechariah 11 in 13:7–9. The close parallelism characterizing the sequence of the eschatological events in the two chapters is seen also in 14:21b, where the rare word for "dealers" again appears.

Once the wicked leaders of the people have been eliminated and the cult has been purified and reopened to all of the faithful, there shall no longer be present in the temple the agent of destruction supported by a defiled priesthood, the sheep trader who eagerly sells the flock to damnation in exchange for his own wealth and comfort. Purged from the restoration community forever will be the defiled priesthood and its agents of corruption and oppression. Thus the restoration hopes of the visionaries, long deferred and yet so fervently longed for, would finally be realized, inaugurated by a pure act of Yahweh the Warrior, and guaranteed forever by the permanent elimination of the opponents who repeatedly had frustrated the restoration efforts of the visionaries.

We arrive at the conclusion, therefore, that the same visionary tradition which produced the program of restoration in Isaiah 60-62 and which continued to reapply the hopes embodied in that program in the oracles which we have studied in Third Isaiah and Second Zechariah produced Zechariah 14 as well. Those belonging to this tradition here continue to cling to their restoration hopes in spite of total alienation from existing structures. They condemn totally those structures, and the hierocratic guardians of those structures. In opposition to the continuity with earlier temple structures characterizing the hierocratic group, these visionaries produce a vision dedicated to utter discontinuity with the structures of the past, reaching back for their models instead to ancient myths and archaic native traditions. Viewing their situation from the perspective of loss of power and oppression, they are able to conceptualize restoration only as a complete reversal to be effected by Yahweh alone, without their own efforts to reform existing institutions or to convince contemporary leaders to share their vision. They thus abandoned the stubborn insistence of their prophetic predecessors to relate the vision of Yahweh's saving action to the events of history. Historical events record only the left hand of God's activity, his judging activity as defeats and calamities come to be interpreted as the horrors of the end-time which will find their full expression before salvation draws near. The vision of that salvation, meanwhile, has broken almost completely from the historical realm, being described in cosmic terms in no way limited by the contingencies of history. The temptation eschewed by Second Isaiah has seduced these later disciples into escaping into the timeless repose of a view of salvation which is largely mythic in nature.

To the extent allowed by the evidence furnished by this composition in its relation to other oracles of the visionaries, we have described the context of Zechariah 14. We turn finally to the application of the typological aspect of our method of inquiry to establish the position of this oracle in the history of apocalyptic eschatology.

Little can be said concerning stylistic matters, except to make the general observation that the composition is written entirely in prose. If Zech 11:4-17 (13:7-9) was transitional, including sections of both poetic prose and prosaic poetry, Zechariah 12 and 14, both being written in normal prose, could perhaps be seen as typologically later.

The evidence on the level of the history of genres is more substantial. The tendency toward hybridization reaches a more advanced stage in this oracle than in any considered earlier. To the ritual pattern of the conflict myth, which in Zechariah 9 was used to carry a promise of salvation to the whole nation, has been fused the salvation-judgment oracle which limits the threat to one segment within the community while promising deliverance to the other. The pattern is altered, moreover, to allow the decimation of the temple mount, normally impregnable in the earlier versions of the pattern. Finally, the promise of the shalom attendant upon the victory of the Divine Warrior is complemented by the curses of the covenant directed against those survivors of the end-time attack who are to be denied participation in the salvation. These formal characteristics place the oracle typologically later than Zechariah 10, which was in turn later than Zechariah 9. The addition of the salvation-judgment oracle in verses 1-2 would have taken place after the development of that genre, a development which occurred in the last third of the sixth century. These considerations definitely place the oracle after the end of the sixth century. How long afterward must be asked in relation to what follows.

The move toward fully developed apocalyptic eschatology is seen dramatically on the level of concepts and ideas. Very close to the surface one senses, in relation to historical realities, a deep pessimism and a hardened vindictiveness born of the disillusionment and defeat suffered by the visionaries. It seems evident that this oracle represents the latest stage found in Isaiah 56-66 or Zechariah 9-14 in the struggle between hierocratic and visionary elements in the post-exilic community. The other side of this coin of historical pessimism is an incredibly brilliant picture of hope displaying the great upheaval "on that day" when all of the existing conditions would be reversed. The wedge has been driven ever so deeply between those two elements of the prophetic tradition which in the classical period were held in a lively relation of interaction, the elements of vision and reality. Indeed that wedge has become lodged so close to the heart of Jewish eschatology that one now must characterize the resulting composition as apocalyptic eschatology, without stricture or qualification. Internal development would continue to occur, but the essentials of apocalyptic eschatology are all present. This is in large part true because of one important fact: the dichotomy between vision and reality made profound dependence upon mythopoeic thought (a mode of conceptualization predicated upon the dichotomy between cosmic and mundane) inevitable.

The move toward fully developed apocalyptic eschatology can be seen even by comparison with another relatively late composition which we studied earlier, Zechariah 12, for there the dichotomy between historical realities and the vision of the oppressed was not so extreme. True, hope had been abandoned concerning the participation of the faithful in the restoration; only Yahweh's intervention could inaugurate the change. But the suffering of the people and the trials of the end-time would have an effect on the entire nation, including those who were the oppressors, for through repentance and purification the nation would once again be made whole. No vision of restoration for the entire nation remains in Zechariah 14; no hope for a national repentance which could lead to purification of Israel; only a bloody purge whereby the wicked would be exterminated, leaving those who were destined to be recipients of the salvation to come. Thus the last ties with a conception of salvation along the lines defined by nationalism seem to be severed, yielding to a new dualism distinguishing not between nations but between evil and good on a broader scale. In the wake of this development is a strong impetus toward universalism in a much more radical sense than that found earlier in the tradition (e.g., in Second Isaiah). For if the distinguishing division of the end-time is not between the Jew and the foreigner, but between the righteous and the wicked, then that division could not easily be confined to Israel, but would extend outward to include all the nations of the world. It is no accident that the collapse of the political aspects of the prophetic office is followed closely by strong expressions of universalism unprecedented in earlier biblical tradition (Is 56:3–8; 66:18–23; Zech 14:16, 20–21; Mal 1:11).

But the dualism spawned by the deepening pessimism of the age penetrated beneath the social and political fabric of the world to the realm of nature, with the result of a blending of ethical dualism into ontological dualism. Conditions were so grim that the situation could not be righted by a change within human hearts alone, not even by a universal assize dividing the righteous from the wicked. The corruption had permeated the natural order itself. A notion found in Second Isaiah and developed in Isaiah 65 here is broadened to portray a full-scale reordering of the natural realm. The full impact of mythopoeic thought expresses itself at this point. The world is locked in a struggle between two orders, one ruled by sterility, corruption, death, the other by fertility, vitality, life. It is a struggle that effects not only the political sphere, but also the functions of nature. The end-time would have to produce new sources of energy to recreate a context which would once again be life-sustaining rather than life-destroying. As we shall see below, the legacy of classical prophetism to apocalyptic eschatology forced the exclusion of the endless cycle which was an original part of the mythopoeic pattern, for only one act of recreation was envisioned, not endless recreative acts. But that one recreation was conceived of in terms drawn heavily from mythic modes of thought.

The rigidifying of dualistic thinking also leads to a strengthening of a feature tracing back in Hebrew thought as far as Second Isaiah, the division of history into epochs. In Zechariah 14, the old era would culminate soon in the apocalyptic woes described with shocking vividness. These apocalyptic woes would be ended by Yahweh's final intervention and defeat of the hordes of the nations. Then would begin the universal reign of Yahweh, inaugurated by a new creation terminating the ancient polarities of the universe, and leading to a period of uninterrupted fertility, prosperity, and peace. This essential division provides the basis for the further elaboration of the notion of world epochs in later apocalyptic writings, and also provides compatible soil into which the notion of the four world empires could be transplanted and could flourish.

Once again, in this development of the notion of historical epochs we sense the impact of mythopoeic thought on Zechariah 14. The various periods into which the final events are divided reflect the cycle of the conflict myth: the onslaught of the rebellious gods against the dominant order, the battle of the warrior god against those disruptive powers, his victory and ascent to the mountain of his dominion, and his reordering of the universe issuing forth in the fertile waters which restore a primeval paradise bringing an end to the frightening threat of sterility.[72] It is obvious that *Urzeit* and *Endzeit* have drawn close together in this drama, seriously threatening the basic linear view of history developed by the classical prophets. Later apocalyptic writings will add nothing essential to this schema, but will further refine it by subdividing the world epochs into sub-units, and by enlarging the cosmic scope by broader inclusion of the heavenly bodies and various supernatural beings.

Within this picture of the end-time events, a picture dominated by the images of myth, it is not surprising to find almost complete abandonment of the attempt to relate the vision of the eschatological events to the affairs of the politico-historical realm. The nations of the world,[73] the ravished women, the exiled people, and the escaping remnant are mentioned, but they are passive objects in a drama acted out exclusively by the Cosmic Warrior, Yahweh.[74] This abdication of all responsibility to and interest in his-

72. The closest parallels for the basic scenario underlying Zechariah 14 are found in the adventures of Baal as portrayed in the Ugaritic literature (the reappearance of these images in the royal psalms draws attention to the mediating role of the royal cult in relation to later apocalyptic borrowings). For he is the storm god who engages in battle against Yamm/Mot, is victorious, establishes dominion from his newly constructed temple, scatters his enemies in an earth-shaking theophany, and from his holy mount sends forth the rains which fertilize the earth. At this late date, however, mixing of images is to be expected. In Zechariah 14 we are therefore not surprised to find that the closest parallel to the twin rivers flowing from the temple mount is the mount of El, "at the source of the two rivers," "in the midst of the pools of double deep" (3.5.13–16; 4.4.20–24; 6.1.32–36).

73. Even in Zechariah 9 mention of the nations is more firmly rooted in the historical realm than is the vague and inclusive term here, "all the nations," for in Zechariah 9 the traditional enemies of Israel are specified.

74. In Zechariah 9 and 10 Judah and Ephraim participate at least to the extent of being drawn into Yahweh's host for the battle (9:13; 10:3–5). Even this tenuous connection with history is lost in Zechariah 14.

torical realities bespeaks total loss of control over existing structures on the part of the visionaries. Dominating the scene is a vision of the restoration which loses all specificity, both in relation to the oppressors and the brethren, and dwells on the gruesome details of the final conflict issuing forth in the extermination of the enemy and the restoration of a brilliant paradise.[75] The powerful ethical consciousness of prophecy, which directed efforts toward bringing the sinner to repentance even in the very act of announcing judgment, has been swallowed up by a morbid preoccupation with the damnation of the oppressor. Such are the lamentable results of the polarization within a community between the bearers of power and the disenfranchised; to the latter remain only visions of what has proven impossible in history, visions which consequently remove themselves further and further from the realities of the community within which the visionaries live but are not a part.

With regard to the final level on which we have conducted our typological inquiry, we can point out that the struggle within the community between the hierocratic temple group and the visionaries, which we have traced as the matrix of the development of apocalyptic eschatology, reaches its most desperate level in this composition. In the oracles of Third Isaiah (e.g., chapters 58, 59, and even 65 and 66), the adversaries were at least taken seriously enough to be attacked specifically on the basis of their cultic and moral faults. Although the tendency toward hyperbole and generalization was evident, it had not led to the total disregard of all particulars which characterizes Zechariah 14. Even in Zechariah 12 this utter detachment from the particulars of the historical situation is not equalled. In that oracle, Jerusalem, though attacked by the foreign hordes, was yet delivered in the last moment by Yahweh and his host. After that deliverance, the inhabitants of Jerusalem

75. The morbid mentality with regard to the enemy manifested by Zech 14:12-15 is found also in the latest addition to Third Isaiah, in 66:24. Here the desire for punishment of the oppressor is not satisfied with final extermination, but develops the notion of perpetual punishment, perdition.

repented for their sin against the visionary group. In the present chapter no such deliverance and repentance occur. The hordes, gathered by Yahweh, penetrate Jerusalem itself, plundering, ravishing, removing one-half of the people. One can hardly imagine a more desperate and vindictive vision of Yahweh's dealings with the opponents of the visionaries within the post-exilic community.

All of the above typological considerations set a *terminus a quo* for Zechariah 14 of about 475 (the date suggested for Zechariah 12). It is very difficult to suggest a corresponding *terminus ad quem.* Noticeably absent are some of the features of the writings from the second century B.C. which develop further the tradition of apocalyptic eschatology. The division into world epochs has not yet been embellished by the four kingdoms theory, the lists of secrets of the universe have not yet become elaborated, the cosmos is still quite empty of supernatural adversaries, guardians, etc. Since all of the features of Zechariah 14 can be seen as unbroken developments from the visionary writings of the period from 520 to 475, and since the inner-community struggle between the visionaries and hierocrats which abetted the development of these features of apocalyptic eschatology seems to have abated toward the end of the fifth century (as indicated by the tolerant spirit of the Chronicler), we believe that a *terminus ad quem* of 425 recommends itself.

In the period following the missions of Nehemiah and Ezra, which seems to have been characterized by an amelioration of the animosity between the opposing elements within the community, the development of apocalyptic eschatology seems to have come to rest. In that period the writings of the visionaries, through various alterations and editorial arrangements, were drawn into the prophetic corpus. Isaiah 56–66 was attached to the Isaianic corpus by virtue of its close relation to the prophecy of Second Isaiah. Zechariah 9–11 and 12–14, having first been redacted into two booklets, were attached, together with a related booklet (Malachi), as anonymous documents onto the end of the collection of the "minor prophets." Thus they were preserved until the second century when community struggles similar to those which produced Isaiah 56-66 and Zechariah 9-14 again tore the Jewish community, leading visionaries of a new era to meditate upon those older visions, to reinterpret their significance for their new age by drawing typological connections, and to gain inspiration from them which produced additional works carrying the stream of apocalyptic eschatology into new periods and new stages of development.

CHAPTER V

An Allegory and Its Explication

Apocalyptic Eschatology was not born on Jewish soil of foreign parents. Both parents were natives. Somewhere in her training Persian magi or Egyptian wisemen may have fascinated her with their clever use of numbers and impressed her with their knowledge of the heavens; indeed she seems to have appropriated some of their learned teachings. But she used them to embellish a system of belief which was Jewish, for her birth occurred centuries before her contact with their learned secrets and calculations, and her early training was in the traditions of her own people. Though impossible to date with precision, her birth seems to have occurred in the latter half of the sixth century; by the close of the fifth century she had already come close to maturity.

The details of her birth are not clear, for it happened during troubled times in the Jewish community, times inaugurated by the disappearance of the Kingdom of Judah within the maelstrom of international politics, times shaken by the blows of a bitter struggle within the surviving post-exilic Jewish community between contending parties. Even her parentage is disputed among the scholars, although our research convinces us that her mother was Prophecy. The identity of her father is less clear; what evidence exists suggests that he was of royal birth. He was at any rate a man whose forms of thought were cosmopolitan, betraying the influence of the ancient Near Eastern royal courts.

A cloud of ambiguity veils the circumstances of the conception and birth of Apocalyptic Eschatology, as well as the early years of her development. Apparently the union bearing the child became possible only as a result of the father's fall from the throne, for in those earlier days of royalty his family and the family of Prophecy were not often on good terms, excluding the likelihood of close friendship and making marriage an impossibility. But the demise of his dynasty made the mating of Prophecy and fallen Royalty possible, leading finally to the conception and birth of Apocalyptic Eschatology.

The announcement of the birth was accompanied by rumors of death which persist to this day. Some claim that with the birth of Apocalyptic Eschatology, mother Prophecy died. Others assert that the death was only apparent, for in actuality the spirit of the mother lived on in the child. Those holding the latter view speak not of death and birth, but of metamorphosis. What seems certain is that the father asserted increasing influence upon the child as the latter approached maturity, for his predisposition toward the lore of myth became powerfully seductive to the young girl as she became introduced to the cruel realities of her post-exilic community, a community whose rulers harshly oppressed her and all like-minded people. There seems to be no question that both of her parents were religious, but their teachings differed in one important respect. Mother taught that their nation's God, Yahweh, acted on behalf of the oppressed within the events of history, a teaching which she found hard to accept as she grew amidst events which seemed to deny either God's power, or this concern for the oppressed, or both. Father's belief seemed more plausible, namely, that history belonged to a fallen order which would be supplanted on the day when Yahweh acted to save his people. Though never abandoning the basic belief of her mother that Yahweh would finally act to save his people, increasingly she came to express that belief in the mythic modes of thought which were favored by her father.

Let us now explicate our allegory by reiterating several cardinal features of the early history of apocalyptic eschatology which have become clear in our study. Repeatedly we have found evidence that apocalyptic eschatology derives from prophetic roots. Those roots were not petrified ones, however, maintaining their exact shape over the centuries. They were charged with life, and readily developed into new forms adapted to the changing post-exilic setting. The contextual-typological method which we applied was thus able to determine the approximate position of the various oracles studied within the continuum reaching from prophetic eschatology to the eschatology of fully developed apocalyptic.

In studying the history of the genres used in Third Isaiah and Second Zechariah, we were made aware of deep dependence upon the classical prophetic genres of the pre-exilic period, the oracle of judgment, the oracle of salvation, the oracle against the nations, etc. Equally apparent, however, was the rapid growth of new forms. Only Isaiah 60–62 and 57:14–21 remained close in form, as well as in style and theme, to Second Isaiah. The first important new genre to develop was the salvation-judgment oracle. In it the originally separate salvation and judgment oracles were fused into one hybrid oracle, thereby enabling the visionary to deliver a word which was simultaneously a word of salvation and a word of judgment. The *Sitz im Leben* of this hybrid oracle was a new situation in the post-exilic community within which there was no longer *one* Israel being promised either salvation or judgment, but *two* Israels, one the object of Yahweh's saving acts, the other of his wrath and judgment. The next notable development was the increasingly heavy borrowing of a genre dating back to the period of the league which had been preserved by the hymnody of the royal cult in Jerusalem, the Divine Warrior Hymn (e.g., Is 59:15b–19; 66:15–16; Zechariah 9). Stressing the cosmic aspect of Yahweh's acts and thus contrasting sharply with the austere historical orientation of pre-exilic prophecy, these hymns revivified themes which pointed toward an ultimate source of origin in ancient Near Eastern myth. In its fullest form these hymns incorporated the complete scenario of the ancient conflict myth (e.g., Zechariah 9 and 14). Thus on the level of the history of genres, a dynamic was visible which was recasting the prophetic oracle in radically new forms, and thereby transforming prophetic genres into the genres of apocalyptic.

What was clear on the level of genres was equally clear on the level of religious ideas. As a point-for-point comparison between Isaiah 60 and Zechariah 14 (the earliest and the latest compositions studied) indicated, the basic vision held by the disciples of Second Isaiah remained constant throughout the material which we studied: it was a vision of a righteous and holy community restored to a glorified Zion, in which all would be priests of Yahweh possessing Israel as their inheritance and secure from the threat of enemies whether from without or within; according to this vision, the glorious restoration would occur on the day of Yahweh's saving action on behalf of his people. While the vision remained constant, the conceptual modes utilized to verbalize it underwent profound change, as can be seen especially when one considers the degree to which that vision was integrated into the categories of history and politics.

Increasingly the view of the classical prophets that God's promises to his people would be fulfilled within the context of historical events yielded to the belief that fulfillment would be imposed upon a fallen world in a cataclysmic display of force by the Cosmic Warrior Yahweh. By the mid-fifth century the visionary group's evaluation of the capacity of historical events as carriers of the salvation hope had grown so bleak as to engender the conviction that restoration could occur only after a disruptive and devastating series of events in which Yahweh would annul the order established at the creation of the world, supplanting it with a new paradisiacal order of harmony and prosperity. Within this dualistic view of reality, which moved the religion of the visionaries dangerously close to the worldview of myth, history began to lose the salvific significance with which it had been impregnated by the classical prophets in their effort to translate the cosmic vision into the idiom of historical events. In apocalyptic eschatology we detect historical events being used less and less frequently to construct a *Heilsgeschichte,* increasingly as data for learned speculation regarding the cosmic timetable: according to the events of the world, how close do we stand to the day of Yahweh, that turning point from the old era of decay to the new world of shalom? This speculation on the cosmic timetable is not yet full-blown in our material, for it would ultimately produce the elaborate historical resumés, specifying for the faithful the precise point at which they stood in the sweep of history from creation to the eschaton (e.g. 1 Enoch 85-90, 93:3-10; 91:12-17; Assumption of Moses 2-10; 2 Esd 3:4-27; Apocalypse of Baruch 53-74). But as Zech 11:4-17 (+ 13:7-9) and Zechariah 14 indicate, we already have in the fifth century the periodization of history which supplied the basis for the later elaboration.

From this view of historical events of the past as episodes in the progressive degeneration of the old order springs the powerful sense of determinism which characterizes the late apocalyptic writings. Yahweh is still suzerain, as he was in classical prophecy, but the arena in which he is active to redeem his elect is no longer primarily the historical realm. Salvific events have detached themselves from history, and have moved closer to the cosmic events of ancient myth. Historical events at most record the judging actions of Yahweh which prepare for the saving events, and even this role of history is eventually replaced to a large degree in late writings by the great assize before Yahweh's throne. At any rate, according to the apocalyptic vision, on the day in which the saving events would be manifested to the faithful the structures of this world would yield before the breaking-in of a new order. Within this otherworldly orientation, historical events and figures were not seriously reckoned with as agents of Yahweh's saving actions. That is to say, the heirs of the prophetic tradition by the fifth century had largely abdicated their role of responsibility to the historical realm, and had virtually given up their mission of translating their vision of Yahweh's cosmic acts into the idiom of history and politics.

After all of these points of contrast with classical prophecy and points of similarity with myth have been recognized, however, it is still obvious that in the early apocalyptic writings as in the late, we have not returned full circle to the mythopoeic religious systems of second millennium Canaan. The great cataclysm and cosmic transformation does not recur seasonally in apocalyptic eschatology, locking the world in an endless cycle, but is envisioned as a once-and-for-all event of the eschaton. History, while losing much of its primary salvific character, still takes the form of a linear development according to divine plan toward a promised goal. The lives of the faithful are still lived out within the covenant framework between promise and fulfillment. While primordial events and eschatological events closely approximate each other by drawing on the images of the same mythic ritual pattern, they never merge, being separated by a memory of the history of the nation which the apocalyptic seers could never remove fully from their thinking. Even in a composition like Zechariah 14, where the eschatological events are described in terms reminiscent of the primordial, a significant fact maintains the separation: the new creation will initiate an order which is genuinely new in contrast to the creation in the primordial times; in fact the new creation will supplant the old creation with a new order. While the description of the *Endzeit* resembles closely the ancient descriptions of the *Urzeit,* closer comparison therefore reveals not identification which reduces to a circle, but a distinct movement from *Urzeit* to *Endzeit,* via the history of the nation Israel, which can be diagramed only on a linear scale.

Inquiry into the history of genres and the development of religious ideas has thus revealed both an undeniable continuity with the traditions of the past (especially those of the "school" of Isaiah) and a powerful impetus toward new modes of expressing old promises and hopes. But another aspect of our contextual-typological method remains to be considered, for without it the phenomenon of the development of apocalyptic eschatology out of earlier prophetic roots remains in many respects incomprehensible. For example, the literary influence of the Divine Warrior Hymn does not in itself furnish sufficient explanation for the profound influence which that genre had upon the eschatological thought of the sixth and fifth centuries. Nor can the transformation of the historical orientation of the prophets into the otherworldly orientation of the visionaries be explained on the basis of some dynamic of inevitability. Israel's earliest hymnic literature indicates that in a time of optimism and vitality the faith of Israel was able to take mythic forms and ideas and force them into conformity with the beliefs of Yahwism. Why at this later period were those same mythic forms and ideas able to assert such force in bringing *Yahwism* into conformity with *them*?

Our study has emphasized that an adequate explanation of the rise of Jewish apocalyptic thinking must take into full account the historical and sociological forces impinging upon the post-exilic Jewish community. Before the influence of the Divine Warrior Hymn could be felt, before the otherwordly orientation of myth could reassert itself, the community situation had to be one which spawned in some of its members a profound sense of the inadequacy of old forms and conceptual modes, and a deep need for new forms of expression and modes of thought. It is this sociological dimension in our method which demonstrated the uselessness of static definitions of apocalyptic, whether of a literary or a theological sort. Apocalyptic eschatology represents a certain perspective, a distinct way of looking at reality. Its protagonists do not one day decide to adopt apocalyptic modes of thought, nor do they adopt them because of their membership in a given religious party. Rather, their position within the institutions and structures of their society condition their perspective on the world, until the point is reached where they find that their beliefs can best find expression in the vision of a more perfect order which will one day be imposed on a degenerate world. Apocalyptic modes of thought are thus not the property of one religious party in Israel. In the sixth century the opponents of the Zadokite priests expressed their faith with the use of apocalyptic forms and were oppressed by the Zadokites; in the second century the Zadokite priests expressed their faith with apocalyptic forms and were oppressed by the Hasmoneans. What did the visionaries of the sixth century and the Zadokites of the second have in common? Not party affiliation, but a common status in the community.

Our study indicated that that status was one of disenfranchisement and alienation from the institutional structures of the community which made peers of disciples of Second Isaiah, defrocked Levitical priests, and likely other minorities within the community which remain anonymous to us. This sociological position led the visionaries to a growing pessimism regarding the adequacy of historical structures as carriers of the salvation hope. This pessimism in turn called into question some of the modes of thought of earlier prophecy. By the same token, it awakened within them a fascination with the mythic forms which were used by Second Isaiah as metaphors adding a dimension of universalism and theological depth to his proclamation. These metaphors, however, they read increasingly as literal descriptions of the cosmic events which would finally extricate them from a situation which in historical terms had grown bleak and intolerable. The dynamic thereby set in motion was self-accelerating, for as their pessimism deepened, their vindictiveness toward the powerful, hierocratic leaders of the community increased. The response on the part of the latter was further oppression, leading the visionaries to even deeper pessimism vis-à-vis the historical order and further flight into the timeless repose of a mythic realm of salvation. Our study has suggested that the period in which the polarizarion between the hierocratic leaders and the disenfranchised visionaries was the most severe was from about 520 to 420. After that efforts by the hierocratic leaders (including Ezra's mission) to restore inner-community peace seem to have ameliorated the situation. Not until two centuries later did new inner-community strife provide the impetus for the further development of apocalyptic eschatology.

Although the present writer has begun a study of the implications of Jewish apocalyptic for contemporary theology and ethics which will be published at a later time, certain observations can be made here which point beyond the analysis of apocalyptic eschatology toward broader concerns. First, in the face of evidence which has exposed a much wider polarization within the post-exilic community than most earlier studies would suggest, it is our hope that the theological solution to this phenomenon will not be found in endorsement of the theological position of one of the parties in the struggle and condemnation of the other. We have sought to make heroes of neither visionaries nor hierocrats, and have posited as the ideal neither an oppressed apocalyptic seer nor a powerful hierocratic leader. Insofar as we dare suggest a model for a position which adequately takes into account the rich visionary dimension of early biblical tradition at the same time as it upholds responsibility to the realm of history and politics, we would suggest that a prophet like Isaiah comes close to the ideal. In his prophecy vision was integrated into politics without thereby losing its normative character. Isaiah, however, lived in a period in which priest and prophet, while often engaged in controversy, were yet able to draw upon the traditions of the same cult and to claim membership in the same nation. The situation which we have studied in the sixth and fifth centuries was different, characterized by a severe split of the community into two contending factions and by extreme polarization of the visionary and realistic aspects of biblical faith. The danger attending this development was that the faith of Israel would be divided into a flat theology of expediency on the one hand and a utopian theology of escape on the other, with both lacking the element of tension present in the proclamation of Isaiah, a man of faith living out his career within the field of tension between the vision of Yahweh's Kingdom and a sense of responsibility for his earthly community.

For a community or an individual who takes the Bible seriously as the word of God, the theological questions raised by our interpretation of the early post-exilic community are serious. The preponderant emphasis upon Israel's historical confessions in works dealing with biblical theology has helped establish the impression in the minds of many that the Old Testament comprises one normative theological current recording a smooth, uninterrupted disclosure of God's will to his community, an impression which is rudely shattered by the discordant voices of the late seventh, sixth, and fifth centuries delivering irreconcilable messages in the name of the same Yahweh. What interpretation can one offer, in the face of conflicting messages from Haggai and the visionary of Isaiah 66, one proclaiming God's will that the temple be built, the other rejecting the temple plan and condemning the practices and leaders of the temple cult?

According to methods of interpretation prevalent in the past, we are faced with unpleasant alternatives: either deny that such internal polemic exists in the Old Testament and attempt to harmonize the "apparent" discrepancies or try to establish the truth of one of the claims over against the other(s). We suggest that this approach has elevated the concept of biblical revelation to an indefensibly high level of abstraction. Revelation in the Bible is not the announcement of immutable truths, but is a record of Yahweh's involvement in the crises and struggles of his human community. The theological thrust of the Old Testament cannot be grasped by dealing with words extracted from their community setting, for Yahweh's will breaks through to the faithful not in isolation from the struggles of the Jewish community, and not on one side of the struggle rather than the other, but amidst such struggle. For as different factions in Israel contend with each other, they are reaching for the God who is at once too near and too far to be encompassed by any theological system, too much present in the midst of his people and yet too remote to be comprehended by any individual. Revelation thus is found not in an unbroken progression stemming from the creation to the eschaton, but occurs in a dialectical movement often marked by tension and dissension, frequently tottering between the extremes of desperate escape into the repose of the cosmic vision and myopic preoccupation with the day-to-day control of cult and community.

If the confession of Scripture is true, that it speaks of "the Lord, who stretched out the heavens and founded the earth and formed the spirit of man within him" (Zech 12:1), can we expect a more transparent, convenient mode of revelation? When one juxtaposes the history of the Deuteronomists, the outcry of Job, the vision of the "school of Second Isaiah" and the prophecy of Haggai, one becomes sorely aware of the fact that Scripture offers no facile solution to the heart-rending and mind-boggling questions raised by human experience. It offers instead a faithful record of men and women addressing those questions from different perspectives within the community of faith, and moving their hearers closer to a proper stance before God often as much by virtue of the points of incongruity between their messages as by the points of accord. That record, moreover, becomes more than past history for those that stand within the contemporary extension of that same community of faith; it becomes an invitation to appropriate and internalize the very tensions which tore at the fibers of the early Jewish community and brought it closer to the One whose name the faithful dared not utter, the incomprehensible YHWH; an invitation to become a part of a community which still struggles within a field of tension midway between a vision of God's righteous and perfect Kingdom and the harsh realities and incredible needs of this world; and not merely an invitation, but a reiteration of an ancient promise as well, that in that community of faith, God is still active, and that ultimately his Kingdom will be realized among men and women.

Within that record are found both positive and negative instances of the challenges raised by the dialectic of faith. For example, balanced against Isaiah's courageous mission of integrating vision and reality is the post-exilic community's polarization into a vision-oriented group and a pragmatically inclined party. Especially for our generation, whose young and disenfranchised are beholding visions of the dawn of a new apocalyptic era, we dare not exclude from the canon those writings which offer the community of faith greater pain than comfort. For the pain of those writings perhaps can convey to our generation a more poignant message than the comfort of the classical oracle of salvation: God's Kingdom will draw closer to us when those in positions of power become receptive to a vision of a community in which distinctions between lords and slaves, oppressors and oppressed dissolve into a new unity in which the "people shall all be righteous . . . , guardians of the plantation of Yahweh" (60:21); and when those with visions of God's order of righteousness struggle tirelessly, even when faced with persecution, to translate that vision into the structures of a suffering society. At that point the dialectic of faith will not only be upheld in the hearts of individual saints, but will be woven into the fabric of the human community. "Thy Kingdom come. . . !"

Select Bibliography

Indexes

Appendix

Select Bibliography

(The brackets contain shortened references used in the text and the footnotes.)

Ackroyd, P. R. *Exile and Restoration.* Philadelphia: Westminster, 1968. [Ackroyd, *Exile*]

Adams, J. L. "The Pragmatic Theory of Meaning." Presidential Address, American Society of Christian Ethics, Washington, D. C., January 24, 1969. [Adams, "Theory"]

Block, J. *On the Apocalyptic in Judaism. JQR* Monograph Series 2. Philadelphia: Dropsie College, 1952. [Block, *Apocalyptic*]

Brownlee, W. H. *The Meaning of the Qumrân Scrolls for the Bible with Special Attention to the Book of Isaiah.* New York: Oxford University, 1964. [Brownlee, *Meaning*]

Chary, Th. *Les Prophètes et le Culte.* Paris: Desclée, 1955. [Chary, *Prophètes*]

Childs, B. *Myth and Reality in the Old Testament,* SBTh 27. London: SCM, 1960. [Childs, *Myth*]

Clifford, R. J. *The Cosmic Mountain in Canaan and the Old Testament.* Harvard Semitic Monographs 4. Cambridge: Harvard University, 1972. [Clifford, *Mountain*]

Cross, F. M., Jr. *Canaanite Myth and Hebrew Epic: Essays in the History of the Religion of Israel.* Cambridge: Harvard University, 1973. [Cross, *Myth*]

Dentan, R. C. *Zechariah 9–14,* IB 6. New York: Abingdon, 1956. [Dentan, *Zechariah*]

Duhm, B. *Das Buch Jesaia,* HAT. Göttingen: Vandenhoeck und Ruprecht, 1922[4]. [Duhm]

Eissfeldt, O. *The Old Testament: An Introduction,* translated by P. R. Ackroyd. New York: Harper & Row, 1965. [Eissfeldt, *Introduction*]

Elliger, K. *Deuterojesaja in seinem Verhältnis zu Tritojesaja.* Stuttgart: Kohlhammer, 1933. [Elliger, *Deuterojesaja*]

———. *Die Einheit des Tritojesaia.* Stuttgart: Kohlhammer, 1928. [Elliger, *Einheit*]

Fohrer, G. *Das Buch Jesaja* III. ZB. Zurich: Zwingli, 1964. [Fohrer]

Frost, S. B. *Old Testament Apocalyptic: Its Origins and Growth.* London: Epworth, 1952. [Frost, *Apocalyptic*]

Gese, H. "Anfang und Ende der Apokalyptik, dargestellt am Sacharjabuch." *Theologie und Kirche* 70 (1973): 20–49. [Gese, "Anfang"]

———. *Der Verfassungsentwurf des Ezekiel (Kap. 40–48). Traditionsgeschichtlich Untersucht.* BHTh 25. Tübingen J. C. B. Mohr (Paul Siebeck), 1957. [Gese, *Verfassungsentwurf*]

Glahn, L. and Koehler, L. *Der Prophet der Heimkehr.* 2 vols. Giessen: Töpelmann, 1934. [Glahn, *Prophet*]

Habel, N. C. "Yahweh, Maker of Heaven and Earth: A Study in Tradition Criticism." *JBL* 91 (1972): 321–337. [Habel, "Yahweh"]

Hanson, P. D. "Jewish Apocalyptic Against Its Near Eastern Environment." *RB* 78 (1971): 31–58. [Hanson, "Jewish Apocalyptic"]

———. "Old Testament Apocalyptic Reexamined." *Int* 25 (1971): 454–479. [Hanson, "Old Testament"]

Janssen, E. *Juda in der Exilzeit.* FRLANT 69. Göttingen: Vandenhoeck und Ruprecht, 1956. [Janssen, *Juda*]

Koch, K. *The Rediscovery of Apocalyptic,* translated by M. Kohl. SBTh 2nd Series 22. London: SCM, 1972. [Koch, *Apocalyptic*]

Kraeling, E. G. H. "The Historical Situation in Zechariah 9:1–10." *AJSLL* 14 (1924–5): 24–33. [Kraeling, "Situation"]

McKenzie, J. *Second Isaiah,* AB 20. Garden City: Doubleday, 1968. [McKenzie]

Mannheim, K. *Ideology and Utopia,* translated by L. Wirth and E. Shils. New York: Harcourt, Brace and Co., 1936. [Mannheim, *Ideology*]

Miller, P. D., Jr. *The Divine Warrior in Early Israel.* Cambridge: Harvard University, 1973. [Miller, *Divine Warrior*]

Muilenburg, J. *Isaiah.* IB 5. New York: Abingdon, 1956. [Muilenburg]

Otzen, B. *Studien über Deuterosacharja.* Copenhagen: Prostant Apud Munksgaard, 1964. [Otzen, *Studien*]

Parsons, T. "Introduction" to M. Weber's *The Sociology of Religion,* translated by E. Fischoff. Boston: Beacon, 1963. [Parsons, "Introduction"]

Plöger, O. *Theocracy and Eschatology,* translated by S. Rudman. Richmond: John Knox, 1968. [Plöger, *Theocracy*]

Rad, G. von. *Old Testament Theology II,* translated by D. M. G. Stalker. New York: Harper & Row, 1965. [von Rad, *Theology II*]

Russell, D. S. *The Method and Message of Jewish Apocalyptic.* Philadelphia: Westminster, 1964. [Russell, *Apocalyptic*]

Schmidt, J. M. *Die jüdische Apokalyptik. Die Geschichte ihrer Erforshung von den Anfangen bis zu den Textfunden von Qumran.* Neukirchen-Vluyn: Neukirchener, 1969. [Schmidt, *Apokalyptik*]

Sellin, E. *Das Zwölfprophetenbuch,* KAT. Leipzig: Deichert, 1929². [Sellin]

Smart, J. *History and Theology in Second Isaiah.* Philadelphia: Westminster, 1965. [Smart, *History*]

Stone, M. "Lists of Revealed Things in the Apocalyptic Literature." Forthcoming in the G. Ernest Wright Festschrift. [Stone, "Lists"]

Torrey, C. C. *The Second Isaiah.* New York: Charles Scribner's Sons, 1928. [Torrey]

Troeltsch, E. *The Social Teaching of the Christian Churches,* 2 vols., translated by O. Wyon. New York: Harper & Row, 1960. [Troeltsch, *Teaching* I]

de Vaux, R. *Ancient Israel: Its Life and Institutions,* translated by J. McHugh. New York: McGraw-Hill, 1968. [deVaux, *Israel*]

Volz, P. *Jesaia* II, KAT. Leipzig: D. W. Scholl, 1932. [Volz]

Weber, M. *The Sociology of Religion,* translated by E. Fischoff. Boston: Beacon, 1963. [Weber, *Sociology*]

Weiser, A. *The Old Testament: Its Formation and Development,* translated by D. M. Barton. New York: Association, 1961. [Weiser, *Old Testament*]

Westermann, C. *Isaiah 40–66,* translated by D. M. G. Stalker. Philadelphia: Westminster, 1969. [Westermann]

Wright, G. E. *The Book of Isaiah.* The Layman's Bible Commentary. Richmond: John Knox, 1964. [Wright]

Zimmerli, W. *Ezekiel.* BK. Neukirchen: Neukirchener, 1956. [Zimmerli, *Ezekiel*]

———. "Zur Sprache Tritojesajas." In *Gottes Offenbarung,* pp. 217–233. München: Chr. Kaiser, 1963. [Zimmerli, "Sprache"]

Indexes

PASSAGE INDEX

AUTHOR INDEX

SUBJECT INDEX

Appendix: An Overview of Early Jewish and Christian Apocalypticism

Jewish and Christian seers of antiquity were not the last to gaze out over a world engulfed by war and desolation and discern behind human armies the presence of demonic hosts. Amos Wilder, as a soldier caught in the throes of World War I, concluded, "Our strife was but the mimicry of heaven's and we the shadows of celestial foes."[1] Dietrich Bonhoeffer, as he watched from his prison cell a world driven toward destruction by madmen, wrote, "There cannot be anyone who has not either in his work or in his private life had some sort of experience of the increasingly impatient attacks of the forces of the Antichrist."[2] The apocalyptic perspective, the perception of human plans and endeavors shattered by forces of superhuman size and the abandoning of all hope save that which focuses on divine intervention, is as alive today as in bygone ages. In fact, no longer are war and desolation prerequisites for the apocalyptic response. A vague feeling of dissatisfaction with modern life seems sufficient basis for laments over "the late great planet earth."[3]

Since biblical apocalyptic writings have always been the favored source of support and authority for latter-day seers, it is important that those writings be understood aright, which is to say, within their historical-social setting. For only if their original setting and function are understood can they be related in a responsible manner to contemporary crises. The need to understand biblical apocalypticism within its original setting provided the impetus for the study in this book. What better place to begin in the effort to understand this elusive phenomenon than with its very dawning?

While the subject area still stands in need of specific textual and historical studies—there being sufficient works addressing the phenomenon of apocalyptic with generalizations which neither ad-

1. Amos Wilder, *Battle-Retrospect and Other Poems,* The Yale Series of Younger Poets (New Haven: Yale University Press, 1923), p. 31.

2. Cited by Eberhard Bethge, *Dietrich Bonhoeffer,* tr. E. Mosbacher (New York: Harper & Row, 1970), p. 489.

3. To use the title of Hal Lindsey's best-seller.

vance our understanding nor base conclusions on careful research—it is needful as well to keep clearly in mind the overall phenomenon of biblical apocalypticism as specific phases of its development are examined in detail. With this latter need in mind, the present appendix seeks to offer an overview of biblical apocalypticism.[4]

From the start it must be recognized that scholars divide over the definition of apocalypticism. At root are Greek words meaning "to reveal" and "revelation." Since this root is found in the book of Revelation, it has been extended to designate other writings which share features with that biblical book. But as is often the case with casual classifications, with this extension came confusion, for there was from the start unclarity over which characteristics of the book of Revelation defined it as apocalyptic. Were literary features the distinguishing marks? Or a particular perspective on reality? Or is the book of Revelation apocalyptic because it was the product of a certain type of socio-religious movement?

Such questions suggest that *apocalyptic* and related terms imply several levels of meaning. Once these are sorted out, the book of Revelation contributes to definitions on these several levels. First, Rev 1:1 indicates that *apokalypsis* (apocalypse) designates this book's literary genre. Rev 1:1–2 gives the bare essentials of that genre: it is a literary vehicle used for the revelation of future events by God through the mediation of an angel to a human servant. While an organic view of literary genres will not impose this definition rigidly on all candidates for this classification, the book of Revelation, as the classical example of the genre apocalypse, must be taken carefully into account in attempts at classifying related works according to literary type.

Secondly, study of the perspective of the book of Revelation indicates that it grows out of a way of viewing reality in relation to divine providence which reaches back to Hebrew prophecy. Its author does not hesitate to use the word prophecy in referring to his message, and the repeated references to prophetic books firmly establishes this line of connection. Clearly the book of Revelation fits into a developing perspective which we can designate as eschatology.

Thirdly, the fact that scholars reconstruct the historical setting of the book of Revelation in the Roman persecutions and find its

4. This appendix was added at the urging of several colleagues in the field who report that they have found it useful to assign my articles "Apocalypticism" and "Apocalypse, Genre" from the Supplementary Volume of the *Interpreter's Dictionary of the Bible* (Nashville: Abingdon, 1976), pp. 27–34, as the first reading assignment in courses using *The Dawn of Apocalyptic* as a textbook.

function in the nurturing of hope and comfort among those suffering for their faith leads to recognition of another dimension of definition to which this book draws attention, that designating the type of religious movement of which it is a product.

Apart from the book of Revelation, the Greek root in question is used in the New Testament primarily in reference to the divine disclosure of saving plans which up to that time had been hidden. Central to such revelation was the series of events recorded concerning Jesus' life (Matt 16:17; Eph 3:1–5). But included as well was a forward look toward the consummation of those events in the parousia (Luke 17:30; Rom 2:5; 2 Thess 1:7; 1 Pet 4:13). According to Paul, this gospel was received not from the apostles but through a "revelation" (Gal 1:11–17).

Such usage does not amplify the definitions we have begun to develop on the basis of the book of Revelation, but it does indicate that broader parts of the New Testament fit into the perspective of apocalyptic eschatology, as Ernst Käsemann and others have pointed out. For these various other New Testament passages relate the root to the unveiling of divine plans amid history's unfolding, especially within that series of events which inaugurated a new aeon, events participating in a cosmic drama of salvation derived not from human planning but from divine initiative.

From the book of Revelation, corroborated in a general way by broader New Testament usage, we have a basis for evolving three levels of definition. While other works will be taken into account in these definitions, the historical priority of the book of Revelation's designation as apocalyptic gives to it a primary position. That is to say, careful attention must be paid to this work in defining the genre *apocalypse,* the perspective of *apocalyptic eschatology,* and the type of religious movement we call *apocalypticism.* While being precise in our definition and use of these three terms, we can apply the adjective *apocalyptic* when referring to the overall phenomenon in a less differentiated manner.

The attempt to understand the apocalyptic phenomenon has been inhibited by repeated efforts at definition through the compilation of lists of characteristics which supposedly constitute an apocalyptic writing. Not only do such lists indiscriminately mix the three levels mentioned above, but they include features which are randomly distributed among the writings in question. This serves as a warning that we are dealing with a multifaceted phenomenon, and a phenomenon which is undergoing constant development and change. Lists, be they of literary features or of concepts, are too abstract to define such a living entity. The definitions we use, therefore, address three different levels and attempt to preserve the organic nature of apocalyptic in its relation to socio-religious and historical realities which, ever changing, leave their imprint on all stages of its development.

The term *apocalypse* should be applied strictly as the designation of a literary genre. It is one of the favored media adopted by apocalyptic seers for communicating their message, though it is not the exclusive nor even the dominant genre. Rather, it takes its place among other genres such as the testament, the salvation-judgment oracle, and the parable as a means of giving expression to the perspective of apocalyptic eschatology and as a vehicle for expressing the ideology of an apocalyptic movement. As in the case of all genres, the apocalypse is not rigid but underwent a history of development over the biblical and post-biblical period. A typical example is found in Rev 1:9–20, where the revelation of God occurs as the seer is allowed to peer into the heavens (cf. 4:1), where he beholds a drama which is determinative of future events in human history. Ecstasy is involved, as indicated by the phrase "in the Spirit" (1:10; 4:2). The Lord may address the seer directly in the apocalypse, as in Rev 1:17–20, though in other apocalypses the revelation is through the mediation of an angelic interpreter (1:1; 17:1–18; 22:6). A motif commonly incorporated in the apocalypse is rapture, in which the seer is guided by an angel through heavenly places, which constitutes another medium of revelation (21:9–22:5). The response of the seer is one of awe (1:17; cf. 22:8), commonly followed by a word of assurance or admonition from the angel or the Lord (1:17; 22:9). While the media used may range from a "literal" description of a heavenly drama to revelation in the form of elaborate symbolism, the revelation of the apocalypse always has bearing on events to come (1:19; cf. 1:1; 4:1). Finally, we can note that the usual function of the apocalypse is that of giving comfort to those tested by persecution and giving them encouragement to remain steadfast in their faith. While the book of Revelation serves quite well in illustrating this genre, the reader may wish to consult the broader sketch of the development of the apocalypse found in the Supplementary Volume of the *Interpreter's Dictionary of the Bible* referred to in footnote 4.

The undeniable connections between writings commonly designated apocalyptic and prophetic writings leads to the second level of definition, what we designate apocalyptic eschatology. This level of definition must take into account two facts. First, the stream of tradition flowing from prophecy through apocalyptic does not constitute the whole; for alongside this traditional material are found materials deriving from Greek, Hellenistic, and possibly other foreign sources, as well as indigenous sapiential materials. Secondly, the perspective which we define with this term, while rooted in prophecy, is not identical with the prophet's perspective. For these reasons we find it useful to identify apocalyptic eschatology as *one* current (even if the dominant one) among others in the complex phenomenon called apocalyptic, which perspective, while growing out of is yet distinct from prophecy, a connection and distinction preserved by the contrast between prophetic eschatology and apocalyptic eschatology. This manner of definition enables one to trace the organic growth of apocalyptic out of prophecy while allowing both for the obvious changes in the prophetic perspective and for the equally obvious addition of other perspectives and materials which flow into apocalyptic works. Only careful literary and historical studies of the works in question can trace this complex growth by giving close attention both to continuities and to new directions.

Apocalyptic eschatology, therefore, is neither a genre (apocalypse) nor a socio-religious movement (apocalypticism) but a religious *perspective* which views divine plans in relation to historical realities in a particular way. Some scholars have made the mistake of identifying it with a particular religious party in Israel. It is not, however, the exclusive property of any particular group, and in a given period its adoption by a given party is determined less by the past history of that party than by its status in a given period. As a perspective, moreover, it does not describe a posture which a particular party or individual espouses or rejects completely, but may be incorporated in varying degrees in combination with other perspectives, a phenomenon with parallel among modern individuals who can combine religious, superstitious, and scientific views. Apocalyptic eschatology, thus defined, allows one to account for the eschatological elements held in common by groups as diverse as Qumran sectarians and rabbinical commentators, even as it allows one to be open to the diversity of perspectives present in the so-called apocalyptic writings. Rigid distinctions such as that drawn by Dietrich Roessler between the legal orientation of the rabbis and the historical perspective of apocalypticism[5] thus are replaced by categories more sensitive to the contents of the texts themselves.

The line of connection between prophetic eschatology and apocalyptic eschatology can be seen in the orientation of both

5. Dietrich Roessler, *Gesetz und Geschichte,* WMANT 3 (Neukirchen-Vluyn: Neukirchener Verlag, 1960).

toward the future as the context of divine redemption and judging activity. The two are differentiated by the degree to which that activity is regarded to be integrated into the structures of historical realities and mediated by human agency. Though prophetic eschatology had its starting point in a vision of divine intention (e.g., Isaiah 6), that intention was grasped very much amid the events and persons of the political world (e.g., Isaiah 7). But in the period between 587 and the Maccabean era the harsh realities of this world made discernment of divine intention amid historical events increasingly difficult for persons taking their directions from a vision of divine drama. With nationhood lost, prophetic and priestly offices taken away, and social and religious institutions controlled by adversaries, world-weary visionaries began to recognize in a mythologized version of eschatology a more promising way of keeping alive a hope for final vindication. As a more transcendent view began to break with prophetic integration, the tension between bleak realities and brilliant promises began to dissolve as the perspective of prophetic eschatology gave way to that of apocalyptic eschatology. The fulfillment which a world fallen to evil powers denied the present order was now envisioned for a future order in which all evil would be banished by the Divine Warrior/King/Creator Yahweh: "For behold, I create new heavens and a new earth; and the former things shall not be remembered or come to mind" (Isa 65:17).

What is the relationship between apocalyptic eschatology and the next level we shall define, apocalypticism? While the two are not to be identified, one should note that apocalypticism as a socio-religious movement is latent in the perspective of apocalyptic eschatology. At the point where the disappointments of history lead a group to embrace that perspective as an ideology, using it moreover to resolve the contradictions between traditional hopes and frustrating historical realities and to establish the identity of that group vis-à-vis other groups as well as the Deity, we can speak of the birth of an apocalyptic movement. Such a birth is described in this book. It occurred in the early post-exilic period. Similar births were to occur again in the second century B.C.E., in the second century C.E., in the Middle Ages, and in subsequent centuries as well.

We come to the third level of definition by describing apocalypticism as the system of concepts and symbols in which an apocalyptic movement codifies its identity and gives expression to its interpretation of reality. Such a system may be called a symbolic universe. The symbolic universe of any given apocalyptic movement will be determined by complex factors including the past traditions of the group developing into an apocalyptic movement, the particular socio-political conditions within which it lives, materials with which it comes into contact from surrounding cultures, the beliefs and attitudes of rival parties, etc. Therefore it is not possible to give a single cognitive definition of apocalypticism, a point reinforced by the fact that typically an apocalyptic universe of meaning develops not in a state of tranquil reflection but as a protest against bitter opposition from the dominant social system or foreign power. Systematic consistency is hardly a priority in such a setting. In the pressing need to define spiritual identity in the face of challenge, and to sustain hope, a basic perspective is nevertheless identifiable around which apocalyptic systems grow: it is the perspective of apocalyptic eschatology, which furnishes a way of viewing reality which denies the apparent superior position of opposing groups of any ultimate validity vis-à-vis divine purpose. The chosen suffer and the ungodly prosper only because the present era stands on the threshold of a great reversal, when God will intervene to vindicate the righteous and oppressed visionary party.

Ancient apocalyptic movements were able to assimilate very diverse materials, so long as those materials could be used to develop the eschatological perspective of the group in question. Hence we find materials drawn together from ancient Canaanite myth, neo-Babylonian astronomy, Greek myth, Hellenistic historiography, Jewish and Egyptian wisdom, Persian religion, alongside copious reference to and commentary upon biblical writings. Small wonder that the impression often made upon the reader is that he or she is dealing with compositions which seem baroque, highly eclectic, esoteric, even bizarre and arcane.

What, however, unifies such diverse material sufficiently to allow us even to speak of apocalyptic literature? We have seen that identification of apocalypses by form-critical analysis only isolates a small proportion of the literature produced by apocalyptic movements. Study of the texts must reach further and can be guided by the fact that all ancient apocalyptic movements were characterized by (a) an identifiable type of social setting and (b) a related group response.

First, the social setting shared by apocalyptic movements is the group experience of alienation. Bleak conditions call into question traditional socio-religious structures and their supporting myths. Life is situated precariously over the abyss. This can be the result either of the destruction of cultural customs by a foreign invader or of the exclusion of one segment of a society from participation in normative structures and institutions. A vacuum is created which seeks a means of warding off the threat both of social disintegration (Isa 24:1–13) and cosmic collapse (Isa 24:17–23).

The vacuum caused by the group experience of alienation explains the nature of the response. Unless a new symbolic universe is constructed to replace the old, life will lapse into chaos. From traditions of the past, from neighboring cultures, and from everyday experience images and concepts are drawn into the central perspective of the group in the critical process of reconstruction. What determines whether the response of a given group develops into an apocalyptic movement is whether it embraces apocalyptic eschatology as the perspective from which it constructs an alternative universe of meaning and to which it assimilates the various types of materials mentioned above. The central view of apocalyptic eschatology, namely, that God, who guides all reality toward a goal, was about to intervene to reverse the fortunes of the prosperous wicked and the suffering righteous, was the rallying point around which an oppressed visionary group could maintain its sense of identity and its vision of ultimate vindication in spite of experiences seemingly denying both. All appearances notwithstanding, such a group could claim, the real direction of history was being determined not by those enjoying positions of power and privilege but by events already under way in the heavenly sphere which soon would be manifested on earth for all to see: "For behold, the Lord will come in fire, and his chariots like the stormwind, to render his anger in fury, and his rebuke with flames of fire" (Isa 66:15). From this perspective, the structures of this world were denied any ultimate significance. For all things were soon to be absorbed, via purgation of all that is evil, into a higher reality: "The kingdom of the world has become the kingdom of our Lord and of his Christ, and he shall reign for ever and ever" (Rev 11:15). The construction of a new symbolic universe, which is the response to the vacuum created by the group experience of alienation, thus begins with denial of any abiding significance in mundane structures and proceeds to a vision of a "higher" order of reality and what it promises for the future.

Since apocalyptic movements are diverse in nature, it is helpful to recognize some distinctions. First, one can distinguish between two types in relation to the dominant system against which the group is reacting. One type involves the response of marginal persons reacting against a dominant party *within* their own nation which has disenfranchised them from meaningful participation in societal and religious structures. This book deals with such a type.

The second type involves a broad segment of a nation reacting against a symbolic universe imposed upon it by an invading or infiltrating foreign power. To this type belongs the Maccabean response to the Hellenism imposed on the Jews by Antiochus IV (Dan 7–12).

Another set of distinctions describes the *form* of response, which varies depending on the status of those involved, the intensity of the conflict, and the goals and tactics adopted by the leaders of the specific apocalyptic movement. (1) If the group believes that reform of the dominant society is possible, it may generate what we may call an "alternative symbolic universe." As bitterness increases in later stages of a conflict, oppression and disenfranchisement may heighten the sense of alienation, leading to one of the following responses: (2) Withdrawal and founding of a new society based on a "utopian symbolic universe"; (3) retreat into secret sectarian existence, leading to a subsociety expressing its identity in a "symbolic subuniverse"; (4) violent opposition in reaction to persecution, generating a revolutionary community constructing a "symbolic counteruniverse." Such categories must be understood as ideal types, and while examples can easily be found for each (e.g., (1) the early followers of Second Isaiah, (2) Qumran, (3) the early *ḥăsîdîm,* (4) the Zealots), commonly a mixture of types is found. For example, while the Covenanters of Qumran withdrew and constituted themselves as a new society, they drew up and refined plans for the day of battle in which God would lead them against their enemies.

Although attempts to define apocalypticism by the construction of random lists of features is misleading, the mixture of materials drawn into any given apocalyptic work does not defy analysis, if understood from the central perspective to which these materials were drawn by the apocalyptic communities, the perspective of apocalyptic eschatology, and if interpreted within the social and political setting within which the particular composition was written. Specific settings will vary in clarity, though there is no reason to despair, for new finds and further research promise to continue to shed light on even the darker periods of apocalypticism. Here, by keeping in mind that—albeit in a general way—apocalyptic movements shared a central perspective (that of apocalyptic eschatology) and social setting (community experience of alienation), we shall illustrate how certain features found in apocalyptic writings relate to that perspective and setting. Commonly, the group experience of alienation and the need to establish the identity of the group vis-à-vis human antagonists and the Deity lead to the drawing of a sharp distinction between the elect and the condemned (e.g., 1 En 5:6–7). The fallen state of human structures is often extended to include the entire order of this world, leading to denigration of the mundane in favor of the drama unfolding on the cosmic level. The result is a heaven/earth dichotomy: "Rejoice then, O heaven and you that dwell therein! But woe to you, O earth and sea, for the devil has come down to you" (Rev 12:12). From a vantage point where mundane realities are shunned in favor of events initiated in heaven, time is divided into the era before the inbreaking of heavenly realities, and the blessed era which follows: "the Most High has made not one Age, but two" (4 Ezr 7:50). From the perspective of apocalyptic eschatology all history is viewed as a part of one unified drama, which leads to efforts to order the vast sweep in various ways, including the division into distinct periods (e.g., the four-kingdom schema) and literal or symbolic historical résumés. In both cases, all history is seen as determined by the divine Purposer, and since the movement of history is thus revealed to the seer, the future, including the imminent inbreaking of divine power, can be predicted with confidence.

The harking back to a more transmundane perspective than had characterized the prophets prepared the way for a reappropriation of many archaic mythical materials by apocalyptic seers. Indeed, something of the heart of mythopoeic thought reemerges in the notion that the end-time will resemble in important ways the primordial events (*Endzeit wird Urzeit*). There is much evidence of the type of radical experimentation with temporal and spatial categories which one would expect of groups disillusioned with traditional historicizing traditions and seeking to establish their own systems of values and symbols. For example, in Daniel 7 the notion of world history as divisible into four kingdoms seems to order reality in a chronological chain; yet the four beasts which symbolize those kingdoms emerge from the (primordial) sea *together,* and *together* they appear before the throne of the El-type judge. Or again, the Qumran community lived with a lively expectation of future events but at the same time celebrated the realities of the new age proleptically in their own rites. Thus spatial and temporal categories blur as the past (whether presented in historical résumés, chronological schemata, or in the form of pseudonymous writings attributed to ancient heroes), the present (whether conceptualized in terms of cosmic woes, deadly polarities, or universal calamity), and the future (whether perceived as a harking back to *Urzeit,* as rebirth of the new from the old, or as intervention of the Divine Warrior on the Day of Yahweh) are all caught up in a cosmic drama defying logical ordering. Within such experimentation there arise various versions of a messianic kingdom, diverse notions of paradisiacal glory and prosperity, and different understandings of the transcendence of death or of the transformation of life into new forms of existence. While such experimentation, abetted in time by the influx of sapiential traditions and various foreign materials, led to significant modifications in the basic historical orientation of Hebrew prophecy, the eschatological perspective which remains at the heart of Jewish and Christian apocalypticism never abandoned entirely the historical orientation out of which it was born. History, to be sure, was drawn into a far wider context than known to earlier writers, but this fell short of the level of abstraction on which the mundane concepts of space and time would be dissolved entirely. Where such an abstract level was reached, we no longer are dealing with the symbolic universe at home in apocalyptic movements, but with that arising within Gnosticism.

While it is not possible to give a simple definition which will comprehend the entire complex phenomenon of Jewish and Christian apocalypticism, we have seen that there is an identifiable perspective as well as a recognizable type of social setting and response which gives us the basis from which to pursue our study of the subject. Here we wish to proceed one step further by offering a brief sketch of the history of Jewish and Christian apocalypticism in antiquity on this same basis. Specifically, the perspective of apocalyptic eschatology supplies the line of continuity which makes such a sketch possible. With its roots in prophetic eschatology, it can be traced from the sixth century B.C.E. down into the period of the early church. In periods of calm it coexists alongside other perspectives (hierocratic, sapiential, pragmatic, Hellenistic, etc.). In periods in which some groups come to experience the pain of alienation from the dominant society, this perspective is elevated to the status of an ideology and utilized in the construction of a universe of meaning opposed to the normative one from which those groups feel disenfranchised. The result is the emergence of an apocalyptic movement, that is, what we can identify as apocalypticism in the strict sense of the word. Such movements die or fade away as the result of eradication by or conversion into the dominant system, or through transformation into a more pragmatic, established movement as the result of victory. In any of these cases the disappearance of a movement espousing apocalyptic eschatology as an ideology usually results in this perspective once again being drawn into the fabric of the society as one perspective alongside others. There it can reside as a potentiality awaiting new crises, new polarizations, and new opportunities to abet the rise of new apocalyptic movements. Study of the history of apocalypticism in antiquity must be carried on in the full light both of all available literary sources and of the religious, political, and cultural conditions which contributed to the social ferment within which the apocalyptic spirit was awakened in the hearts of the oppressed.

The study of the antecedents of apocalypticism goes behind biblical prophecy to the great cosmogonic myths of the second millennium B.C.E., whence many of its concepts and motifs ultimately were derived. To be sure, borrowing from these sources was not direct. Rather, elements were mediated in attenuated form by the Israelite tribal confederacy, royal cult, and prophetic movement. In certain cases foreign—especially Greek and then Hellenistic—carriers may have functioned as transmitters of such ancient materials. But it was in the first instance within Israelite religious experience that such materials combined with concepts born of Hebrew experience to engender a perspective in many ways unique in the ancient world, that of prophetic eschatology (e.g., Isa 29:5–7). The emergence of this perspective can be traced back all the way to the experiences of a mixed group of tribes of the Mosaic period who fostered a new world view drawing on ancient ancestral sagas of Amorite derivation. This was their response to the group experience of alienation which they suffered in the face of the collapse of the credibility of the mythopoeic universe of meaning sponsored by the Pharaohs. Thus was born a perspective which subsequently was refined amid the tensions between royal, sacerdotal, and prophetic circles during the age of monarchy in Israel.

Prophetic eschatology developed within the framework of Israelite nationhood. With the collapse of kingship, temple, and nation under the blows of the Babylonians culminating in the destruction of Jerusalem in 587, a pervasive sense of calamity prompted prophets like Jeremiah and Ezekiel to envision redemption increasingly on a cosmic level. In this reorientation the increased use of mythic motifs becomes apparent (e.g., Isa 4:23–28 and Ezekiel 47). The most creative response to the vacuum of alienation to emerge in the exile came from the prophetic voice we call Second Isaiah, who put together pieces derived from prophecy, royal court, and myth in a manner which prepared the way for the transformation of prophetic eschatology into apocalyptic eschatology. Although this prophet did not cut off moorings from historical realities entirely, he was drawn to a lofty vision of cosmic transformation. This infused the prophetic tradition with mythopoeic symbolism (e.g., Isa 51:9–11), which in turn abetted the development of heaven/earth and past aeon/future aeon dichotomies (e.g., 43:18–19). These dichotomies became central features of later apocalyptic movements.

Beyond Second Isaiah, all that was required for the dawn of apocalyptic was the final demonstration to a group of alienated disciples that their vision of a restored Israel could not be realized within mundane structures or through human agency. That demonstration came in the years following the Edict of Cyrus (538). With the return of the first waves of exiles, the Zadokite priests seized the initiative in restoration activity, basing their rebuilding activities on the program for restoration devised by the prophet Ezekiel (Ezekiel 40–48). But progress did not go at all smoothly. Not only was all in disarray as a result of the earlier destruction by the Babylonian armies, but hostility from neighboring peoples and economic reversals exacerbated an already grim situation. This was the type of climate which is conducive to apocalyptic movements, and such in fact arose.

The first actually did not develop into a full-blown apocalyptic movement, for it retained some of the marks of earlier prophecy, especially in partially integrating its vision with historical events and persons. From its inception this movement had a nationalistic flavor, fired by the enthusiasm of the prophets Haggai and Zechariah, who transformed Ezekiel's program into an apocalyptic vision (e.g., Hag 2:6–9 and Zechariah 1–6). It took the form of a counteruniverse to the Persian overlords by envisioning the cosmic intervention of Yahweh and the establishment of a messianic kingdom under a Davidide (Zerubbabel) and a Zadokite High Priest (Jeshua), events portrayed vividly by Zechariah in the earliest examples of the genre of the apocalypse in the Bible. This apocalyptic movement was short-lived. It would seem that it was interpreted by the Persians as a violation of the generous terms of their treaty, which prompted them to remove its revolutionary leaders (Zerubbabel disappears from the scene never to be heard about again) and to cooperate with its more pragmatic members in evolving a hierocratic program which supplanted all apocalyptic elements with a pragmatic social system cooperating fully with the Persian overlords. The apocalypses of Zechariah were reedited from this perspective and given the new function of legitimizing the Zadokite hierocracy and its leadership.

The other apocalyptic movement growing out of this crisis was more resistant to assimilation, partly because it was further removed from the dominant social system to begin with. Its program was much more cosmic in orientation (Isaiah 60–62), leading to tensions with the protagonists of the Zadokite program from the early period of the restoration. The alienation which its protagonists suffered was not ameliorated by collaboration with the Persians but was increased by the oppression to which they were subjected by the Zadokite leaders (Isa 66:1–5). As oppression was followed by excommunication, their symbolic universe increasingly broke with history, and hope for vindication was lifted to the heavens as they interpreted their experience from the perspective of apocalyptic eschatology: "Truth has fallen in the public squares" (Isa 59:14); this was a situation to which they responded not with renewed efforts at reform of the social system but with a vision of Yahweh coming "like a rushing stream" to "repay wrath to his adversaries, requital to his enemies" (Isa 59:18b–19). This was an apocalyptic movement with momentum deriving from a deeply felt sense of alienation, which sense increased in intensity during the last years of the sixth century and through most of the fifth century as well (cf. Zechariah 12 and 14). Resigning to the necessity of abandoning a disintegrating social order, they greeted the arrival of Yahweh's new act: "For now I create new heavens and a new earth" (Isa 65:17a). It is not surprising to note that the responsibility to the present political order which was characteristic of prophetic eschatology yields to abdication of concern for this world in favor of the world to come. The supermundane orientation expressed itself in dichotomies which developed beyond those already detected in Second Isaiah: past history = an epoch of evil/imminent future = a new order of salvation; opponents = evil/visionaries = God's chosen; this order = degenerate/heavenly order = source of a new life.

A sizable corpus of literature produced by this movement has been preserved among the writings of the Bible (Isaiah 24–27; 34–35; 56–66; Malachi, Zechariah 9–14, final version of Joel). From the beginning of the fourth down to the middle of the third century B.C.E., however, we have no known apocalyptic writings. It seems that the reform measures carried on by Nehemiah and Ezra led to the reintegration of the diverse perspectives of that time into one dominant socio-religious system based on "the law of your God, which is in your hand" (Ezr 7:14). This new assimilation of perspectives is expressed by the classical work arising from this reform, the Chronicler's History, which unites under one hierocratic canopy priestly and prophetic elements alike. Apocalyptic eschatology ceased to generate an apocalyptic movement for a time, existing instead as one perspective alongside others.

Then came the battle with Hellenism, which threatened to cut from Judaism its very heart as the cost of entering into the new cosmopolitan culture of the time. The first indications that latent apocalyptic eschatology was again being appropriated as a means of generating an alternative symbolic universe are found in the section of 1 Enoch which stems from the late third century B.C.E. (chapters 6–11). In the first half of the second century the situation hastily degenerated into a chain of shattering events involving political and ecclesial intrigue, military destruction, and harsh measures to eradicate Jewish Torah in favor of Hellenistic practices. The experience of anomie and alienation which resulted led circles like the early *ḥăsîdîm,* who had preserved a strong eschatological perspective, to respond in the manner of earlier apocalyptic movements. They interpreted the devastating events of this earth as reflections of cosmic events, and they turned to visions of the cosmic drama to predict the nature of the denouement which would destroy the wicked and raise the righteous to everlasting glory (Daniel 7–12).

Subsequent happenings had a sifting effect, as the breadth of the nationalistic apocalyptic movement caused by Antiochus IV's severe measures began to diminish following the military successes of the Maccabees. The most stringent of the *ḥăsîdîm* were the first to leave the Maccabean camp. Others were alienated as the dominant social system of the Hasmoneans evolved into a pragmatic system of making peace with the Romans, or any other power which could enhance their earthly power. This was interpreted as a betrayal of the transcendent vision by certain groups, whose growing sense of alienation caused them to withdraw further into the symbolic universe of apocalypticism. It is within this polarizing climate that we can place the various apocalyptic writings of the second century B.C.E. (including those scattered throughout the apocrypha and the pseudepigrapha as well as certain of the writings found at Qumran), although much more research is needed before the specific apocalyptic movements producing them can be adequately defined and distinguished from one another and from other parties current at that time.

The perspective of apocalyptic eschatology, which proved so useful to wide circles of Jews in the trials of the second century, lived on into the Common Era under the sponsorship of the Pharisees, the Essenes, and various other sectarian groups. From this perspective John the Baptist preached repentance. Though the question of degree of dependence is hotly debated, Jesus' announcement in parable and sermon of the coming Kingdom of God develops certain aspects of apocalyptic eschatology. Beyond question, the way in which the person and message of Jesus were interpreted in the kerygma of the early Church was strongly influenced by this perspective, though in mixture with other perspectives, including biblical prophecy, Gnosticism, and other views of Hellenistic and Roman culture. The important thing to remember is that here as in earlier periods the perspective of apocalyptic eschatology bore with it the potential of providing the basis for apocalypticism, and we have a few examples of its thus coming to expression (e.g., Mark 13 and 2 Thess 2:1–12). In times of an aggravated sense of alienation, certain Jewish and Christian communities responded to crises like the destruction of the temple and persecutions by Roman emperors by embracing the perspective of apocalyptic eschatology as the ideology of new apocalyptic movements. This brings us back to the point of departure of this excursus, back to the most famous of all apocalyptic writings, the book of Revelation, but it also calls to our attention works like 2 Baruch and 4 Ezra. For the spiritual descendants of the Jewish visionaries of the sixth and fifth centuries B.C.E. had inherited from their ancestors a perspective which allowed them to look squarely at the success of their tormentors, and yet, with courage and in hope, to proclaim that the prosperity of the ungodly was only apparent. For there was a God in heaven whose ways the visionaries alone could comprehend, and that God had in mind their vindication.

The perspective of apocalyptic eschatology lives on today, and occasionally it is embraced by groups alienated from their environment as the basis for an alternative universe of meaning. But recent memories of Jonestown, Guyana, join a chain of other memories from the history of apocalyptic of dreams which led not to a heavenly Jerusalem ruled by a gracious messiah but to an earthly Gehenna ruled by a human demagogue. And together these memories evoke serious questions vis-à-vis modern appeals to focus attention heavenward and follow the visions of a seer. The problem of contemporary apocalypticism is of the magnitude to invite not the casual comments of a concluding paragraph but full-scale treatments. Nevertheless, the insightfulness of such treatments will be dependent to a large degree on knowledge of the history of apocalypticism, especially the biblical apocalypticism to which modern movements most often make their appeal. In this connection it will be important to recall that biblical apocalypticism did not involve the exercise of self-conscious theological system-building by individuals enjoying relative security and repose, nor did it rest on the unquestioned word of one authoritarian leader. It involved the community response of the oppressed and afflicted to a world on the edge of the abyss. The apocalyptic movement studied in this book generated its symbolic universe in a period when faith could be maintained only by retreat from the dominant society, which was the source of its sore oppression. Since retreat was tactical, however, it was followed by reentry and renewed involvement in the affairs of everyday life once a climate of normalcy returned. In the case of ancient apocalyptic movements where such reentry did not occur, the result was a degenerate sectarian dogmaticism which failed to challenge life to greater levels of faithfulness and human compassion. Had we time, we could demonstrate instances, especially from medieval history, where pseudoapocalyptic movements did not generate alternative symbolic universes in response to alienation, but where they took the symbol system of an earlier movement and exploited it programmatically, often for nationalistic, racist, or dogmatic purposes. Such phenomena are a mockery of genuine apocalypticism, for they involve blind imitation which is bereft of the pain and struggle of attempting to keep faith alive amid the crumbling structures of a degenerate social universe.

The study of ancient Jewish and Christian apocalypticism will thus remind students of modern religious phenomena of the extremely adverse social and political settings to which apocalyptic universes of meaning were a response. Amid a vast array of modern myths of salvation, many of them utilizing apocalyptic rhetoric, historical study will aid in the search for a fitting response to those many systems which offer to deliver world-weary moderns from their struggles. Of such systems it must be asked, Do they grow out of a responsible attempt to relate a sensible view of reality to contemporary life in a manner which is constructive, creative, and compassionate, or do they draw elements from various earlier sources into a program aimed at heroism, deification, and self-aggrandizement, whose final motivation can be traced to a pathological death wish for the mass of humanity and contempt for the entire created order?

While studies of ancient apocalyptic movements will contribute to such ruminations, an even more useful guide than the model of the Hebrew seer will be the model of the Hebrew prophet. For in a world which still seems to be situated somewhat short of the abyss, we do well to remember the prophetic dialectic. While subjecting all mundane structures to their visions of an order of justice wedded with peace, the prophets resisted two extremes: that of abdicating social and political responsibility in favor of an escape into the timeless security of their vision, and that of reifying existing institutions in the name of pragmatic expedience. Indeed, it can be argued that the creative dynamism of our religious heritage has developed especially under the tutelage of those carrying forward the prophetic tradition of being guided by a vision of the Kingdom but being equally zealous in integrating that vision into the realities of the everyday world. This posture does not imply a denial of the authenticity of the apocalyptic response. It merely reserves it for those for whom it is intended, those suffering from a sense of alienation which threatens to cast life into the abyss.